# Praise for *The Art of Planned Giving:*

"Doug White is the philosopher prince of planned philanthropy."
—Conrad Teitell

"This remarkable book should be required reading for every planned giving professional."
—Charitable Gift Planning News

"What we really like is the accessible and extensive discussion of topics we have not seen addressed in other books on charitable gift planning."
—Charitable Sector Letter

"A comprehensive and deeply sensitive look at the realities of its subject, *The Art of Planned Giving* is a necessary guide for all those newly entering the gift planning field, and an essential reference for experienced fund-raisers and philanthropists alike."
—Marilyn M. Montgomery
Director of Gift Planning
University of Washington

"*The Art of Planned Giving* sets forth a compelling argument for bringing a broader perspective to the pursuit of planned gifts—encouraging us to balance technical knowledge and skills with a deeper understanding of what truly promotes philanthropy."
—C. Alan Korthals
Manager, Gift Services
The First Church of Christ, Scientist

"The Art of Planned Giving leaves no stone unturned in defining the human as well as the technical elements which constitute the ingredients for successful solicitation and implementation of planned gifts."
—Susan Moore
Marketing Director of Charitable Giving
New York Life Insurance Company

"Doug White's *The Art of Planned Giving* is an eloquent and thoughtful voyage through the myriad human challenges that confront all of us in the field of philanthropy."
—Caleb B. Rick, JD
Director of Planned Giving and Charitable Gift Counsel
The Sierra Club

"Doug's discussion implicitly educates the reader on technical gift structures, but keeps the focus where it belongs: on the rewards of practicing philanthropy."
—Nancy Herrold Strapp, JD
Director of Planned Giving
Children's Hospital Foundation

# NONPROFIT LAW, FINANCE, AND MANAGEMENT SERIES

# The Art of Planned Giving: Understanding Donors and the Culture of Giving

## Douglas E. White

**John Wiley & Sons, Inc.**
New York • Chichester • Weinheim • Brisbane • Singapore • Toronto

Copyright © 1995 by John Wiley & Sons, Inc. All rights reserved.

Published simultaneously in Canada.

This publication is designed to provide accurate and authoritative
information in regard to the subject matter covered. It is sold with the
understanding that the publisher is not engaged in rendering legal,
accounting, or other professional services. If legal advice or other
expert assistance is required, the services of a competent professional
person should be sought.

*Library of Congress Cataloging-in-Publication Data:*
White, Douglas E.
    The art of planned giving : understanding donors and the culture
of giving / Douglas E. White.
        p.  cm.—(Nonprofit law, finance, and management series)
    Includes index.
    ISBN 0-471-29846-8 (paper)
    1. Deferred giving—United States.  2. Fund raising—United
States.  3. Charities—United States.  I. Title.  II. Series.
HV41.9.U5W48   1995
658.15'224–dc20                                        95-16207
                                                       CIP

Printed in the United States of America.

10  9  8  7  6  5  4  3  2  1

# Dedication

I dedicate this book to Charles L. Terry, Lewis Perry Professor of the Humanities and Instructor in English at Phillips Exeter Academy. To Charlie, teaching—that is, enabling others to learn—is the noblest profession. Charlie taught me much of words and, therefore, life. To my former teacher and life-long mentor and friend, thank you.

# In Memoriam

David Donaldson was a partner at the law firm of Ropes and Gray in Boston, Massachusetts. When Dave died in the fall of 1994 the world of planned giving lost a remarkable mind and a great friend. The profession of planned giving, however, will forever benefit from his vibrant optimism and vigorous spirit.

# Foreword

I first met Doug White on paper. Specifically, I read his "My View" column in *The Chronicle of Philanthropy*'s March 21, 1989 issue. In that column, Doug wrote that "planned giving has reached adolescence. After 20 years of unitrusts, annuity trusts, and pooled-income funds, fundraisers are mastering the mechanical and technical part of planning giving. My days are filled with conversations similar to the one above [a typical conversation with a donor about the tax and economic aspects of a gift]. Philanthropy today can be a complex and rewarding process. But, as with children growing into adulthood, philanthropy, particularly planned giving, is reaching a pivotal stage. Our technical knowledge may be overwhelming what we have always known on a human level. By marketing planned giving incorrectly we may be selling our souls and, ironically, our futures for the sake of a superficial level of success today." How true! How well it describes the dilemmas that we in planned giving face! That column expressed more eloquently than I could ever hope to express the simple but critical truth that we, as planned giving professionals, have some way, somewhere along the way, lost our bearings and our sense of purpose.

Now, with *The Art of Planned Giving: Understanding Donors and the Culture of Giving*, Doug has written the definitive analysis of what excellence in the field of planned giving requires. This book is most assuredly not a technical book on planned giving. Heaven knows we have enough of those! It is not a book on how to raise more money and thus earn more money. There are other books on that. *The Art of Planned Giving* is about doing planned giving *right*: understanding donors as human beings; understanding the many factors that cause people to emotionally connect with a charity's mission; appreciating their life experiences and how these experiences affect their motive to give; understanding, as if you were there, how it feels to be in the donor prospect's shoes during a planned giving visit; and appreciating the role of the other planned giving team members.

Rest assured, *The Art of Planned Giving* gives technical issues their place. And the fact that success is often measured in dollars raised is clearly recognized in this book. But the human dimension, so often missing or diminished in other treatises on planned giving, takes center stage in *The Art of Planned Giving.*

Philanthropy, in the Greek, means essentially "to love humanity." To give to further a charitable cause is an act of love toward humanity. The reality of that truth is occasionally apparent, but more often is shrouded and hidden by the experiences of a lifetime. But unless we can master that truth and all of its complexities, all of the technical knowledge and all of the fund raising skills that one can possess will fall short of the goal we each should aspire to: being a successful planned giving *professional.*

Doug White has applied his skills as a planned giving professional, both as a planned giving officer and as a for-profit advisor to planned giving officers, to give us a unique view of planned giving. His experience born of many years in this profession, combined with his understanding of and sensitivity to the human condition, qualify him to write this book. *The Art of Planned Giving,* with its real-life approach, reads much more like a novel than a planned giving treatise. The reader cannot help but identify with the characters, and you will recognize many familiar shortcomings in the lifelike situations played out in the book. But the only better way to learn than through one's own mistakes is through close identification with individuals in a fictional but realistic situation. It doesn't hurt as much, and the lessons are learned just as well.

In *The Art of Planned Giving,* Doug White has challenged each of us who make up the planned giving community—planned giving officers, lawyers, accountants, financial planners, trust officers and life underwriters—to look more deeply into the process of philanthropy and into the concerns and motivations of philanthropists, and to look more deeply into ourselves and how we approach each day and each challenge of our professional lives. I challenge you to meet Doug White on paper through the pages of *The Art of Planned Giving.* His experiences, the depth of his knowledge, and his unparalleled gift for bringing words on paper to life combine to take us on a matchless professional literary journey—one that will profoundly affect how you approach your work and will forever change how you perceive and do planned giving.

Terry L. Simmons, JD, LLM
General Counsel, Baptist Foundation of Texas
Vice President and General Counsel, Thompson & Knight, P.C.

# Preface

If we claim the right to ask for money we need to understand the ancient and honorable instinct of charitable giving in the context of a modern world, whose philanthropic sector finds itself questioning donative intent, tax incentives and the purpose of many charities, all at once. Planned giving provides such a forum precisely because it embodies the ambiguities inherent in asking for gifts in return for a life income and other benefits. This book was conceived as a result of my need to examine and address those ambiguities. It is no cliché; planned giving is a mix of art and science, and the competent planned giving professional must balance the two.

But there's more. Planned giving is still a myth for most charities. For all the talk, for all the conferences, for all the seminars, for all the newsletters, for all the consultants, planned giving is for a vast majority of the nearly 600,000 public charities in the United States nothing more than an unrealized dream. This is largely because most efforts to be educated on the technical merits of the various gifts exceed, by far too much, efforts to understand the role charity plays in our society and the reasons donors donate. For what feebler reason can the executive of a charity offer in defense of a planned giving program, or, for that matter, any fundraising effort, than its tax deductible status? Or the income benefits derived from deferred gifts? Yet look at the agenda of any planned giving course and you will find tax-related items prominent among the topics. The science. Fine. Learn those things, for they are important. But too many who learn planned giving do not learn well enough the importance of mission. Good things would result if more donors demanded an apologia from the charities they support. The art. Although the science and the art in the profession of planned giving each depends on the other, one—the science—garners all the attention.

Although federal and state tax regulations undoubtedly inspire almost all who practice planned giving to continuously probe the legal and mathematical particulars of this curious form of fundraising, its technical world is not, for the most part, a profound one. Creative ideas emerge each year, but they are often mere byproducts of the tax code, held hostage to the strong but mundane forces of Congress and the IRS.

Much more important, in my opinion, are the human dynamics of planned giving. As our legal system embraces more than what can be found in Black's law dictionary, the world of planned giving is much broader than its mathematical or legal components. It is as big as the human soul itself.

Technical knowledge is important, of course, but I liken that to dates in history. That a student of American history knows the Civil War began in 1861 and ended in 1865 is good and necessary, but that knowledge alone does not begin to explain the issues that led up to the bloody conflict or its role in the many societal struggles since. In fact, there would be no point in knowing there was a Civil War if 1861 and 1865 were the only points of reference. So it is with any serious undertaking, including planned giving. Formulas and technical knowledge play the same role as dates in history—important, useful, and necessary, but only the supporting elements in the complex and unending process of true understanding. How important can a planned gift technique be without a donor upon whom to employ it? No matter the discipline, to know only the superficial elements is to comprehend almost nothing. Thus, this book, an admittedly immodest effort to address what I think is missing in our profession: a look beyond the formulas, as well as a look inward. A painting with accurate lines but no depth is empty. Something is also missing when the profession of planned giving teaches formulas without a human component. Perhaps these chapters will fill part of that void.

This book has been written for anyone whose interest in planned giving goes beyond the technical. I assume some legal and mathematical knowledge, but only as a bridge to the human interplay. Dealing with others, no matter what the profession, is an important but difficult skill to master. In truth, it is never fully mastered, but those who seek to improve that skill routinely examine the nuances of their interactions with other people. Often the examination is introspective. In addition to seminars and formal presentations, learning the art of planned giving involves experience and much self-education. I am optimistic that when you finish this book you will feel refreshed and rejuvenated about one of the world's wonderful professions. I hope you will find thought-provoking inspiration in these pages. Because the ideas examined in these pages stand well against time, I also hope you read *The Art of Planned Giving*, or parts of it, more than once.

One of the technical themes in this book is planned gift investments. Most planned giving professionals do not deal with asset investment or administration after the gift is acquired. I do not expect fund-raisers will ever control planned gift investments any more than treasurers will ever dictate the solicitation process; nevertheless, I do believe this knowledge is important.

   *The Art of Planned Giving* flows from philosophical to personal to technical to organizational to ethical. Chapters 1 through 5 embrace what I feel is the essence of planned giving: why donors donate, and what takes place during encounters with donors and their advisors. The next three chapters, 6 through 8, broadly review various technical concepts, including specific questions that arise often during a gift solicitation, as well as investment and administrative concerns after the donor makes the gift. Chapters 9 through 13 address some of the internal and public challenges charitable organizations face when operating or implementing a planned giving program, such as trustee involvement, consultants, and crediting policies. The final chapter, using the *Model Standards of Practice for the Charitable Gift Planner* as a guide, probes some of our profession's ethical dilemmas. While dramatized, every situation described in this book is based on an actual event, and every character you meet has a real-life counterpart.

   The unique and powerful force of philanthropy has measured well against time, and planned giving, which is broader by many measures than simple deferred giving, has become the lens through which we in the profession of raising money to support charitable causes view almost every capital and endowment gift. *The Art of Planned Giving: Understanding Donors and the Culture of Giving* is a small start in the process of looking at this profession, if not in its current entirety, at least with an eye on the human drama associated with planned giving. If you're looking for the action, the real action in planned giving, forget the Internal Revenue code. Peer instead into the soul.

Douglas E. White
April 1995

# Acknowledgments

No book is written by only one person.

First, Terry Simmons of Dallas, Texas. Terry is my role model in planned giving. One does not practice this profession for long without knowing who he is. An attorney and among this nation's handful of genuine experts in planned giving, he champions the causes of charities in the often cynic-laden halls of Congress and at the offices of state officials in Austin, Texas, as well as among many in the private sector. Terry is among the brightest, most caring individuals I know, and, planned giving being the profession it is, I know many caring and bright people. Terry is vice president and general counsel of the Baptist Foundation of Texas and is Of Counsel with Thompson & Knight, as well as co-editor of *Charitable Gift Planning News*. He is a past president of the National Committee on Planned Giving (NCPG), and a past chair of the important NCPG Government Relations Committee. For good reason Terry was named the Planned Giving Professional of the Year in 1994 by the newsletter *Planned Giving Today*. He continues to work tirelessly to make this a better profession and, in my view, a better world. Anyone even remotely connected to planned giving or interested in the fate of philanthropy is indebted to Terry Simmons. I especially; Terry helped edit this entire work with an eye on the planned giving and legal concepts, and I have him to thank for its undoubtedly greater breadth and accuracy than it would have enjoyed without his thoughtful eye.

I am forever indebted to Katelyn Quynn. Katelyn is the director of planned giving at Massachusetts General Hospital in Boston, Massachusetts, a past president of the Planned Giving Group of New England, a member of the board of the NCPG, and a lecturer and teacher as well. She and Ron Jordan co-authored the comprehensive text, *Planned Giving: Marketing, Management and Law.* also published by John Wiley & Sons, Inc. Most important, however, she is a close friend. During my darkest hours of solitude and angst (a necessary hazard of writing), Katelyn somehow found the time to provide more encouragement with her smile and her heart than I should think I have ever deserved: quite literally, this book would not exist without her support.

The graphs found in Chapter 4 on pages 102, 104, 105, and 106, and in Chapter 7 on pages 184 and 185, were provided by Kaspick & Company. Scott Kaspick, the managing director of Kaspick & Company, has dedicated his professional life to helping charitable organizations understand the value of lower payout rates for charitable remainder unitrusts. I also thank Scott for enduring my diversions more frequently, and for a longer time, than either of us expected.

All the remaining planned giving illustrations were provided by the Windows-based planned giving software program *ParaGon*, written by Blackbaud, Inc. I thank Suzanne Schaffner and Mark Terrero for their assistance and friendship. I also thank Blackbaud's president, Tony Bakker, and Blackbaud's product manager of design and architecture, Lou Attanasi, for their support and good will. Each has a combination of more mathematical ability and human qualities than most of us have of either. I have admired their talents and have valued their friendship and professional camaraderie for more than a decade.

For assistance on the chapter dealing with trustees, I thank Elizabeth Lowell, vice president of Arthur D. Raybin Associates, Inc. in Harvard, Massachusetts. I know Elizabeth as a trusted counselor to many charities who have benefited from her insistence that board members exercise their long-range vision, not only for fund-raising but for all aspects of a charity's activities. For help on the chapter dealing with consultants I thank Ellen Estes, who makes the incomprehensible comprehensible to her many students of planned giving. During our many years of friendship Ellen has always been honest and thoughtful, and therefore indispensable, on several of this profession's important and difficult issues.

The following people also displayed early enthusiasm about a project whose successful completion required a great deal of imagination: Richard Carey, the director of communications at the Holderness School in Holderness, New Hampshire; Charles A. Johnson, the retired vice president for endowment at the Lilly Endowment, Inc. in Indianapolis, Indiana; and Betsy A. Mangone, the vice president of the University of Colorado Foundation, Inc., in Denver, Colorado, and a past president of NCPG.

I also belatedly thank Marcia, David, and Christa for their patience. Family members must too often tolerate the inattention associated with pursuing another's dream quest.

Finally, the words in this book would be much more loosely constructed and the ideas much more flabby without the stern but sweet discipline of my editor Marla Bobowick. Marla, because she is the better student, learned much more about planned giving from this enterprise than I did about writing well. That the book has structure is the result of her influence; where it is lacking my shortcomings, and mine alone, are responsible.

As I say, no book is written by only one person.

# Contents

# Contents

# Contents

# Unexpected Gifts

*Now comes the mystery.*
**Henry Ward Beecher**

## THE WOMAN WHO FOUGHT BEYOND HER DEATH

The old woman was weak, but determined. She was only in her mid-sixties, but anyone so close to death is old, no matter the age. Cancer. Although most of us have suffered another's death, few of us have suffered one so profound. In the fifth and final phase of the dreaded disease, she enabled herself to see an opportunity to help beyond her lifetime.

One hundred thousand dollars for the Sierra Club in San Francisco. Who was this person? Someone who previously had given no money to the club, yet devoted her life to saving the California environment. Although she was frail, the woman wanted to fight: against those who would ruin the land, and for water rights in Arizona. She lived her life vigorously and was determined to end it by making a difference. In a world of million-dollar gifts and higher, it was a modest gift; but to her it was a big, meaningful gift.

As a young woman she saw a large company buy many acres in her town to build a factory. The factory produced chemicals that were bought by other companies and the government. Some chemicals were not bought, however, and the company disposed of them in the ground. Next to the river. The company knew not to dump them directly into the river because that was against the law. It was also against the law to bury them in the ground, but the company thought that no one would

1

ever know. But when some people in the town began to get sick, and when some of those died, people began to wonder. And they did find out. The company did not admit guilt; instead it fought its cause in the courts. Although the company lost, the victory was shallow because much harm had been done and the punishment was small. Two of the people who died were the young woman's parents. Their deaths were never officially connected to the company's chemicals, but the woman knew.

Anger. The woman never forgot. After exhausting her frustration on petitions and speaking out at town meetings, she discovered a movement that worked to save the environment, a movement that fought the big companies that, in her view, thought more of profits than of health. From that moment of discovery until her death more than 20 years later, she fought what she considered to be the biggest injustice of all: the assault on the environment. Sometimes, charitable intent is easy to identify.

The woman, aware of her limited time, summoned the club's planned giving director, wishing to explain in person why she would help. When he walked into the woman's apartment in Sun City, she was only another name on a prospect list, unmarried and childless. He reacted to their first minutes together with dismay, noting primarily the death in her face, a sight she had learned to ignore in the mirror. Death would be, she assured him, positive and uplifting. But he was not uplifted. He unconsciously subsumed what the woman had intended to be her good news with his sorrow at her impending death. Then, when she told him her story, he understood, and was more moved by the woman's sincerity and focus than by her generosity; she had an agenda that death would not prevent her from completing. The moment became powerful because she recognized in her mortality the opportunity to make a difference. She led him to the gift, not the other way around. When she died two days later, the planned giving director was reminded that he had one of the most important jobs in the world.

## THE MAN WITH A LONG MEMORY

No one had any idea.

On a cloudy morning in 1977, Phillips Academy, the eminent independent secondary school in Andover, Massachusetts, was bustling with its normal activity. The phone call that day from an estate attorney, however, was anything but normal.

"Is the name Mr. Walter Leeds significant to you?"

"No, I'm afraid it isn't," said the person who answered the phone. "Is he associated with Phillips Academy in any way?" Andover was not unaccustomed to estate attorneys informing the school that a graduate had died and had provided for Andover in his will.

"I'm calling to inform you that my client has bequeathed Phillips Academy the sum of five million dollars."

No one had ever given such a large sum to Andover. Even with its $140-million endowment and healthy annual fund, this news was momentous. Was the call a joke? How could anyone have left so much money? And who was this person, this generous benefactor? "I'm sorry," said the development officer, "Would you tell me again the person's name?"

"Leeds. Walter S. Leeds."

"Do you know in what year he was graduated from Andover?"

"I'm sorry I don't. His will, although precise and clear about his intentions, does not provide any reason why he would make such a generous gift. His will says, and I quote, 'I hereby bequeath upon my death the sum of five million dollars to the Trustees of Phillips Academy in Andover, Massachusetts.' Period." By the time the estate was probated a year later, however, the amount transferred was six million dollars.

Beginning that day, beginning that moment, researchers in the Office of Academy Resources searched their records for information on Walter Leeds. At the end of one week they knew that he was a member of the class of 1908 and often supported the annual fund and capital campaigns. He never visited the campus, however. Andover researchers, after exhaustive study, discovered three additional facts about Mr. Walter Scott Leeds: that he was a member of the class of 1908; that Alfred Stearns, the headmaster at the time, had befriended the young Leeds; and, most surprisingly, that he was *asked to leave* before the end of one year because, they were later to learn, of a misdemeanor.

That Walter Leeds would die a multimillionaire having productively controlled LaSalle Steel Company in Chicago, one of the nation's richest steel empires, probably would have surprised those who in 1905 decided that Andover was not right for this youngster. That he made a gift of such substance more than 70 years later unquestionably surprised those at Andover. Everyone wondered why.

Why indeed? Why does anyone leave such a large amount to a charity? Why does anyone leave anything at all to charity? Those on the Andover campus did not enjoy the luxury of being told why this particular charitable impulse was directed their way. Yet, for whatever reason, Mr. Walter S. Leeds, at the age of seventy-eight, made good on a promise, one he made years earlier in the unique, confidential air between a client and an attorney. His was not Andover's most significant gift—Samuel Phillips, the school's founder, started the tradition almost two hundred years earlier in 1778—but it was by far the largest at the time. If anyone had thought to ask Mr. Leeds his motive, he might have said that it felt good—nothing profound—and for all anyone knows, his generosity continues to make him feel good. Knowingly or not, however, he participated in the oldest form of planned giving: He made a bequest.

# CHAPTER ONE

# The Fragile Seeds of Altruism

*Take egotism out, and you would castrate the benefactors.*

**Ralph Waldo Emerson**

Not everyone has a donor who seems to emerge from nowhere to make a major commitment to a charity. Those who do, however, including the Sierra Club and Phillips Academy, continue to encourage donations. Since the late 1970s, charities have seen an explosion of activity and professionalism in their development and fund-raising efforts. The annual campaign, because of sophisticated goal-setting (where the goal is almost always a higher dollar amount as well as a higher participation percentage than the previous year) and heavy reliance placed on the annual fund to balance the operating budget, has been transformed into a process more resembling a large corporation's quest for quarterly profits than it does the plea for funds to keep the lights on. Also, capital campaigns, which usually include the annual fund as well as endowment and building projects in their totals, have grown so much that tax attorneys, accountants, and consultants—all professionals and usually well-paid—are omnipresent. Fund-raising is a big business.

Planned giving is becoming a big part of that big business. As donors become more sophisticated and appeals for large amounts of money are broadened to include those who cannot or choose not to part with an asset *and* its income, planned giving plays a major role in the fund-raising offices of more and more charitable organizations in the United States. Once the exclusive domain of the large and well-established,

planned giving is a file to be found in almost every development director's desk.

## PHILANTHROPY

To understand planned giving, we must understand the concept of philanthropy. But who can understand that? When the charitable representative visits a prospective donor, presumably to discuss philanthropy,
the discussion is usually dominated by what the charity needs or, for
planned gifts, the various technical ways a contribution can be made.
Either of these approaches employs an assumption that the prospect
wants to assist the charity to fulfill its mission, but anyone who has seriously committed himself to the practice of fund-raising knows that such
a motive cannot be assumed; the real task in convincing the prospect to
give to the degree desired by the charity is connecting the prospect to
the charity's mission.

Much of what is written about charitable giving, and planned giving
in particular, implores the reader to understand the technical aspects of
giving and receiving. Some planned giving materials discuss donor
motives, but these usually are sadly superficial:

> Mary and Bill Happy want to make a gift to ABC Charity, but,
> sadly, they are concerned about paying a capital gains tax. Lucky
> for them, ABC's planned giving director comes along to rescue
> them from big, bad Uncle Sam and ushers them into paradise with
> a life-income trust.

Of course, everyone lives happily ever after. (And don't think that
was invented; those very words can be found in a 1987 planned giving
brochure.) Yet what else might be said in trying to explain the logically
unexplainable? So much more simple is the task to cloak the process in
easily understood terms. Few people in this one-dimensional world ever
have a terminally ill parent or an unhappily married daughter or a suspicious second spouse or mortgaged property or a need to retain access
to the assets—complicating details found all too frequently in the real
world, conveniently but unfortunately left out of almost every discussion involving the acquisition of a planned gift.

### Technical Challenges vs. Human Relations

Yet, is it any wonder that we write about and communicate what we
know, the technical and not the psychological? The technical is impor-

tant and, apparently, always changing. Who can know what Congress will do in its next session? The Alternative Minimum Tax (AMT) was a huge problem for six years; might it be so again? Is the Generation Skipping Transfer Tax going to be revised again? (Will anyone ever *really* understand it?) Might charitable deductions someday be lost to higher-income individuals because of the floating floor under itemized deductions? Even the technical aspects that do *not* constantly change require constant attention by practitioners. Bargain sale rules will always be perplexing and the four-tier system of trust income distribution will always remain exceptionally complicated. And what exactly do you mean when you say Charitable Mid-Term Federal Rate? Perhaps you never say it.

These intricate portions of the problem pale, however, when compared with obstacles presented in the multidimensional world in which solicitors are daily required to work. Yet, what resources are made available to prepare for this world? Understanding—and then dealing with—human motivation has never enjoyed the status of lesser challenges. And make no mistake: As challenging as understanding the technical aspects of planned giving is, it pales by comparison with understanding what makes donors donate.

Although the idea of life-income gifts was officially created with the first meeting of the Committee on Gift Annuities (renamed in 1994 the American Council on Gift Annuities) in 1927, just before the Depression kept many minds away from philanthropy, it was given substance by an act of Congress with the Tax Act of 1969. But even that, in the world of tax changes, was a long time ago. As with the young adult to whom we owe our insight and not the mere tolerance reserved for a child, those who solicit planned gifts owe it to themselves as well as to their donors to understand what really happens during such transactions. As gift planners need to understand the impact a gift of appreciated property will have on a person's actual cost of a gift (by potentially saving capital gains taxes) or what the Charitable Mid-Term Federal Rate means (the higher it is, the higher the remainder value of a life-income gift), they also need at least a sense of *why* people give. The terms are usually abstract: "donative intent"; "satisfaction"; "a shared mission"; "love." What can these mean to mere technicians? Like sermons, these words do not go far toward much besides satisfying the already convinced. Too many people do not believe and, worse, too many do not even understand the language—not the technical language of planned giving, but the more elusive language of philanthropy.

Those who teach a foreign language usually take one of two approaches: illustrative or technical. The teacher with the technical approach will be certain the students first learn vocabulary and sentence structure; the teacher with the illustrative approach will act out words and phrases so students learn by example and participation. The technical instructor of Spanish has the students open the first page of the textbook and look at the word "Hola," which means "Hello." She will say precisely that: "'Hola' means 'Hello.'" Yet the illustrative teacher may, on the first day of class, wait a few moments for all the students to arrive and, theatrically opening the door, wearing a warm and welcoming smile, bound into her classroom, shouting with arms outstretched, "Hola, clase!"

Students in each classroom undoubtedly learn what the word means, but the two groups are taught differently. In the course of a semester, each approach uses a little of the other, but the emphasis is the opposite in each case. Whichever approach is used, however, inherent in each is the assumption that learning the language is useful; that speaking the language will help the learner not only to be more knowledgeable about the language but to better understand the cultures where the language is spoken. In this sense, the language—the words, the grammar, and the syntax—is merely a tool to be used for a higher purpose.

Charitable giving employs a language, and to many people—even to those who *solicit* gifts professionally—it is not a native tongue. The language of philanthropy speaks to a person's heart and soul before it speaks to anything else. It must. If it did not, the tax benefits and the increased income so often touted as incentives to make a planned gift would add up to no incentive at all. And similar to a real foreign language, charitable giving has two elements: the mechanical considerations of how to make a gift (the technical component for the donor and the marketing component for the charity), and the less technical, the much more elusive part that makes the donor feel good about giving. These two dialects inevitably become hopelessly intertwined in the process of obtaining gifts, but fund-raisers must realize the importance of each and why the two are separate.

## The Role of Charities in Society

Philanthropy is a phenomenon. Charitable organizations provide services for which the public is generally unwilling to pay a market rate. Yet the services are judged by Congress and the IRS to be beneficial to society. Philanthropy has come to be called the "third sector" of our society; the other two are business and government. Government cannot provide those services because it does not have the capacity, the resources, or the clarity of direction (despite well-meaning proposals to the contrary, federal and state bureaucracies have not yet been focused enough to be effective); and business will not provide them because there is no money to be made (efficiency is mainly driven by the reward of profits). Nonetheless, this third sector is a big sector. According to *Giving USA,* charitable organizations received over $124 billion in 1992, with over $100 billion from people in all economic categories (although giving as a percent of income is *highest* in *lower-income* households; that is, the rich give less than the poor when gifts are related to income and assets), and the amount continues to grow.

What is so special about charitable giving? The unabridged second edition of the *Random House Dictionary of the English Language* defines "philanthropy" in the following manner:

> Altruistic concern for human welfare and advancement, usually manifested by donations of money, property or work to needy persons, by endowment of institutions of learning and hospitals, and by generosity to other socially useful purposes.

No wonder charity is the work of neither government nor business. We also need not wonder why most people are not charitable: altruism is not a regular in daily vocabulary. Most people are too concerned with their own household budgets and savings to be concerned about charity. Even many who have benefited from charity—and everyone who has been in a hospital, or has been educated at a college, a university, or an independent secondary school, or who goes to a church or a synagogue has benefited in some way from a charity—do not always see the need to give charitably. Only the most successful annual campaigns at colleges and universities see results of 50 percent or more as a measure of participation. Most see much less participation. This may mean that the nation's large and growing philanthropic support from individuals can be viewed as increasing support from the same people. If that is any gauge, it is not surprising to conclude that most people are not kind, not in a charitable sense. Although most of us will hold doors open for others and in general try to get along with people even without a financial incentive to do so, being merely mannerly is quite different from being charitable. Charity usually requires sacrifice, sacrifice of time or sacrifice of money. Most of us, when confronted with the elderly woman who feebly asks for alms for the poor, will usually wonder, "Why should I be bothered? It's not my problem."

Yet there are those for whom poverty is a problem—not because they are poor but because they are moved—and those people are charitable, either by giving directly to the old woman or by supporting more organized charitable causes. Although not everyone can be another Mother Teresa, why are some people more inclined to help than others? Why are some people charitable? Why do many people—busy, budget-conscious people—give away their money when nothing tangible is returned?

Who knows? Ask some donors. They may say they feel obligated to help those institutions that helped them. The stories that surface when charitable representatives ask their donors why they made a gift are endless and usually anecdotal, each with its own personal drama. The Visiting Nurse Association learns that it, and no one else, cared for a mother dying of cancer; one particular nurse seemed to give to the patient more heart and soul than she possessed and made the patient's last months comfortable well beyond expectation. A private secondary school, who ages ago kicked out an unruly freshman, learns 70 years later that the erstwhile sloth not only became a successful entrepreneur but credits in large part the school that taught him a lesson by kicking him out, and that he is now at his death, expressing his gratitude with a large gift. The synagogue learns that family members credit their ability to cope with a father's drinking problem to the spiritual dimension they feel they would not otherwise have received. The hospital, war-torn from malpractice suits and unreimbursed Medicare expenses, learns that one patient, operated on five years ago, now lives happily and healthily, and today thanks the medical staff for being on call at two o'clock in the morning after a drunk driver ran him off the road and into a tree at 70 miles per hour. The world of philanthropy hears thousands of these stories each year, stories that provide interesting clues to what really constitutes the motives for philanthropy.

## ALTRUISM

Motives of some sort drive every major gift, motives as compelling to those who make the gift as to those who receive it. We like to think of the "goodness" factor in those who give, and undoubtedly most donors are compelled by virtue. But some virtue is more Machiavellian than praiseworthy. A large part of any donation pool for a capital campaign meets regularly at the charity: the directors or trustees. These individuals serve without pay and donate much more than their money; they donate services and time that remain largely unappreciated by the larger constituency. Yet when the fund-raising challenge comes the trustees will usually look inward to start things off.

"Well now. I'm going to get things going by putting on the table a pledge of $100,000." The board member—not the chair—looks around the room to see how his declaration plays. Everyone, a professional at maintaining decorum, smiles and begins to think how wonderful that is.

"Now the catch is, the rest of this board has to cumulatively match that amount by a factor of two before I'll make the gift."

The chairman of the board hears this to the accompaniment of more than a few deep breaths. The math pros look around the table to see how many must be divided into $200,000. Fifteen. A little more than $13,000 each. But some here can't afford to make much of a gift, at least not compared to the average, so that means even more for the others. The chairman of the board, the president of a local bank whose stock has been plummeting in recent months, feels the pressure and begins to worry. Sure, he wanted to give but not to the tune of $20,000. But how can he, the leader of this group, fail to respond? If he does not give, what kind of example will that set? And how would that look, not only to the board, but to the rest of the community? These things are supposed to be kept confidential, but somehow board gifts never are. And why was this matter not discussed in private prior to the meeting?

The relationship many people have with charities can sometimes dictate what the charity can expect from those people. Charitable boards are socially correct. To serve is truly an honor as well as a social statement. Those who are capable—and it is also true that many modern boards are looking beyond the pocketbook to define leadership—cannot, without loss of dignity, refuse to financially support a charity's cause at what is known as a leadership level. In fact, the capital campaign counsel will determine whether the effort can be successful in part by how much the board is willing and able to support the campaign. For those who are capable, part (although certainly not all) of leadership is digging deep. To not rise to the expectation might be nothing short of embarrassing. Sometimes motives are astonishingly recognizable.

## Communicating a Charity's Needs

After embarrassment, what is left? Only those closest to a charitable organization can actually be *expected* to support it. The others of whom solicitations will be made must be otherwise motivated. Defining a charity's needs is a common strategy. Often fund-raisers find themselves designing their appeals around the needs of the charity. While this approach has the same effect on most prospects that a tedious person has on a cocktail party, it does have the advantage of simplicity: simple for the fund-raiser. How easy to explain what the administration says are its needs. We need a new library. We need a new wing. We need a gymnasium. We need a student center. We need more money for scholarships. We need to pay our faculty better. We need better equipment. We simply need.

The approach also has the advantage of accuracy. Charities do in fact have needs. We really do need a new stage for the symphony. Let's say we figure out how much it will cost and then go raise the money? Yet, even at the level of needs, only the exemplary charity is capable of fashioning its appeal beyond the clarion call to keep it in business. Studies both formal and informal have shown that supporters do not list a charity's needs as a primary motive for giving. This should surprise only those intellectually lazy enough to actually believe that people of means will throw their money to a failing cause. Say to someone with even the slightest hint of desperation that you need the money, and you will most certainly be denied. Despite misleading marketing efforts and advertising campaigns, no bank has ever lent money to someone who actually needed it to stay solvent. Instead, the money goes to those who will use it wisely, who already have means, who will enjoy a return on it, and repay the bank.

In this regard, donors are better asked to *invest* in a charity. The need for a new library should translate to an opportunity for students, a gateway to the future. Thus the need does not suffer a loneliness, which makes it negative, but is directly linked to an opportunity, which makes it positive. This line of thinking is not mere euphemism; it conveys an attitude. We instinctively reject beggars.

Once interested in the general mission, however, donors need to know the economics of why a charity needs support. For example, take almost any service a charity provides—educating a student at a private secondary school, for example—and you will find that the cost to the consumer is less than what it costs the school to provide the product. That is, if it costs $20,000 for tuition, room, and board, the school quite likely actually spends closer to $25,000 or $30,000, and in many cases more than $30,000, to educate the student. Using a simplified approach, this is determined by dividing the budget (what is spent to run the school) by the number of students. If the budget is $30 million and the school has 1,000 students, the cost per student to run the place is $30,000. Yet the school charges only $20,000. This equals 67 percent of the real cost, which means the cost for each "full paying" student, before considering financial aid for those who cannot pay the total bill, is subsidized by 33 percent. Businesses have been known to declare bankruptcy employing similar financial practices.

All other charities find themselves in the same predicament. Hospitals, for example, find themselves providing services for which the customer does not always fully pay. Even insurance coverage that pays all the physician and other medical bills does not, as tuition does not at schools and universities, cover the expenses. Clearly, this is a money-losing proposition. Just as clearly, because charities, like everyone else, must balance their checkbooks, they need income from sources other than their customers. Donors will respond to a well-communicated need.

Enter the need and the willingness to give.

## Endowment Income

Some of that difference may come from the charity's endowment. An endowment can be thought of as a large (or sometimes small) savings account. The interest is usually used to offset operational expenses. For example, an endowment of $50 million earning 5 percent in dividends and interest will create an additional income of two and a half million dollars. This supplements income generated from fees—tuition in this case—so that the charity's bank is not placed in the uncomfortable position of bouncing checks when the bills come due. But most charities, even those with large endowments, do not have enough endowment income to completely offset what they do not receive in fees. Only a fraction of the approximately 600,000 charities in the United States have endowment income large enough to factor in next year's budget. And even those that do need more income.

What many people might feel is a rich charity is not necessarily rich. If "rich" can be thought of as having more money than is necessary, Texas A&M's multibillion-dollar endowment does not make it rich, no more so than concluding that Romania is rich because its gross annual income is larger than that of a wealthy American family. The university's graduates are asked annually to contribute to the operating fund to help make up the difference between actual costs, and tuitions, fees, and endowment income. Some charities have more than others in terms of measuring assets, but this wealth is tempered by the commitments against those assets. Like all responsible charities, Texas A&M carefully scrutinizes its budget each year (and many times during the year) to reduce waste.

Currently, only one private school in the United States—the Milton Hershey School in Hershey, Pennsylvania—has enough endowment to completely offset the need for *either* tuition or annual giving. Hershey's endowment exceeds one billion dollars, far in excess of those independent secondary schools ranked closest: Andover, St. Paul's, and Exeter, all with endowments well in excess of 200 million dollars.

It is important to remember that endowments—at colleges, secondary schools, hospitals, or anywhere else—do not simply happen. In the vast majority of cases, they are the result of the efforts of past donors so possessed of a charitable commitment and of the financial ability to help preserve the charity's mission that they contributed to a cause they wished to see perpetuated. In general, well-endowed organizations have been able to communicate their needs convincingly to their publics, and convince their donors that their missions are important.

Although vital, endowment income does not normally supply sufficient dollars to supplement income from fees or tuition. This is why charities need donations to be used for current operations. Charities need people, businesses, and foundations to contribute extra money to pay the bills. In the example above, if the endowment is $50 million dollars and creates an income of two and a half million dollars, the charity whose budget is $30 million still needs another $7.5 million each year. The calculation is more complicated for schools and colleges when accounting for financial aid students, those who are not able to pay the full tuition. This is also true for any charity that is able to provide services to those who cannot afford them but need them for less than the stated price.

## Tax Incentives

Unfortunately, except for private foundations who are legally required to give away their money, no tangible incentive exists for other donors to help out: They receive no services or goods in return for their money. When they send their checks, they are rewarded with a nice thank-you letter (sometimes) and a mention in the annual report (sometimes). The government rightfully doesn't allow much else (although the phrase *quid pro quo* is a pretty hot topic around IRS coffee machines these days) because of what it perceives as the public nature of the charitable deduction. No one has much material incentive to be charitable to either an annual fund drive or a capital giving effort.

But what about saving taxes? Is that not incentive enough? What of those many financial planners who glorify the virtues of charitable giving on the basis of saved taxes? The public is being taught that giving to charity, especially in the form of a life-income gift, is much the same thing as taking from Uncle Sam. To say "it's tax deductible" is so common that today the implication is that a person actually saves money by getting a deduction.

Not so. Not unless a deduction is worth more than the gift; that is to say not unless a tax bracket is higher for deductions than for income. A deduction, any deduction (as opposed to a tax credit), saves taxes equal to only a percentage of the deducted value. A person in the 30 percent tax bracket, if she itemizes, saves only 30 cents for every dollar given to charity (or otherwise deducted); this means, of course, that she still pays 70 cents for each donated dollar. Even at a 90 percent tax bracket (looking back to the early 1960s), a donor still pays *something*—10 cents—to make a gift. Without making the gift, the donor has a dime more in her pocket. Not exactly high math, yet many charities inexplicably offer tax savings as the bait to inspire donations. Even factoring in the saved capital gains taxes, one still does not rob the government.

One may hear that a person has a tax problem and that the solution lies in a gift to charity. But how can this be so? A tax problem often means the person feels that she has too large a tax bill and would like to reduce it. Finding deductions against money already *spent*, such as interest on the mortgage, saves tax dollars; but spending or giving away money, even though it is deductible, does not help the person's net income after taxes for the year. If a person is otherwise charitable, paying 70 cents to donate one dollar is inexpensive; otherwise the person parts with 70 cents that could have gone for other, personal purposes. Charitable gifts generally do not *solve* tax problems.

## A Message from Washington

Yet tax policy is social policy, and social policy is threatened by uncaring social caretakers in Washington. Regardless of our day-to-day feelings, we depend on Congress to enact laws. Tax policy is where the action is in Congress, for determining what to tax and to what extent determines so much about our society. There exists few more powerful tools than a tax—or the absence of one—to alter a society's behavior. A tax discourages behavior: A tax on the purchase of cigarettes is thought to deter smoking. Conversely, a tax deduction encourages behavior. A deduction, determined by Congress, is a social statement. This is why home mortgages survived the deduction decimation in 1986. A home, of course, is in every American's dreams; it represents reward for hard work. The charitable deduction, a uniquely American way to further the advancement of our civilization, should be viewed in the same positive way as a mortgage deduction. Unfortunately it is not.

When Congress, which generally acts on what its members feel is a fair representation of public opinion, looks at the charitable deduction as one way to help balance the federal budget, something is terribly wrong, but to explain what is wrong and why would require a complex language, a foreign language that for general use, and certainly for commercial consumption, has not yet been translated. As a result, we are left with the metaphor, the story. We relay the message through examples and hope to speak a language convincing enough for other similarly minded people to understand. Yet, when the story is told before a Congressional subcommittee looking for sources of money, too many do not understand. Congress, at least in this context, is comprised of normal people, the general public. When the House Ways and Means Committee was charged with addressing an error in the Tax Reform Act of 1986, one that inconceivably linked otherwise tax-favored charitable gift annuity provisions to commercial—and taxable—insurance activity, the representatives were incredulous when told the benefits of a charitable gift annuity. "Why," they asked, "would anyone want to do one of those?" And, of course, the question always asked by those who do not understand the joy of giving: "Where's the motive?" Then the more revealing question: "Doesn't the donor understand she can do as well at her insurance company?" Even though the Tax Reform Act of 1986 predated the great savings and loan debacle—when greed was headlined as a dominant characteristic—years later it is still true, and probably always will be, that donors *never* personally benefit economically from making a charitable gift. This is a point lost on a budget-balancing Congress and, unfortunately, on those who offer charitable gifts, particularly deferred gifts, on the merits of personal economic benefits. Despite popular opinion, the seeds of philanthropy cannot be purchased from the IRS.

## A COMMITMENT TO THE FUTURE

From where, then? The seeds of love and loyalty are planted and nurtured somewhere. People do give, and they usually give out of motives more commendable than embarrassment and tax savings. For the technicians among us, this is a complex question, but to the many who have made development their life's labor (by giving as well as by asking), to those who have created relationships with donors as well as with the charities where they have worked, the question almost answers itself. In a document that bore the seeds of revolution and democracy, Thomas Jefferson held some truths to be self-evident: that all men are created equal (if only he said "people" instead) and that they are endowed with certain unalienable rights, such as life, liberty, and the pursuit of happiness.

As Thomas Jefferson avoided a detailed apologia, perhaps so can we. Another self-evident and perhaps even more universal truth is this: Philanthropy is the result of a long and good relationship. It cannot be bought or quickly manufactured in response to tax laws, financial gimmicks, or even a good marketing program. Like the love between a married couple, or between a child and a parent, the love and altruism in philanthropy take time to nurture. A mother loves her son because of a mature sense of pride and relationship. After years of trust, the mother spends—invests—what is needed to educate him and further his responsible goals. She would normally have no such desire to do the same for the neighbor's child.

The disparity of training—and therefore of expectations—among individuals who thrust themselves into the profession of planned giving is enormous. Although different organizations are differently capable of seriously looking at planned giving, it seems everybody wants to start a program, especially in light of the almost star status planned giving enjoys in today's world of development. Stars not celestially created, however, quickly lose their luster when they are embroidered with little more than formulas to save taxes, and summarized with catchy slogans—the artificial tinsel of this particular star. Hope for success in planned giving cannot hinge on the false assumption that the tax code is an ally unique to any one organization.

Nor can hope hinge on the quick expectation of large assets. The excitement of beginning a new venture in planned giving must be accompanied by a commitment to continue—forever. For the star's shine not to tarnish, as it has for the organizations who have demonstrated genuine concern for their prospects (which is to say genuine concern for their own futures), seeds must be planted and roots must be formed, quietly and without fanfare, below the ground and out of sight. Even then, care and nurturing must outweigh the desire for immediate satisfaction if even a small result is to be produced from the effort. Further, deferred gifts create an additional waiting period, beyond that already consumed with developing the proper attitude. Even *established* deferred gifts do not help the charity by producing actual money until a later time, sometimes much later.

Add to this the feeling common to many planned giving professionals that many donors who establish planned gifts outlive their statistical life expectancy. The reason, to the degree the feeling has merit, may have something to do with more than the ability of the wealthy to afford good health care. Although no statistics are yet available to confirm this, some feel that people of means who share their souls as well as what they produce know that higher goals than their own personal concerns exist in this world, and they therefore tend to live with an inner peace that might be thought to extend life. The insurance companies, who help determine life expectancies, measure all lives regardless of circumstance, wealth, or philanthropic customs. To the dismay, perhaps, of impatient keepers of the budget, many donors enjoying the fruits of deferred gifts do not die on schedule. The practice of planned giving, like so many other worthwhile activities, requires the passage of time.

Remarkably, a number of charities that historically have paid little attention to the development and cultivation of constituencies have recently alerted themselves to their impending financial doom, budget crises being what they are, and have woken up to desire at once the fruits thought to be born of a planned giving effort. Such wishful thinking is not unlike the parent who ignores responsibility for caring and nurturing a child and who, after 18 years of practicing neglect, claims to have assembled a mature, responsible young adult who, naturally, is expected to love the parent for all he has done for the child. American businesses might artificially produce stature and sales through aggressive and misleading television and newspaper advertisements—indeed, our society's marketing leaders might believe that satisfaction can be accelerated without limit—but asking for the "ultimate gift," to which a planned gift has been appropriately likened, can never be anything other than the product of well-earned trust.

"Look at many large universities, like Harvard, Northwestern, and the University of Washington; look at that well-known hospital and look at the Baptists," a seminar leader tells her students. "These organizations do planned giving well, very well, and you can too." Indeed, let us do that. Let us look at them carefully. Let us look at them with an eye more discerning than for the simple and obvious image these particular organizations evoke, that of the established and successful, that which affixes pride to the very thought of possibly becoming the fundraising equal of such prestigious charitable organizations. Instead of—or at least in addition to—casting such a superficial glance, planned giving practitioners should understand that these and many other organizations, many less well known but as successful, have at least one other common characteristic: They all have raised funds well *for a long time.* Holderness School, a coeducational boarding school in New Hampshire with approximately 260 students, earnestly began a planned giving program in the early 1980s, and realized immediate success not because of sophisticated brochures, computers, and consultants, but because for many years the headmaster, other administrators—in particular, the director of development—and trustees stayed close to the school's friends. Although the fund-raising lexicon has changed over the decades, the feeling that someone is a part of the Holderness family forever has never changed. This might explain why so many parents of students and parents of alumni, as well as Holderness alumni themselves, participate in the annual fund every year. Like respect, loyalty, the lifeblood of any planned giving program, cannot be earned in a short period of time.

Inherent in the need for time to pass is the need to educate people about how to be charitable. Although many people so educated will still find no place in their hearts for giving, those who do or will must be taught the value of returning something to society. Our government, with all its faults, allows us each to help the organizations we want. The deduction is allowed for all qualified charities. Thus, each charity must educate its own constituency, not about tax savings or the technical advantages of life-income gifts, but about its mission and why it is important to help.

It has been observed that alumni of Dartmouth College are taught how to love their college from the day they first step on campus as freshmen. They learn that life exists after graduation and they are early exposed to the college's greatness and traditions. Before classes begin in September most freshmen participate in a camping trip that introduces the new students to the college's history and bonds the class forever. Students also often participate as solicitors in annual fund (Dartmouth calls it the "Alumni Fund") drives. They are exposed from an early time to a large picture, a picture that today they help paint, and learn that someday they will be called upon to help purchase the paint. A sense of family and of pride is instilled early, never to be broken, always to be nurtured. This truth became evident by example when, in 1987, an elderly alumnus and donor expressed his dissatisfaction with Dartmouth's policy on apartheid because the endowment, at the risk of less growth, liquidated its holdings of the stock of corporations that conducted business in South Africa. After continually complaining about the college for two years, he was asked by a friend why he simply did not rid himself of his curmudgeonly misery by terminating his annual giving. "What?" he asked in bewilderment. "You mean stop supporting the place I love so much? Never!"

Dartmouth is not alone in cultivating its constituency—many hospitals, museums, religious organizations, social service agencies, and other colleges and universities do a similarly admirable job—but not nearly enough of the nearly 600,000 charities do what is needed to justify high expectations of major gifts or even a decent annual fund. For a planned giving program to realistically materialize, board members must be thoughtful and caring, which is to say fiscally responsible, and they need to look toward the future, for what are they if not the keepers of the cause for future generations? What are planned gifts if not financial lifelines to the future?

Over time the mother will undoubtedly disagree with her son and the son will disagree with his mother, but they will never stop loving and supporting each other; the relationship is too strong. Properly cultivated donors may express their love critically, but they never stop loving. ("Love it or leave it," the slogan often heard during the Vietnam War imploring dissenters to change their minds or leave the country, required a feeble and unexamined love.) Planned giving solicitors and all other fund-raisers might look more intently on the real meaning of the word "development." It does not mean mere fund-raising, which can be characterized as one result of development. It also means planting the seeds and harvesting the product when the time is right. Such patience and education add credibility to the hopes that donors will invest in a particular cause, as opposed to expecting unrequited aid. Because the altruism required for philanthropy is a fragile child and not a normal outgrowth of society's value system, the right time usually will be a long time. Fortunately, many fragile seeds are being planted even at this moment, ultimately to grow into a harvest of philanthropy within the souls of thousands of people. Unless those seeds die—and you, reader, in your heart, know they will not—the IRS will have nothing to do with a donor's personal decision to be charitable.

# CHAPTER TWO

# The Initial Interview

*Where ask is have, where seek is find,*
*Where knock is wide open.*

**Christopher Smart**

Although the job of the planned giving professional starts long before the first interview, the opening moments of encountering a prospect for the first time are normally full of angst. Such is the currency of dealing with people. With the smile and radiant personality must come a technical proficiency to make the visit credible. With a knowledge of planned gifts, taxes, and law must come a desire to meet new people and to deal with their situations. Few professions require such an even and significant dose of both personal and technical skills. The attorney needs to know the law, and no matter how poorly he deals with people, when his clients need him his personal skills are the less important. Or the accountant? She, like the attorney, needs to know many technical things—numbers and taxes—yet her clients usually need her more than she needs them. At the other end of the skills spectrum, the minister needs to know people but usually does not need to possess many technical skills. The life insurance agent comes close, with a need to know finance as well as people. But society rewards technical skill. Perhaps that's why a good attorney earns far more than a good minister. Yet a good attorney needs to understand people, at least a little. The planned giving professional must both understand people and possess technical skills.

We are going to visit three prospects with an eye over the shoulder of each of three planned giving professionals. They will seem at once typical but atypical, for how many planned giving visits can truly be termed typical?

## ALAN ENNICO

### Professional Advisors

At the Learning Arts Museum in Santa Fe, New Mexico, Alan Ennico, a prospect, presented himself to Suzanne Bradley, the planned giving director. Alan's attorney, Jonathan Hopkins, came along.

"My client is interested in making a gift to your museum." The attorney sat in the chair next to Alan's, both of which were in front of Suzanne's desk. "We are thinking of establishing a Charitable Remainder Unitrust with a valuable piece of property that Alan has had in his family for many years."

These words were almost incomprehensible to Suzanne. She had sent many letters and brochures. She had written articles in the museum newsletter. She even organized an estate planning seminar a year before. Yet this had never happened. A potential donor had never simply showed up at her office offering to make a planned gift.

What a wonderful opportunity. The Museum was in the third year of a five-year, $50 million capital campaign and needed a little over $10 million to reach its goal. Board members had given as much as could be expected—about 30 percent of the total goal—although one trustee had indicated that she would possibly be able to help with another gift, a significant and additional amount, if at the end the goal had not been reached. This new gift could be very helpful.

"My client's property is valued in excess of two million dollars, and he wishes to donate it to the museum."

Just like that. This "client" walks in off the street and wants to donate more than $2 million. Suzanne wondered why but she was excited nonetheless. Wouldn't it be nice if Mr. Ennico would say something? She had done her homework. When the attorney called to make the appointment, she researched her files in the fund-raising software program, "The Raiser's Edge," and discovered that Mr. Ennico had been a $100-a-year contributor to the annual fund for the last five years. Last year he had also attended one private reception following the opening of an exhibit by a local artist. He owned a privately held company that supplied airplane parts to the major builders, Boeing and McDonald Douglass. He was 69 years old and his wife, Ruth, was 65. Until the call from the attorney, however, she had never thought of Alan Ennico as a potential planned giving prospect; he just had never seemed that interested. And now, here he was with an offer to make a gift of $2 million.

It was time for Suzanne to talk to Alan. "Mr. Ennico, I'd like to be the first to thank you for such a generous gift. As you know we are trying to complete a capital campaign and your gift could help a great deal. The trustees have authorized that planned gifts be counted at their full value for campaign credit, and, as I say, this would be a fabulous opportunity for the museum."

"Well, thank you. I would like to do something for a place I have come to admire a great deal, and my attorney, Jonathan, suggested I donate the land in exchange for an income for the rest of my life. Actually, although I did not come in sooner, I got the idea about a year ago after reading your excellent planned giving newsletter, where someone else did pretty much the same thing."

"You must be thinking of the Kurzmans. They made a gift of appreciated securities to fund a unitrust. As I recall, that was a gift of about $195,000. That was a nice piece. They were so kind to allow us to interview them both. Ultimately, they want to set up a fund to pay for young artists to study for a term in Paris. They intend, by the way, to add to their trust each year with hopes of getting it past a million dollars by the time the fund is actually established." By that, she meant by the time they die, but Suzanne had such a difficult time saying things so bluntly about death. "They really are generous; they also, as you may remember from the article, gave us some outright money to get some activity going right away. Plus they're both very nice people." She stopped there thinking that she was talking too much about the Kurzmans and getting away from Alan Ennico's visit. "I'm glad that article inspired you to think of the museum in the same way, Mr. Ennico."

"Alan, please. And yes, I'd like to see what we can do here. As Jonathan says, I've got some land with a low cost basis, and I'd like to see about turning it into an income-producing asset."

"Low cost basis is an understatement," said the attorney. "The land has been in Alan's family since 1947. His father bought it right after World War II, and then gave the land to Alan in 1975. His father died just a few years after that, but Alan's cost basis is his father's original 1947 price, which—and stay in your chair for this—is just under $7,000. Seven thousand dollars!" The attorney seemed to explode with this revelation. "Do you realize how much money my client would have to pay in capital gains taxes if he were to sell the property? Well over half a million dollars." Then he repeated himself, "Well over half a million dollars."

Suzanne knew that the original cost basis was carried to the new owner when a lifetime gift was made but chose not to reveal this knowledge because the attorney was almost orating at this point. And who could blame him? A half-million dollars is a lot of money to send to the government unnecessarily. She did not want to break the spell. Anything she said in agreement would be extraneous anyway. The point is, Alan had a valid economic argument to make this gift. By making the gift, he would be able to avoid the capital gains tax because the charitable trust would be tax-exempt. This is not a bad motive, but Suzanne wanted to know a little more about Alan Ennico's plans for how the museum would use the money in the future. That could wait, however, until some of the other issues were ironed out. She still could not believe that someone had just come in, almost literally, off the street offering a gift of $2 million.

The attorney continued. "The land is in New Hampshire, on Squam Lake. I know that's far from here in Santa Fe, but you won't have any problems selling it. I've seen the property myself, in fact, and it's beautiful. That's where they shot the film *On Golden Pond* in the early eighties, and it's just as pristine as could be. And the land values have shot up incredibly. My client used to summer there with his family, but now everyone is scattered about so much that it's difficult to get the whole tribe together for that much time, and health has prevented Ruth, his wife, from traveling much in the past few years. So I advised them to consider making a gift of the property." Almost true, thought Alan. The attorney first advised them to sell the property. Not until Alan had told him of his interest in the museum and had shown him the newsletter on the Kurzman gift—and of course brought to his attention the capital gains tax problem—had the attorney considered a gift.

"Now, my client was thinking of establishing a Charitable Remainder Unitrust paying a tax-exempt 10 percent income for the rest of his life and that of Ruth. Alan is 69 years old and Ruth is 65. The trust will be funded with the land. In fact, I have taken the liberty of drawing up the document for your own legal people to review."

## Dealing with a Difficult Advisor

Every profession requires its practitioners to respond to challenges delicately and tactfully. This moment defined one of Suzanne's. In one sentence, Jonathan Hopkins had drawn the line and defied the museum to cross it. Despite the well-meaning words and the graciousness of the visit, Alan's attorney was proposing no gift at all. If she could be charitable for the moment she would have thought that the attorney did not know better, but she could not help but believe that the attorney had no intention of searching out a charitable motive for Mr. Ennico. The income expectation was simply too high. And tax-exempt at that. How should she respond? What should she say to this request? A simple no would convey what she wanted, but she was unsure of Mr. Ennico's motives. He seemed as if he sincerely wanted to help the museum, and was legitimately using an asset that would be in his best interests. The tax laws do, after all, provide taxpayers some benefits when they make gifts to charity. Suzanne felt uncomfortable at this moment because it seemed as if a line had been crossed, the line from giving to planning. Or was giving ever an option?

"Well, Mr. Hopkins, I want to reiterate how deeply moved I am by Mr. Ennico's generosity. As well, I would like to thank you for taking such a keen interest in seeing that this gift takes place. As I say, the museum will be a better place for it."

"I also need to stress, however, that if we are going to work with you on this gift, it must be one that meets our needs as well as those of Mr. Ennico."

"By which you mean?" he asked, wearing a smile.

"By which I mean, at the start, that a 10 percent payout is much too high. The Ennicos are in their sixties and their life expectancy is at least twenty and perhaps as long as thirty years. To expect us to maintain such a high payout for such a long time would be unreasonable."

"Then what would you recommend?" asked the attorney. The smile was gone. To this, Suzanne did know how to respond. Although the museum's board of directors had not addressed this question—the maximum payout for a charitable remainder trust—she knew that 10 percent was too high. Whether the attorney was truly asking or just amusing himself she did not know. But now, she must say something. She could say she would get back to them with an answer, a maximum payout rate for their ages, but that might make it seem that she did not know what she was doing. Besides, anything less than 10 percent would be an improvement.

"I'd say we would not be comfortable with anything higher than 7 percent." She felt uncomfortable saying that, but there it was. Now it was the attorney's turn to respond.

After quickly punching some numbers into his calculator, he said, "That's $60,000 a year less than what I had hoped." He then turned to the donor, who was looking less and less like a donor, to ask, "How would you feel about an income of $60,000 less than what I told you would be available?"

What a question! thought Suzanne. How to set up the poor guy with an answer that could be only one thing, and make the museum look cheap. Who was the attorney, anyway, to have presumed to speak for the museum on what kind of payout agreement would be reached? This angered Suzanne, but she kept a cool demeanor as the attorney spoke to her.

"I'm afraid my client's best interests won't be well served with such a proposal. I don't know why you can't pay 10 percent. During the last ten years, the stock and bond markets have been up. Who do you have managing your money, anyway? And haven't they been able to get a modest 10 percent on their returns?"

Another issue. Suzanne had intended to learn more about the way planned gifts were invested and administered but had not yet taken the time to do so. She had many other commitments since the campaign had begun. In fact, although she knew that the local bank had been managing the money—about $5 million in deferred giving assets, including the pooled income fund, the gift annuities, and the three other charitable remainder trusts—she knew nothing about the way the bank had been performing. She received statements each quarter, but they were full of numbers that meant nothing to her. She was not able to answer the question well.

"Of course they've been able to get 10 percent, but—"

"Well, then," the attorney interrupted, "what's the problem?"

The problem was not easy to articulate. She simply *felt* that 10 percent was too high. She had been at a seminar the year before where the question of payout rates was discussed and she remembered that several charities had policies that restricted the rate. She also remembered that many said that 10 percent was too high. She was not on firm footing on this question, however, and felt uncomfortable against this challenge. Yet she did not want to lose the gift. "Mr. Hopkins, I know that many charities would feel the same as I do, that 10 percent is an unreasonably high payout, especially for people the ages of the Ennicos. We must take into account several matters. Besides, the income tax deduction would be much higher if the payout were less than 10 percent."

## Payout Rates and Remainder Values

She then stalled, by offering to show the deduction for the two rates. "Now how old did you say you and your wife are, Alan? 69 and 65?"

"Yes."

She turned around to her computer and punched in some numbers. "OK. I'll put you in for those ages and make the gift $2 million. Now, let's see," she said as she entered some more information. "The cost basis was what? About $7,000? And we'll put this in for quarterly payments . . . and the interest rate we're using this month is . . . "(her computer showed the best rate for the month prior) "6.0 percent."

"I thought we were talking at least 7 percent," said the attorney.

"I'm not speaking of the payout rate, Mr. Hopkins. I mean the Charitable Mid-Term Federal Rate. The rate that changes every month when you calculate remainder values, that is potential deduction values." She was glad he did not press her on what that meant because she would not have been able even to bluff. She only knew that the higher it is, the higher the deduction is, although for unitrusts, it seemed not to make much difference. "OK. For the 10 percent payout, the deduction is $340,760, and for the 7 percent payout the deduction is a lot larger—$557,820. More than $200,000." She then took her calculator to determine the difference more precisely. "Actually, about $217,000." Then, because she was nervous, she stayed with the numbers, even though she did not think this was making an impact on the attorney. "And, at Mr. Ennico's tax bracket—" she thought the blended federal and state rate had to be over 40 percent, so she used that number—"the tax savings on the difference alone would be a little under $87,000." She looked up to see their reactions.

"That sounds pretty good to me," said Alan. "But does that offset the extra income?"

"Exactly my point," said Hopkins jumping in. "Although the deduction may be higher, in a little over a year that would be offset by the extra income from the 10 percent payout over the 7 percent payout." The attorney was calculating that the difference in income was $60,000, the difference between $200,000 (10% of $2,000,000) and $140,000 (7% of $2,000,000), which was only $27,000 less than the tax savings with the higher deduction provided by the lower payout. He reasoned that during the second year the extra income would outweigh any deduction benefit.

Suzanne did not feel good with this. She knew that 10 percent was too high but could not now show it, and here she was, feeling bullied by this advisor who thought he knew everything. Or at least that's how she thought things were going. Yet, and this was inescapable, a man was sitting across her desk right now offering to make a $2 million planned gift. She decided to address another nagging issue. "By the way, did you say something about tax-exempt income?"

"Yes." The attorney answered dryly, as if that were the most obvious expectation of all. "We would instruct you to invest in tax-exempt securities so that the income would be tax free. My client here felt that this would best suit his needs." Of course, everyone would prefer to have tax-exempt income over taxable income, but that's why the IRS exists. Suzanne had heard this before and knew the issue. Who would be instructing whom? she wondered.

"Aside from the question of whether we could get a 10 percent tax-free investment, Mr. Hopkins, I'm afraid that the income from the trust to Mr. Ennico here would not be tax-exempt. At best, the income would be capital gains income. Which would be better than fully taxable income, but it would not be tax-exempt."

"And why is that? I was under the impression that these trusts were tax-exempt, and that if the investments produced tax-exempt income, the beneficiary would not have to pay taxes." Here was another delicate situation calling for a tact Suzanne was not certain she possessed. The donor and the advisor were sitting right here in the same room. How could she explain the problem without making the advisor look like an idiot?

## The Four-Tier Rule

"There's a little known provision in charitable trust law, commonly known as 'the four-tier rule.' Basically, it says that income is first ordinary, then capital gains, then tax-free, and then return of principal, which is also tax-free. It applies here in that the asset is highly appreciated, and even if we were to invest in tax-free securities, the income would be capital gain until all the capital gain in the asset is depleted." She then returned to her calculator for a number she knew would sober the attorney. Even she was surprised at the result. "Even if we could get a 10 percent income from completely tax-free investments, it would take almost ten years before Alan would be eligible to receive any tax-free income."

Alan Ennico looked confused and his attorney looked miffed. "Don't you think a lawyer should be interpreting that for us, one who knows, as you say, this little-known provision?"

"I don't know that a law degree is a prerequisite for reading and understanding the tax code, but, actually, yes, I do think Alan should consult with his legal counsel on that point, and that advisor is obviously you. But you should know that I have my law degree and know the rule fairly well. It comes up a lot in this job, as do other matters of legal interpretation."

Now it was out. Suzanne knew she had to tell Jonathan Hopkins this fact at some point, but she was sensitive to when and how. He was at least twenty years her senior and she felt uncomfortable. She found that, as before, when she was uncomfortable, she talked. "Of course, I am not now giving you any legal advice as defined by the American Bar Association." She was now speaking to Alan Ennico directly. "I can't act as your attorney. I can't act on your behalf at all, actually, because I'm working for the museum. But I can tell you what the code says and how it applies to planned gifts. Mr. Hopkins is your ultimate advisor." And how unfortunate, thought Suzanne. He apparently has twisted the idea of a charitable gift into the most unrealistic financial gimmick she had ever been exposed to in her three years in planned giving.

"Well," said Hopkins, "we'll have to look into that." He knew he was wrong but did not know how to deal with it.

"Just a moment," said Suzanne. She then stood up and walked across the room to her filing cabinet, where she looked through several files, and returned after a few minutes. "Here's an article on this very matter. It was written by an attorney who sits on the board of the National Committee on Planned Giving. I refer to it all the time. I'd be glad to photocopy it for you so you can have it for your files as well." She was now speaking to Hopkins. "I have found that the tax code has become so complex that no one can be an expert in all of it. It seems that several attorneys who work primarily in the field of planned giving have created their own little area of expertise, and several of them write articles from time to time dealing with specific issues. This is one of them." She looked at Hopkins as he scanned the article. "Although I'm not an expert on this particular provision, I think you'll come to the same conclusion after reading the article." And that was the most tact she could muster. She knew very well what the four-tier provision was all about, but for $2 million she could dig pretty deep to find some humility.

The attorney actually looked pleased. "Thank you, Suzanne. I think I will take a copy." Then, as if to collect and recompose himself, he asked about the gift. "So what do we do next?"

## Gifts of Land

"Several things. I appreciate your taking the trouble to work up a draft of the trust agreement. You will need to get a qualified appraisal on the land, and because of all the interest in land these days, I think someone from the museum will have to actually see it before deciding if we can accept it. Since it's on a beautiful lake in New Hampshire, I'm sure that'll be no problem, but we have to see it anyway. Then, the trust document has to be signed, and there are a couple of issues that need to be looked at there. And yes, I will have another attorney look at it with me. For one thing, I'll be interested in seeing how the trust is structured; we usually accept illiquid property into a net-income unitrust. Whether you want a makeup provision is up to you, but most people do. Then, I'll want to see who the trustee is. We prefer to act as trustee, by the way. I'm also interested in seeing if anyone else is a remainderman in the trust, and if we are an irrevocable remainderman. Then we'll take a look at it to make sure it conforms to federal and state law. On that point, I'm sure there'll be no problem since you have written the document.

"After we both agree that the trust document is valid and good for the museum as well as for Alan we need to have him sign it and transfer the property. That's done by going to the register of deeds in the town where the property is located and executing the transfer. We'll have to contact an attorney there who is qualified to work on our behalf." She paused to be sure she had thought of everything. "Once that's done, the gift is made. There may be one or two things that don't come to mind right now, but that's basically it."

The donor and the attorney were now both studying her intently. It was as if she had taken complete control of the interview. Where Hopkins began the meeting with his suggestions, demands really, he was now carefully listening to what was being said, clearly accepting the fact that he was in the presence of someone who knew what she was talking about.

## The Importance of the Appraisal

"Has the appraisal been done yet?"

"No," said Hopkins. "Not yet. Although I wanted to discuss that with you."

Suzanne again walked to her files and retrieved another document. "The IRS is pretty particular these days. Ever since the beginning of 1986 donors who make noncash gifts of over $5,000, except for publicly traded securities, must have the property appraised. There's a slight exception for closely held stock—a $10,000 amount instead of $5,000—but that's not an issue here. What is an issue is that the appraiser know what he or she is doing, competently complete the appraisal, and then fill out this IRS Form 8283." She slid a copy of the form across her desk to Hopkins, pointing to the appraisal summary section on the back. "It looks complicated—and it is, a little—but it's not that big a problem. The bottom line is that you get someone who's good at appraising this type of property, someone who will come up with a number that the IRS will probably accept. Alan, do you know any appraisers in that part of the country?"

"No, but I know several real estate people who sell homes on Squam Lake, and I'm sure they could find someone."

"I want to emphasize that this will be an expense borne by you and not by us. As I read the law, and the way many of my colleagues in planned giving look at it, a charity should not pay for the appraisal. I know it seems odd to ask someone who, in this case, is giving away two million dollars to spend money to do it, but that's the way the law works. Even if the gift were outright and not a life-income gift, the charity is not supposed to pay for the appraisal."

"I know of a charity that would pay for it," said Hopkins.

"Really?"

"Really." The two attorneys looked at each other for a moment before Suzanne broke the silence. She spoke directly to Alan.

"Are you telling me that there's another charity involved?"

Alan looked uncomfortable. "Not exactly. Jonathan was just telling me that it is common for charities to pay for the appraisal and that you probably would do that."

"Fair enough, as far as expectations go. But we have a policy here not to pay for appraisals. I think the weight of experience at other charities is overwhelming and, as I say, so do most of my planned giving colleagues who are attorneys. Our position is this: The idea of "quid pro quo" is a popular topic these days at the IRS. If we pay for that, we feel the deduction may be reduced by the amount of the appraisal. Further, you can deduct it, not as a charitable deduction, but as a deduction to determine tax liability. It is subject to the 2 percent of AGI floor, however, and so the deductions, to be allowed, must exceed 2 percent of your income."

She then returned to Jonathan Hopkins with her newest concern. "Surely, you're not telling me that if we don't pay for the appraisal you will take this gift elsewhere. I know we're not rich but we can't bend the rules simply to suit the situation. We don't operate that way. Further, I admit that we could do a lot of things better around here but I won't get into a bidding war with another charity. I'm afraid you'll have to accept that it is our policy not to pay for appraisals."

The attorney considered what had been said. "All right. Let's move on. You mentioned something about a net-income unitrust. What do you have in mind there?"

## Net-Income Unitrusts and Gifts of Land

"A net-income unitrust is a variation of a regular—or straight—unitrust. Congress had just this type of gift, land, in mind when it created unitrusts in 1969. Otherwise, we couldn't accept nonliquid assets to fund a unitrust. We would be forced to sell the land to generate a payment within a year of the gift. And as you know, we don't know when we will be able to sell it. We certainly want to sell it as soon as possible, but we both also want to get as much as possible for it."

"But what does the net income part of it mean?"

"That means if we ever get more than 7 percent—if that's what we decide the payment should be—then we can pay that extra out to Alan and Ruth to the degree that there was any deficiency." The two men looked confused. "OK. Let's look at it with a simple example." She then wrote the following as she spoke:

| Year | Trust Value | Actual Income | Amount Paid | Deficit |
|---|---|---|---|---|
| 1 | $2,000,000 | $ 0 | $ 0 | $140,000 |
| 2 | $2,000,000 | $140,000 | $140,000 | $140,000 |
| 3 | $2,000,000 | $200,000 | $200,000 | $ 80,000 |

"Say we go with 7 percent and don't sell the property for one year. During that year, the trust, if it were liquid, would have paid $140,000. But it's not liquid, so the money is not paid out. In fact, with a straight unitrust, actual land would have to be distributed. And that would be a nightmare. A net-income unitrust keeps track of that fact and puts that amount in a column to be paid whenever possible. Say we sell the property in the second year and earn 7 percent in income during that year. Also assume that we have exactly $2,000,000, too, although that's probably not going to be the case. During the second year, the trust pays $140,000, the amount of income available, and the amount the trust says should be paid out. All this time the $140,000 'debit' from what was not paid out during the first year stays on the books, so to speak. We haven't forgotten that it exists.

"Now, assume in the third year the trust is still worth $2 million and investments show income earned to be 10 percent, which is 3 percentage points more than the trust payout. That's highly unlikely, but I use the number to help me illustrate. That's $200,000, which is $60,000 of excess income. In the third year, Alan would receive that extra $60,000 because of the deficit, in addition to the $140,000. The deficit would then be reduced to $80,000. As time goes on, if there is a deficit and there is extra income to make up the deficit, it would be made up. Of course, if there are years when 7 percent is not earned, the deficit grows by the difference." Suzanne stopped there, hoping that she had clearly explained the idea.

"So what you are saying is that Alan can recover what is not paid out during the time the land is being sold?"

"That's right."

"I don't think I have any further questions," said the attorney. "I'm going to leave you a draft of the document I have prepared, but I also want to discuss this meeting in private with Alan. At issue are the payout rate, the nature of the income, and the appraisal. I don't believe we are far apart, Suzanne, on any of these issues but I want time to talk it over." He looked at Alan, who smiled but said nothing.

"I would also appreciate your running some numbers for us, if you will. Your software can certainly project Alan's income based on a few assumptions?"

"Yes."

"Well, let's assume that the land doesn't sell for a year and that we make up the income as soon as possible." The attorney looked through a file on his lap. "Is there anything else?"

"Just the appraisal, I believe. Getting it done, that is. You've got to make the gift within sixty days of the appraisal if it's done prior to the gift, and you have until the date your taxes are due—that's April 15, unless there are any extensions—if the gift is made before the appraisal is done. It's all there in that article on appraisals I gave you."

## The Charitable Purpose

After everyone ingested this information, Suzanne spoke again. "I want you to know that I appreciate your visit. I also want to know, however, Alan, what your thoughts are as to the ultimate disposition of the trust assets. That is, what do you want the money to be used for? Assuming all the details can be worked out, and the trust is established, how do you want us to spend it when it becomes available to us?"

Alan looked perplexed, as if he had not thought about this question before. After a few moments, he responded, "I can't really say right now. I mean I know that's important, but I've been so caught up in the mechanics of the gift that I haven't considered how the money should be used." Then, as if he had just thought of something, he said, "No offense, but I hope that's not for a long time."

The matter of how the gift ultimately will benefit the charity is too often the last thing on the minds of donors and planned giving officers. Certainly Suzanne has a great deal of technical work to do in preparing for the gift, but she is right to ask the donor what his motives are. Just because a donor has not given the question much thought does not necessarily mean that he does not want to make a gift or that his motives are suspect, but as the world of planned giving becomes more technical and the literature emphasizes technique over the value of philanthropy, everyone needs to pay attention to how the charity will benefit.

## PHYLLIS EMERSON

Except for the bequest, the charitable gift annuity is the oldest planned gift. It is by far the oldest life-income gift in the United States. According to a history of the Committee on Gift Annuities (now the American Council on Gift Annuities) written in 1991 by Charles Bass, it is believed that the first gift annuity was established in 1843, predating by over 125 years the Tax Reform Act of 1969 that created unitrusts, annuity trusts, and pooled income funds. Gift annuities are popular because they provide a fixed dollar income for the person's lifetime, usually a higher income than is available from most other investments. Also, depending on the circumstances, some of the income is free of tax, making the tax-equivalent income even higher than is actually paid to the donor. This is, in fact, one of the major advantages of the gift annuity when it is compared to the charitable remainder annuity trust.

This was the information Donald Butler stored in his head as he traveled to the home of Phyllis Emerson. Don was new to planned giving, a recently retired teacher who had been volunteering at the hospital for the last four years. His wife had died after a valiant struggle with cancer, a disease first diagnosed at the hospital. Although she lost her exhausting, difficult battle, Don would be forever grateful to the doctors who did everything possible to save her life. The hospital had become his second home. When the development office advertised an opening in its newly created planned giving program, Don was immediately interested and applied for the job. Although his technical background did not include taxes and trusts, he did teach math and impressed the development director with his willingness to learn and his ease with people. Phyllis Emerson was his first prospect.

Phyllis had not been well known to the hospital. Don's predecessor established a mailing program asking for people to respond to an inquiry about estate planning. She did not return the card but called Don's office one day.

"I was looking over the brochure on planned giving," she said after introducing herself, "and was wondering if I could receive some more information." This was the first time Don handled such a call and he did not know how to respond. Further, he had no other information beyond the brochure.

"Thank you for calling, Mrs. Emerson. What was it in particular you wanted to know?" She explained that the gift annuity idea intrigued her, especially the part about the guaranteed income and that some of it would be tax-free.

"That's right. The hospital has 45 other people who have so far established gift annuities, and almost all of them for the same reasons you are outlining now."

He asked some questions about her and learned that she had been widowed about a year earlier, that her husband had left behind a sizable estate, and that she wanted to help the institution where he had been treated before his fatal heart attack. After that, he discussed some of the aspects of the way the gift annuity worked and then made an appointment to visit her at her home, a townhouse about a twenty-minute walk from the hospital. He was reciting to himself the highlights of the gift annuity when he neared her home.

## Getting to Know the Prospect

"Why, yes, thank you."

She had asked if he wanted any coffee or tea. He hated coffee and tea but always accepted the offer, and he was determined to continue that level of courtesy in his new planned giving job. He had learned long ago that when someone offers something, a refusal is not the polite response. He once thought that the other person would have to do more work by making the coffee, but was taught that people want to extend favors, that to refuse them is a sign of discourteousness. It would be another matter had he a health or even a religious reason to avoid caffeine. In that case he might ask for something else instead. He did not, however, ever accept a mixed drink or even wine when visiting at a time and occasion other than dinner. Thus he learned to tolerate coffee and tea. "Coffee. Milk and sugar, please." If he was going to drink the stuff it was going to be as diluted and sweet as he could get it.

He brought along some gift annuity charts and a graph to review while he was talking to his prospect, but put his briefcase aside as he began to discuss other things. Small talk was not his favorite activity; he knew there was a point when some people in his situation sounded insincere, asking questions too quickly or with clearly no purpose other than to follow some textbook formula on selling. He had himself been the victim of that several times in his life: when buying a car, life insurance, and his home. Salespeople tend to want rapport but have difficulty finding it. As a teacher, he determined long ago that if nothing natural came to mind as he was talking with parents about their child, he would get right to the point.

But this situation was different. He was invited into the personal realm of someone from whom he wanted a gift. In a sense, he was a salesman, although he was loathe to think of himself as one. Instead, he found comfort in viewing his job as helping the hospital. He was not on commission, after all, and whether this person or any other gave any money to the hospital mattered not at all to his paycheck. Sure, if enough people said no and if enough tasks were left unaccomplished he might find himself without a job, but he felt no pressure in this home during this visit to witness her signature at the bottom of a gift agreement.

The matter of commission income was not, he heard recently at a planned giving conference, a moot point. Although some organizations had agreed to support fund-raising principles disallowing an employee's pay to be determined directly by solicitation success, several organizations did allow it. And hadn't he read an opinion article in the *Chronicle of Philanthropy* about this matter just a month ago? The writer said that he thought that soliciting funds for an organization was no different from the commission paid men and women who sell securities or cars or anything else. Although the responses to the editorial all agreed that such was not the case, that soliciting funds for a charitable cause was somehow different, the logic was not complete. He felt that the issue would have a long life before it would be resolved. At any rate, he thought, he was glad to have a job helping the hospital for which he was paid a salary. Less pressure. Less need for manufactured small talk.

What a coincidence, he thought, that this woman's husband had died at the hospital at about the same time as his wife. This topic, close to them both, absorbed them for well over an hour, several cups of coffee, and almost an entire coffee cake. They discussed the doctors and nurses they came to know well. They talked of the accommodations and the frequent visits to the hospital, especially during their spouses' final days. They laughed about the food, especially the never-fulfilled promises of acquiring a new caterer. They found themselves crying too, as they were able—perhaps as they could not before—to put words to their thoughts of loss and grief and emptiness. No, in this case, small talk was not a problem. Before much time had passed, Donald Butler knew that he had begun a friendship. This *was* textbook, he thought, as he remembered that the phrase "friendraising" had been used somewhere in describing what the development world was really all about.

The sun had sunk below the city's buildings, and shadows cast themselves over Phyllis Emerson's living room. Not until then did Don realize how large and well furnished her townhouse was. Outwardly, she appeared to live comfortably. Thoughts of her husband's estate crept into his mind as she apologized for taking so much of his time and asked if they might now begin to discuss the real purpose for his visit.

## The Charitable Gift Annuity

"I know you didn't come out here to discuss me. Or perhaps you did, in a way. So let's get on with it. You mentioned a charitable gift annuity, or something. A way to receive a guaranteed income from my gift to the hospital."

"That's right, Phyllis. A gift annuity provides you a fixed dollar amount each quarter from the hospital."

"Then where's the gift?" How innocent, yet perceptive. Had he come across too much the salesman on the phone? Had he sold the benefits before the mission? He knew this was a common danger, to talk too much about what the donor would get from the gift and not enough about what the hospital would get.

"The gift is the part that we receive." She looked confused. And who wouldn't, he thought, with that kind of stupid answer. He quickly tried to make up for what he thought was an unnecessary mistake. "What I mean by that is the income is less than what you would get from a commercial insurance company, if you were to transfer the same amount of money."

"Which reminds me. I was going to ask on the phone. How much income would you pay me?"

"That depends on your age." He felt awkward here. She looked about his age, but she could be older. He found that wealthy people tended to look younger than they were, at least to him. Here he was, not at all poor, but dressed in a tweed jacket and trousers that were not new. His shoes were several years old, but they looked decent, he thought, because he shined them regularly. He looked average but certainly she could see that he was not wealthy. This was a part of the job he was not yet used to. As a high school math teacher, he dealt with colleagues and parents who were for the most part in similar economic circumstances and dressed as he did. The students, although children of those parents, dressed in a way he did not care to think about for very long.

"I'm 65." She said it so firmly and directly that he must have seemed surprised at her forthrightness. "No, I'm not going to hide it. For a long time I did, but after I turned 60 I decided that age wasn't a big deal to me, that I couldn't hang on to my youth forever, despite what I try to do with my outward appearance. And now that I'm a widow, all the more reason to be up front about it." Then she paused and said with a wry smile, "But don't ask me how much I weigh." They both laughed, and Don noticed, not for the first time, how comfortable she made him feel.

"OK. Sixty-five it is. Actually, even though I looked you up on our computer before I came, I did not know that. I assumed that you would be about that age, so I took the liberty of preparing some information based on a person who is, as it turns out, exactly your age." He then brought out a single sheet of paper from his briefcase, looked at it, and said, "The hospital would pay you an annual income of 6.5 percent of the gift." She asked to look at the paper herself. What he had pulled out was a deduction computation for a gift of $10,000 (see Exhibit 2.1).

"Oh, my. I don't have any idea what this is all about."

"I know this looks confusing; at first glance all of these reports are. But let's go through this—it's only one page—and see if it doesn't make sense as we go along. Let's start with the amount you would receive each year. That number is in the information grouped at the top—'The Annual Annuity Amount.' It's also at the right in the group of numbers at the bottom. This is actually a calculation showing your annual income from the gift. It also shows how much you would be able to deduct from your taxes."

"Deduct?"

"Yes. In addition to receiving an income from the hospital, you would be entitled to a deduction of about . . . let's see," he said referring to the paper, "of about $4,170. On a gift of $10,000."

COMMUNITY HOSPITAL
IMMEDIATE GIFT ANNUITY
Profile of Income

**Donor's Name: Phyllis Emerson**

**GIFT INFORMATION:**

| | |
|---|---|
| Value of Gift | $10,000.00 |
| Type of Gift Asset | Cash |
| Annual Annuity Amount | $650.00 (6.5000%) |
| Payment Frequency | Quarterly |
| Date of First Payment | 7/1 |
| First Payment Amount | $113.97 (Pro-Rated) |
| Beneficiary's Age | 65 |
| Charitable Mid-Term Federal Rate Used | 7.0% |
| Charitable Deduction | $4,169.79 |

**INCOME INFORMATION:**

| | |
|---|---|
| Number of Full Payments this year | 1 |
| Amount of Income this year | $276.47 |
| Amount of Annual Annuity | $650.00 |
| Amount of Regular Quarterly Payment | $162.50 |
| Amount of First Partial Payment | $113.97 |

**BREAKDOWN OF ANNUITY PAYMENTS:**

| | Ordinary | Tax-Free | Total |
|---|---|---|---|
| This year | $151.78 | $124.69 | $276.47 |
| Next 19 full years | $356.85 | $293.15 | $650.00 |
| 20th year | $510.85 | $139.15 | $650.00 |
| After 20th year | $650.00 | $ 0.00 | $650.00 |

After 19.9 years, at the end of the beneficiary's life expectancy, all annuity income becomes fully taxable.

**Exhibit 2.1**    Gift Annuity Income for a Gift of $10,000

This illustration was prepared using the planned giving software ParaGon™, developed by Blackbaud, Inc.

"Ten thousand dollars," she said thoughtfully, but without indicating the number's relevance to her. She could be thinking this is too much, or too little. Or it may be about right. At the seminars he had attended he learned to go with an example using a round number, one the prospect could easily divide or multiply based on what felt comfortable. Still, he felt uncomfortable not knowing what she was thinking. If only she would say that the number was about right, or that she was thinking of giving more, or less. Some indication would be helpful.

## Income Categories in a Gift Annuity

What she said next did not relieve his anxiety. "And how did you say this worked? I'm particularly interested in those lines showing how the income will be taxed."

"Certainly. As you can see, I am showing what you would get this year, as well as for every year during the rest of your life. For the first 20 years, you would receive $293.15 of tax-free income, and the rest would be fully taxable. If you make the gift today, the date on this example, you would receive $276.47 this year, which represents a pro-rata payment of $113.97 and a full quarterly payment of $162.50. Then, next year you would receive the full $650, assuming the gift is $10,000." He looked at her to see if she understood what he said. She seemed fine, but had one question.

"Why does the tax-free portion of my income evaporate in 19.9 years?"

"That's because your life expectancy is about 20 years."

"Life expectancy? According to whom?"

This is a question that comes up occasionally and, of course, no one knows for certain. It is especially complicated because the life-expectancy tables used in planned giving are different from the more accurate life insurance tables. They are less accurate because they are single-sex based, following (although not required by) a 1983 Supreme Court ruling—Arizona vs. Norris—that said that pension payments were unfairly smaller for women than for men because of women's longer life expectancies. That is, if an equal amount is available for a man and a woman in a retirement account and the money is to be distributed over the actuarial lifetime of each, the man would receive a larger payment because the total income is divided into fewer years because his life expectancy is shorter than hers. The Court said that this system was unfair. Following this logic, perhaps as a preemptive measure, the life expectancy tables used to determine the exclusion ratio in gift annuities have been single sex since 1984. Don was able to recall that the one-life table was known as Table V and the two-life table was known as Table VI. Although he tried, he was not able to recall that the tables are described and shown in IRS Regulations 1.72-9.

"We must use government tables in the calculation to determine the tax-free portion of the income, but, of course, many people live longer." He did not say that many people die sooner. Then, as if she were wondering about something even worse, he said, "But please be assured that no matter how long you live, the hospital will pay you this amount of money every year. It's just that the tax-free portion will stop after 20 years and all of it will become ordinary income." She pondered this for a few moments.

## Funding a Gift Annuity with Appreciated Property

After a while, seeming content with this explanation, another thought occurred to her. "Your brochure mentioned that many planned gifts are funded with appreciated property. Will you explain?"

"Certainly. In fact, most people do not make gifts of cash to establish a gift annuity. They use assets that have grown in value over the years. By making a gift of highly appreciated property, they save a capital gains tax."

"Save a capital gains tax?" She looked confused.

"Yes. Remember when I said that a gift annuity is partly a gift because it pays less than a commercial annuity? Well, the problem with a commercial annuity is that the insurance company does not accept anything other than cash, certainly not stocks or other property. You would have to sell the asset to get the cash, and, with an appreciated asset, you would have to pay a tax on the appreciation. Here, instead of selling the asset and then paying a capital gains tax on the appreciation to create more income, you establish a life-income gift with the hospital, and all the assets continue to work for you." He did not prepare an illustration on this so he began to write on a blank piece of paper. He showed her an example using an asset worth $10,000 with a cost basis of $5,000. "If you were to sell this asset you would pay 28 percent capital gains tax on $5,000, or $1,400. This means that only $8,600 would be left to invest. Assuming both paid 10 percent—I say that because it's a round number, not because we or anyone else would pay that right now, especially to someone as young as you—then the return on $10,000 would be $1,000 and the $8,600, the amount left after paying a capital gains tax, would create $860." He punched a few numbers into his calculator and then said, "That's an increase in annual income of over 16 percent. Money that's not going to the government, but is being reinvested with a gift annuity on your behalf."

"Would that be the same percentage advantage with the—what was it, 6.5 percent—as opposed to the 10 percent payout?"

"Yes." He said this quickly and with certainty. He had been a math teacher, after all, and percentages did not faze him. Percentages were, among other things, relationships, and the difference between 6.5 percent of one amount and another was the same as a 10 percent difference of those same two amounts. What scared his newly acquired planned giving colleagues, in fact, was that he had a fairly full understanding of how the remainder value factor is calculated in all the deferred gift vehicles. "You would receive the same advantage."

He looked at her as she seemed to be pondering the advantage of making a gift of appreciated assets. "Are you thinking of something other than cash?"

"Why, yes, I am. You are making a good case for it right now." Of course he was, and he mentally kicked himself for not bringing along an illustration showing the benefits of using capital gain property. Yet he knew from the phone call that she was recently widowed, which he took to mean that she would have few, if any, appreciated assets. He had learned that the cost basis of property is stepped up to its fair market value when a person dies. Her husband had died just over a year ago, she said. Thus, he reasoned, all of her assets would have little or no appreciation.

## The Danger of Assumptions

"I didn't think you would have any appreciated assets. The cost basis of everything your husband owned has now been increased to their value at death. Certainly they could not have appreciated that much in a year?"

"So, I take it that you believe I have no assets that were solely or even jointly in my name to begin with?" she asked. If it had not been for the small talk at the beginning of the visit, Don might have found himself on the street right now without a gift and without a friend. The three sentences he just pronounced were as derogatory as anything he had ever said, and he did not even realize it. Until her response, that is. Then he wondered how foolish he could be, making such an assumption. In today's world no less. Of course she probably had assets, and could very much have been a partner in her husband's—or their, he should say— financial affairs. She even could have had her own separate financial affairs all along. He should have realized from the way she called, her vocabulary, her education, and the way she presented herself. She was much too sophisticated for him to have ever behaved like that. Not that any level of perceived sophistication, no matter how small, should encourage such an assumption. He deserved to be thrown out, he thought, and was lucky they had established a rapport earlier.

"I am so sorry. Will you ever be able to forgive me?"

She looked at him and then smiled. Then she laughed softly. "Of course. No, no, no. I'm the one who should be sorry. I'm the one who offended. I'm the one who knew the impact of my words. You were only trying to be helpful, and for that I thank you. I was only wondering if this gift would be better made if I used appreciated securities, and you've led me to think of something I had not thought of before. Actually, this whole idea of making a life-income gift is new to me. I really do want to explore it, but time is running out on me at the moment. I have a meeting to attend this evening and I need to get myself ready."

"Of course," Don replied. "Can we meet another time? Say, in another week or two?"

"Yes. In fact, that would be an excellent time. I'll be leaving on a cruise in three weeks, and I would like to make a decision and have it executed before I leave. One never knows when one's last days have arrived. I should only *hope* for twenty years." She said that with such a graceful tone, he thought. "I'm partly joking but I do want to get going on this. The hospital is such a wonderful place and I want to do whatever I can to support it." She paused to think about her own schedule. "What about Tuesday in two weeks?"

"Same time? Same place?"

"Yes, to both questions. That's perfect. I look forward to seeing you again."

As Don walked back to his office—slightly slower than his brisk pace to her home—he could not help thinking about his mistake. If it had been anyone other than this graceful, charming woman he might be looking for another job. Well, maybe it wouldn't be that bad, but he kept scolding himself for such an egregious blunder. This profession relied so heavily on personal communication skills that he could not afford to make that kind of mistake. And wasn't she just wonderful to make him think *she* was at fault. Nor did she ask, as he knew now some people are wont to do, about special treatment at the hospital in the event she had to be admitted. This was a touchy issue, and his response was always the same, the response approved by the board for such a situation: The person would be treated as any other important person would. If the hospital started promising preferential treatment, it would find itself in a public relations nightmare. The board was already fending off charges that its endowment was too large, that it did not provide enough charity care to those in need, to say nothing of the IRS's position on quid pro quo, a newly invigorated interest the government had in cracking down on charities who gave something in return for gifts. Although this was most publicly the problem of educational television and radio stations who give something back for their pledges, such as mugs and umbrellas, it was a problem every charity had to face. New guidelines and interpretations were sent every day, it seemed, from the hospital's legal department.

Although he knew these things, they were not in the front of Don's mind during his slow walk back to the office. Nor was he reviewing, as he should have been, the meeting's discussion of the charitable gift annuity. He knew what had to be done there. He would prepare another page or two showing the benefits of using an appreciated asset instead of cash. That would reduce the tax-free income and turn much of it into capital gains income, but that would be offset by the complete avoidance of capital gains tax on the transfer. He also would bring along a copy of a gift annuity agreement for her to see. And perhaps sign.

So certain was he that she would make the gift, he did not question whether she should establish a gift annuity. He was not even thinking that the gift might be a unitrust or a gift to the pooled income fund. Nor was he thinking that he did not even find out how much the gift might be. He had shown her an example based on $10,000 but he had no idea what she might be able to do. It could be a million dollars for all he knew—but he was blissfully unaware of all of this.

No. He was thinking something very different. Instead, he was thinking how long it had been since his wife had died, that since that day he had not been interested in another woman. Until now.

## SAMUEL LIVERMORE

The first visit is always the most difficult. The ideal situation is to make contact either in person or by a long telephone conversation and become well acquainted with a prospect in advance of the solicitation visit. Getting to know the donor and his reasons for considering a gift are the most important parts of the conversation, and age and financial expectations from a planned gift are two of the most basic technical pieces of information a solicitor needs as part of becoming acquainted. Many planned giving officers will want to know the prospect's giving history—if he has supported the charity's annual fund, or volunteered for it. Knowing whether the prospect is married and to whom is important, as is knowledge of children. Almost always, the planned giving officer should have a specific sense of why the prospect is interested in helping with a planned gift. Not all situations follow such a pattern, however, and many first visits are the result of only the briefest cards, letters, or telephone calls. Because many planned giving prospects are not already well known to the charities they ultimately benefit, the initial interview is often held with only the scantiest information available to the planned giving person. In fact, even with proper, long-term preparation the typical first visit remains filled with anxiety.

Any planned giving professional could attest to that, but how many know the anxiety also experienced by the donor? Although he has sent in a response card calling for further information and has accepted a request for a visit by someone in the development office, the prospect—a suspect, really, at this point (to use sales-office terminology)—does not necessarily feel comfortable about the upcoming visit. Despite feeling close to the charity, a prospect many times will feel guarded against being sold anything he might not want. Usually, although not always, the first visit is an exploration of what is possible, not one of commitment. Most people solicited for a planned gift are not among those closest to the charity.

## Consider the Prospect

Frequently, despite the confirmation letter and phone call, by the time the actual visit is about to take place the prospect is too busy to have remembered or prepared for the appointment. This is not always true, of course, especially when the person is retired, as are many planned giving prospects, but it was true for Samuel Livermore. At the moment of the scheduled visit, Mr. Livermore wondered why he mailed back that little card on planned giving. This temporary remorse on the part of the donor is not uncommon, or even undesirable, because successful people tend to be busy. They juggle many activities and thoughts at once. They also are able to list their priorities, and it would be the strange person for whom giving away money is more important than making it.

This prospect was busy. It had not been a good day. By 9 A.M. Samuel Livermore had already lost two contracts he was counting on before his fiscal year ended. Not that his salesmen were delinquent; they had stayed on top of the prospects all the way through the decision-making process. But for some reason, and he was determined to find out why, Digitex, one of the larger corporations in the state, had decided to do business with someone other than Sam's All World Travel Agency. The other, a church group that had been traveling to Hawaii each spring for several years, decided that it was time to stay home this year. The economy apparently was having its delayed effect on the area.

The business had been good to Sam and his family for over thirty years, and to Sam's father—who started the agency after World War II—before that. At first it was a small two-person shop, just Sam's mother and father, but by the early 1960s, shortly after Sam bought the stock from his father and took control of the business, the agency had grown to be the largest in the state, rivaling the highly regarded and seemingly omnipresent AAA Travel Agency. And the business continued to flourish under Sam's guidance. Even in the dark days after President Carter oversaw the deregulation of the travel industry in 1978, Sam's agency prospered. Today, despite this morning's bad news, he could be proud of his 23 All World travel agencies throughout the region.

He had not taken the time that day, and he usually did not until his quarterly meeting with his accountant, to think of net profits, projected this year to be about $200,000 for his closely held company. Nor had he thought of his accountant's advice to begin declaring dividends for himself or his warning that the agency's excess earnings could create new and unnecessary taxes.

It was now two o'clock, past lunch time without lunch. A crisis arose with his group-travel manager; it seemed a traveler in eastern Europe was unhappy with her hotel accommodations and had called to complain at midnight the night before. Although the manager essentially did all that could be done, the traveler threatened to sue the agency on breach of contract upon her return to the United States and wished to inform everyone of that. This was particularly irksome, because all the literature describing the journey explained that eastern European standards of comfort were not the equal of those to which well-heeled travelers accustom themselves in the United States and the more developed and commercially aware foreign countries. The woman was in Prague, after all, not Tokyo or Paris or Barcelona. Although Sam routinely adapted himself to irrational people in this business—thankfully, though, complaints were uncommon at All World—he did take time to review the matter thoroughly with his manager during the only available hour on his calendar, lunch time. The manager had just left Sam's office when he wrote a note to remind himself to bring this problem to the attention of the legal department in the unlikely event that something messy should develop.

## Professionalism

Like a bullhorn, the intercom interrupted his thoughts. "Yes."

"There's a Mr. Lee here to see you, sir. Your two o'clock appointment."

For a moment Sam could not recall a Mr. Lee, or an appointment for that matter, the day had been so hectic. Not that chaotic days were rare in this business; it was just that Mr. Lee did not represent an airline trying to lure his business with false promises of higher commissions, or another insurance carrier with unrealistic claims of lower premiums and more coverage for his employees. Representatives of these services and dozens more necessary to run a travel agency were ubiquitous and seemed to demand all of Sam's attention. No, Mr. Lee, as Sam quickly recalled last week's unusual phone conversation, represented Old Ivy, of which he was an alumnus. Class of too long ago.

Old Ivy was mostly a place at this point in Sam's life to retreat to a football game that most of the time knew no talent, not like the kind seen on television most Saturdays. When they could, he and Elizabeth would pick a weekend in the fall to enjoy the New England scenery and then go to campus to see a game. Harvard was always important and so was Dartmouth, although each year when he would see Old Ivy play an opponent he could not, for all the excitement of the prior year, remember who had won. He supposed sports was simply not his major interest and had long ago given up feeling embarrassed about not knowing the Mets' starting lineup or who defeated whom in the Super Bowl for any given year.

The college games on this level were different, not because he could remember anything about them but because he took an almost backward pride in seeing such ineptitude on the field. He could not, for example, remember anyone ever kicking a field goal from more than 40 yards out. He had seen plays that would be almost spectacular except for a missed block or a stumbling interior lineman. The games were, simply put, badly played—which, of course, was the point. Sam felt that Old Ivy and other colleges like it were destined to bad play because of their emphasis on academic training. No spring workout schedule, unless you call one day a "schedule"; during the season the players missed practice before they missed class. So, when Sam watched Old Ivy play Dartmouth in a game with no long bombs and no long field goals, he felt a pride in knowing that his was not a football school or a sports factory of any kind, but was ranked among the top 20 in the nation academically. His annual purchase of season football and basketball tickets did not mean that he shared in a sports hysteria that demanded that his team win every game. In fact, he gave away all but three sets of game tickets during the last ten years, he was so busy most weekends. He simply wanted to stay close to the college where he played varsity football and freshman basketball and where he received what he thought was a fine education. So fine he had wanted his two sons to go to Old Ivy. Back in the days when they were applying to colleges. Back before each was denied admission.

"Mr. Livermore?" Mr. Lee was at the door with Sam's secretary. While asking his secretary to fax the agency's attorneys his notes on the Prague problem, he took note of how young Mr. Lee was. He couldn't be more than 40. Sam was trying to remember last week's telephone conversation. He envisioned George Lee to be at least 50, yet here he was, a mere fortyish man, to talk about—what did he say, something about including charity in his estate plans?—making a gift to Old Ivy in, as he recalled the conversation, "a way we'll both be able to benefit from." How that would be was beyond Sam.

## The First Phase of a Planned Giving Interview

"Yes. Mr. Lee, I take it?"

"Please, call me George."

Whatever you want. George, despite his relative youth, carried himself well. He also carried a small briefcase, which he put to the side of the chair to which Sam had motioned him a moment earlier. "Please, sit down."

"Thank you." A pause, a little awkward, Sam thought. Most of the people who wanted to sell anything to him would begin talking right away, a definite sign of nervousness. Most also failed to look him directly in the eye. But George Lee didn't begin to talk right away. He looked Sam directly in the eye, and sat down. He smiled a genuine smile, but he did not say anything.

Sam was momentarily lost for words. He had been disarmed with a mere few seconds of silence and found himself disobeying his own rule of allowing—requiring—the salesman to speak first, thus allowing him, Sam, to take control of the interview. But he had not built a multimillion-dollar business and a substantial personal estate by letting the unexpected put him for long in an awkward position. So, he filled the silence with a neutral question. "How's Old Ivy? I hear the kids are taking well to the new president."

"They are," George responded. "Have you been to campus recently?"

A question! When would this man begin to talk on his own? "Yes. I come up for a football game once in a while and I happened to be there shortly before Thanksgiving. That was a good game against Columbia." He was going to say he was glad Old Ivy beat Columbia, but then realized he had forgotten the outcome of the game. "A fun game." He smiled knowingly, as did George, referring to the ineptness of the players. "Too bad it had to rain during the second half. But I love the team, even though it's no good. In fact, I take some pride knowing that gridiron talent takes a back seat to the classroom." But enough of this. "George, how can I help you?"

"When we spoke last week, Mr. Livermore, you said you were interested in helping Old Ivy beyond the annual fund if there was a way that would be beneficial to us both."

"Did I say that?" Again, only George's smile. "Well, I suppose that's true. Although I can't for the life of me think of a way that can happen, and, to tell you the truth, I agreed to see you because I'm intrigued by what you said you could offer me." This time Sam smiled. "You see, I could understand if you wanted me to raise my annual commitment to the school. I feel very indebted to Old Ivy, although you'd never know it by the level of my contributions." A chuckle.

"Your level of contributions each year is fine with me, Mr. Livermore." Had the people over at the Annual Giving Office heard him say that, they would have disagreed of course, but so what? He was here to discuss something else. "When looking through your file I did notice that since you graduated you have not missed one year's contribution to the Annual Fund. I think that's remarkable."

Yes, indeed. Young George had apparently taken the time to look that up, and was putting forth a compliment, subtle and fitting directly into the conversation, unlike most who aim to impress. The barrier was beginning to come down now, and although Sam realized this, he almost didn't care. This George was okay and he could simply postpone the 2:15 appointment with the Coastal Air Shuttle representative. They were probably going to go out of business or be bought out anyway, so it really wouldn't matter what commission structure would be promised. After asking his secretary to cancel his appointment and to hold all but the most important calls until further notice, he came back to the conversation.

"You know, George, and this is the truth, when I was in the army stationed in Germany over 30 years ago I called my mother to have her send in the contribution for me on June 30 of that year. June 30, the last day to be included, the last day of the fiscal year!" As if suddenly noticing his pride and enthusiasm, Sam sat back again in his chair and stopped for a moment to collect his thoughts. After a half-minute or so, during which George did not say one word, Sam continued. "It's meant a lot, the education I got at Old Ivy, and although this business was handed down from my parents, I think I've contributed a lot to its growth. In fact, I remember one of the best lessons ever was from my history teacher—his name was Mr. Bragdon, never knew his first name—who gave me a "D" on a paper I thought I did pretty well on. He said I should have provided not only correct information, but relevant information. That's exactly what he wrote. Relevant information. I remember it to this day and always will because of how right he was. You can't imagine how often I use that standard with myself today, as well as with my employees when they have a problem to address. And that was a history course." Sam then spoke to himself as much as to his visitor, "Who could have known that I would learn something I've used all my life in an American history course?"

George Lee was smiling, still silent, but Sam was on a roll now, and thinking good things. After an exchange about what students today expect from a college education—and Sam learned that it's quite different from what he expected—he decided to ask George a question. "So, what have you come to tell me?" Finally. Now Sam was certain that young George was not about to answer with a short statement or another question. You could bet on it.

## The Life-Income Concept

"Sam, as I mentioned on the phone, Old Ivy has a program to help its donors make a larger commitment to the college than they otherwise might have thought possible. You remember the mailing you received describing our life-income program, the mailing where you returned the postcard saying you wanted more information?"

Oh, yes. It was all coming back now. The letter that said, and he could remember this clearly—he always remembered this kind of thing clearly—"If you own any of these stocks, we can double your income." That was it. There was a list of about 40 stocks, mostly blue chip stocks, and he owned a little of some of them. Many were given to him by his parents a long time ago. He hadn't paid much attention to the income they produced and used the money primarily to spend on Christmas and summer vacations. He did not need more income, but he was interested in seeing how any place, especially Old Ivy, could take those stocks and double his income. And make a gift. Now he remembered the reason for responding with the postcard: He wanted to learn if the college had lost its senses, allowing donors to get their money—and more—back. "Yes, I remember. I remember very clearly now." Pause. Doesn't he ever just start talking? "Go ahead."

"This may sound incredible, but you can donate those stocks, all of them or just some of them, to us and then we—Old Ivy—will pay *you* an income for the rest of your life, and the income will be about double what you're getting from any one of the stocks mentioned in the letter." George stopped for a moment to determine if any of this was sinking in. Sam's eyes were noncommittal but alert. Although he had apparently not heard of this before, he was not uninterested.

This was one of the difficult parts of getting to know a prospect. At this early stage, George had learned, most prospects not sincerely interested in helping the college will see him, but mostly out of courtesy. These people do not see the visit as a call to discuss a gift; they instead want to talk only about the campus or how their classmates are doing. When you start talking about the gift structure, even the basics, many prospects reveal their lack of interest when they claim already to know of several noncharitable ways to increase their income. Sometimes they think of it as a scheme, something they are not interested in getting involved with. It is not a scheme, of course, and George knows that thousands of people make gifts this way, even if some of his prospects and their advisors are not aware of the many tax and income advantages of a planned gift. Determining who is serious about making a gift and who is not is one of the many difficult parts of the job. For now, Sam seems interested.

## Measuring Philanthropy Against Personal Gain

An even more difficult part of the job must be played out at this point. When a person does show interest in a gift, but primarily on the basis of comparing the gift's economic benefits to those available from other forms of investing, George meets the issue head-on. The hook in the ad, after all, was the implied promise of a 100 percent income increase. He would like to be able to politely end the persuasion portion of the conversation and spend the time getting to know the prospect. The economics of the gift structure, he was certain, should not drive the gift. Yet that's not altogether realistic. At least it hasn't been in George's life. The battle between personal benefit and charitable impulse is not won or lost at this stage, and except for the rare greedy individual, the conversation continues. There is no harm in cultivating even a seemingly nonphilanthropic person; no one knows when someone else might want to make a gift. At this point of the conversation Sam was interested, and he seemed to be interested for the right reasons. George decided to go easy on the explanation, though, so he wouldn't lose his prospect in details.

## The Fact-Finding Process

"Do you own any of the stocks listed in the letter?"

"Yes. I own a few shares of IBM, and some of the others." A few shares of IBM. Say, about 20,000. Sam's childless aunt and uncle were among the first of Tom Watson's employees in Endicott, New York, who bought the stuff with cents—no, fractions of a cent—on the dollar. And with all those splits since then.

"IBM's dividend was hovering a little over 3 percent for many years, Sam, and now it's about 2 percent." George knew that Sam would know this, but he said it anyway so that he could build his case for a life-income gift. It also did not hurt to show Sam that he was following the stock market. "Our life-income plan, the one discussed in the letter, currently provides a little over 6 percent."

This interested Sam a great deal, but he felt something coming and decided to play coy. "So? I read that much in the alumni magazine advertisement."

"So, if you are interested in helping Old Ivy, yet would like to continue receiving an income from the asset, I can help you do that. I can even help you *increase* your income. In this case, about double it. Actually a little more than double it."

Sam fell silent and thought about George's statement. So far, what he said didn't make much sense. A gift that pays me income. More income than I had before. Sounds like no gift. But if that's the case, then why is Old Ivy out here *selling* these things? "I'm not sure I follow you. What I mean is, I don't know how you can pay me more on stock I own."

"Let me ask you a question, then, to get a start on this." Another question. This guy's good at getting me to talk, thought Sam. "Would you be interested in helping Old Ivy beyond the annual fund if you could?"

The hesitation was the result only of skepticism, nothing more. "Okay. Sure. Like I said, I love Old Ivy and will do anything I can within reason to support it."

"And I mean to be clear about this, too. Your annual fund gift is very important and I would not want to see that diminished or replaced by any other type of gift you might want to make."

"I understand."

"All right. Now, based on what you've heard so far, are you interested in pursuing this idea?"

"Yes. Yes, I am."

"On the card you checked off, there was mention of replacing a modest income from some of the more well-known blue chip stocks with a higher income from one of our life-income plans." Sam was not familiar with the terminology of "life-income" but decided to hold his question until later. "This can be accomplished by transferring the stock to us." George stopped there.

"So I give you some, say, IBM stock, which is paying me a little under 2 percent right now, and you give me an income of . . . what?"

"That depends on a few things, not the least of which is how much you want to get back each year."

"But I thought you said you were paying about 6 percent."

"You're right. We are, in the Pooled Income Fund, but that's just one choice. Depending on a lot of things, most of which I don't know right now, one choice will be more attractive to you than any of the others." Progress. Sam is asking questions *and* he's listening to the answers. The moment of truth. When a prospect is not interested, this is when polite reserve is exhausted. The prospect's attention will return to other matters of the charity, take a side road to another topic and then, after an appropriate time, the visitor is whisked away. Sam is interested in both Old Ivy and a way to make this gift.

## Know Your Prospect

But George knew very little of Sam at this point. He did not know his financial affairs or even if he was still married. Visibly located on Sam's desk, however, was a picture of Sam and a woman. Although he had never met her, he assumed it was Patricia, the name on the development office's computer program. George had visited too many people not to know that for this deferred gift ever to materialize, at least if it is to be a significant one, he would need to know Sam's—as well as his wife's—comfort level with this type of transaction. Who knows? Sam may not make a planned gift, despite his early apparent interest, or he may say he would like to make a $5,000 gift to the Pooled Income Fund, or he may be interested in something much greater. George had no way of knowing.

Although the information on the office's database revealed that Sam owned this travel agency and the 22 others in the state, research could not provide him with any financial information about the agency. Dun and Bradstreet could report only that no one had ever reported late invoices, indicating only that Sam paid his bills on time. The Better Business Bureau did have three complaints on file within the last two years, but all three were addressed satisfactorily by the agency's legal department. George learned that it is not uncommon for any business, but especially a travel business transporting over three million people around the globe each year, to have a few complaints lodged against it. Anyone, including that precious slice of society who delight in complaining about everything, can blot a business's record with the Better Business Bureau.

But nothing about Sam's finances. What he held in public corporations was too little to be noted on the companies' financial reports, and his own corporation was closely held, not traded on any exchange. Even his annual revenues were not known, and his profits were anyone's guess. Most business owners learn that they are successful if they spend a dollar to net 10 cents. So if his gross expenditures were three million his net profit might be $300,000. Maybe more. And he's *got* to get some of that money out of the corporation or he'll be taxed on excess earnings. Yet if he does that by taking an extra paycheck or an irregular increased salary, the IRS might see the extra income as a dividend and tax it twice—once when it is not tax deductible by the company and again when he takes it as dividend income. And his salary might be deep into six figures. That, and his kids are through school. They did not go to Old Ivy, however; he would have to check on that. Probably the house was all paid off and . . . and what is there to spend it all on? George was getting excited just thinking about it. But on the other hand, what if the business was not doing well? The commissions on travel were less these days with deregulation; and with all these unethical hotel and tour operators on the loose, the agency might not be making any money at all. Also, the travel agency business is heavy on service and the cost of people, unlike technology, just keeps going up. Had Sam trimmed expenses without trimming service?

Research did show that Sam lived in a comfortable but not wealthy neighborhood. George had driven through the area on his way to the office from the airport and saw many modest houses on the street where Sam lived, most of them well-kept. The house itself was a one-story, brick ranch built, it looked, in the late 1950s or early 1960s. Had Sam lived there all his adult life? Was there a mortgage? Probably not. Had the home appreciated a great deal during his time there? Probably. Did he own a vacation home somewhere? There was so much that he did not know about Sam, and here he was, trying to get a substantial deferred gift for Old Ivy.

## Suggestions on Structuring a Planned Gift

"Much of what might happen, Sam, will depend on what you want, and that, to some extent, depends on what resources you currently have to fund the gift."

"What do you mean?"

"Well, for example, how much of that IBM stock do you own?" This question was too direct for many people, but George thought it best to ask this type of question right out. The information from research was so skimpy, especially when it came to owners of closely held businesses, and many planned giving prospects owned their own businesses or were otherwise elusive from the standpoint of getting any financial information. At one of the seminars he attended several years ago, George remembered someone telling him that the best research on a prospect is conducted by asking the prospect directly. Since George became comfortable with asking financial questions of people, he was always amazed at how open most of them were.

"I'm not sure. My accountant knows all this stuff. But I would guess I have somewhere in the neighborhood of 20,000 shares. Maybe a few more."

Twenty thousand shares! Well, that would be, say, a little over a million dollars, plus a little more for whatever IBM was trading for these days above $50 a share. About $20,000 of income, give or take a little at 2 percent. All taxable. So about $12,000 or so after taxes, assuming Sam was paying about 40 percent in taxes. And that's not taking into account the state income tax. Not much on such a huge asset. But what now?

Congratulate him on his large holdings? Tell him he could do better with our Pooled Income Fund or a life-income trust? Would he give it *all* to Old Ivy? Maybe half? But he also said earlier that he held "a few" shares in some of the other blue-chip companies. Could this mean he has several types of stock, each valued at about a million dollars? What kind of gift could we be talking about? Let's not get ahead of ourselves here, George silently warned himself. Let's just get through the basics.

## A Planned Giving Illustration

"Well, Sam, I'd like to show you an example of what we might do. This illustration is simple and, I think, will demonstrate how transferring some of that IBM stock to create a life-income gift might help you financially."

"Help me financially? I thought you were here to talk about a gift. Are you saying I can make a gift and be helped financially?" Despite being told that his income could increase significantly and acknowledging this information, Sam reacted as many other prospects do, especially those who are more charitably inclined than financially motivated by the potential transaction. They hear the fact but have difficulty believing it.

"Actually, Sam, these numbers are going to give you exactly that impression. Yet, what you say is true, and I misspoke just now. This gift will not help you financially in the sense that you'll be better off than not making the gift or that a life-income arrangement is better than investments made outside the charitable arena. You should know, though, that many people who make these kinds of gifts—we call them planned gifts because of the amount and type of planning donors and we do—the people who do this are surprised many times by what benefits they receive."

"Okay. So let's see what you have." At that moment the intercom buzzed and Sam answered his secretary's interruption. After he finished dealing with the matter he said, "George, we've got to wrap this up pretty soon. My attorneys are calling back in a few minutes to discuss a problem we had last night with one of our clients in eastern Europe. I'm sorry."

If only he had not spent so much time talking about Old Ivy at the beginning of the conversation, George thought. But that was necessary to get Sam in the mood to discuss a gift. Not for the first time, George wondered if a formula could be designed, defining the proper amount of time a person should spend on preliminary information—no more than idle chit-chat most of the time—before getting down to the issues of making a gift. He'd been here a little more than an hour, yet was just getting to the substance of the visit. But now, Sam's attention was diverted and the meeting had to close soon. This is an ongoing problem with meeting prospects during business hours at their offices.

"Well let me just show you this one page then. As you can see, the financial benefits are really quite remarkable. You'll note that this example assumes a man of approximately your age, 58, and a gift of $100,000 to a Charitable Remainder Unitrust." (See Exhibit 2.2.)

"A what?"

"I'm sorry. The gift is technically called a 'Charitable Remainder Unitrust.'"

"What's that?" And then, after a second or two of silence, Sam followed with, "No, don't explain. I don't have time anyway. I'll just look at it with my accountant." George then quickly reviewed the financial impact of the gift's income tax deduction, increased income, and the savings of the capital gains tax—none of which, George could see, was making an impression on Sam at this point. Clearly he had other things on his mind.

"So, let me simply leave this with you," George said as he placed one lonely page on the desk. "I would like to call you in the next few weeks to get your reaction to this and our talk here today, as well as to answer any questions either you or your accountant might have."

"Fine, fine. I'll look forward to hearing from you." Sam was short, and then caught himself. "No, George, hold it. I'm sorry. I want you to know that I'm glad you came. You've come a long way and have made time for me on your busy schedule. I do appreciate what we've discussed today and I do want to look this over. We—Elizabeth and I— would be very interested in talking this over more thoroughly, and I think this makes a good start. I apologize for being rude, but I do have a late-breaking issue I need to address before it becomes a big problem. Please, be sure to call me in a few weeks when I hope you'll join us at our home, perhaps for dinner, when things won't be so hectic."

## Reviewing the Meeting

*Elizabeth.* George wrote the name in his notepad the moment he sat down in his car. The name was not familiar; Patricia was the name that came up in the computer search as someone who at least once was married to Sam. As George drove to the hotel where he was checked in for the evening he mulled over his talk with Sam. Despite its abrupt ending, it had gone well. Sam clearly liked Old Ivy and was open to new ideas about how to help. Yet one question kept nagging: What else was there to know about this man—especially about his finances? He had so much work still to pull this off in a good way. And what about Sam's accountant and attorney? How much pull did they have over this man?

---

OLD IVY
CHARITABLE REMAINDER UNITRUST
Comparison Report
Gift vs. Sell and Reinvest

**Donor's Name: Samuel Livermore**

## GIFT INFORMATION:

| | |
|---|---|
| Value of Gift | $100,000.00 |
| Type of Gift Asset | Appreciated Securities |
| Cost Basis | $40,000.00 |
| Fixed Unitrust Percentage | 6.0000% |
| Length of Trust | Lifetimes of Beneficiaries |
| Beneficiaries' Ages | 58, 56 |
| Charitable Mid-Term Federal Rate Used | 7.0% |
| Charitable Deduction | $21,249 |

## GIFT COMPARISON:

The following information is useful if the donor wishes to examine the potential initial income difference between making a gift to a Charitable Remainder Unitrust and selling the asset and reinvesting the income:

| | GIFT | SELL AND REINVEST |
|---|---|---|
| 1. Value of Gift | $100,000 | $100,000 |
| 2. Charitable Deduction | 21,249 | 0 |
| 3. Value of Deduction (41% Tax Bracket) | 8,712 | 0 |
| 4. Donor's Investment | 91,287 | 100,000 |
| 5. Capital Gain | 60,000 | 60,000 |
| 6. Capital Gains Tax Paid (28% Tax Bracket) | 0 | 16,800 |
| 7. Investment Amount (Line 1 – Line 6) | $100,000 | $83,200 |
| 8. Reinvested Income (%) | 6.0000% | 6.0000% |
| 9. Reinvested Income ($) | 6,000 | 4,992 |
| 10. Effective Yield (Line 9/Line 4) | 6.5726% | 4.9920% |
| 11. Increased Yield With Gift | 31.6627% | |

No planned gift should be made in the absence of a charitable intent or solely on the basis of financial expectations.

---

**Exhibit 2.2**   Gift Comparison

This illustration was prepared using the planned giving software ParaGon™, developed by Blackbaud, Inc.

Not much, he hoped, which was quite possible. George had observed that self-made people, entrepreneurs, usually were able to make up their own minds when they wanted to do something. Not like some others who pretended they couldn't go to the bathroom without their attorney's permission. No, Sam seemed okay. The matter now was to do some more research on this man, maybe by checking him out with his class agent or someone else from the college who knew him, and by preparing a proposal that would make him want to make this gift. Research, proposals, and another visit, maybe two. And the proposal had to be simple.

He intentionally left a single sheet with Sam, one with very few numbers at that. He found that too many pieces of paper with too much information had an adverse effect. Keep it simple. Even at a place like Old Ivy, donors were not immune to the disconcerting aspects of planned giving proposals. Keep it simple. He reminded himself of that over and over. Not keep it simple stupid, for he had met very few stupid people. But simplicity has its virtues. The problem was how to convey complex information in an easy-to-understand format. His planned giving computer program, installed in his notebook computer, would be able to help only a little. It would provide the easy part, the numbers— the potential deductions and the cash flows. The rest—matching Sam's interests and his ability to give with what Old Ivy wanted—could come only from George's ability to understand Sam. That would take some time. And it would have to be kept simple and short. This reminded George of a quote he first heard in college, which is often credited to Lincoln although Blaise Pascal said it first: "I have made this letter longer than usual, only because I have not had the time to make it shorter." George hoped that he would be able to take the time to make the proposal short enough.

George had a lot to think about. He learned quite a lot from just being there, things that research might never be able to tell him. The amount of stock Sam owned, for example, assuming he got an accurate indication from Sam. With a little more work the name of his wife could be obtained, through his class agent most easily. In fact, as George thought about it, that was a pretty simple bit of information not to have acquired before the visit. Luckily he didn't ask about Patricia. A first-hand look at the size of the office and a drive by the house gave George a fairly good idea that Sam was not a flashy person, that he, as so many others who have made a success out of a business, did not live lavishly. And how about the Old Ivy chair in Sam's office? The talk, despite the time of day and the location, was relaxing, as far as these types of talks go, especially for the first time. He must like the college.

What to do now, though? What does a planned giving officer do at this point? How should George proceed? So much can be discussed in a short time, so much more than might be gleaned from sterile records. The interview with Sam was no exception. How many points of potential consideration had Sam brought out? He said he loved Old Ivy, an important start. And that he had never missed an annual fund gift. George knew this already, but Sam pointed it out proudly. He said he owned a few shares of some publicly traded stock, but upon direct questioning he admitted to owning many more than a few. And who knows if he was even then being forthright? He might own a lot more. George knew that Sam owned a large and apparently prosperous business, a business with closely held stock, stock that might be worth a lot of money. George had yet to learn how Sam acquired the business, and the stock, presumably, from his parents. It was "handed down" he said. Did he buy it or did his parents give it to him? He also said that about some of the other stock. What did that mean?

It could mean that Sam could fund a large trust. He could use the IBM stock and increase his income. Or he could use some of the closely held stock from the business to fund an outright gift. Or he might want to set up a lead trust, although he didn't mention anything about his kids. A lead trust would be complicated with private foundation rules to consider, and George would have to make sure that Sam knew about capital gains taxes if the trust ever sold the stock. But you never know. He might need to replace whatever he gives, if he were to establish a life-income trust, with a life insurance policy, so his children would not be sacrificed to his generosity. He was certainly young enough to get good rates. But maybe he didn't like his kids. People have many different attitudes about taking care of their grown children these days.

George had added Sam to the list of visits after he arranged the others in the city, but now he felt that Sam had the most potential of all. This was exciting. And it all came from a simple mailing that included a response card. The biggest potential negative, among several, was that his kids were denied admission to Old Ivy, but that did not seem to matter to Sam. After all, he had never missed an annual fund gift, and he said that he loves the place. So maybe that wasn't so much of a negative. What about Elizabeth? It would be important to see her the next time George is in town. Dinner at his house was a good idea. Spouses, he thought, especially newly acquired ones, tend to be a bit possessive about things. What if she saw this as an attempt to get Sam's money? But that shouldn't be too much of a problem because she would, of course, share in the income; it would be provided until the second of them dies. But that didn't always assuage the spouse, especially if he or she wasn't charitable.

George pulled off the road well after he was out of sight of Sam's building to write a few things down before he forgot them. Underneath the word "Elizabeth," he wrote:

POINTS HE MADE TO ME:

- Annual Fund donor forever
- Loves Old Ivy
- Liked idea of life-income plan
- Owns various blue chip stocks, could be a lot of each
- Admitted to owning 20,000 shares of IBM and may own more
- May have income tax problem
- May have estate tax problem
- May have alimony woes
- Wants me to return for dinner (this is good)
- In fact, made a point of not being rude at end of conversation
- Thinks the football team is great because it stinks

Then he added the following thoughts:

OPTIONS:

- Pooled Income Fund is probably too small a gift
- 7% payout may be too high
- He may not want or need 7%, though
- What about a 5% unitrust?
- Don't forget about buildup unitrust, for retirement
- Or the deferred gift annuity
- Annuity trust and gift annuity out of the question—too young
- Lead trust? Possibly—has closely held stock and may wish to transfer to children someday; however, unlikely gift option

He then wondered why he so immediately discarded the lead trust. He didn't know and promised himself to think about it. There was much left to do, he knew, as he pulled back on the road to the hotel. Now, however, a run would clear his head. Then he would prepare for his two appointments tomorrow. Then dinner. Then sleep, unless the Celtics game against the Knicks was on television tonight.

Try as he might, George Lee, whose education included undergraduate and law-school years at Northwestern, a place he loved just as dear-

ly as anyone loved an Eastern school (although he did miss a few annual fund gifts), could not understand why so many of these Easterners
were so proud of their terrible football teams. Didn't any of them wish,
even just a little bit, for more talent on the gridiron? And why were so
many so sure that a good football team meant poor academics? George
Lee loved his job and came to love Old Ivy, but he never lost his love
for the midwest and the hope that one day he too might make a
deferred gift of his own.

# CHAPTER THREE

# The Challenges of Persuasion

*And, if we care to listen, we can always hear them.*

**W. H. Auden**

## PERSUADING

The line between safety and danger is fine and subtle. Most know after they cross it, and then become uncomfortable. Yet most cannot prevent themselves from crossing the line. At some point a discussion changes from informing to persuading, but the change is often awkward. The discomfort evolves—it does not normally jolt—and even the untrained mind senses, although not always precisely when, that the line separating the world of comfortably representing from that of pushing too stridently has been crossed. The speech is slightly more shrill, the brain starts to race and the thought process is suddenly not paced or at times even reasoned. The voice overtakes the mind. The speaker knows this, but the listener senses it. The speaker then senses that. Anxiety arrives.

The situation does not have to be formal; all of us have experienced the angst of trying to convince people of something in which they are not interested or do not want to hear. But what is fund-raising if not persuading? Don't fund-raisers convince others to part with their money or other assets? Isn't the line *always* crossed? Yes, but the nuances of the process, largely determined by the confidence and maturity of the person who is asking, make all the difference between whether the line separates safety and danger or whether it marks the natural evolution from informing to persuading. In fact, the *effect* of awkwardly charging across the line is not at all subtle, and the discussion immediately takes on a different, darker hue. We think that we do not take the money and run. We're better than that. That's what separates us from the whores on Seventh Avenue. We think. Who among us has never experienced the feeling one gets when outside of the psychological comfort zone, the fear of hearing someone say *no?* When the planned gift has been characterized as the "ultimate" gift, the gift planner had better be careful; careful to communicate the right concepts, careful to ensure that donor and mission are closely aligned, certain that the money is put to a good and lasting use. We find comfort in talking about the mission and the gift structure and many other things, if needed to accomplish the goal of communicating.

## LISTENING

What is communicating, if not listening? Despite the odds, two ears are no match for one tongue. The art of listening, so important for learning, communicating, and persuading, is deathly ill and unlikely to survive. A radio commentator, who himself was being interviewed on the radio, confessed that he had not learned the art of conversation until late in life. He said that for many years, through his fortieth birthday, instead of listening to what was said, he listened not at all and thought only of what he wanted to say next. This was not just on the radio but with friends at dinner or during the short talks that take place in the grocery store or at the bank. Forty years wasted without listening to much of anything. Listening, one might think, can be learned earlier—perhaps in school when children learn arithmetic and spelling. The crucial diplomatic meetings between the United States and Iraq before the Gulf War were characterized not as a dialogue but as two monologues. Nothing was accomplished. Professionals trained to sense the subtleties of communication failed to communicate. How much more hopeless is that which passes as daily discourse between people untrained in diplomacy? Give this problem some thought. It is the cause of much harm.

An insurance sales manager, inquiring on the outcome of a meeting one of his new agents conducted the previous evening with an insurance prospect, became discouraged upon hearing of the agent's failure to make the sale. The sales manager, who was not upset with the new agent, perceived that the prospect did not listen when the agent explained how insurance worked. After being told the details of the conversation, the manager said, "You were getting the yup-yups."

"I was getting the whats?" asked the new salesman.

"You were getting the yup-yups. You know . . . you must know.

Haven't you ever been talking with someone—apparently you were last night—when you sense he fades away, the eyes are not with you, and then, when you make a point, all you hear is 'yup, yup'?" The yup-yups are not uncommon. People tend to be much more interested in themselves than they are in other people. As a result, what passes for dialogue and engaged (to say nothing of engaging) discourse is usually nothing more than a prefabricated language pattern. Like the homes in some neighborhoods, things look pretty much the same from location to location, from discussion to discussion.

"How are you?" Many of us are asked that every day. But how many care how we are? The other person might be thought to say to himself, "I don't really care, but I rely on clichés to get me through the day. Something must be said, you see, but nothing consequential, so please don't answer, or if you do, at least follow through with another cliché, like 'I'm fine.'"

"I'm fine, thanks." Unthinking yet safe words. The cheap currency of what passes for communication.

What consequences would the poor answerer have encountered had he told the truth? Imagine the following response: "Thank you for asking. I appreciate your concern. Actually, I'm glad you asked. I went in for an operation last month; gall bladder, but they say I'm fine now. But the good news is that just a week before, my wife received a judicial appointment to the appellate court."

"Yup. Yup. Well, I'm so glad. I really must be going now." Concern for another is furthest from the person's mind. People are not so obtuse as to not understand this, but the ritual proceeds anyway. It is the ritual, however, that pretends to give the meaningless words and phrases dignity, as if they mattered. But they don't. Instead they are cheapened, and as words are cheapened so are our relationships.

When we glaze over or answer with the yup-yups, we convey an attitude of indifference. But we certainly are capable of expanding our concerns to others when our sensitivities and prejudices are assaulted. Providing incontrovertible evidence are those unfortunate barometers of American sensitivity and intelligence—television and radio talk shows. The economy, the Soviets (before the revolution in the early 1990s,) college curricula, and civil rights are all of interest to so many who know little of substance of the issues. The same person who does not care about your personal health will likely care a great deal, and have several opinions on, how the nation's health crisis should be corrected. This, of course, is not the result of caring, but of blaming. How much easier it is to blame a faceless government (or some not-so-faceless politicians) than to take the time to care about someone else's circumstances.

## The Dangers of Categorical Thinking

Black or white. Hot or cold. No gray and no warm. Although almost all of life's questions involve subtleties, many of us ignore the shades, the offsetting consideration that would make the answer less easy. Instead, we think categorically; the person or idea is either good or bad. Never mind different circumstances at different times imposed on different people in different situations. Because of an ability to react, despite an inability to think, nothing is beyond the assault of the common talker. Who is worse on the radio, the host or the caller?

> CALLER: "You know, of course, that homos—gays, lesbians, whatever—are ruining the country and the whole AIDS thing is a message from God."
>
> HOST: "You don't know what you're talking about. You sound like an idiot. Don't you know anything?"

Two monologues do not equal one dialogue.

Sometimes, at equally great peril, a reasoned caller disagrees with the host.

> CALLER: "I think the media gave short shrift to those who opposed the war. Why didn't the opposition have the same opportunity to express their views as those who favored the war had?"
>
> HOST: "What do you mean? Those terrorists are nothing but yellow-bellied freaks who know how to do nothing else but complain and criticize. And I suppose you're one of 'em!"

No exaggeration. Extreme, maybe, but not untrue. The words in the latter conversation were heard verbatim on a metropolitan radio station in a large Midwestern city, and the words of the former could be heard on a syndicated program. And the extremism is not only from conservative voices: "You know of course that until we rewrite the dictionary, women—make that womyn—will always be suppressed."

It is a good thing that such forums were invented, for how else would inarticulate, unthinking people publicly dispense their wisdom? The other popular medium is no better. On the television set the pretense of a serious discussion of issues is sadly outweighed by the mockery audience participants, pathetically encouraged by their well-groomed if uneducated hosts, make of respectful dialogue. They, hosts and audience alike, can be seen or heard screaming into the microphone to make their piteous points. Nothing of consequence happens, of course, because nothing possibly could under such circumstances. Instead of shedding light on controversial matters, nothing but conceit is delivered by such programs. Geraldo, Sally, Phil, Rush, Howard, and their ilk are today's beacons for enlightenment on current affairs. Children, who today watch and listen to more than they will ever read, are learning that serious issues can be debated and easily resolved with clichés and, if they fail, threats. Adults learn this same lesson. Absolutism—a black or white view of the world's problems—is easier to understand than the thoughtfulness required of fully (or even partially but significantly) comprehending an issue. Categorical thinking has its superficial benefits, if not many results.

## Planned Giving Professionals and Communication

What has this to do with planned giving? After all, the world of fundraising is a world where, for the most part, intelligent, caring people talk and correspond with other intelligent, caring people. The world of extreme political opinions and discourtesy is not one in which most fund-raisers live. Perhaps. But the public world, where the ways of communicating are constantly being redefined, affects us all, and at the least we must be aware of what others are doing and feeling. We cannot bury our heads in the sand or pretend we can rise above the disputes to a point where they do not affect us. If enough discourtesy showers the airwaves and other halls of discourse we all will hear of it at some point. We all will need to deal with it. None of us is immune to the world—we would not want to be—and we are all affected by what happens in it.

Even the most thoughtful person is a person of her era, and when society establishes a norm we all react with that norm in mind. We either agree with or oppose what we see and act accordingly, but even if we act against the norm we still conscientiously act in response to something. That something is internal, the product of our experiences and beliefs, and is not usually fluid, or at least as fluid as society's norms, which tend to shift more frequently. Look at two norms of other eras, for example: premarital chastity and regular church attendance. Many individuals, moral by today's standards, subscribe to neither norm. Neither is a norm in the sense that getting a job or marrying someone, for example, depends upon a prescribed behavioral pattern relative to either issue. In the context of today's societal standards the absence of either is not viewed as harmful. Yet the change is the result of public discourse and a broad acceptance of the revised behavior.

This of course begs the question: Are today's changes in communication levels bad in the broader scope of things? Perhaps, but perhaps not. As with so many other changes in society, whether their effects are detrimental can be determined only after many years have passed. But the profession of planned giving, as with so many other person-dependent professions, would have a difficult time if people stopped listening to each other.

Not that this is new to this decade or even this century; we have always been a people more comfortable with reaction than reflection. But modern technology has stolen the time required for reflection and urges us to expect instant answers. Kindness would steer us to the conclusion that the worst of human nature is brought out at such times; the objective observer, however, might differently conclude that this behavior is not the worst, but *representative* of how people conduct verbal intercourse. The radio commentator who recently learned the art of discussion says he learned not to talk, but to listen—not intently, where the eyes are *so* piercing and the facial expression *so* intimidating that the exchange is unnatural—but casually and respectfully. Of course, the challenge is inherent: We talk because we want to say something, yet saying too much makes the conversation one-sided and loses the point of the exchange: communication. That is why there is so little, aside from common sense, to guide us. Remember that you feel good when another asks about you; thus, you can make another feel good when you take a sincere, respectful interest in him. In this context, those who mean to persuade reasonably intelligent people to support a purpose or a cause without material gain must do so in a struggle. The salesman must bite his tongue. He must listen. He must be alert. He must persuade without offense. He must hear what is said, and he must see and sense what is communicated.

Go to a play and observe the characters. Although the dialogue and the reactions are tightly scripted, the effect is instructive. When one person talks, the other listens. For the most part, characters do not interrupt each other. Further, and more instructive, when someone does talk, he is actually responding to what was said. Imagine the quality of discourse between two people when what is said is in response to what was previously said. This happens when people actively listen and care. This happens not enough. You may not care about the infirmities of your prospect; your own troubles that day may be overwhelming. But a crucial part of the job of asking for planned gifts—asking for anything, actually—involves caring discourse. If this is too often troublesome, then the profession of planned giving is not for you.

## Overcoming the Technical Barriers

But establishing a caring demeanor is not the only hurdle. People throw up other hurdles willingly and forcefully. The profession of planned giving, like so many other technical professions, already has enough difficulty conveying complicated concepts even with the best of intentions and communications skills. Reasoned people will disagree because even though the facts may be understood and agreed upon, the importance of those facts may be in dispute. The numerical value of a potential deferred-gift deduction is easy to calculate, but the planned giving director may think this is wonderful while the prospect may not care. Not only does the planned giving person need to communicate the technical aspects of a gift, she also needs to understand what the donor thinks is important. This is done through listening.

Getting another to see things your way is a difficult process, one for which there are no precise rules other than those dictated by common sense. In a scene familiar to anyone who has ever asked for a charitable gift, the woman leans to the back of her chair with folded arms. The lips are pursed. Unwelcoming, she says with her body language: Prove to me you are worth my time. Tell me why your hospital deserves more of my support. You know her husband died on the operating table three years ago, and you know that she has since generously supported the annual fund anonymously. The thoughts flash by in nanoseconds: Why can't she be friendly? Why can't she say she wants to make a gift? Why is she making me feel uncomfortable? Why can't she act nicer? I am uncomfortable, and I don't like the distraction from my own comfort while I am talking. I keep talking, and the sound of my voice is muffled by the screams of my doubt. This is why I keep talking. Faster and faster. What will it take for me to assemble my thoughts and confidence—to shut up—and let her talk?

Maturity. Listening is not an easy job. Getting her to talk is not an easy job. Some development directors would consider themselves successful by merely being invited to sit in the same room with this prospect; getting out of there with a gift might be too much to ask. The required level of maturity to conduct a discussion during which you listen *and* persuade is more than most of us possess most of the time. We know, after the fact, that the line between talking too much and saying too little has been crossed. But, because this is an art and not a strict science, perhaps the flow can still be established so there is comfort on both sides of the table. The way to unfold her arms and unpurse her lips and move her forward toward you is to ask her a question: What are your impressions of the hospital? This cannot be asked unnaturally, either. Everyone has experienced the discordant sound of another's insincerity. If the solicitor is talking rapidly, stopping quickly to ask a question out of context is worse than not asking at all. No rules exist to tell us when the satisfactory moment arrives; relating to other people is, after all, an art. Of course, after the question is asked, the answer must be awaited. None of us likes dead air; silence during a conversation frightens us. During the downtime, the other person might be thinking of reasons not to like what we just said, so we are compelled to keep talking. The one tongue is victorious over the two ears. Avoid this at all costs. Bite the tongue and stay silent.

Because the charitable representative is usually an educated, caring person talking with other educated, caring people, the disrespect found among those who take part in talk shows (talk shows, you will note, not talk and listen shows) usually will not be found in discourses about helping charities. Yet the need to listen actively and respectfully persists. The interviewed radio interviewer came to terms with this problem and declared himself better for having done so. Now, he contended, he could enjoy his life more and learn more. Donors would appreciate this person, and, by the way, with a little training on the particular mission of the charity, he would be an excellent fund-raiser. A disinclination to listen is a warning, like failing grades in medical school, to withdraw from the profession.

## MARKETING

Another part of the persuasion equation is marketing, specifically advertising. In planned giving and even in the larger arena of development, people are needed to wave the flag saying, "Yes, we are here and we deserve your support." Even places like Haverford College and Whitman College, both with loyal alumni bodies, and the American Red Cross, whose fund-raising successes are legendary, feel a need to connect donors with the mission. If a successful program would not need to sell or advertise, why does Dartmouth continue to emphasize the Class Agent program and its Alumni Fund mailings? Why does the Red Cross constantly remind its supporters of its good works? Indeed, why does Coca-Cola or McDonald's feel a need to advertise? Because the message needs to be instilled regularly. Or, as someone once responded while aloft in an airplane, after being asked why a successful company continues to advertise, "The same reason the pilot keeps the engines going." Samuel Johnson, the great eighteenth-century philosopher, once said, "Men need more often to be reminded than informed." At nonprofits, we so often do what McDonald's or Coke, despite all their success at keeping our attention, would never do: stop advertising. Similarly, charities cannot stop telling people about their mission or stop asking for support. One of the saddest examples of giving up is when trustees or a development office stops sending planned giving newsletters because, after a year, the rate of new gifts or inquiries has not risen.

The effect of continuing the mailings would be to continue placing planned giving ideas and opportunities in front of future prospects; the effect of discontinuing the mailings is to send a message—the wrong message—that the charity no longer places importance on the effort. Keep the engines running.

Part of the process of persuading involves a common connection with, if not knowledge of, the product. Both the seller and the buyer need to speak the same language. They need to understand the product. This is where charities are singular. Unlike Coca-Cola, which sells soft drinks, or McDonald's, which sells hamburgers, a charity's product is not tangible. A charity's product is its mission. Planned gifts are tangible vehicles that accomplish the donor's goal of helping the charity's mission.

## The Relationship Between Planned Giving and Selling

In addition to marketing, charities must take the initiative to confront potential donors face to face. Asking for gifts is, really, an act of selling. Let us be crystal clear on this point: Those who raise money sell. They represent or "sell" charities, and donors are their constituents or consumers. It is another matter that some fund-raisers don't know the product they sell—mission, not trust vehicle—if they at least understand they are selling when they talk with prospects about making a gift.

This is not so much an issue for those charged with managing an annual fund drive; the annual fund solicitation is couched in the written format of a letter that need only be passively responded to. Also, annual fund volunteers on the phone, class agents at colleges, universities, and independent secondary schools—generally not the professional fund-raiser—are present at the point of sale, when the decision is made. The annual giving fund-raiser manages a program and generally does not directly raise funds. But capital and deferred gifts are not raised in the same fashion; they require one to thoughtfully research and visit a person, and then ask that person—in person—for money or other assets.

Few speak of salesmanship. For some reason some people don't think of sales as a respectable endeavor, as if it were several notches below the activities of those employed in real professions. Even though everyone seems to have had at least one disastrous experience with a salesperson, sales is still and probably always will be a major and driving economic force. Are there no MBAs or attorneys to be found among the ranks of those who sell? Insurance certainly has its share. So do many other professions, including planned giving. Perhaps, in the minds of many, the problem is that selling equals desperate aggression. The image of Willie Loman looms. The mind's eye sees someone hawking cheap watches on the sidewalks of Fifth Avenue. Distasteful. Bad. Not for me. I'm a professional and I do not sell.

## Overaggressive Persuasion

Those in the insurance profession, admittedly at times among the many who are guilty of misrepresentation, are told numerous times that aggression in sales is counterproductive. Although aggressive tactics are capable of producing marvelous short-term results, aggressive salespeople do not sell much for very long. Hostility, the psychologist will inform us, is really a form of defense; in sales, aggression is so blatantly defensive that all but the most naive prospects know what is really going on and will react accordingly—by not purchasing the product, or at least by waking up the next morning with a changed mind.

Some insurance agents steal customers from other companies. "Did you see our new product 'WizBang Life'?" This illustration shows that, assuming a 15 percent annual return on your money for the next thirty years, you will receive a cash value benefit of over seven times what you put in."

"Really?"

"Really. Now, does your current insurance program do that for you?"

"I don't know."

"Well I can assure you our product is better than the one you have now from that stuffy old company licensed in New York State, and I recommend you drop that policy and buy ours. It's less expensive and gives you more."

Replacing insurance policies, while it takes place often, is illegal. Further, there are no guarantees, at least none that anyone likes to talk about. The prospect will see that the fine print on the policy says perhaps 3 percent annual growth on the basic cash value is guaranteed and nothing about a guaranteed dividend. It is no wonder that people not only do not understand insurance, but do not want to. Much the same can be said of those who sell stocks and bonds. Despite regulations on the federal and state levels, aggressiveness in sales thrives. Aggressive tactics sometimes win the battle but seldom the war.

Planned gifts have their fine print too, and some prospects are suspicious when approached about making a gift that pays them an income, a higher income than they have been collecting, while avoiding capital gains tax and receiving an income tax deduction and an estate tax deduction and at the same time helping charity. The successful planned gift transaction, much like the successful insurance sale, is preceded with a great deal of dialogue and other effective communication. One person has been persuaded. Sold.

## Reacting to Solicitation

There are always those who irrationally refuse to admit they are "sold" anything. They're the ones who always buy solely on the basis of informed decisions, uninfluenced by advertisements or other outside pressures. The majority of people, if they were polled, would say they have purchased most products on the basis of reasoned, disinterested research. That and references from friends. Most intelligent people have many flaws, the most obvious of which is a well-developed, if unconscious, sense of self-deception. The process of knowing oneself never ends, but for some it never begins. Call it arrogance or fear, but when some people create an image of who they are, that image endures far beyond any connection with reality. To at least some degree, we all can be rightfully accused of some self-deception, especially when we are confronted with the issue of being persuaded; instead of embracing the ideas of others, we have merely—and, for our egos, safely—confirmed what we knew all along.

"I have always felt that cash value life insurance is superior to term insurance," the owner of a recently purchased whole life policy will say. The State Farm television advertisement, which shows a family of four happily agreeing to purchase coverage and thanking the insurance agent for rescuing them from financial ruin, is viewed with disdain among those who think they already know everything. A debate on the relative merits of each point of view—the totality of the problems solved by the purchase of insurance (or any other product), and the purity of decision making—might generate a great deal of heat, if not light. But what if the agent never showed up? Would the now insured and satisfied individual have taken the initiative if Mr. State Farm had not already taken it for himself, and therefore for the insurance purchaser?

Only the rare individual on his own actually telephones or visits the local life insurance office. And then that person usually has a reason to take the initiative—a recent diagnosis of cancer, for example, which usually does not endear him to the insurance company. Only those who cling to deceit will deny that the function of a salesperson is almost always necessary and most of the time, with unfortunate and notable exceptions, admirable. Someone must connect a person with a product and some products do not sell themselves well through the media. Insurance is one of them. A charitable cause is another. Someone must take the initiative to personally contact the public, an action most people would not undertake with any enthusiasm. It is a difficult job.

The reality is that a salesperson connects a potential buyer to a product. Look at it this way: Would donors have made the gift if you had not spoken to them? If not, you have placed the product in front of the consumer, which is what a person who sells does. This is not bad. This is good. And you do a service to philanthropy by doing this. Most planned gifts are not made without this effort on the part of the charity's representative.

## Positive Uses of "No"

The effort at persuasion does not always succeed, and as with anything with the potential for failure, we have come to fatally desire soft, comfortable words in our discourse, often to the detriment of real progress or understanding. We live with euphemisms. We no longer resolve problems, we address issues; we know of no mean people, just those with personality disorders; a bad person has never been born, just those who have from time to time behaved poorly. Thus, with such a mentality, we fear being told *no*. An outright *no* is bad. It means rejection, and we have grown away in comfort from rejection. Many college rejection letters, for they are still called that by real people, take on an almost congratulatory air as students, bad students who perhaps would have done better not to have wasted their or anyone else's time by applying in the first place, are relieved to learn that the only reason they have been denied admission was the "high number of quality applicants," which, of course, made the selection process all the more difficult for the poor admissions staff. The lack of initiative, low grades, or a disagreeable personality, while almost always an overwhelming contribution to one's image and persona during an interview, is never communicated as a reason for rejection. It is therefore a wonder that more rejected applicants don't write letters of sympathy to the overworked admissions director offering consolation for an unappreciated job well done. Euphemisms are not necessarily bad; when they communicate accurately *and* better, they should be used, but when they communicate less accurately and more confusingly, they should not be used. A spade is still a spade.

*No* is a simple, two-letter, one-syllable word that says quite a lot, a lot that people do not like to hear. Yet, in some cases (fund-raising in particular), there is really no getting around it. This word, in response to many questions, can and should be considered complete all by itself. The mind's natural inclination is not to give away money but to keep it. This is true for everyone concerned: the donor, the attorney, the accountant, and most certainly the spouse and children. For the person ever to part with his money, the solicitor must ask for the gift. But in asking, is there not the chance that the person asked will refuse? Might he say *no?* Might this be another, often unspoken, reason to dislike selling?

## Persistence and Perseverance

One of the older motivating stories circulating around sales training rooms is the one about Babe Ruth—how he, one of the best hitters in the history of baseball, retired with a lifetime batting average of .325. That means 325 hits for each 1,000 times at the plate. Awesome. But it also means 675 strikeouts or nonhits (except for walks, which don't count) for those same 1,000 times at the plate. The best batter ever in baseball failed about two times for every one time he succeeded. One part achievement to two parts failure. A recipe for success.

Another story told to budding prospective sales forces to keep them awake and feeling good about themselves during training classes concerns Abraham Lincoln: He was essentially a failure. He twice failed in his own business, was defeated in a run for the Illinois state legislature, was twice defeated for the House of Representatives, was twice defeated for the United States Senate, and lost when he ran for Vice President. His personal life had its misery, too. His first fiancee died and he suffered a nervous breakdown. Looking at it that way, the man was a loser. In the eyes of many, however, he became the greatest president, the greatest leader, the greatest humanitarian, in the history of our country. The story is usually told for inspirational effect with Lincoln's identity revealed at the end, when surprised looks and wet eyes are most stirring.

The obvious lesson is this: Lincoln and Ruth were successes not because they did not fail, but because they never gave up. Any imbecile can claim victory, which is to say avoid defeat, when the effort was never or too infrequently made. The true hero in our culture is the person who keeps trying, the person who strives against odds to succeed. There are no supermen, no superwomen, who with ease conquer all problems. Those who accomplish tasks, great and admirable tasks, are those same who fumble, stumble, and keep trying until they get it right.

So it is with fund-raising, particularly in the arena of planned giving. We can surround ourselves with all of the best ancillary weapons—brochures, tax services, and clean desks—but nothing can take the place of calling or visiting a prospect. And nothing (okay, very little) in planned giving will happen otherwise. This means that the fund-raiser must get used to hearing the frequent *no*. If only she would hear *no* a mere 675 times for each 1,000 people she asked; if only she asked 1,000 people.

The distance between the phone's receiver and its bank of numbers is large and made larger by the fear of *no*. Yet that distance must be traversed for progress to be made. Mr. State Farm did it, and so do thousands of others who are employed to sell. Most do not do so easily, despite the common misperception that those who perform well are so skilled that the inherent tasks in the performance are successfully completed without toil. Babe Ruth must always have hit a home run, right? In fact, the truly skilled are truly trained; they work at their craft endlessly. As with all professionals, so it must be with those who practice planned giving.

## The Unasked Question

You do not answer the question about air conditioning if you do not want to buy the car. In the sales training room, this is known as getting the big sale with the little question. "Do you want air conditioning in your new Thunderbird or not?" Either an affirmative or a negative response to the little question—it does not matter—equals an affirmative response to the big but unasked question: Do you want to squander your hard-earned income on this piece of glitz that surely will not outlive the required sixty payments? Answer: yes. The decision about the air conditioning, an afterthought, is revealing. Another form of little decision is yes or yes. Do you want the black or the red model? Either color equals a model. The sales manager (for cars, stocks, insurance, frozen foods, magazines, whatever) will earnestly defend this manipulation, saying that the little questions provide the customer the right perspective; the little pieces are easier to embrace than the whole, big piece.

You do not need a Thunderbird with air conditioning to get from one place to another; a horse will do that. You do not need a fancy car to transport things; a wheelbarrow will do that. Support to a charitable organization can be either a wheelbarrow or a Thunderbird. Like the automobile salesperson with several types of options to sell, once an objective has been determined, the planned giving director relies on many benefits to accomplish the objective. Thus, the benefits of a planned gift are similar to the attractions of any other purchase: A tax deduction might equal air conditioning; increased income can be thought to equal more miles per gallon; the Thunderbird (and not the Volkswagen or a horse) could equal a unitrust (and not a modest annual fund gift).

## THE MISSION AS PRODUCT

But benefits do not equal product. In planned giving the product being sold is not an income for life or increased income or tax benefits or anything else so agreeably tangible. Perhaps the point is not stretched too far to say that the car salesperson's product is not actually a car: A man walks into the dealership showroom not to buy a car—after all, he probably used a car to get to the showroom—but to add to his self-worth. Similarly, life insurance salespeople do not sell policies; they sell peace of mind. Almost every purchase, no matter the product, is the result of an examination of self-worth: a car, a life-insurance policy, a new suit, perfume, shoes, a computer, this book. So it is in fund-raising. The planned giving director sells and Samuel Livermore (you met him in Chapter 2) knows it, the *mission* of Old Ivy, its reason for existing: to educate students to become active, caring, and responsible adults. What is purchased is that faint, intangible heartstring between the soul of a supporter and a charity's programs or buildings or future. (The IRS does not yet recognize this as a quid pro quo transaction, but no one knows if someone untrained in the subtleties of donor intent is trying to determine the value of that powerful heartstring.) A hospital might have a high-tech heart center; the Boys' Club, a unique ability to bridge the gap between boys and men; the church or synagogue, a road map to otherwise uncharted destinations. Buying into such a noble mission satisfies a vacant spot in Sam's feelings of self-worth.

But most charities, like most salespeople, do not yet articulate their missions well. Too many board members are afraid to ask what their town would be like if their charity ceased to exist at noon the next day. Even Old Ivy, having articulated its mission well, still has not made much of an impact on the majority of those from whom it wants support. This is why George Lee, the planned giving director at Old Ivy, and all the other planned giving officers, must continually retell the story of what is happening with the charity. From the telling of the story emerges the mission—the real product being bought, even if it is sometimes clumsily sold.

## Selling a Sense of Mission

Even for so noble a purpose, however, sales tactics must be employed. By inquiring about the amount of income, Samuel Livermore is slowly making a decision. He is not yet (in Chapter 2) at the point of affirming air conditioning, but George Lee is making progress. Here, however, a difference emerges between this sale and others. Contrary to everything that most will ever know about the art of persuasion, George is selling, as he should be, primarily by conveying information. By his manner and his attitude, as well as through the strength of the mission of the charity he represents, George will allow Sam to *lead himself* to the decision. This blend of selling and informing is the essence of persuasion; in a perfect world all interviews would incorporate the give and take between the two, a give and take that requires more listening than talking.

## Setting the Stage

The world is not perfect, however, and far too many planned giving interviews are long on selling and short on informing. In fact, George enjoys the luxury of managing a discussion on the more comfortable side of the line between informing and persuading for a reason other than his abilities to conduct an interview. Before George ever shows up, Sam is already willing to support Old Ivy. Persuasion, an essential ingredient in selling, has preceded George to the interview. Even if they are unaware of the many benefits a planned gift offers, many donors, unless they are unconcerned with the charity's mission, are still willing to talk earnestly with the charitable representative because they are predisposed to help. That feeling is created well before the visit, often many decades before. Some donors simply want to revive their youth, hoping to help others enjoy similar experiences; others are less emotional but committed nonetheless because of a need to give back to society in a particular manner. These are the seeds. Then, many discussions might occur before a decision is made to give. It is not an exaggeration to recognize that those who occupy the cushy chairs in today's development offices must, if they possess integrity, credit their predecessors, whose seats were probably much less cushy, for today's open doors. And major gift solicitors today instill feelings to be awakened to action during one of the many tomorrows.

## UNDERSTANDING THE MOTIVES OF DONORS

Remarkably, even when ghosts of the past have not paved the way for the future, unsolicited loyalty is not uncommon. Why else would charities who do nothing to cultivate donors, whose missions are unclear, attract what they do? Some people, without persuasion, are willing to help a particular cause. The charity's trustees may bicker about everything and provide no direction, its staff may be detrimentally political so that no worker is happy, and its customers may frequently complain about its services, but people support the hapless charity nonetheless. This inexplicable willingness on the part of people to be charitable is essential to the process of raising money. The subjective, internal, and highly personal feelings donors have for their preferred causes, untraceable to any tangible activity or effort, are important elements in the decision-making process.

Yet George has never read about this—why people give—in the professional literature. Not in any substantive format. Even the more psychologically oriented literature on giving does not explain this. The examples in otherwise excellent newsletters and textbooks are lifeless cardboards: the widow who has a chunk of land, the childless couple with low cost-basis and low income-producing assets. Where do these people come from? Although stories abound, relatively few who have actually conducted an interview with a real prospective planned giving donor come back to the office to say, "Gee, I've just talked to someone, my first visit, in fact, who wants to set up a $100,000 unitrust with IBM stock, and he gave me the stock on the spot and everybody was happy." Instead, any gift of substance, as will Sam's before it is made, usually requires more than one interview, and most of the time the interviews will include more than the donor and the spouse. Advisors are always part of the process, as they should be, as are children and others who might have an interest in whether the loved one gives away a great deal of money. (For reasons not fully explained, protective love, many times after years of dormancy, has a habit of appearing rapidly, like the cavalry on the horizon, when such decisions are made.) The purpose of the newsworthy journals and newsletters is to transmit information on what has recently happened: the latest on gift annuities, life insurance funding a unitrust, the latest private letter ruling from the IRS, the hottest gift. The real human dramas, because of space and the time most readers do not have, are never scrutinized, yet we all miss so much by their absence. Life with uncertain donors, greedy heirs, and obnoxious attorneys can be so much more cruel and interesting and useful than cardboard cutouts.

But before the gloom sets in too heavily on this point, it must be noted that it is also true that nothing academically oriented can fully prepare the planned giving practitioner for the real-world problems encountered when actually seeing donors in their homes and offices. Little of substance is available for George Lee to read. Besides, reading does not equal doing. We use the cardboard merely as a useful launching pad into reality. That is not the fault of the cardboard. Just don't be lulled into thinking that the practice round equals the real thing.

Although some gifts by donors—products of intense, personal feelings—are made without effort on the part of the charity, no sincere fundraising effort relies solely on chance, and a properly run planned giving program will not thrust unwanted visitors on unsuspecting innocents. The efforts to market and follow through are such that many supporters, by responding to advertisements, *ask* to be visited. The prospect knows the visitor arrives with a purpose; naiveté is not a common characteristic of someone in possession of substantial assets. Thus George does not need to spend time selling the idea of support. Unlike other salespeople intruding on the lives of others, George does not ask, "Why am I here?" only to be told, "I don't know. Perhaps because you caught me in a weak moment on the telephone."

Some insurance agents are also uniquely capable of making the most basic idea unnecessarily complicated. (Does anyone really know what "interpolated terminal reserve" is? And that's an easy one.) But planned giving professionals are similarly culpable. Too often, prospects do not make a gift because no one explained the concepts well enough.

George comes to Sam as a teacher comes to a willing student. George possesses the technical knowledge, but success will be determined by his ability to deal with people; he is able to make Sam feel comfortable without letting him control the interview. How many instructors are academically capable but still poor teachers? Everyone has been exposed to one of those somewhere, no matter at what school or college. The ability to clearly convey information is rare. Although communicating the tax implications and the other mathematical aspects of the gift is essential to the process, practitioners of planned giving serve no one by exciting themselves over technicalities; they are not the primary players in such dramas, but merely the supporting cast. The technical knowledge is, as a mathematician would say, a given; the ability needed to apply the knowledge is the variable. Each interview is unique. Each interview has as its sole purpose to determine if the prospect is willing to make a planned gift, to encourage the prospect to talk about his experiences with the charity. The art is persuasion and the product is the mission.

# CHAPTER FOUR

# Following Through

*'Tis known by the name of perseverance in a good cause ...*
**Laurence Sterne**

W hat do prospective donors think about after a meeting, after the planned giving director has gone? The prospect is alone, perhaps with her spouse, thinking about—what? The tax benefits? The increased income? A new way to help a charity? Dinner? Perhaps there are as many answers to that question as there are donors, but clearly some sort of evaluation process takes place. Unless a person knows that she is unable or unwilling to make a planned gift, a great deal of thinking surely takes place about both the satisfaction of making a significant charitable gift and the personal opportunities that the gift provides. The purists and those most naïve among us might like to think that the donor is solely motivated by the opportunity to help, that the personal benefits are incidental to the decision-making process. But that, of course, is not true. The visit takes place because of an interest in the charity, and its success is built upon the commitment the person has for the charity, but to make a gift actually happen, the planned giving professional must understand that at some point the difficult questions— both of the gift's structure and of charitable intent—not only must be raised, but must be answered.

This is why a second meeting, and often a third, a fourth, and sometimes even more, must take place before a donor is completely satisfied with a decision to make a planned gift. It is, after all, an important decision. During the meetings following the first, the prospect will air concerns she did not express at first, perhaps because she did not know enough to ask, or did not feel comfortable discussing them. Hearing that a deduction is available, for example, does not readily trigger a question about the ability to use it all, at least until the idea has had time to sink

**79**

in. Although it seems counterintuitive, time is often the ally of the planned giving professional.

## ALAN ENNICO

### The Gift of Land

Suzanne had just hung up the phone with Alan Ennico, and she still had no idea, because he did not, how the gift would be used after his and his wife's death. Since the first meeting six months ago, the Learning Arts Museum had raised a significant amount of money toward its $50 million goal, but still found themselves $10 million short. The Ennico gift would go a long way toward meeting that shortfall, as well as inspire others to make a similar gift, if only she could get the principals to agree to the terms.

### The Payout Rate

The payout rate remained a problem. The attorney, Jonathan Hopkins, continued to insist on the higher trust income. After he had discussed the matter with Alan, he called Suzanne to reiterate that a payout of 10 percent would be most appropriate for his clients. Suzanne said she would have to discuss the matter with her trustees and that she would get back to him as soon as possible. She still felt this was too high, but she could not argue with his logic that the museum's investment managers would be able to receive at least that much, so there was little likelihood that the trust would ever lose money. In fact, the more the trust grew, the more the Ennicos would make. After Suzanne took this matter up with the development committee, which was willing to approve the 10 percent payout, she concluded that if the Ennicos were willing to make a gift worth $2 million to the museum she would be glad to accept it.

Besides, the attorney kept talking about other charities that might be interested in the gift. In fact, he specifically mentioned two—the colleges of Mr. and Mrs. Ennico. He told her that either of the colleges would gladly take the gift and provide a 10 percent payout. If they would do that, she thought, there was no reason the museum should not take it. Besides, it would get her that much closer to the capital campaign goal. Unfortunately, she did not consult with the planned giving director at either college, both of which were located in the Northwest, to determine their policy on payout rates. Neither would have agreed to pay 10 percent. She knew the names well enough, and therefore felt that their planned giving programs were well established and healthy. They have enough, she thought, and we don't have much. It will mean so much more to us. She wanted this gift badly.

When she discussed the payout rate on the telephone with the attorney, she decided to fight one last time for a lower rate, despite her trustees' approval of a 10 percent payout. "If for nothing else, think of the amount that would come to the museum," she began. "Every increase in payout rate decreases the amount coming to us."

"Well, as I already told you, my client needs the income."

"But they're both so young."

"Yes. And you're getting a gift valued today at $2 million." She could not argue that point, so stayed silent. After a few moments Hopkins continued. "So what's the problem?"

"I don't know. But it just doesn't feel right."

"I know what you mean," he said in an uncharacteristically understanding tone of voice. "But feeling right is not enough here. Alan has a legitimate need for income, and I know that many trusts are written for that amount and more." She thought this was true, but that did not make it right in this case. He continued, "Look, this is what I'm willing to do. Let's make the payout 9 percent. That's a lot of sacrifice on our part, and it adds to whatever amount that will come to the museum. That way, if your investment managers get what they've been getting these last several years, you'll be in great shape. You'll have much more than $2 million, probably closer to $3 million or even more. So don't sweat it."

Suzanne was at once happy and angry. It seemed as if the attorney was dictating the terms of the gift. Telling her not to sweat it was paternalistic and completely inappropriate, in her view, and she wanted to strangle him with the telephone cord. On the other hand, he did concede a full percentage point on the payout rate. This was good, she thought. She also thought of the two colleges who might instead receive the gift if she made her anger known to the attorney. "Thank you," was all she could say. "I think the trustees will accept your offer." As she returned the phone receiver to its cradle, and for a long time after that, she couldn't help thinking that he had taken advantage of her.

## Paying for the Appraisal

The appraisal was another problem. The attorney continued to insist that the museum pay for the appraisal, which was expected to exceed $1,000. The cost was not at issue, but the museum's trustees felt, as Suzanne had explained to Mr. Hopkins and the donor, that the expense should be borne by the donor. But she could not find anything specifically speaking to that matter in the Internal Revenue Code or the Regulations. She thought payment of an appraisal would amount to a quid pro quo, where the charity provides a service of value to the donor. She called an attorney she knew in Michigan who was in private practice but on retainer to a large university active in planned giving, and frequently dealt with this problem. Surely, she would know, if anyone did, what the rules were. No, Suzanne was told, she could find nothing that specifically prohibits the charity from paying the appraisal fee, but her friend's understanding of the intent of those in Congress who wrote the appraisal rules in 1985 was for the donor to pay for the appraisal. During the first visit, Suzanne explained to Alan Ennico's attorney that the donor can deduct the fee not as a charitable deduction in its own right but as a miscellaneous itemized deduction paid as part of determining the amount of a tax. That was a Schedule A deduction, however, that was limited to amounts over 2 percent of the donor's adjusted gross income. It was also included in the amount that is reduced by 3 percent of adjusted gross income in excess of a certain amount, something a little over $100,000. This was all she had to go on when she talked with Jonathan Hopkins. That and a board policy, which she knew that he knew could be overridden with enough persuasion.

"We won't pay for it," she found herself saying. Perhaps it was all the bravado he brought to their meeting to which she was now reacting. She did not want to give in on this point, partly because of what her friend in Michigan had told her but also as a matter of pride. She was trying to maintain control of the process. Although donors needed to feel good about making a gift, they could not dictate the terms of the gift. Planned giving was becoming increasingly blurred on this point, and she worried that while charities were advertising what they could do for donors, at the same time they might be relinquishing some much-needed control over the gifts. Who pays the appraisal fee was a small point in the scope of the overall list of issues, but she thought it was necessary to remain firm. "The policy of the trustees is clear, and we can't pay for the appraisal." She expected him to erupt or maybe hang up on her, but he was surprisingly soft in his response.

"I see. Well, boards have their policies and this is one of them. I'm not going to fight that. We've given this a lot of careful thought and I don't think Alan will mind paying for the appraisal. It's really not that much, and I don't want us all to get consumed by that. We do, after all, want things to go smoothly."

And that was it. To Suzanne's surprise, the matter of who would pay for the appraisal ended quietly and without controversy. She did wonder, though, if a concession was what had taken place. What if the appraisal cost had been significant? Why should a higher cost justify having the charity pay for the appraisal? she wondered.

## Property Valuation

Deciding who paid the appraisal costs, however, did not help decide how much the property was worth. The value of the appraisal came in at $1,650,000, $350,000 less than the expected $2,000,000. Not that $1,650,000 was insignificant, but everyone was surprised.

"I knew that if I asked a friend of mine to do the appraisal, he would have been able to figure out how to make the land worth closer to $2,000,000, if not even more," argued Hopkins.

"But that probably would have violated the appraisal rules," Suzanne countered. "I'm thinking of Section 1.170A-13—somewhere in paragraph (C), I believe—of the IRS regulations, which says that a person acting 'as an agent' to the transaction would disqualify the appraisal. Although it doesn't say so specifically, I'm afraid a friend of yours would not qualify." She was not certain of this, but she said it anyway. In anticipation of the gift and this very question, she had read an article on this topic just the day before. "Besides, if that's what the land is worth, why try to dispute it? Remember, we have to sell it, and we want to be as close as possible to the appraisal value because if we sell it within two years, and I definitely want to do that, for too little, then we could run afoul of another part of the rules that say that we—read, the donor—might be fined for fraud. That's in Section 6662, I believe." Again, she referred to the previous day's reading material. Suzanne stopped for a moment, surprised at the knowledge on the code and regulations she could muster in front of Hopkins. "At least I think that's where the information can be found."

The attorney wanted to hear no more. "All right, all right. I'm simply saying that it would be nice if Alan's land were worth more." That's not what Suzanne heard him saying, at least at first, but she decided not to argue the point. The attorney was actually questioning the validity of the appraisal, she thought. That he would concede on this matter also was good enough for her. She had, after all, essentially conceded on the payout amount.

Suzanne did open a discussion on the sales prices. "Now that we have a value of $1,650,000, I'd like to talk to a real estate broker to find out what we ought to list the property for. After the gift is made, of course." She had no idea what the market would actually bear, especially since she was not familiar with land in New Hampshire, where the property was located. She tried to argue for some flexibility, to let the broker give her an idea of the likelihood of selling the land at that price. She had convinced her trustees that she should visit the site, and she did meet a real estate agent whom she trusted, yet she could not know what the final sales price would be.

"We at least have similar interests," Hopkins told her.

"What do you mean?"

"I mean that we both want to sell the land for the highest possible price."

"That's true, but it seems to me that you have simultaneously conflicting interests. Yes, we both want to sell the land for the highest price, but your client also would like to get income as soon as possible. We don't really care about the income, except that we want the trust to be everything the Ennicos are looking for. Theoretically, we could keep it on the market for years before we accepted an offer."

"But that would not make my clients happy," replied the attorney.

"Exactly."

They decided to let the matter of the sales price rest mainly in the hands of the planned giving office at the museum. Suzanne thought this wise because the museum was the trustee and she knew that aside from considerations of donor relations, she, representing the museum, had complete authority to sell it for any price she wished. The matter of representing the museum, however, was problematical. Neither she nor any of her predecessors had dealt with a gift of land to a unitrust, or any outright gift of land for that matter, and the chair of the finance committee questioned whether Suzanne had the right to represent the museum on this matter. The executive director, on the other hand, said that because Suzanne accepted many other gifts—cash and stock, for example—he had no problem with the arrangement.

The finance committee chair made clear that he was not questioning Suzanne's competence. Just the opposite. He said he simply wanted to give her the proper authority to accept the gift and to negotiate other matters with donors and their attorneys, as well as to decide the ultimate sales price, so the board would not have to be involved. In fact, the board member said, if anything ever goes wrong—if the donor sues the charity, for example—Suzanne would be personally protected. Because of this concern, the trustees voted unanimously at their next board meeting to allow Suzanne, as director of development, in consultation with the business manager and the executive director, to accept the gift and negotiate anything else pertinent to this or any other gift. Suzanne, who attended board meetings, felt relieved because some decisions had already been made—the appraisal and payout rate issues, for example—although the big one, actually accepting the land, technically had not yet been made. That would come in three weeks.

## Inspecting Gifted Property

During that three weeks, Suzanne traveled from New Mexico to New Hampshire and visited the site. She was surprised at how little so much money would buy. Although the lake was beautiful, the parcel of land was small and the rustic house might most generously be described as a handyman's delight. While she was there, the next door neighbor, a wealthy banker from Miami, showed some interest. His house was big, and Suzanne thought she might get an easy sale, especially since the real estate broker's contract had not been signed. He asked what the property would be selling for, and she told him that it was not yet for sale, that it was about to be given to a charitable trust. She did, however, share with him the appraisal value. When he learned that, he said he could not afford it, that he only wanted to have the property as a second lakefront home for overflow guests on summer weekends. His own home, built eight years earlier, had cost about that much, and his was almost twice as big and was winterized as well. He knew, however, that the film *On Golden Pond* had been filmed at the lake after he had purchased his property, and this undoubtedly had increased the value of its homes. When he told her this, she realized that the lakeside home might be worth every bit of the $1,650,000 appraised value, despite the property's stark appearance. Before she left, Suzanne visited a real estate agent, recommended by a friend of a museum trustee whose son and daughter-in-law used to live in New Hampshire near Squam Lake.

After Suzanne reported to her executive director that she saw no problems with the property, the museum hired an attorney in New Hampshire to act on its behalf. He drove to the registry of deeds in Moultenboro, where the land was located, to do a title search. He also recommended a Level I environmental audit, which turned up nothing. This was not surprising for waterfront property on one of New Hampshire's prettiest, most pristine lakes. It was a formality, an important formality, when the deed was actually transferred.

## A Transfer of Deed

The meeting at which the gift decision was consummated and the trust document was signed was anticlimactic compared with all the negotiating and other activity that had gone on before. This was good because Suzanne had asked the executive director of the museum and the chairs of the finance and the development committees to attend the meeting. The Ennicos had met the executive director but she thought that inviting two trustees would be an added bonus. Plus, she thought, the attorney would be less likely to raise any last-minute stumbling blocks with so many museum representatives gushing their thanks at what was a remarkable gift. If this had been an outright gift, it would have qualified as the sixth largest of the campaign. One million, six hundred fifty thousand dollars was a lot of money no matter how it came and Suzanne intended to publicize it as much as possible.

The deed had been transferred just days ago. The real estate attorney in Moultenboro made certain that all the papers had been transferred correctly. One last-minute snag arose when it was discovered that New Hampshire had a transfer tax, but the attorney quickly determined that a charitable trust is exempt from having to pay its share (although he did not know about the laws in other states), so the donor paid only his share, a fact that the donor's attorney originally objected to but soon came to realize was inevitable. After the signing, the museum's attorney attached Schedule A to the trust document, which consisted of the deed to the property, duly signed over from the donor to the Alan Ennico Charitable Remainder Unitrust.

## When Is a Charitable Remainder Trust Funded?

Transferring land to a charitable remainder unitrust raises a niggling but important question: When does the trust take effect, especially when the transfer is not on the same day the trust is signed? If the property is transferred to a trust that is not yet signed, technically it gets transferred to nothing. Yet if the trust is signed before the actual transfer of property, the trust is empty. The museum's legal counsel opined first, that there was no real, solid rule on the matter, and second, that it was permissible to allow for the discrepancy and that the trust would exist on the latter of the two dates. With land, this is not much of a problem because the appraisal was conducted on a date within 60 days of the gift date (or, if the appraisal is conducted after the gift, up until the donor files his tax return), but with publicly traded stock, for example, knowing the specific transfer date is crucial because the value of the stock is determined on the basis of when the donor no longer owns—the day the donor loses control of—the asset.

## The Celebration

Everyone left the meeting happy. The Ennicos were happy because they had finally made a gift to a worthwhile cause, something they had wanted to do for a long time. They were slightly concerned, however, about the income. Would it be enough and would it begin soon enough? And, for all the celebration and fulfillment of a longstanding desire, was this the right thing to do with their most valuable asset? Jonathan Hopkins was happy because he had done right by his client. He had fought the fight, and he thought he left the impression that without him the gift would not have been made correctly. The executive director and the trustees were happy because they were $1,650,000 closer to their goal. (Fortunately, they had not questioned whether a trust whose life expectancy was over 20 years should count as current money to a capital campaign.) And Suzanne was happy. Despite her duels with the attorney, she was glad she completed the gift, her first charitable remainder unitrust funded with land. She then wrote a list of points relating to a gift of land to a unitrust, which she placed in her files:

Points and questions to consider when accepting a gift of land in a charitable remainder unitrust:

1. An appraisal must be conducted.
2. Who pays for the appraisal?
3. What should the payout rate be?
4. What about environmental concerns?
5. Who at the charity should accept the gift?
6. Get the name of an attorney located near the gifted property.
7. Get the name of a good real estate broker.
8. Talk with the donor about expected income.
9. Determine who pays the real estate tax bill until the property is sold.

She did not worry, although she should have, about who would pay the next real estate tax bill. She worried a little bit, and mentally reminded herself to talk with the investment managers of the museum's charitable trusts, about a 9 percent payout. For now, however, she contented herself with the knowledge that because it was written as a net-income unitrust the principal would never be eroded, and that in all likelihood the trust would be able to maintain a good income for the Ennicos. On this point she should have worried a great deal more.

## PHYLLIS EMERSON

### Gift Annuity Rates

Donald Butler, the planned giving director at Metropolitan Hospital, returned from his successful visit with Phyllis Emerson, the widow who indicated an interest in a charitable gift annuity. Don, happy about her desire to make a gift, told his treasurer about his visit.

"You promised her what?"

Scott Corliss, the treasurer at Metropolitan Hospital, once again wondered why the planned giving office was out selling gift annuities for such an outrageous price. The treasurer thought of the income he would be responsible for paying annuitants for the rest of their lives, and each annuity agreement represented one more obligation into an indefinite future, an obligation he was sincerely afraid he or his successors would someday not be able to meet.

"All I did was quote her the rate recommended by the American Council on Gift Annuities. Six and a half percent."

"Six and a half percent." When the treasurer said it the number sounded ominously high, but Donald Butler had thought the number to be quite modest, especially since the recommended rates had just been reduced because of the economy. "And do you know where I can go to get interest like that? For her lifetime?" Actually, even though 6.5 percent is not a lot of income, the treasurer did have a point. When this gift was made, bond rates were low, and the benchmark 30-year treasury bond was providing a yield of only 7 percent annually. This was higher than the amount promised from the gift annuity, but Scott was concerned that yields were too low to follow the rates the American Society on Gift Annuities established.

## Communication Between the Development and Finance Offices

Donald Butler could not answer the question because he knew little of finance and investments. But he did know that many other charities were writing gift annuities, and they were following the Council's rates. In fact, although he did not know why, some charities were promising even more than that. He stumbled through his thoughts and he sounded less certain of himself with the explanation than he should have.

"We're going to have to go buy a bond that will pay that," said Scott, "and I'll just have to go out and buy the long bond. She's got, what, at least a 20-year or so life expectancy? And no bond, other than the long bond, will pay very much. Not today anyway."

Don had come to recognize this as a common dispute. Why, he asked himself, couldn't the development and finance offices get together on this question and develop a policy? This way he wouldn't have to guess about what rate to offer every time he went out to see a donor about a gift annuity. He had not yet visited many prospects in his new career, but his predecessor had told him about his constant conflicts with the treasurer. Don's predecessor had not formulated a solution to the problem, but surmised that the answer was not mysterious. His predecessor kept talking about better communications. Which is why, Don himself surmised, there had been a vacancy recently in the planned giving office.

Don was concerned about that. He was told at the planned giving seminar he attended in Memphis that turnover was a serious problem facing the development profession. Too many planned giving officers stay with an organization for too short a time; because planned gifts are generally the result of long periods of personal cultivation and developing relationships, many charities do not receive as many planned gifts as they might if the tenures of planned giving people were longer. His own predecessor had been employed at Metropolitan Hospital for only two years and was now at another charity, not even a hospital, nearby in the same city. He thought that if only planned giving people stayed longer they could develop better relationships not only with prospects but with other staff members at the charity. Right now, for example, he had to fight for this gift annuity and he really wanted no part of that. He told himself that very soon he would take the initiative to set up a meeting or several meetings—no matter how many it took—to develop policies on accepting gift annuities. First, however, he had to understand the profession more. He knew that this was not the time to bring up new suggestions.

He did know that the treasurer had threatened to reduce the rates on gift annuities at the hospital. He even had suggested that gift annuities be discontinued altogether because of the obligation the hospital undertook in issuing them. Fortunately, this decision had not been made. The hospital's literature described them and Don was asking people to enter into gift annuity agreements. This discussion about annuity rates, however, worried him. Don knew he could not under any circumstances return to Phyllis Emerson to tell her that the hospital would not honor his commitment of an annual payment of 6.5 percent on her gift.

"You'll simply have to go back and tell her we can't do it. I've put up with this long enough, and this is the final straw. When are development types going to learn to start getting money and not giving it away?" Harsh words from a man at least twenty years younger than Don. "Has it ever occurred to you that planned giving is a scam, a stupid way to get people to do something that's great for them, but not in the best interests of the charity?" Clearly, the treasurer was having a bad day. Don tried not to take it personally. His long teaching career had taught him many people, especially the younger ones, tried their mettle with displays of bravado and even temper at times. This was, he was sure, an example of that. Who knows? Maybe next year's budget was still unbalanced and he was getting some pressure from the president of the hospital or the board's finance chair. But the fact was that his promised gift annuity was at best uncertain and at worst history. He had to save this somehow. He could not let Phyllis down, not for any reason.

"I can't tell her that, Scott. I've already promised her. Besides, she may not make the gift if I tell her we won't pay that much."

## The American Council on Gift Annuities

"All the better," the treasurer responded. "If you haven't noticed, there's no gift in this deal anyway."

"Look, I know that I'm new here, new to planned giving, too. But I was only doing my job. I was only doing what over a thousand charities around the United States are doing right now. And that is paying what the American Council on Gift Annuities recommends. No, I don't know much about the finances involved, and I'm not an actuary, but I do know that 6.5 percent is not a king's ransom, as you're trying to make it out to be." Don was calm during this response, calmer, he thought, than the treasurer had a right to expect. "Look, I'd like to sit down with you on this and discuss it rationally. Let's have a meeting. But right now, I've given this woman my word—based on nothing personal or extravagant—that we will pay her 6.5 percent. And as far as "no gift"—as you put it—is concerned, there is in the IRS's view. It's about half the amount she's using to fund the annuity. So if she gives us $100,000, that means we'll get about $50,000." He had not done the calculation yet but he knew that 50 percent was about right for the amount remaining for the charity at the time a person dies. He was also surprised to hear himself say $100,000.

"I wish I knew what the IRS is thinking. I suppose no one ever knows that, though. Besides the IRS doesn't know squat about investing." Don fleetingly had the image that his treasurer also knew nothing about investing. Balancing budgets, perhaps, but not investing. He remembered something in the Memphis planned giving seminar about the concept of total return, that total return consists of both income and capital growth.

"Look, I promise that I want to correct this misunderstanding as much as you do, Scott. I don't like knowing that you think that I'm out there giving away money instead of raising it for the hospital. This place means a lot to me, Scott, perhaps even more to me than to you, and I would never, ever try to do it a disservice. Perhaps we can invite Ellen in for the meeting, as well as the finance chair and the development director." His mind was racing to include everyone relevant he could think of so the meeting would take place with as little confrontation as possible. Ellen was a planned giving consultant who had been hired four years earlier, when the hospital began its planned giving program. At first she had been used extensively, a certain number of days each month, according to the records Don reviewed when he started, but now she was available on a case-by-case basis. Don had not used her since he began, but his predecessor said that she could speak the language of development as well as finance and had been helpful in talking with donors and their advisors. Even though this was no donor visit, this was, Don decided quickly, the kind of case where she could be useful. "Besides, I'm not really trying to push unrealistically high payout rates for gift annuities. Perhaps the meeting will result in us all agreeing that we should have lower rates than those recommended by the Council."

## Keeping the Gift

Scott Corliss looked startled at Don's self-assured response to his tirade. He knew that Don meant well, and until this moment had thought of him as a harmless elderly man who lost his wife and needed a job to keep busy, someone the development office hired more out of sympathy than on the basis of any professional acumen. Perhaps he was wrong. Still, Scott felt he knew the numbers—and he knew he did not like gift annuities. He was powerless to stop them, though; the trustees voted to be more aggressive with a planned giving program and the hospital had been issuing gift annuities for 12 years now. So far they were very successful. Why shouldn't they be? he thought. They were practically giveaways. But, perhaps a meeting was best. After all, Don was being reasonable, and everyone wanted to stop the bickering.

"Okay. Let's do it. But remember, I'm coming at this a little differently from you. You may not know it, but payments to gift annuity donors are backed by this hospital's assets. There's no trust to protect us. That's why I don't care as much about high-payout trusts as I do about annuities. Trusts can go down the tubes and we'd never lose a dime, but if the gift assets can't back up a gift annuity, then we start paying out of our own pockets. Do you understand where I'm coming from?"

"Yes, I do, Scott. And I respect your position, too. I'd like to know more about it, actually, because I can't imagine why the development and finance offices can't agree more often." Don knew that his situation was not unusual, that conflict existed between the two offices at many charities, but he did not know why. He was determined, even at this early point in his planned giving career, to resolve the problem. "But for now, can we at least agree to pay Phyllis 6.5 percent?"

Would he never let up? Scott wondered. If a meeting could eliminate this problem, of course this donor could get whatever she wanted. "Yes."

Then one of the unfortunately rare meetings between the planned giving director and the treasurer ended.

## The Gift Annuity's Perceived Capital Gain Problem

"Is that what he said?" Don was in his office with his prospect, Phyllis Emerson, several days after his visit with the hospital's treasurer. He bore good news, but he was being told something disturbing.

"Yes, it is." Phyllis had just told Don that the planned giving director from her college had also talked with her about a gift annuity. She said that she learned that there is no capital gains tax advantage with gift annuities, which was why he was recommending a charitable remainder annuity trust rather than a charitable gift annuity.

"But that's not true." In the three months since his first meeting with Phyllis, Don had learned a great deal about gift annuities. And, yes, people did say that the capital gains tax distribution was a problem, at least for gifts that were funded with appreciated property. But *why* it was not a problem still eluded him. That's why Ellen, the planned giving consultant, was present at this meeting in his office. He had no idea this question would arise, but he knew he needed Ellen's help to explain the gift and its impact on the woman who had decided to entrust the hospital with her money. Now that he had asserted himself on the point about avoiding a capital gains tax, with a confidence born only of the consultant's presence he turned to Ellen for the explanation.

"I know the argument well," Ellen began. "One central result of a gift annuity funded with appreciated property is that part of the income the donor receives includes capital gain." Both Don and Phyllis were listening intently, but neither with much comprehension.

"Let's look at it this way," continued Ellen. "A gift annuity is really a bargain sale." This seemed to confuse them more, so Ellen quickly explained: "That's not very confusing, actually. A bargain sale is part gift and part sale. Mrs. Emerson, if you had a $10,000 asset that you 'sold' to the hospital for $6,000, you would be making a gift of $4,000. The other part is a sale. That's a bargain sale." Phyllis nodded her head in understanding. Seeing this, Ellen continued. "Let's take a this a step further. Suppose the asset had a cost basis—what you paid for it—of $5,000, or 50 percent. You would be responsible for paying a capital gains tax on 50 percent of the sale part, the $6,000 part. And 50 percent of $6,000 is $3,000, so you would pay a capital gains tax on $3,000. The other $3,000, by the way, would represent a return of principal and therefore would not be taxed at all."

"And the other part, the gift part?" asked Phyllis.

"The other part—the $4,000 that goes to charity—is not subject to capital gains taxes because it's a gift to charity."

"But I thought that even gifts to charity sometimes were subject to the capital gains tax."

"They used to be. The law between 1987 and 1993 said that the appreciated portion of gifts of property was subject to the Alternative Minimum Tax as a 'preference item,' but that's been changed."

"So the 50 percent gain on the $4,000 gift—$2,000—would not be taxed?" asked Don.

"That's right."

Phyllis and Don thought about this a moment and then Phyllis asked

Ellen, "I think I understand that, but how does this relate to a gift annuity?"

"Look at the sale part of the $10,000 as the income going to the donor. Instead of getting a check today for the $6,000, assume you were paid a total of that amount over the rest of your life. You would actually probably receive more than $6,000 because spreading it out over a long time means that the $6,000 amount will be worth less in the future than getting it today." Phyllis nodded her head vigorously. "So, because the IRS takes that into account, in actual money you would probably get $8,000, $10,000, or maybe more. I don't know right now. The important thing to realize is that we are equating the sale portion of an outright bargain sale to the income you get from a gift annuity. Thus, a gift annuity can be thought of as a bargain sale with the sale part paid in regular increments over a long period of time.

"The next step is to realize that when the asset has appreciated in value, those income payments—just like the sale part in an outright bargain sale—include some capital gain."

"So," said Don, "the gift annuity does *not* avoid a capital gain."

"Not exactly," responded Ellen.

"But you just said that part of the income represents the capital gain the donor has acquired in the original asset. Except for the gift part, the donor pays the tax on the gain."

"Yes, that's true," said Ellen, "but that does not mean the donor does not avoid a capital gain." This was not working as well as she hoped, so Ellen decided to change the example slightly. "Let me try to explain this a little differently. Say a person has to include a total of $1,000 of capital gain in her gift annuity payments—that's like the $3,000 we were just talking about—and her life expectancy is 20 years. Let's further say that the donor is getting an annual income of $500 per year. Some of that is ordinary income, some is tax-free income, and the rest is capital gain income. For purposes of our example, we simply divide the $1,000 of capital gain by the life expectancy of 20, which is $50. That means that of the $500 income, $50 is capital gain income. The other $450 is divided into fully taxable and tax-free income. Actually the tax-free income and fully taxable income are calculated first, and then whatever capital gain income needs to be paid reduces the tax-free portion."

"So how is that a problem?" Don asked.

"It's not, really."

"Really?" Don looked very confused. "Then why are we having a problem?"

Ellen could see that this wasn't going very far. "Let me use a real example." She then pulled a sheet of paper from a file (Exhibit 4.1) and placed it on the table.

"I've used an example of a gift of $100,000 with a cost basis of

$25,000. As you can see from this illustration of how the income is taxed, each year, of the $6,500 that is paid to you, Mrs. Emerson, almost $2,000 is taxed at capital gains rates. This amount is taxed for approximately 20 years, and represents the gain of the income portion of the gift." Knowing that would have little impact, Ellen explained that point again. "The gift portion is what we're calling the charitable deduction—$46,970. That means the nongift portion, the value of your income for the rest of your life, is the difference between the gift of $100,000 and the charitable deduction. That difference is $53,030. The capital gain represented in

---

**METROPOLITAN HOSPITAL**
**IMMEDIATE GIFT ANNUITY**
**Profile of Income**

**Donor's Name: Phyllis Emerson**

**GIFT INFORMATION:**

| | |
|---|---|
| Value of Gift | $100,000 |
| Type of Gift Asset | Appreciated Securities |
| Ownership of Asset | Asset Owned Solely by Donor |
| Cost Basis | $25,000 |
| Annual Annuity Amount | $6,500 (6.5000%) |
| Payment Frequency | Quarterly |
| First Payment Amount | $534.25 (Pro-Rated) |
| Beneficiary's Age | 65 |
| Charitable Mid-Term Federal Rate | 8.4% |
| Charitable Deduction | $46,969 |

**INCOME INFORMATION:**

|  | Ordinary | Capital Gain | Tax-Free | Total |
|---|---|---|---|---|
| This year | $1,274 | $664 | $221 | $2,159 |
| Next 19 years | $3,835 | $1,999 | $666 | $6,500 |
| 20th year | $4,987 | $1,135 | $378 | $6,500 |
| After the 20th year | $6,500 | $0 | $0 | $6,500 |

The donor must report a total of $39,773.24 of capital gain in annual installments of $1,998.66 over 19.9 years. After 19.9 years, at the end of the beneficiary's life expectancy, all annuity income becomes fully taxable.

---

**Exhibit 4.1**   Immediate Gift Annuity Income Report

A report showing the frequency, categories and amount of annual income from an immediate gift annuity.

This illustration was prepared using the planned giving software ParaGon™, developed by Blackbaud, Inc.

that number is $39,773. This follows because the capital gain is 75% of the total income."

This real-life example appealed to Don's mathematical acumen, and he followed the logic instantly. "So what you're saying is that Phyllis would have to pay capital gains taxes on the $39,000 number."

"Exactly."

"And that is divided up into Phyllis's life expectancy, which, according to your table is about 20 years?"

"Yes again."

"So we in fact do not avoid capital gains on a gift annuity," Don said as more of a question than a statement. Despite being shown three examples in the past half hour, his otherwise acute math abilities did not yet let him understand this point.

"That's technically true," replied Ellen, "but that's not the way to think of it."

"Then how should we think of it?" asked Phyllis. "It seems that from what you are saying, the gift annuity comes with a burden that an annuity trust does not."

"Or even a Pooled Income Fund," said Don.

"Okay, you're both right. Technically. But let me have you look at it this way. Suppose you transferred $100,000 to both a pooled income fund and a charitable gift annuity. You get an income tax deduction for both, right? In fact, because of the difference in the calculation formulas the pooled income fund would probably provide a lower deduction than the gift annuity. So far the annuity is winning, or is at least equal, right?" Both listeners nodded their heads in agreement.

"So now let's look at the capital gain issue. If the property has a $75,000 gain, as in this example, which gift makes the donor pay the gain *up front?*"

"Up front?" Don responded. "Neither, of course."

"Of course," Ellen replied.

"But we're not talking about up front. We're talking about the taxation of the payments to the donor."

"Exactly. But I want to be certain we all agree that so far, the gift annuity provides the same benefits as the pooled income fund, or the annuity trust for that matter. They both provide an immediate income tax deduction and neither under usual circumstances forces the donor to pay a capital gains tax up front." Again, the two nodded their heads in agreement.

"Then we are left, as you say, with the income question. How is the income from a pooled income fund gift taxed, Don?"

"It's fully taxable. It always is. It's a provision of the law on pooled income funds."

"That's right," Ellen said, even though she had no idea what he meant by "the law on pooled income funds." She hoped he meant that the Internal Revenue Code clearly states that pooled income funds are prohibited from accepting or investing in tax-exempt assets, and that all beneficiary income is fully taxed. She was familiar with Internal Revenue Code Section 642(c)(5)(C), but doubted that Don was. "But a gift annuity's income is not fully taxable, is it?"

"No." Don sounded less sure of himself on this point. "No, it isn't."

"So where's the problem?" asked Ellen.

"The problem, I think, is that the donor does not get to avoid the capital gains on the gift."

"Capital gains is part of the income," Ellen said. "You're right. The donor does not avoid a capital gains tax. But how does that mean that the gift annuity is somehow hindered in its ability to provide benefits? We've just shown that the gift annuity is just as beneficial, perhaps more beneficial from an income tax *deduction* perspective, as a pooled income fund or a charitable remainder trust." She paused to see if what she was saying was being comprehended. Then she continued. "Even if the gift were a charitable remainder trust and the appreciated assets were placed completely in tax-free investments, under the four-tier rule—where income is taxed at the highest rate, based on the character of the income distributed from the trust—the donor would still receive a great deal of capital gain income. No tax-free income. And requiring—I should say asking—a charity to do that—invest in tax-free assets—would do it no service because the asset would be worth very little at the end of the donor's life. Especially someone who's right now only 65 years old."

Don and Phyllis took this in. Don spoke first. "So what you're saying is that the gift annuity has as many or more benefits than some of the other gifts, especially the fixed-income payment of the annuity trust."

"And," said Phyllis, "that means that the fellow from my college was wrong."

"I wouldn't go that far, Mrs. Emerson. After all, the capital gain—at least that portion attributable to the life annuity—is repaid during the donor's lifetime. It's just that its effects are not as devastating as many people in this profession are led to believe."

## The Problem of Fixed Income

Ellen paused for a moment, and then continued. "But if I may introduce another concern about the gift annuity. . . ."

"What's that?" her two students replied in unison.

"Well, a 65-year-old person has a long life expectancy." She was speaking to Phyllis directly now. "Are you certain that you want a fixed income for life, an income that will erode against inflation as time passes?"

"I'm glad you asked," said Phyllis. "Don brought that up for me a few meetings ago. He said that a lot of widows haven't balanced a checkbook their whole lives and when they get a lot of money from their husbands' estates they have no idea how investments work. They therefore like the security of a guaranteed amount of income, even though it's not in their best interests financially. Yes, I'm familiar with that situation. And yes, I'm sure I'm doing the right thing now, although for a different reason. I've invested other money in securities that will provide a hedge against inflation. I know this is a fixed-income arrangement, but I'm glad to be getting the income, and, to the degree possible, I'm glad that the hospital will realize the benefits of the growth of my gift. After my lifetime I hope that the money will in some small way be used to help finance heart research efforts here. My husband died of a heart attack a little while ago."

Don thought that this was the way a gift should be made. Phyllis had the right intentions and the right situation. And she knew what she was doing. He also wished that his treasurer could understand that despite what he clearly thought was a high payout, the hospital would benefit in the end, if, as Phyllis pointed out, it invested wisely. Although he did not know why, he felt that investing better meant buying something besides, or at least in addition to, bonds. But that was a fight for later.

Don looked at Ellen, wondering what to do next. Ellen spoke. "Well, Mrs. Emerson, do you have any other questions about the gift annuity?"

"No. I think you've answered my remaining question, the one brought up by the man from my college. Actually, I think I'll make a gift to the college despite his warnings against the gift annuity. I have a great fondness for the place."

"Is that to say you've made a decision about making a gift to Metropolitan Hospital?" Ellen asked.

Phyllis looked at Ellen for a moment, and then she looked at Don for a few moments, before she responded. "Yes. Yes I have. I'd like to use some of the highly appreciated securities I've owned for many years, and establish a gift annuity at the hospital for $100,000, or as close to it as I can with a block of stock."

## The Personal Relationship

Don and Phyllis did not stop seeing each other after the gift annuity was established. Instead, although Don did not feel fully comfortable, they developed a personal relationship that continued to grow. As a result, Phyllis pledged the rest of her estate to the hospital at her death *so long as Don was never fired.* Her attorney drafted her will with that provision, taking into account a trust fund in the event she died before him. Don was hesitant to tell the development director, and certainly did not want to discuss this with Scott Corliss, the treasurer. Her provision, however, made it necessary for the hospital to learn of her intentions, so Don went directly to the president of the hospital. He told him that a multimillion-dollar estate would be forthcoming at the death of someone currently 65 years old, but that for the bequest provision to hold up, the hospital would be forced to continue to employ him, at least until he was ready to leave. Don said that he was uncomfortable with the provision and that he did not know what to do. He thought of leaving voluntarily but that would not do the hospital or him very much good; technically he would not have been fired, but he knew that her intended bequest was the result of her friendship with him, not her loyalty to the hospital, despite its good works. He also thought of discontinuing his relationship with Phyllis, but he knew that he could not now do that; besides, he thought, that would not benefit the hospital either. He could ask her to remove the clause from her will, but then the hospital would not receive the gift. He did not know what to do, but he wanted to do the right thing.

Don's honesty impressed the president, who reassured him that the hospital's good fortunes were less important than personal relations. He also told his planned giving director, however, that if the hospital ever felt that he was not doing a good job or if the department would have to be reorganized without him, then that simply would have to be. The hospital could not be held hostage to the whims of a widow, no matter how generous she might be.

Don was pleased with the discussion, especially because they had both been honest with each other. He wanted to marry Phyllis, but felt that a permanent personal relationship with her might be unethical, especially if the hospital's president felt that her bequest intention was being offered as a way to restrict the hospital from doing what it might someday have to do. He was pleased to know that the money, while important, was not so important that it would force the president to make a promise the hospital would feel uncomfortable about keeping. The gift annuity was irrevocable, and he had earned that gift. The bequest—well, who knew?—that was unimportant right now. He did, however, make a mental note to call the chair of the ethics committee at the National Committee on Planned Giving, as well as others in philanthropy who might have thought about ethical dilemmas, to find out if this problem had ever come up before.

That would be later, though. Now, he turned his attention to a much more important matter. As he walked across town to a home with which he had become intimately familiar, he was reminded of a time more than

40 years earlier, when he was 24 years old, the only other time he had asked such an important question. Experience, he was discovering quickly, provided no comfort; as he formulated his plan to ask it for the second time in his life, he realized that he was no less nervous now than he was the first time, and he knew the question was no less important.

## SAMUEL LIVERMORE

As is true in all of development, planned giving is all about relationships. The hard-earned soulful connection between a donor and a charitable cause is what transforms good feelings into financial support. Developing relationships takes time, as well as sincerity and a well-defined mission. Although George Lee, the planned giving director at Old Ivy, is sincere, and the mission of Old Ivy well-defined, we cannot deceive any reader about the time that must pass between a first visit, such as the one between George Lee and Samuel Livermore, the successful travel agency owner, and the moment when a planned giving prospect decides to become a donor. Even a well-written novel cannot properly scope the time it takes to live a life, the story told in so many pages, the reader condensing a lifetime or lifetimes into several evenings—the problem of the medium.

In real life, statistics show that from beginning to end, a planned gift takes about 18 months to gestate—twice as long as it takes something infinitely more complex. But this does not take into account the time donors have taken during their lives to come to terms with connecting themselves to the charity's mission, or the time taken to read through brochures sent from the development office about how the charity is in the business of planned giving. This may be changing, as planned gifts are marketed more and more for their personal benefits and not for their philanthropic payoff, but even the quickest planned gift decisions—with exceptions to be found everywhere, of course—generally take a long time. For the purposes of our saga with Sam, let us think of the final solicitation meeting as taking place a year and a half after George first met Sam. When we left George he had much to think about.

### A Spouse's Concerns are Important

George did confirm from Sam's class agent that Sam had remarried—he and Patricia had divorced five years before, and Sam married Elizabeth just two years ago. At first, George worried that this might complicate matters. It did. Elizabeth, it seems, enjoyed Sam's lifestyle and was reluctant to see her husband give away anything substantial to charity because she felt such charity would affect their ability to travel and live well. During their first meeting, Sam invited George to dinner the next time George was in town. The dinner, held at Sam's home two months later, was awkward.

Although he knew better, George found himself defending charitable giving to Elizabeth. If it was to be such a big deal to her, he thought, then he simply should have walked away from the possibility of receiving a planned gift from the Livermores, a possibility that seemed less and less likely as the dinner wore on. A relationship, however, was growing, and time might have the effect of winning her over to her husband's dreams of helping Old Ivy. She did say that since she was a graduate of Mills College, a well-known and highly regarded women's college near San Francisco, it would be nice if something could be done there. Seizing upon that newly found but slight hope, George discussed with Elizabeth how this could be accomplished, but she continued to emphasize that giving away money at their young ages would require too much sacrifice to their lifestyle.

Fortunately, Sam was clear on that point: He would do whatever he wanted with his money and Elizabeth would not sway him. During the tense discussion, which took place in George's presence at the dinner table, Sam reminded his wife that he was solely responsible for their lifestyle. He also reminded her that meddling was one of the reasons why he was no longer married to Patricia. Such are the moments when planned giving officers earn their salaries. No amount of money, George thought as he uncomfortably focused on his dessert and not the discussion, could balance the tension he observed as Sam and Elizabeth argued. But this was not unique to George's visit with Sam and Elizabeth. This, in one form or another, had taken place several times during the ten years George had been in planned giving at Old Ivy, with a spouse, a child, or another interested and caring relative. The awkwardness was not eased when Elizabeth reminded Sam that he was quite incorrect by asserting he was the sole provider of their lifestyle; *she* reminded *him* that she was the sole beneficiary of her late husband's substantial estate, and that their lifestyle was funded by both of them. The debate could have raged for the entire evening had George not gently and with good humor reminded them that he did not want to be a party to any marital disputes, that he was not an attorney or a religious figure.

Yet, at the dinner, when the discussion on the possibility of a gift did begin, George was surprised by the specificity of their thinking. Only two months ago, he had introduced Samuel Livermore to the idea of a planned gift, and that meeting had been cut short due to an emergency at the travel agency. Despite their disagreement, Sam confessed that he and his wife had seriously contemplated a life-income gift.

"Yes, we've discussed the trust proposal and we were hoping that we could arrange to receive an income of 8 percent. This would increase our income, as you said it would, and we feel that even in today's economy the trustee will be able to earn at least that much. Do you think we can arrange for that?"

George Lee, as was his habit, sat silently and listened. He listened to every word as he was ingesting the information Mr. and the new Mrs. Livermore were imparting, getting a sense of their needs as well as trying to formulate a response. A few moments before he had listened to reasons why the gift could not be made, and now he was listening to their request for a high payout of income from a charitable remainder trust. This, combined with tension between a husband and wife, made George's job interesting.

## The Donor's Advisor

Although this meeting, a dinner, was to be primarily social, much planning and other activity took place in preparation for it. The road to this point was not rocky but it was not smooth either. The problem for Sam began when his attorney had reluctantly said, "Well, if you want to do this, go ahead. But I'd be very careful if I were you."

"Very careful." Words to still a heart. When an attorney, one whom you have known a lifetime and whose advice you have always trusted, indicates his legal reluctance, you sit up and take note. Samuel Livermore was merely mortal and even though he was a successful entrepreneur with a lifetime of making independent decisions about his business under his belt, cautionary words about his and his wife's future were meant to be taken seriously.

## The Payout Rate's Effect on the Income of the Unitrust

Careful the couple both were, and during the two months before the dinner, several further discussions were needed to address the issues involved with a charitable remainder unitrust paying an income of 8 percent each year to the two of them for their lifetimes. Now, George found himself in the Livermores' home, hoping that they would further their thinking about a planned gift. At this point he was thinking of a lower payout, a 5 percent unitrust. George was not comfortable with a payout as high as 8 percent because he knew that because they both

were so young—Sam in his mid-sixties and Elizabeth in her early sixties—they would actually lose income when measured against inflation,
even if the trust's total return could exceed 8 percent. Using a gift value
assumption of $1 million, he showed them a graph of their expected
income, a presentation of their expected income increase over their life
expectancy, comparing the 8 percent annual income they desired with a
5 percent annual payout (see Exhibit 4.2).

"You can see," George said to both Elizabeth and Sam, "that after
about 17 years, the lower percentage payout actually begins to pay you
*more* money each year."

"Why is that?" asked Elizabeth.

"Because each year, the lower payout allows more to be reinvested.
Assuming a 10 percent total return annually, the 5 percent payout allows
for the other 5 percent to be reinvested, which has the effect of helping
the trust grow by that amount each year." He added, "Your income
would grow by that amount as well." George then focused on the 8 per-

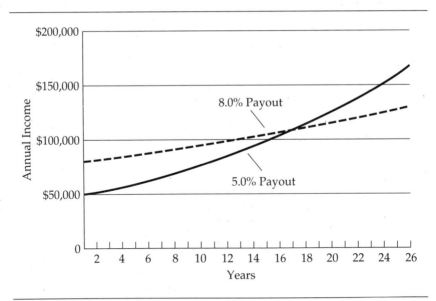

**Exhibit 4.2   Annual Income in Nominal Terms**

A graph showing the annual income from two unitrusts, one paying 5%
annually and the other paying 8% annually, without taking inflation into
account. Total return is 10%.

This illustration was prepared using the Donor Model software developed by
Kaspick & Company.

cent income line. "In this situation, however, again assuming a total return of 10 percent, the trust has only 2 percent left to reinvest, so it will grow more slowly. So will your income. This has the effect of providing less annual income over time—in this case about 17 years—than the lower-percentage payout." Then, because of the importance of his next thought, he spoke the following words slowly and deliberately: "Although the income starts out higher, it grows slower."

"That's very interesting," said Samuel Livermore, looking intently at the graph. "Very interesting indeed."

"You are, in the planned giving world anyway, considered to be very young people," said George. "As you can see, your joint life expectancy is almost 30 years. The effect of the payout decision can be quite dramatic when measured over a lifetime." George then let them examine the graph uninterrupted, knowing it made an impact on them.

After a full minute had passed, George explained that although the income lines increased for both payout rates, the actual buying power—measured by taking inflation into account—would be greatly reduced with the higher payout. He then showed a second graph (Exhibit 4.3). It used the same information as the other, but the results showed the effects of an annual inflation rate of 4 percent.

"Clearly," said George, "this is at least as dramatic as the other graph. Most people I talk with are interested in preserving their income's buying power—the amount left after battling inflation—during their retirement years. As you can see, the 5 percent income maintains its purchasing power, where the 8 percent payout loses its buying power rather quickly." He looked at them both to see if they understood. Showing the effects of inflation on income, while important, usually confused most donors.

"So you mean to say that the higher income, the 8 percent payout, would lose its purchasing power *that* quickly?" asked Sam.

"That's right," responded George. "Not a pretty picture, is it?"

"No, no it's not."

Elizabeth then asked what would happen if inflation turned out to be more than 4 percent. "That would make both lines fall," said George. "But that is not an argument for the higher payout," he added quickly. "Although the 5 percent payout would provide less purchasing power than you see here, the 8 percent payout trust would provide even less than that. The line that you see dropping so dramatically in this graph would drop even more dramatically." He then said, "The only way for the 8 percent payout to be to your benefit would be for you both to have a very short life expectancy." Then, after a slight pause, he said, "But I don't think that either of you are contemplating that."

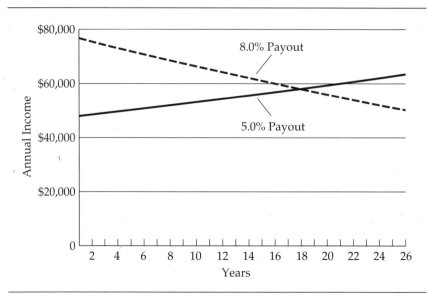

**Exhibit 4.3**    Annual Income in Present Value Terms

Graph comparing the annual income from two unitrusts, one paying 5% annually and the other paying 8% annually, taking 4% inflation into account. Total return is 10%.

This illustration was prepared using the Donor Model software developed by Kaspick & Company.

## The Payout Rate's Effect on the Charitable Gift

Satisfied that they both understood the effect of the payout decision on their incomes over the years, George then wanted to show them the effect of the payout decision on Old Ivy. "Of course, the more a person takes from a trust, the less will be in the trust. Let me show you the difference the two payouts make on what would ultimately be available to us." (See Exhibit 4.4.) Then he showed them what Old Ivy would receive with a 5 percent payout compared to an 8 percent payout in inflation-adjusted terms. (See Exhibit 4.5.)

He explained that the people who manage their trusts could reasonably expect to receive an average of about 10 percent of total return—yield plus capital appreciation—each year. If inflation is 5 percent, he said (it is often higher for charities than for individuals), they would lose 3 percent of purchasing power each year with the 8 percent payout unitrust. He explained the 3 percent loss of purchasing power this way:

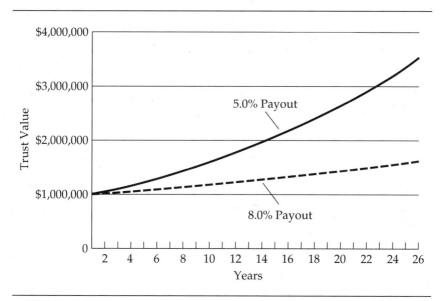

**Exhibit 4.4**   Nominal Remainder Value

Graph comparing the amount left for the charity from two unitrusts, one paying 5% annually and the other paying 8% annually, without taking inflation into account. Total return is 10%.

This illustration was prepared using the Donor Model software developed by Kaspick & Company.

Total return is 10 percent but the payout is 8 percent and, therefore, must be subtracted from the total growth. This leaves a net of 2 percent growth. But the purchasing power of that growth is affected by inflation. Assuming an inflation rate of 5 percent for the charity, the positive 2 percent growth becomes a negative 3 percent growth, or a *decline* in purchasing power of 3 percent annually. To keep things simple, he incorporated the annual management and administration fees into the trust's total growth. Then, using the same steps, he explained how the 5 percent trust would provide for consistent, unchanging purchasing power: The 10 percent total return minus the 5 percent payout minus inflation of 5 percent equals zero percent. George knew that the Livermores would readily understand that the higher trust payout would provide less to Old Ivy. But he also suspected that they would not know, intuitively at least, that they, the income beneficiaries of the trust, would also eventually be provided with less each year. Few donors are aware of that. Few advisors, too. After studying the reports and the graphs for a

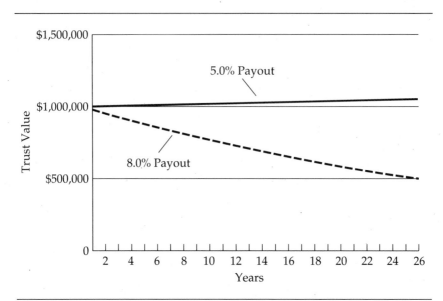

**Exhibit 4.5**   Present-Value Remainder Value

Graph comparing the amount left for the charity from two unitrusts, one paying 5% annually and the other paying 8% annually, taking into account an institutional cost increase of 5%. Total return is 10%.

This illustration was prepared using the Donor Model software developed by Kaspick & Company.

while, Sam and Elizabeth became comfortable with their new knowledge. Although nothing had been decided, George felt that the dinner meeting went well.

Yet Sam's attorney still insisted, in a discussion several weeks after the dinner, that more immediate income would better serve the Livermores' short-term interests. And who knew how long they would live? They both might die tomorrow in an automobile accident, and then what? It would be better, he advised, for them to take as much money as they could up front and worry about the future later. This disturbed George all the more because he saw that they had no need for more income. He did not know how to approach the matter, but silently settled with himself that despite the attorney's bleak assessment of the future, he would not allow a charitable remainder trust to be written for this relatively young couple at such a high payout. He also maintained confidence in the effect his graphs would have on Sam and Elizabeth. Ultimately, George thought, they would agree with him.

Seven months passed after the dinner before George and Sam talked again, George calling from his office to Sam's office. Although the unitrust income problem was not yet fully settled, they decided to move on to other issues during that discussion. The question arose of what other charities should benefit. Again, George was not alarmed. He knew that many times Old Ivy would not be the only remainderman of a charitable trust. He anticipated the question, actually, because so many spouses wanted to help their colleges and other charities. Sam reported that Elizabeth wanted both Mills College and the local Visiting Nurse Association, for which she volunteered regularly, to receive some part of the remainder.

Another nine months passed before the three of them met again in person—this time in Sam's office—and before the Livermores made a final gift decision—a decision, in view of the content of the discussions to date, that earlier would have surprised all of them, especially George.

## The Lead Trust

The major issues did not, after all, center on the need for income. George, a seasoned planned giving professional, had learned from their meetings that the Livermores were not strapped for income. They were, in fact, making so much income that they did not need all of what they were earning. Neither George nor Elizabeth was born into wealth and so they were just learning where their comfort level was. George had first thought of the lead trust possibility at dinner almost a year and a half earlier, but decided not to pursue it because the three of them were so focused on the benefits of a remainder trust. Also, George did not know then, as he knew later, that without further planning the Livermores would have an estate tax problem. He also thought a lead trust—with its income going to charity for a number of years before the trust's assets reverted back to Sam or to his children—would be too good to be true for Old Ivy. George had first learned of the lead trust in a seminar, but not much time was spent on the topic because, the instructor said, not many organizations have lead trusts.

The instructor explained that a charitable lead trust was the reverse of a charitable remainder trust, with the charity instead of a person receiving the income. He also explained that there were two types of lead trusts: the kind whose assets reverted to the donor, called a *grantor lead trust,* and the kind whose assets reverted to someone else, most typically the donor's children or grandchildren, known as a *nongrantor lead trust.* George was told that only the wealthiest donors, who did not need an income tax deduction—the nongrantor lead trust provides no income tax deduction, but it does allow for a potential transfer tax savings— would be prospects for the lead trust.

All the ingredients seemed to be in place with the Livermores. Adequate income. A desire to transfer assets to his children. A potential estate tax problem.

"The problem is, George, that I'm concerned about my family."

"You mean Elizabeth?" They both looked at her.

"No." When he saw George's reaction, he quickly added while looking back at her, "What I mean is, she and I will be all right. It's hard for her to realize—it's hard for me to realize—that we have enough money right now. We'll never starve. No, I'm more concerned about the children, especially after we're gone. I mean, I'd like to be sure they're going to get something from my estate but the remainder trust we've been discussing won't help them. I've given some thought to an outright gift, but I couldn't possibly simply give away $1,000,000 outright. Not now. I just don't know what to do." During the telephone meeting with Sam nine months earlier, George discovered that the Livermores would be able to make a gift larger than $1,000,000, as long as it would provide an income. Although the idea of $5,000,000 subtly emerged as part of that discussion, they were all thinking of $1,000,000 as the operating number. George knew, however, that he would try to introduce the larger number with a lead trust gift.

George decided to try out the idea that so far in his career had eluded him. Perhaps now was the time to determine if the concept had any validity. "Have you ever been told about a charitable lead trust, Sam?"

"A what?"

"A charitable lead trust." Seeing that this meant nothing to Sam, George explained the concept. "It's like making a current gift to Old Ivy, but ultimately the asset comes back to your children." George did not assume that the nongrantor lead trust would necessarily be best, but he did sense that simplicity would be best; he did not at this point confuse his prospect with the intricacies of the differences between the nongrantor and the grantor lead trust. "In the meantime we get the income."

Sam looked perplexed. This was something brand new to him and he had no idea what George was talking about. "So how does this work? And how does Old Ivy benefit?"

"The first thing here is that you are saying that you and Elizabeth don't need an income from a charitable trust, that you already have too much income, right?"

"That's right. I wouldn't say we have too much income—nobody has too much income—but let's say that we're comfortable and always will be."

"Fair enough. So the remainder trust idea, even with its increased income to you, is probably not what you're looking for. Yet you still want to make a major commitment to the campaign here at Old Ivy, right?"

"Yes. Actually, that's my problem. I feel that if I don't go ahead with the remainder trust idea, I won't be fulfilling what in essence has become a pledge."

"Well, let's get that straight right away. You haven't pledged anything. There is no commitment, so do not feel obligated, at this point anyway. Yet I know you want to help. But let's figure out the right way to help, the right way for you as well as Old Ivy. If the remainder trust is not the right choice, then let's forget about it right now. I can assure you that we'll work something out. But let's keep your interests foremost in mind.

## Reducing Transfer Taxes

"Now, we're getting into the idea of a charitable lead trust. This might actually work quite well in your circumstances. During one of our first visits, during that wonderful dinner I believe, you talked briefly about your attorney's concern that you will have an estate tax problem." George had learned from that meeting, and confirmed later with the attorney, that Sam's estate was valued at slightly in excess of $30,000,000. Much of it, about 75 percent, consisted of the travel agency stock, and another large portion consisted of publicly traded securities. He had also learned that one of the two sons wanted to continue on in the business, that the current plan was to freeze the estate—a technique not previously known to George—so that the asset could be transferred with minimal estate taxes. But Sam's attorney hadn't discussed the possibility of a lead trust, probably because Sam hadn't made it clear that he would like to make a major gift to Old Ivy.

"Yes. I'm not going to be ridiculous about not paying any taxes. A man of my financial position owes something back, but I'd like to pay as little as I legally can." George was reminded of the great judge Learned Hand's remark: "No man should pay more than he has to in taxes."

"Well then, I think a lead trust just might be appropriate for you. In general terms, it allows you to make a substantial gift to Old Ivy, a current gift I might add; you pass the asset to your sons, and you could save a great amount of estate taxes."

"This sounds too good to be true. So far, you've not steered me toward hype, George. That's why I like you so much, but this sounds like a lot of hype. Be honest with me. Please."

This type of moment is when a planned giving officer pauses to realize his impact on another's life. Here was a prospect, a wealthy, intelligent person, who was asking that George be honest with him. Sam was admitting that he was deferring to George's judgment about one of the most important decisions in his life. George did not feel powerful at this moment. In fact he felt scared, scared he would steer Sam in a direction that did not suit his needs. At points like this—and there had been many in his career—George asked himself whether he was working for the donor or for Old Ivy. He always justified the answer to be Old Ivy because that's where his paycheck came from, but he was always a little uneasy with such a simple explanation. He thought it was more complicated than that, which is why he did not consider the question often and continued to live with the dilemma.

## How a Lead Trust Works

"Sam, I know this sounds like a good deal for you, and it is. But I must tell you also that you do not receive an income tax deduction for this type of gift. In fact, you might pay a tax, a gift tax, for making the gift."

"You mean I could save taxes—like you said a moment ago—but I might have to pay them as well? I don't understand."

Explaining a lead trust is not easy. "Let's look at it this way. You have an asset. Say that asset is $1,000,000, the amount we've been talking about lately. Only this asset is your closely held stock—"

"Wait a minute, George. I never said anything about giving away my agency stock. That stuff is near and dear to me. Someday I want to leave that to the boys. I want them to continue running the place."

"I understand, Sam. In fact, I'm taking all that into account right now." Sam looked more puzzled than ever. George took a piece of paper and drew boxes to illustrate what he was trying to explain (Exhibit 4.6).

"This concept is the opposite of a charitable remainder trust. The income goes to Old Ivy—and any other charity you and Elizabeth wish—for a number of years. Let's say 25 just to get a number out on the table. At the end of that time, the assets in the trust go to your children. In a way, we are only borrowing the assets and using the income for that time. The income to Old Ivy, by the way, is produced when the company declares a dividend from the stock. That, or the trust can make an in-kind distribution of the appropriate amount of stock each year to Old Ivy. In that case, we would sell it back to the company. After the trust expires, the two boys will own the stock."

Sam still looked confused. "So how does that help me? I think I can understand how Old Ivy benefits, although I'd like some explanation on that, too."

"Let me take Old Ivy first. For example, let's say we get an income of $50,000—5 percent of the value of the $1,000,000 asset—right now and we get that for 25 years. That's $1,250,000. Quite a gift. By the way, we would credit to the campaign ten years of income, or $500,000, and that would help us a lot."

"Okay. So that's how Old Ivy gets the gift."

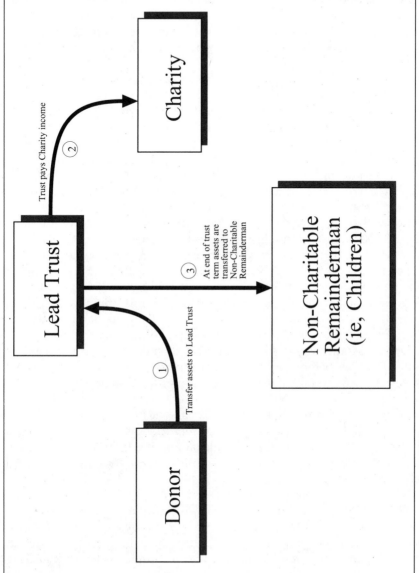

**Exhibit 4.6** A flowchart showing how a nongrantor lead trust works

"Now, you. As I mentioned there's good news and bad news with this type of gift, but the good news usually outweighs the bad news. I mentioned that you might have to *pay* a tax by establishing a lead trust. What I meant is that you would be making a gift to your sons—whatever is left in the trust in 25 years—and that amount would be subject to a gift tax."

"You're right, that's bad news. So why would I ever want to do something like this?"

"Because, as I say, the good news usually outweighs the bad news."

"And that is?"

"The tax you pay today may be less than what you pay at your death when you leave the boys those shares."

"Can you explain that a little more?"

"As you know, whatever you leave to your sons at your death—or your wife's death—will be taxed by the federal government. Most people call it an estate tax. Right now the marginal rate is 55 percent. I don't know what the rate will be when you or Elizabeth dies, but let's assume for now that the highest rate is 55 percent. And believe me, with a $30,000,000 estate, you are in the highest marginal estate tax rate.

"I'll put some numbers on the computer in a minute, but let's just see if I can explain this in general terms first. To do that, I'd like to make the numbers larger. A larger gift means a larger benefit to your estate. Let's assume that the gift is valued not at $1,000,000 but at $5,000,000. I know that this is different from we've been talking about so far, but, as I say, a lead trust provides the most benefits to the donor when the gift is large." George waited for the number to sink into Sam's and Elizabeth's thinking before continuing. "At 5 percent annually—or $250,000 each year, without taking into account any growth—that would provide Old Ivy with about $6,250,000 over a 25-year period. That is quite a lot." Sam and Elizabeth nodded in cautious agreement.

"That's the income to us. Now, further assume that the remainder portion of the gift, using the IRS calculation, is $2,500,000—about half. That means that half the value goes to the income for Old Ivy and the other half goes to your children."

"The remainder portion?"

"Yes," George said, indicating the diagram they reviewed earlier showing how a lead trust works. "The IRS requires a calculation—just like in the remainder trust—to determine how much of the original amount of the gift represents income and how much is left over. This is done in present value terms." George then drew another diagram (Exhibit 4.7).

"Okay, I understand that. But certainly the amount going to my children will be far more. My stock value has grown by over 20 percent annually for the last ten years. That's why I'm in this mess."

"That's right. And you're also right about the value in another 25 years probably being far more than $2,500,000. But we're talking about the *present value* of the asset right now. We can look at the computer in a moment to get an idea of what it will really be worth, given some growth assumptions, but the idea here is that the IRS considers you to be making a gift today of that value to your children."

"Even though they don't get the stock for another 25 years?"

"Even though they don't get the stock for another 25 years."

"Okay. So how is that a good thing for me?"

"Since the value of the portion of the stock going to your sons is essentially frozen at $2,500,000, the 55 percent tax is paid now—this year—on that amount. That tax would be a little more than half, so let's say about $1,375,000. If it is paid now, it is a *gift* tax. At death it is called an *estate* tax. I call them both a *transfer* tax, because they both are taxes on the *right* to transfer assets. It's just that the one transfer is made during life and the other is at death. The same rate applies, though."

"So, that's what I would have to pay today, about $1,375,000?" Sam no longer looked confused, although he did exhibit some astonishment. "So I make a gift that you value at over $6,250,000 to Old Ivy, and I have the privilege of paying one-point-three-seven-five million dollars in taxes?"

"Yes." George was biting his tongue at this point, wondering how to proceed. Sam was someone who caught on very quickly. Math was not difficult for him. George was counting on Sam's ability to get him through this moment. "But," George began cautiously, "that value may

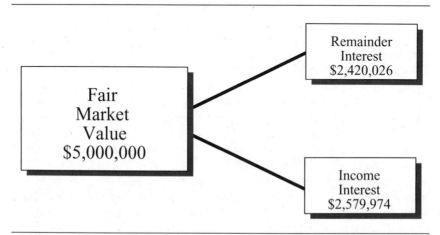

**Exhibit 4.7**   Trust Income and Remainder

be less—it may be a lot less, actually—than what you will have to pay in estate taxes later."

"Let's look at it this way. How much do you think that stock will be worth in 25 years?"

"I don't know. Quite a lot, I imagine," said George as he reached for his briefcase.

## The Growth of an Asset

George retrieved his calculator, one on which he could quickly demonstrate future values. "You say the average growth rate for your company's stock these past ten years has been 20 percent?"

"That's right."

"Well, let's take a more conservative approach and grow the stock by 10 percent a year, net of taxes, for the next 25. Okay?"

"Fair enough."

After a moment punching in some numbers, George said, "That's about $54,000,000." Both stopped for a moment to take in such a large amount. Neither thought it would be that high. "Even in my wildest imagination," Sam finally said. "You mean my stock will be worth that much in 25 years?"

"That's if the stock grows at 10 percent a year. If it continued to grow at 20 percent—let me see. ..." George recalculated, perhaps out of a sense of giddiness, but he did want to know the answer. After a few moments he looked up, puzzled, and said, "I must be doing this wrong."

"Why? What do you get?"

After recalculating the value, George looked up and said, "I still can't believe this, but my calculator says $477,000,000. That's *million*." Both men, each of whom was well versed in money matters, sat still for several moments, trying to comprehend what that number might mean. George thought that $54,000,000 was a lot. Now he was suddenly talking about a figure almost ten times that much. Composing himself to further the discussion, George said, "Well, for the sake of being conservative, let's use the 10 percent growth figure. That's $54,000,000. The point here is that your estate will pay a little over half of that in estate taxes if you want to leave the stock to your sons. That would be estate taxes totaling about $30,000,000."

Even though Sam well understood math and business, he could not imagine paying $30,000,000 in taxes. The amount was simply too staggering. "I know I said I want to be fair to the government, but don't you think that's a bit much?"

"Well, that's up to you, Sam. I do know, however, that by establishing the lead trust, you could avoid paying $30,000,000. Or at least most of it."

"That makes $1,375,000 sound like a bargain."

"Exactly."

"So I make a gift of $5,000,000 to the lead trust, you get the income for 25 years—about six-and-a-quarter million dollars over the length of my lifetime—and I pay a gift tax of about $2,500,000."

"Almost." George knew that part of the success of the discussion so far was Sam's ability to quickly comprehend mathematical and financial questions. "You pay the *tax* on approximately $2,500,000, which is actually about $1,375,000. That would be compared to the tax on $54,000,000, or about $30,000,000."

"That's less than 5 percent," said Sam, quickly calculating in his head the difference between $1,375,000 and $30,000,000. He then saw how the lead trust might help him. If the asset grows in value, he avoids the higher tax later in exchange for paying a tax today on its current value, the value the IRS says is going to his children in 25 years. Then he thought of something else. "But how does that gift tax of $1,375,000 compare with the estate tax of $30,000,000 later on when you take inflation, or the investment opportunity of that $1,375,000, into account?"

"What do you mean?" asked George.

"I mean, let's say instead of socking away that $1,375,000 under the mattress, I put it in the bank to earn interest or invested it more aggressively to get an even better return. What would it be worth in 25 years?"

"Good question." George then went back to the calculator to determine that number. "What do you think you could get if you invested it? Net."

"Let's say 10 percent, the amount we're assuming the stock will grow, although I doubt if I could get a return that good, especially after taxes. But let's use that number anyway, just to see."

George finished punching in the numbers and said, "At a 10 percent annual growth rate, $1,375,000 grows to a little under $15,000,000 in 25 years." George let that sink in for a moment, but then was quick to point out the benefit to Sam. "Even though $15,000,000 is a lot of money, it is still just half of $30,000,000."

Sam was still letting this new knowledge sink in. He had never before heard of a lead trust, and now, less than an hour into this meeting, he was starting to think that this would be the way to help Old Ivy. A huge gift and a way to leave the stock to his boys.

"Now, we've been talking generalities here," said George. "Let me put some of these numbers into the computer." Within five minutes, he had entered the data, received a printout and had photocopied the information so that both he and Sam were looking at the same thing (Exhibit 4.8).

As George put the two pieces of paper in front of Sam, Sam looked incredulously at the product. "You mean you were able to put this together in less than five minutes? I thought we were advanced at the travel agency, but we have nothing like this. Also, my lawyer has never been able to put anything together quite this quickly. I'm impressed."

"We have some software put out by one of the companies that works heavily in planned giving. This is just one of several programs available to charities. Although they are all good, we just purchased this one a few months ago. One of the reasons is this report. What they can do these days astounds me. When I came into planned giving in the late 1970s, we had to calculate remainder values by hand. It would have been inconceivable to do these types of analyses at all, let alone in five minutes."

George laid out the two identical pages side by side so that they were looking at them together. He then reviewed the numbers. "The first thing to note is that line 5 shows the amount the IRS says you will be leaving your children."

"You were almost right on. You said $2,500,000 and it says here $2,420,025. Not bad."

"Lucky guess." Sam sensed, however, that George's experience was substantial and he knew exactly what he was talking about.

"Now if you take a look at line 7, you'll see that the gift tax is actually much smaller than we discussed, only about $800,000—a little less, actually—as opposed to $1,300,000. That's because you are able to protect $600,000 of your assets with something commonly called the 'exemption equivalent.' This means only a little more than $1,800,000 is being taxed, and not all of that at the marginal 55 percent bracket. As you see, the actual tax is a little under $800,000. Compare that to the estate tax paid at your death, assuming the assets—not in the charitable lead trust—grow by 10 percent per year for 25 years. The asset itself is estimated to be worth just under $40,000,000 and the estate tax on that would be over $21,000,000."

"I thought we just figured that the growth would be almost $54,000,000 or something. Why is this different?"

"That's because I forgot to mention that any income the asset produces is itself subject to an income tax. The 10 percent return is a gross, or before-tax return. Our assumption has 5 percent of capital growth, which isn't taxed, and 5 percent of income, which is taxed every year. This reduces the amount that gets reinvested, and that reduces the total growth of the assets. In this case that makes the anticipated amount in 25 years only $40,000,000 as opposed to the $54,000,000." George fin-

# OLD IVY
## LEAD TRUST ANALZYER SUMMARY

**Donor's Name: Samuel Livermore**

### GIFT INFORMATION:

| | |
|---|---|
| Fair Market Value of Gift | $5,000,000 |
| Payment Frequency | Annual |
| Number of Years Analysis Runs | 25 Years |
| Prior Taxable Gifts | $0 |
| Charitable Mid-Term Federal Rate Used | 8.4% |

### ASSUMPTIONS FOR 5.0% CHARITABLE LEAD ANNUITY TRUST:

| | |
|---|---|
| Payment at Beginning or End | End |
| Annual Income to Charity | $250,000 |
| Deduction | $2,420,025 |
| Capital Growth for 25 Years | 5.0% |
| Yield for 25 Years | 5.0% |
| Assumed Inflation Rate for Gift Tax: | 10.0% |

### ASSUMPTIONS FOR NO TRUST:

| | |
|---|---|
| Estate Value, other than Asset | $25,000,000 |
| Appreciation Rate of Estate | 3.0% |
| Capital Growth for 25 Years | 5.0% |
| Yield for 25 Years | 5.0% |

### NONGRANTOR LEAD TRUST SUMMARY

| | 5.0% Charitable Lead Annuity Trust | No Trust |
|---|---|---|
| 1. Original Principal | 5,000,000 | 5,000,000 |
| 2. Total Income to Charity | 6,250,000 | |
| 3. Principal Value at End of Trust Term | 23,386,735 | 39,329,247 |
| 4. Total Income Tax | 2,970,974 | 5,588,482 |
| 5. Present Value of Asset (Using IRS Formula) | 2,420,026 | |
| 6. Present Value of Income (Using IRS Formula) | 2,579,974 | |
| 7. Transfer Tax | 793,812 | 21,631,086 |
| 8. Inflated Transfer Tax | 8,600,723 | 21,631,086 |
| 9. Total Tax (Lines 4 + 7) | 3,764,786 | 27,219,568 |
| 10. Total After-Tax Value (Lines 3 – 8) | 19,621,948 | 12,109,679 |
| 11. Value of Asset for Heirs at End of Trust Term (Lines 3 – 7) | 22,592,923 | 17,698,161 |

**Exhibit 4.8**   Lead Trust Summary: Projected Income, Value, and Taxes

Lead trust summary, comparing projected income, the value of the asset at the end of 25 years, and the gift and estate taxes.

This illustration was prepared using the planned giving software ParaGon™, developed by Blackbaud, Inc.

ished the explanation by saying, "Quite a difference, and a good example to show the effect of taxes on the growth of an asset."

"*Only* $40,000,000," Sam repeated, still amazed at how his estate would grow over the years.

"And there, on line 8, you see an accurate comparison of the gift tax paid today with the estate tax paid in 25 years. You'll see the $800,000 grows to about $8,600,000, assuming an annual inflation or investment rate of 10 percent. That's a lot of growth you're not getting on that money, but look at how much less it is than the amount your estate will pay if these assumptions hold. A little more than a third. Again, just as we discussed."

Sam took a moment to review this point. He was trying to think through the process of adjusting the initial tax amount to the invested amount and then comparing that to the estate tax in 25 years—or beyond, if he lives longer. Once satisfied with that, he jumped to the bottom line, line 11. "Does that say what I think it says?"

"I don't know. How do you read that line?"

"Well, if I'm right about this, it looks like my kids will end up with more by making the gift than if I don't make the gift. But that can't be right."

"Well, Sam, that's exactly right. I should caution you, although I'm sure you're aware of this, but we can't rely on these assumptions to hold true for 25 years. Any one year could and probably will produce different investment results, but over the long term I'm told by our investment advisors that these are not bad assumptions. And remember that any change equally affects both the trust and nontrust sides of the ledger. Given that, I'd say the lead trust gift is not a bad idea. I should also say—and we can't forget this—that you are making a gift here. The downside of this equation, if you need to think of it this way, is that Old Ivy is getting an income. You'll see that on Line 2. You do not have use of the asset for 25 years. That's a long time."

Sam thought about this for a while, and then asked, "But the no-trust side of the ledger shows an accumulation of the income, after taxes, over the 25 years, doesn't it?"

"That's right."

"So, although Old Ivy is getting all this money during that time, the net amount after that is still more for my boys than if I just keep the dividends and reinvest them. Is that right?"

"Yes, Sam, that's right."

"So what were you saying about a downside?"

"Now that you remind me, I can think of two issues. The first is that the company stock in the lead trust retains its cost basis. When the boys get the stock after the lead trust ends, they'll incur a large capital gains tax if they sell it. By then, it will be worth a lot, and the cost basis will be practically zero."

"But the idea is to transfer the stock to them so they can own the business."

"That's right. That's why the lead trust is a viable option for these circumstances. I just wanted you to know."

"Okay. Now I know. The second downside? Did you say something about income going to Old Ivy, or some horrible thing like that?" Sam was having a good time ingesting this information.

The two men looked at each other and began to laugh simultaneously. The logic of the plan hit Sam at the same time the wonder of it hit George. Looking back on that first visit to a person who had fastidiously never missed an annual fund gift since graduation, George now saw an alumnus completely transformed. He had gone from the duty of giving annually, a schedule he promised to maintain, to the love of being an important part of Old Ivy's growth and mission. Never before had Sam considered himself a potential large donor to his alma mater. Instead, until now he had seen himself as simply a small, insignificant part of the whole incomprehensible fund-raising picture at Old Ivy. Now he was the center of a major effort to raise money.

George thought how easily he could have arranged for Sam to establish a charitable remainder trust. He wryly remembered the argument over the income. At first they needed nothing; then Elizabeth and the attorney felt they needed a high income; then it was discovered they had no need for more income, that there was, in fact, more than enough. Then the asset question. George still was not sure how much IBM stock Sam had but he was almost certain it was more than the amount he indicated during their first meeting. How typical it would have been to have looked at the highly appreciated publicly traded stock and gone for the unitrust. Only through the process of talking and listening to Sam explain his growth at the travel agency was George able to infer that the closely held agency stock might be a gift asset. Then, when Sam told George of his desire to have his sons carry on in the business, the idea occurred to George to discuss lead trusts. From Old Ivy's perspective, the gift was immediate and Sam could make a much larger gift than he otherwise would have thought possible. Further, although the other assets would be included in his estate, the sons could sell the IBM and other publicly traded stock without much capital gain (at least according to the tax laws today) because of the stepped-up basis they would have upon Sam's death. They would not pay much in a capital gains tax if they sold the publicly traded stock soon after Sam's death because the stock would have a cost basis equal to the fair market value of the stock as it was valued in Sam's estate. In that sense, the cost basis is *stepped up* from what Sam originally paid for it to its value at Sam's death. When the boys get the stock, therefore, their basis is *stepped up* and they will have little, if any, capital gains tax to pay at that time.

## Adding Another Charity to the Lead Trust Income

The only problem came about two weeks after the meeting in George's office. Sam had called to ask about Mills College, his wife's alma mater. George had already told the chairman of the capital campaign committee about an upcoming gift of approximately $2,500,000, the $250,000 annual annuity from the lead trust amount taken out ten years, the pledge period of the current capital campaign. Although the lead trust would run for 25 years, the campaign would credit gifts for pledges only up to ten years in the future. But George was elated when Sam asked if Old Ivy would still be the trustee if some of the annual income could be paid to Mills and that he would provide for Mills by adding $2,500,000 to the trust for a total of $7,500,000. Sam had explained that his attorney agreed with George and said that the gift tax was lower than they thought partly because Sam had not used up the untaxed amount available in his estate. Looking at it that way, Sam said he felt comfortable adding $2,500,000 to the lead trust to take into account her obligation to Mills College. Mills would be the beneficiary of his efforts, Sam thought, but then he knew that the planned giving director at Mills has probably done the same thing for other colleges when setting up planned gifts. That's just the way the charitable world worked and, he thought, it was the better for it.

All in all, George thought, this is the way a gift should be made.

# CHAPTER FIVE

# The Failed Planned Giving Interview

*Haste in every business brings failures.*
**Herodotus**

One of the bigger myths pervading the planned giving community, especially among those who are new in the profession, is that a planned gift can be acquired quickly. This is not true. As we have seen in Chapters 2 and 4, many meetings, in addition to what is usually a long cultivation period, are needed before most donors feel able to make a gift. The nature of the process is complex; although an annual fund gift decision can be made over the phone, planned gifts require advisors, the staff at the charity, and time. Usually, a great deal of time.

Yet there are enough exceptions to the normally time-consuming process that some in planned giving raise their hopes that a gift can be acquired quickly and without much work. One of the worst mistakes a person soliciting a planned gift can make is to rely on the quick but isolated personal observation or the handy tax detail that, in his mind at least, will make the difference in persuading the prospect to decide to make a gift. This hasty attempt, made at the expense of understanding the donor's needs and expectations, and often unaccompanied by a solid knowledge of planned giving vehicles and the economic and financial culture within which gifts are made, often leads to a failed gift solicitation. This story is about a gift that was not made and a planned giving officer who did not do a credible job. Unfortunately, it represents too many other stories.

## ANXIETY

She was responsive, open, and . . . inviting. No woman had ever before reacted to him as she did, as if he were the only person in her life . . . as if she were attracted to him.

The call to Richard Marks came unexpectedly; they normally did not call him back. She listened to him, too. Not like most of them, who, once he had introduced himself and explained why he was calling, said they would rather not, but thanks for calling and good luck in the future. Sometimes not even that, just a polite good-bye. No, this one was different, and he heard that difference immediately in her voice, the warmth, the caring. That she allowed him to visit her at home after his very first call was almost shocking, except, as he thought about it on the drive over, this is the way he was told it should be.

Was it too soon to think about what might happen? After all, making an appointment had never gone this smoothly, and he might blow it by allowing himself to think past the immediate task at hand. No, he would concentrate on the important things first, and that, in this case, was getting her to say yes. But how best to accomplish that? Charm her with his smile? Act businesslike and professional? He had read somewhere that people like her reacted best to the casual approach, not the heavy-handed way that many planned giving officers attend a first meeting with a prospect. Well, he decided as his car neared her home, he would simply have to approach her in the most natural way he knew; if she didn't like it, that would be too bad. He didn't even blink an eye when she, not a servant, opened the door.

"Good evening, young man." She was beautiful, even at her 82 years. Her eyes were sharp and revealed an intelligence not dulled by age. Her smile was inviting. "Do come in."

Richard Marks first learned about this woman from the most recent *Forbes 500* listing of the 50 wealthiest individuals in the United States. To learn also that she lived in this city piqued his curiosity. She was not known to the Visiting Nurse Association (VNA), the organization he represented. She had never made a gift and never used the organization's services, but he had done his homework and found out all about her. Maria von Rothsberg had been born in Michigan, the daughter of a German immigrant who came to the United States to find a better life. Maria, several times married and as many times divorced, was the heir of a fortune worth hundreds of millions of dollars. She had acquired her wealth upon her mother's death three decades before. Her father had died a decade earlier. The publicity about her family's wealth had subsided during the last few decades, and the recent *Forbes* article was short and contained few newly discovered facts. Richard, the VNA's director of development, noted that the article did not mention anything about her being reclusive. He decided to give her a call.

And to discover she lived right here in town, thought Richard. Certainly, although she had no connection with the VNA, she would be interested in parting with at least some of her money for a good cause, to say nothing of tax and income benefits. So he entered her home and starting talking immediately about the advantages of a planned gift.

## A Tedious Conversation

As he was sitting down and ignoring the scones and tea in front of him, he mentioned the charitable gift annuity, that many people are interested in the gift annuity because of an increased income, some of which would be tax-free; and that an income tax deduction is available. He told her that she could have all this, and make a gift to the VNA all at the same time. Maria had no chance to say anything during Richard's 20-minute description of the charitable gift annuity, but she did listen intently and seemed to comprehend all that was said. When Richard ended by saying that this would be a good deal for her, she asked a question.

"Thank you for coming, Richard. I want you to know that I do appreciate your visit. I have one question, however."

"Yes," said Richard, "and what's that?"

"Maybe you already discussed this point, but please tell me why I might want to enter into such an arrangement."

Richard Marks sat back, not a little stunned. What had he just spent 20 minutes discussing? Wasn't he in the process of describing the charitable gift annuity in rather minute detail? How could this woman, who seemed so inviting just moments before, act as if he had been saying nothing? With difficulty he found the composure to respond. "I know this may sound a little complicated to you," he said, "but perhaps if I show you how the gift annuity works you'll understand it better. Let me show you some material I brought along."

## A Tedious Printout

The woman looked at him politely and nodded her head. From this he inferred that the problem was, in fact, one of understanding. Now that he thought of it, who could blame her? This stuff was pretty complicated. He had taken a long time to master the intricacies himself, and should not have been surprised that this woman needed some printouts. A lot of the business people whom he talked to also needed to be shown how life-income gifts worked. So, despite his initial surprise at her question, he decided that the need to show her material on the gift annuity really was not a problem. He was prepared, after all. She certainly knew a lot less than most of his other prospects. She was, he had to remind himself, only an old woman who inherited her wealth. Her life had been one of privilege, and so her father and her husbands probably did all the thinking for her. She's now a lonely divorcee hoping someone will come along to help with the finances. To supplement what he thought was a perfectly lucid explanation of gift annuities, he turned to another programmed response. He reached into his briefcase and removed a thick file, bound in soft transparent plastic with a hard plastic colored spine. The first page was blue and looked handsome (see Exhibit 5.1).

Inside, the presentation looked even more handsome. No fewer than 23 pages of description and numbers and full-color graphs. The first seven full pages of single-space type contained a detailed description of the characteristics of the charitable gift annuity, and included:

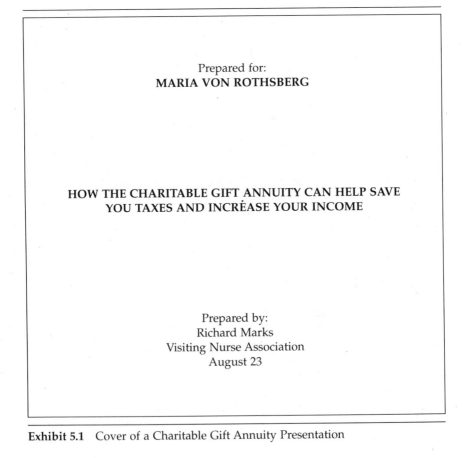

Prepared for:
**MARIA VON ROTHSBERG**

**HOW THE CHARITABLE GIFT ANNUITY CAN HELP SAVE
YOU TAXES AND INCREASE YOUR INCOME**

Prepared by:
Richard Marks
Visiting Nurse Association
August 23

**Exhibit 5.1**  Cover of a Charitable Gift Annuity Presentation

- A description of how the gift works, noting the tax advantages
- Information on how the charitable income tax deduction is calculated
- A description of the limits of the deduction based on a person's adjusted gross income
- A summary of where in the IRS Code and Regulations the definition of the gift annuity could be found
- A full page and a half explaining the bargain sale rules
- An explanation of why part of the income from a gift annuity is tax free
- An explanation of why a gift annuity is a good idea
- A list of the types of donors for whom the gift would be most appropriate

Although Maria von Rothsberg did not understand very much of what her visitor was essentially reading to her, she did see that a gift annuity is most appropriate for donors who are elderly, need tax-free income, need more income than they might receive from their investment sources, and want a significant tax deduction.

Richard Marks thought the following pages would be even more impressive to his prospect. The first three contained just the income tax deduction calculation, showing the deduction value as well as the tax-free portion of the gift. Maria von Rothsberg's elderly eyes caught such terms as "Asset Solely Owned by Donor," "Pro-Rated," "Charitable Midterm Federal Rate," "Present Value of Annuity," "Remainder Value," "One-Life Return Multiple," "Adjustment Factor," "Exclusion Ratio," "Bargain Sale Value," and "Clay Brown Rules." She was also introduced to "Table R(1)," "Table K," "Table V," and an "ACGA Schedule 5." Those three pages of calculation contained a lot of information, different from what the first seven offered.

## IGNORING THE PROSPECT

The information was overwhelming. Not only was the presentation detailed, but from the moment Richard walked into the house he talked almost without stopping about how the gift annuity worked. He did not ask her questions: He did not know if she was interested in a gift annuity or any other type of gift; he did not know what she knew about charitable giving; he did not know if she wanted to make a gift; he did not even know if she cared about the VNA. Instead, he assumed that she would be persuaded by tax benefits and an increased income. To make it worse, he did not pick up on her body language, which almost shouted for him to slow down, to take it easy, that she would be glad to have a discussion if only he would listen a little and get to know her.

So many people avoided getting to know her, she thought, her eyes losing focus as she tried to make sense of the computerized printouts. In that sense, she realized her wealth was a sort of prison. She was certain that people would like her for who she was, but she was seen first as a center of wealth. Without that, she wondered, would she have been able to live a fuller, happier life? Would she have been able to marry for requited love, and today not have the feeling that she bought her husbands and then paid handsomely for their departures? Hers was not a happy life in many ways, she thought, as this young man from an organization she wanted to know more about was babbling on about the tax and income benefits her accountant had already described to her. Not in the detail to which Richard was now treating her, of course, but with enough description that she and her accountant both agreed to discard the option as unnecessary. She did not need extra income. In fact, she needed to reduce her estate and wanted to know more about how charitable giving, particularly outright gifts, would help her accomplish her goal of sending less money to the government.

## CHARITABLE MOTIVES

She also had developed an interest in charity. She truly did want to know about the VNA. She had read in the newspaper a few weeks earlier of the good works the organization was doing for infirm people around the region. The reason for the article, moreover, was that the executive director was announcing an initiative to renovate an old schoolhouse into a day-care center for children whose parents were unable to pay. The story covered not only interviews with the executive director and a few VNA board members, but also conversations with the parents, mostly unwed mothers, who described in heartrending detail how they were so pleased that such a place would now be available.

Maria von Rothsberg was particularly struck by the closeness between the people who were helping and the people who were being helped, and by the minimal level of bureaucracy. She thought that this country did such a fine job of allowing people to help others through organized charity, and thought sorrowfully about how so many other countries were unable to do this. Not that this country had it all correct and was without its social problems, but that those who could help were encouraged to do so through the tax laws. She was not consciously thinking about tax savings, but she did know that more than half of her many, many millions of dollars would be sent to the government on her death if she did not give much of it away to charity. She had no intention of marrying again and her lawyer told her that, as a result, one of the two estate deductions—the marital and the charitable—would be unavailable to her upon her death. So charity it would be.

But which charity, and how to help? As a young woman she did not think much of giving her money away, but in college she had befriended another wealthy young woman with whom she corresponded regularly and visited occasionally over the years until the other's death five years ago. She learned from her friend that giving away money was a serious job, not a capricious, occasional act, that someone with her wealth and potential and desire to give had to do the proper research and decide what was worth supporting. Both decided, for example, to help the college they attended, but neither felt it needed much of their support and that other causes might be more needy. Up until the last few years, though, she did not think much about charity because she was so busy traveling and trying to make a life with her husbands. Now that she was in her eighties and addressing her own mortality, she had discussed charity a great deal with her attorney, and in addition to designing her estate plan in such a way that the federal and state governments would get as little as possible she was looking for ways to help a good cause. When Richard Marks called she was reminded of the newspaper article and was delighted to see him. She did not expect the meeting to focus so much on tax benefits and so little on the VNA, as it had for over 45 minutes now.

"And so you can see how the deduction and the income taxation portion of the gift annuity works," he was saying. "Now I'd like to show you how the estate tax deduction works and why this plan is good from that perspective, too."

Oh, my. Had she missed his review of the income taxation portion of the gift? She must have been daydreaming. The young man, however, continued to drone on. He was now showing her the final pages of the estate plan. He had no idea, of course, what her plans were, although she would have been glad, within reason, to discuss them with him. She yearned for someone other than her attorney, as good as he was, with whom to discuss these things. But Richard was giving her no opportunity, and her interest in making a gift was waning. Before he finished with a summary of the presentation, she interrupted to ask the question again.

"Excuse me, young man, I am so sorry to interrupt but would you be so kind as to explain to me again why you would like me to make a gift?"

This time Richard was more exasperated. He had just spent an hour reviewing the plan in some detail, which to him was sufficient reason. Internally he took a deep breath and responded. "I think I am answering your question, Mrs. Harris."

"von Rothsberg, if you don't mind. I've recaptured my family name and intend to use it until the day I die."

"I'm sorry. I didn't know. I knew you were single, again, but I didn't know that."

"Of course not. How could you?" He shrugged as if to agree. He could have asked. But he did not.

"I thought I had answered the question, Mrs. von Rothsberg. I've been explaining how the gift annuity works. And I put in a lot of time compiling what I think is a first-rate presentation. I think you'd agree that all the information you need to make a decision is right here."

He paused for a moment, the longest he had paused with intervening silence since he arrived. "Now, what do you think?"

"I think you are right. The plan is well thought out." At this Richard smiled, thinking that the $50,000 gift annuity with a 9 percent payout was in hand. "But, and I sense you will be frustrated by this, I still do not have a satisfactory answer to my question."

Frustration was right. Richard did not understand what the woman was talking about. Finally he asked, "Then what could I be telling you to help?"

"From what you've said I have no sense of why you are asking me for a gift. You have told me nothing yet about the mission of your organization, the Visiting Nurse Association."

## AN INADEQUATE MISSION STATEMENT

"But it's right here, at the back. I was going to get to that." He turned to the last page, a single page, where the VNA's mission statement was included. The prospect took a moment to read the one paragraph that explained that the organization dedicated itself to the "humanity" of the community and searched for ways to "help those in need." As she read the short paragraph she decided to be truthful in her response.

"But this does not say very much. Only that you are trying to do good work." She saw nothing concrete, nothing to distinguish this group from several others, and she told Richard what she thought.

"But it's all right here," he responded. "Read it for yourself," he said as if she had not clearly done just that. "I'm sure you'll see what you need. This piece, I'll have you know, is the product of many of our best board members' thinking."

"So it was written by a committee?"

"Well. . . ."

"So it was. And so it reads. Richard, I'm sorry but I know nothing about the VNA from this. It sounds like the trustees wanted not to offend anyone and used pathetic lukewarm words with many syllables that sound good on the first hearing, but which, upon analysis, don't really mean anything, or do anything to distinguish your efforts from, say, the local hospital's. From this I can tell you're not a college or a university, but not much else." Despite her age, thought Richard, this woman has a sharp mind. And a sharp tongue.

She went on. "Now, let's put this away and let me ask you what you would say your mission is. If you can do that, you will answer the question I've been asking since you came in the door over an hour ago."

Richard looked flabbergasted. Never had a prospect asked such a question. And he felt he could not answer the question now. He looked at the one-paragraph mission statement, then back up at her, and said, "We do a lot of good work. Our nurses do what very few people are able to do, especially when it comes to helping those who can't pay the bill."

"Okay," said the prospect. "That's not bad, but tell me more."

He then looked without saying anything back at the mission statement. After a few moments he said, "I can't."

"Why not?"

"Because I think you're asking for too much. I don't know anything more."

"How long have you been working for the VNA?"

"Six months now. Six and a half next week."

"So you haven't been there very long?"

"Well, as I said, almost seven months now. What's wrong with that?"

"Nothing, really. I think, however, that you should know more about your own organization." This sounded like an insult, but he did not say so. "And I've learned that to help an organization I need to know about it. I don't mean just the tax benefits, which, as I understand it, are available no matter which charities I decide to support."

"But I thought that the benefits of the gift annuity would be attractive to you."

"And whatever gave you that idea, Richard?"

He thought about this for a minute and then said, "They are always attractive, and I know a lot of people who have made a gift to the VNA this way."

"Yes?" She asked as if he had not finished his explanation.

"Well, it's just that I thought you might like the idea. As you can see I put a lot of work into preparing for this visit."

"A lot of work. Yes, I see, and I agree," she responded. "But you did not come prepared to tell me anything convincing about the VNA. For example, you did not come prepared with a copy of a very interesting newspaper article explaining the new child-care center you are now running."

"But I didn't think that would be important."

"And why not? Don't you realize that would be one of the most important things someone like myself would want to know?"

## The Prospect Remains a Mystery

No, Richard did not realize that. And he did not realize a great deal more either. The woman was an ideal prospect, more ideal than Richard would ever know. To him she was a name from a public source, a local person who happened to have a great deal of money and who agreed during a phone conversation to see him. He had no idea that her interest was sparked by the newspaper article, or that she knew anything at all about the VNA. He also had no idea how a gift annuity might fit into her plans.

"But, despite that, doesn't the gift annuity sound like the perfect way for you to make a gift?"

"And why would you think that?"

He felt like he had to repeat himself. "Because a gift annuity offers a great many benefits."

"Benefits I may or may not need, young man. And from what I know from my attorney, I do not need more income, tax-free or otherwise. I have stock that I've been selling over the years to get a higher income, but I've been selling it incrementally so as to minimize the impact of the capital gains taxes." She looked at him squarely and finished by saying, "In short, despite all your good preparations, I don't need a gift annuity."

Richard looked anguished. In a short sentence she had destroyed the work of several hours, as well as the dreams he had of taking a deferred gift back to the VNA. His demeanor changed rapidly and all he wanted was to leave. He thought again that he had never had this type of discussion with a donor. Never had he thought, actually, to expand his talk with a prospect beyond that of the technical aspects of a gift. Of course, when he allowed himself to think honestly, he had never really closed a deferred gift, except once. That once involved a younger person who seemed not to be charitably minded but was interested in accumulating a tax-free supplemental retirement fund. That man was in his early fifties, and Richard had discovered him while working at another charity two years earlier. He had worked in the development office at two other charities since then. He had no idea how the gift assets were growing, or even *if* they were growing. That transaction was in a different life. This was a new life.

"I don't need a gift annuity," she said again, as if she sensed that her original response compelled him to think of other things. "I do need advice, however, about my estate plans. Not from my attorney. He's been good, but he can't help me identify which charities are right for me. I want to get to know other charities to see which ones I can feel a part of. I want to make a difference." The unsaid presumption from Richard's perspective was that the VNA was not such a place, although nothing could be further from the truth.

## The Rejection

Maria von Rothsberg then walked to the kitchen and returned with her purse. She retrieved her checkbook. "I do want to help, however," she said as she began writing a check. "I want you to take this back and use it to help that child-care center."

Without looking at the folded check, he put it into his pocket. "Thank you," he said without conviction. "I'm sure this will be greatly appreciated at the office."

When Richard was in his car he looked at the check. She had made a gift of $10,000. At first he was elated. An outright gift of $10,000 would do much more good than a deferred gift with a remainder value of about $7,500. (Even though the gift annuity technically is not a deferred gift, the VNA would invest it to create the donor's income, and so he thought of it as deferred.) The executive director would be happy with his efforts. He was going back to the office with a gift. That's the important thing, he thought.

But an unsettled feeling came over him. Despite the gift, he still felt rejected. He thought for a while as he drove, and suddenly feared that he had been given nothing. A $10,000 gift to her must have been pocket change. It came right out of her checkbook, he realized, and she didn't blink an eye when she wrote it. She was, after all, one of the country's wealthiest people, and here she was giving him a check for $10,000.

## What Went Wrong?

Then he began to rethink the entire conversation. What had gone wrong? He had prepared himself as well as he could. Obviously, he said the right things on the phone because she gave him an appointment. But while he was in her home he was nervous, but not so nervous as to blow the gift, to say the wrong things. But why did she keep asking him that question? Clearly, she could see that the gift would provide benefits to her. These things are true no matter how rich people are. In fact, the benefits are greater for those in the highest tax bracket, and certainly she was in that category.

Could he have addressed her question differently? Could he know or should he know what the VNA is all about? He thought that it would not matter. A gift, after all, is a gift. Once you master the technical aspects of planned giving, what should the mission of the organization matter? He had worked at several places now and this had not come up yet. The more he thought, the more confused he became.

Richard Marks was confused because, despite the technical knowledge he had acquired, he knew nothing—and did not recognize anything—about donor motivations. Although a persistent topic in the discussions of many planned gifts is tax and income benefits, the primary theme is *why* the donor wants to give. Not how, but why. The absence of this simple fact—that the solicitor did not ever learn why the donor wanted to help the charity—made this gift impossible. The solicitor did not hear the prospect.

## UNDERSTANDING WHEN NOTHING IS SPOKEN

When you are on a city street corner asking how to find a certain address, the person you ask needs to know a little about you. Do you know the area? If so, you might know a landmark near the address you want to go to. The person may say, it's just two blocks from the X building. Take a left when you get there. But if you have no idea where the X building is, the person needs to give directions very differently. Well, from here, go straight for five blocks. When you see a restaurant with a blue sign, turn right and go another seven blocks. The directions are much more specific because the questioner knows nothing of the area. The person giving the directions saves a lot of time and effort if she finds out what the questioner needs to know. The search for context is worth the effort.

This is true in almost every conversation we have. Typically, we correctly make assumptions when we talk with people. "John called the other day about the gift," a secretary will tell his supervisor. He does not need to identify John because he knows his supervisor knows who John is. But if a supervisor tells her secretary to expect a call from John, she may say that John is very important, that he just sold his business for a million dollars, and that he's thinking about making a gift. For the secretary who did not know John, the supervisor's explanation was helpful.

Richard Marks did not take the time to hear what Maria von Rothsberg could tell him. He did not listen to her body language. Although she was polite, he did not notice that her eyes glazed over when he began to talk about the gift annuity. He did not take time to accept a cup of tea or a scone. He unthinkingly started to talk. He should not have done that. He also should not have been so detailed in his oral presentation without some response from his prospect, some acknowledgment that she was hearing—and understanding—what he was saying. Further, he should never have prepared, let alone presented, such a detailed written outline of how the gift annuity works. No prospect, until she convinces the solicitor that technical information is welcome, should be exposed to the minutia of a remainder value calculation, especially a prospect who has no intention of making a life-income gift. And where did he get the idea that the gift annuity would be in her best interests? From a book. A manual. From the discussions in a seminar. As true as it is that a gift annuity is most appropriate for an elderly person— because the income is flat and can never change—this does not mean that any person should be solicited without explaining in broad terms what might be a useful way to help the charity. The original phone conversation contained nothing about a gift annuity, or even a life-income gift. In fact, Maria von Rothsberg simply said that she would see Richard to discuss the VNA.

Richard Marks did not realize many things on his confused trip back to the office. The most painful would have been that his major prospect would have been happy to make a significant gift had she been able to learn more from him than from the newspaper account she had read several days prior to the visit. Had he listened, or cared to listen, he would have learned that Maria von Rothsberg wanted to do something significant for a charity—a charity where she could make a difference. He would have discovered that she would be willing to discuss a gift of at least a million dollars, with the possibility—probability—of more gifts. Instead, he concentrated on only one thing: the technical details of the charitable gift annuity. He did not even pause to consider that the gift annuity might be inappropriate. Because he learned at a seminar that the most elderly people are those for whom gift annuities are appropriate, he had simply assumed that this type of gift would be appropriate. He never even considered the possibility that an outright gift would be better for everyone: her, him, and the VNA. To his unfortunate visit he brought only those broad but isolated ideas about how he felt a gift solicitation should be conducted, and he did not make any attempt to connect the prospect with the reason for making a gift.

Instead of beginning a relationship and perceiving the broad and indefinite outline of a major gift, one that could have meant a great deal to the VNA, Richard Marks drove away disappointed.

## THE PERSISTENT DONOR

As it turned out, however, Maria von Rothsberg thought more about the VNA, and when the thank-you letter arrived from the executive director, she called. Two months later the executive director, who knew nothing about planned giving but who knew a lot about the good works of the VNA, invited Maria von Rothsberg to an interview in her office at the VNA. The two women met for over two hours, during which time nothing was mentioned about a gift. The discussion turned to money when the donor wanted to know how much certain things would cost to build, establish, or maintain. Shortly after that warm and friendly discussion, about which, at the urging of the donor, the development director knew nothing, the donor instructed her attorney to establish an immediate gift of two million dollars. She consulted her accountant about which assets would be most appropriate to use for the gift. She also instructed her attorney to modify her will so that the VNA would receive $10 million more at her death, by far the largest gift ever made to the VNA.

A year after her initial phone call, at the formal ceremony announcing the gift, Maria von Rothsberg spoke movingly about what she now considered one of her favorite charities, a community organization doing good work to help some local disadvantaged people get through their days. She told how she was struck by the newspaper article and the subsequent news she received about the good works the VNA had been doing for many years. She only hoped, she said, that her small effort would help.

Many people were in the audience that day, including the newspaper reporter who wrote the original story. Today, he was there to write a new story, about what he considered a remarkably wonderful charitable gift. The executive director was there, of course, as well as several members of the board. And, at the request of the donor, many of the single mothers for whom the child-care center was built were in the audience. Although they felt awkward sprinkled among several of the city's most influential and wealthy people, they were made to feel welcome by the most influential and wealthy person there—Maria von Rothsberg.

Not in attendance was Richard Marks, who was no longer employed at the VNA.

# CHAPTER SIX

# After the Gift

*About tomorrow there's no knowing.*
**Lorenzo de' Medici**

Nothing gets the adrenaline going like an agreement. The excitement when someone finally formally agrees to make the deal happen, almost any deal, is powerful. This is the car salesperson when a buyer says yes; this is the real estate broker during the closing; this is the newly elected president of the United States at 12:01 P.M. on inauguration day. No matter the product, the acceptance and recognition of hard work and success are key ingredients in the commerce of objects as well as of ideas. Whether it be a widget or trust document, when the other person signs on the dotted line distinct feelings of pride and achievement combine to make a person whole, to make the world right.

The planned giving director feels this rush when the gift document is signed. Everyone experiences different levels of excitement, but the feeling of accomplishment overwhelms nonetheless. The good feeling is so good, of course, because it usually follows a great deal of work: talking with the accountant or the attorney, calculating many numbers on the computer, and talking with the donor, as well as with other family members, to ensure that her interests are aligned with the organization's. In planned giving as elsewhere, it is not a coincidence that many people celebrate after such a joyous occasion.

But many celebrations are hard to remember after some time has passed. For example, the Democrats' euphoria after George McGovern was nominated by the party in the very early hours of a summer morning in 1972 was shortlived. Or remember how happy the bride was—the first time to the altar? Some good things don't stay good forever or even for very long. Unfortunately, despite good intentions, this is true about some planned gifts, too. Even for those still around to remember being present when a trust was drafted and the gift made, some life-income donors are remembered less enthusiastically than they might otherwise be because, among other things, they have become disillusioned with the falling or stagnant income or because they are exercising their life-time right to correspond with the development office. Despite the donor's and the charity's initial happiness, an ill-conceived planned gift, or one that is not well managed or administered, can create frustration, despair, and sometimes even anger. The vast majority of planned gifts outlive the tenure of planned giving or development directors.

It is normal to think of successes in the present or near future, but, as with retirement planning, the decisions planned giving professionals make today will affect the incomes of others in the future. How many in this profession are honestly able to say they can extrapolate into the future and imagine the donor's financial life in 20 years? Will the gift arrangement be all that was promised? And make no mistake, when we talk of future income, we talk of promises. The issue here is the promises made during the solicitation. They must be realistic and fully understood by the donor. The process of good relations *after* the gift, of course, begins *before* the gift is made.

## LEAD TRUST CONSIDERATIONS

In the case of Samuel Livermore's charitable lead trust gift (described in Chapter 4), despite George Lee's efforts to determine the best course of action in establishing the lead trust, no one can accurately predict how or if the trust will grow. Because a person (or people)—not a charity—ultimately receives the assets of a charitable lead trust, the trustee must be careful—perhaps even more careful than with a charitable remainder trust—to set realistic expectations for the remaindermen, those who will someday receive the assets remaining in the trust when the income to charity stops. The donor's children are usually the remaindermen of a charitable lead trust. A lead trust allows a person both to be charitable and to pass assets to others, usually children or grandchildren. Assets typically used to fund a lead trust have a great potential to appreciate while in the trust (such as closely held stock), allowing the trust to benefit the donor by reducing potential transfer taxes on the asset.

Samuel Livermore established a lead trust to provide an annual income to Old Ivy for 25 years before its assets are transferred to his children. Not many planned giving people are around today who established lead trusts 25 years ago, so few know yet, from the children's or grandchildren's perspectives, how successful those trusts have been. Certain issues, however, arise with some regularity regarding lead trusts, issues that planned giving officers should recognize.

Planned giving officers need to be as certain as possible that the remainderman's expectations are the same as the donor's. That is, the children (assume for these examples that the remaindermen are the donor's children) should understand the terms of the gift. Although the trust assets will eventually revert to them, they may feel cheated that the assets don't come to them sooner. Even though the charity receives only the income, they may think that their inheritance is whittled away by needless payments to an organization for which they may have no feelings. Further, what happens if the actual value of the trust is less than the children expect? Are they in a position to sue the trustee, typically the charity, for not properly managing what they often consider to be their money? A charitable lead trust is not a tax-exempt trust, and the trustee must carefully invest the lead trust assets to obtain as much growth as possible, while ensuring a proper flow of income to the charitable income beneficiary. This can be difficult and requires clear understanding among the donor, the charity, and a competent asset manager.

If appreciated assets are given to the trust, and the trustee sells the assets, the trust pays a tax on the capital gain. If the donated asset, such as dividend-paying closely held stock, is not to be sold while in trust, the children must realize that their cost basis is the parent's original cost basis; therefore, if they sell the asset after it is returned to them from the lead trust, they will probably pay a large capital gains tax, especially if the asset has appreciated considerably during the trust's term. (See Example 6.1.)

---

### Example 6.1

A donor pays $25,000 for an asset that grows in value by an average of 15% per year. At the end of 20 years, when it is worth slightly more than $400,000, the donor funds a 5% charitable lead unitrust paying charity 5% each year. In trust, after the charitable payments, the assets grow by 7% each year. After 25 years, the trust is worth approximately $2,221,000. If the remaindermen—the children—sell the asset at that time, their cost basis is only $25,000; they will pay a capital gains tax on almost $2,200,000, the appreciation since the day the parent acquired the asset.

---

Conversely, if the company's value has decreased because the original owner has passed control to the children, who may be seen by the company's customers as less capable than their founding parent, the value of the stock during and after the trust term might not be as high as the children expect. The amount the children receive may be far less than what they might have been led to expect 25 years before. These are matters that are best addressed and agreed upon by the donor, the remaindermen, and the charity before the gift is made, not after.

## CHARITABLE REMAINDER UNITRUST CONSIDERATIONS

The charitable remainder unitrust, despite its popularity, has equally great potential to disappoint its beneficiaries. Even the most innocent effort to inform could lead to unrealistic expectations. For example, a brochure on charitable remainder unitrusts explains that the income from the unitrust may vary from year to year because, unlike that of a charitable remainder annuity trust, it is a percent of the trust's value each year: "When the trust value rises, so does the income." When? Is it true that unitrust values increase each year? Has there never been a unitrust whose value has dropped? The prospective donor's first exposure to the idea of a unitrust, which takes place well before she ever thinks seriously about becoming a deferred gift donor, subtly sets expectations. The would-be donor begins to think that there may be some regulation unique to charitable gifts that prevents charitable trust values from dropping. Not bad.

But it can get worse. The brochure's prose continues with an example:

> Assume a 63-year-old man transfers $100,000 of marketable securities to a charitable remainder unitrust in exchange for an 8% income to be paid quarterly. The income in the first year is $8,000. If the trust increases in value to $120,000 in the second year, the income—because it is a percentage of the trust's value—is then 8% of $120,000, or $9,600, an increase of $1,600.

At first glance this is innocent prose; the brochure writer wants to show how the income is a function of the trust's value. A second glance, however, reveals the flaw. The writer creates the unrealistic expectation that the trust will earn a total of 28 percent in one year. Read this text again, and you see that even if only subliminally, it leads the reader to infer that there is a possibility that the trust will earn a great deal during the course of a year. (The 28 percent is a combination of the increase from $100,000 to $120,000 [20 percent] plus the amount paid to the income beneficiary [8 percent]). Some investments occasionally have experienced such a return, but to create that expectation is impractical. The sorry matter of paying as much as 8 percent to a person in his early sixties will be addressed later in this chapter, but for now let us understand that no one should ever expect or cause another to expect such an unrealistic investment return. The point of how unitrust income fluctuates can be more realistically made if the trust's total return assumption is 10 percent, or 9 percent. With a 7 percent payout (again, a high payout for most situations) against a total return of 9 percent, the trust's value in the second year would be $102,000. (This result, shown in Example 6.2, is calculated as follows: $100,000 plus $9,000 [9 percent] of return, minus $7,000 [7 percent] of payout equals $102,000). This is meager compared with the more dramatic $120,000, but much more realistic.

---

### Example 6.2

| | |
|---|---|
| Appraised value | $100,000 |
| Trust payout | 7% |
| First year payout | $7,000 |
| Total growth in first year | 9% |
| Asset value at end of first year before payment | $109,000 |
| Asset value at end of first year after payment | $102,000 |
| Second year payout | $7,140 |

---

Showing an annual asset value increase over the life of the trust may be acceptable in a brochure or a computer-generated example, but trusts do sometimes lose value, and it may not be the fault of poor planning. Suppose the gift consists of one stock trading at $100 a share, and the day after the trust is established (and the assets transferred) the stock's value plunges to only $90 a share. Typically, the investment manager hired by the trustee would gradually and incrementally sell the donated assets to invest in a portfolio with a broader mix. As this takes place, however, the manager has only the $90 value to trade. Although stocks do not always drop so dramatically, it has happened. A decline in stock value between the time the gift is made and the time the asset is sold reduces the efficiency of the trust by increasing the work the remaining asset must do in the first year to make the payout—a payout determined on the date of the gift.

Using this example—and ignoring brokerage costs for trading and assuming the closing price of the stock equals its high and low for the day it is donated—in one day the trust experiences a 10 percent drop to $90,000. If the payout in the unitrust document has been established at 8 percent, the dollar payout for the first year is $8,000—8 percent of

$100,000—but the trustee has only $90,000 to invest and earn that $8,000. This means that the actual percentage payout during the first year will be not 8 percent, but almost 9 percent (8 divided by 90 is 8.9 percent) of the asset's new and lower value. This further means that if the trust, worth only $90,000, earns a total return of 10 percent (ignore management fees here) it will still not equal its original $100,000 gift value, even before the required $8,000 payout. After the beneficiary payment, it will increase to only $91,000 from $90,000 at the end of its first year. ($90,000 increased by 10 percent is $99,000. The $8,000 payout [8 percent of the market value of $100,000] is then subtracted, which leaves $91,000.) (See Example 6.3)

---

### Example 6.3

| | |
|---|---|
| Fair market value | $100,000 |
| Trust payout | 8% |
| First year payout | $8,000 |
| Total growth in first year | 10% |
| Asset value at end of first year before payment | $99,000 |
| Asset value at end of first year after payment | $91,000 |
| Actual asset value when stock is sold | $90,000 |
| Actual payout percent in first year | 8.9% |

---

That first year's decrease will forever affect the beneficiary's income—and the trust's value. This is a matter known most intimately by those who invest trust assets, but it should be understood, at least broadly, by all planned giving professionals.

How many brochures take this into account when describing charitable remainder unitrusts? Of course, they should not explain this possibility in detail, but at least they should not be misleading. This can best be accomplished by using realistic investment projections and language that does not imply unrealistic financial growth. For example, the following should not be said: "If a $100,000 unitrust that pays 8 percent, or $8,000 in its first year, grows to $120,000 in the second year, the beneficiary will receive $9,600 in the second year." The idea of a unitrust is better portrayed by saying: "Assuming an annual total growth of 9 percent, a $100,000 trust that pays 8 percent annually will grow by approximately 1 percent each year. This is an example only. Actual trust experience may be different because of varying investment objectives in each trust." Honest, yet inspiring enough.

Trusts also lose value because of high payouts. In the late 1970s and early 1980s, when inflation was high and the prime rate was at or in excess of 20 percent, many financial plans were based on the assumption that such an economic environment would continue indefinitely. Therefore, many planned giving officers established planned gifts with expectations of that kind of growth. But—and remember this—*life cycles are longer than economic cycles.* We smile at the assertion that a person automatically extends his life expectancy when establishing a life-income gift, but if such a person actually does live longer than the mortality tables would indicate, the reasons for establishing proper financial expectations are all the more compelling. A person with a 25-year life expectancy, as someone in her mid-sixties has, will live through at least one economic cycle, and perhaps several. What were you doing 25 years ago? What was the rate of inflation? Or the prime rate? Or the yield on a 30-year treasury bond? Now look back at a donor who established a unitrust 20 or 25 years ago. Is that person's income, taking inflation into account, equal to what it was then? Is it equal to what it was even *without* taking inflation into account? Is the trust payout meeting the expectations the donor set at the time the gift was established?

## Growth Rates

Predicting how investments will grow is a risky business. In 1980, a life insurance salesman showed a prospect a projection of insurance values using a 14 percent growth rate. The prime rate—the rate major banks charge their best institutional customers—was 21 percent that year and the economy was in trouble. Asked if he felt the projection was reasonable, the life insurance agent said yes, that we would be living with that level of growth for a long time. This from a person whose only claim to financial expertise was a modest course in the training rooms of one of the major insurance companies. He was asked by that prospective life insurance buyer what the prime rate was 20 years before. Not surprisingly he did not know, and was astonished to learn that it was slightly less than 2 percent. Two percent. How the world had changed in 20 years. Although he could not know it, the world of finance would change dramatically again in the following decade. No one can predict the future and, as attorneys are fond of saying, "Although one should hope for the best, one needs to plan for the worst." A 14 percent annual growth rate for 20 years is beyond hope. A 28 percent growth rate for one year is hardly realistic. Yet the financial planner feebly replied that he thought his projections would prove to be accurate. They did not. The best guide available for projecting future growth, although it comes with no guarantees, is history. Every decade will have its aberrations, so look beyond the last ten years to get a sense of how things might grow. Most trusts last for much longer than ten years and prudent people will not base their long-range projections on the current economic climate.

But before we laugh away the folly of those in another profession, a study at the Planned Giving Group of New England shows that in a geographic area that prides itself on philanthropy and fiscal conservatism plenty of trusts were written in the late 1970s and early 1980s with payouts of 8 percent or more. One might wonder how rampant this practice has been throughout the country. Many of those trusts are in trouble today because they are losing their nominal value, to say nothing of their inflation-adjusted value, and incomes generated by these diminished-value trusts are also falling.

Where to begin the list of problems? Donors who were led to believe when the trust was established that their incomes would rise discovered too late that their incomes initially were higher but are now dropping. Donors looking to their retirement years need their income to sustain itself against inflation, not drop. A 10 percent payout with a 10 percent total return on investments may seem balanced, but factor in inflation and the purchasing power erodes. A $7,000 income in a world of 5 percent inflation buys in 25 years what a little over $1,900 buys today. About a quarter on the dollar. The effects of inflation cannot be ignored. Only the most elderly of donors, those whose life expectancies are short, should consider a gift whose income will never rise, such as a gift annuity or an annuity trust. It won't fall but it won't rise either. Think about that.

## Donative Intent

Charities also have an obligation to themselves. Charities have a right to design gifts that are—well—*gifts*. Why go through the elaborate exercise of establishing a deferred gift if little or nothing is left to benefit charity? Donors and their advisors need to realize that half of planned giving is *giving*. The same attorney who argues protectively that "his client" needs an 8 percent income, as did Alan Ennico's (in Chapters 2 and 4), and that the charity ought to be able to invest well enough to provide it, may very well be the same attorney who smells litigation a decade later when his client complains that the trust's income has dropped. An unsolicited piece of advice: If donors demand too much in establishing the trust, begin to analyze their donative intent. If they are looking more to earn income than to make a gift, they are not donors. Turn down the offer, for it is in fact not an offer and will not magically transform itself into a gift. As difficult as it might be to refuse a gift, dealing with a bad gift over the next few decades will be much more difficult. The payout issue is the most revealing of many matters with which the planned giving officer must deal. Donors in their sixties who demand a high trust payout quickly expose their lack of donative intent.

## THE UNITRUST MAKEUP PROVISION

Donors are led to expect much. The makeup expectation in a net-income unitrust is an example of how unrealistic expectations are sometimes created. It confuses a lot of donors as well. A net-income unitrust pays only the income, paid from yield or dividends, and not from principal. A "makeup" provision allows the trustee to pay more than the stated unitrust percent in any one year if (1) in past years there has been a deficit and (2) the yield exceeds the payout percentage.

When land is donated to a unitrust, a donor is normally told that the best arrangement is the net-income unitrust because it allows the trustee to sell the land at (or as close as possible to) its fair market value without the pressure of producing a beneficiary income payment by the end of the first payment period, often the first quarter. This is common, and a good idea as well. As part of the explanation, however, the donor is often told that whatever income is not paid out during the time required to sell the land can be made up through the makeup provision in the trust. For example, if land valued at $1 million is donated to a unitrust and the trust instrument calls for a 6 percent payout, the charity will usually want to establish a unitrust that pays a net income with the potential for making up what was not paid out. (Almost never should land be used to fund a charitable remainder annuity trust because it has no income flexibility, nor a pooled income fund because unsold land depresses everyone else's income. Most pooled income fund documents, in fact, prohibit donations of nonliquid assets.) If the trust sells the land after one year, the donor has received no income during that year and, in a sense, is owed 6 percent of $1 million or $60,000. The donor is often told that this does not present a problem because the trust, once invested in stocks and bonds, will produce a higher income than 6 percent, allowing the donor to shortly make up what is her due. This is a problem. The real problem, though, is saying this—creating the expectation— to begin with. If the donor needs to make up $60,000 in one year (the first year of liquidity and the second year of the trust), the trust would need to earn 12 percent income in that second year to pay the stated 6 percent plus the 6 percent not paid during the first year. This is a ridiculous expectation in any economic climate. Most people know that, of course, but even spreading out the "owed" income for, say, six years, strains the total return. When income is the primary objective, any investment portfolio's total return will be reduced.

Some trusts define capital gain as trust income, allowing capital gain income to be paid out as part of a net-income unitrust. As long as the trust language does not contradict the obvious (such as declaring income to be principal) or violate state law, the attorney who drafts the trust may define capital gain as income. Charitably-minded donors, however, normally would prefer to use only the capital gain built up after the gift was made.

## Total Return

Planned giving people are not usually well enough educated in finance issues to understand the problems inherent in the investment process once the gift is made, but they need to be. J. Scott Kaspick, at the 1993 conference of the National Committee on Planned Giving, prepared a report entitled, "A Financial Tool-kit for Planned Giving Professionals," which outlines what planned giving people should know about the investment issues of establishing a trust. That report emphasizes that investing for high income is done at a cost to total return, which may result in a reduction to the beneficiary's future inflation-adjusted income from a charitable remainder unitrust or a pooled income fund.

Total return in any investment is negatively affected when income is the primary goal, and certainly this is true for a unitrust. The lower the total return, the lower the income will be later in the donor's life. An income based on a percent of an asset grows only when the asset grows. Because a straight unitrust (one that is *not* a net-income trust) is allowed to use capital gain and even principal to make an income payment, the trust manager can invest for a higher total return than if income is the primary need. For example, a straight 5 percent payout unitrust might be invested to realize 5 percent yield and a 5 percent capital growth, for a total annual return of 10 percent. This leaves a margin of 5 percent—the total return of 10 percent less the payout of 5 percent—for growth. For a straight unitrust paying 6 percent, the investment manager can still invest for total return. If the trust is a *net-income* unitrust, however, paying 6 percent annually—and the income beneficiary actually expects a 6 percent payout—the asset manager must keep an eye on the 6 percent, as opposed to the total return. This results in a reduction of the total return, typically by about one percentage point. This means the net growth—the now 9 percent total return less the 6 percent payout—equals only 3 percent (See Example 6.4.)

---

**Example 6.4**

|                 | Straight Unitrust | Net-Income Unitrust |
|-----------------|-------------------|---------------------|
| Payout          | 6%                | 6%                  |
| Yield Required  | N/A               | 6%                  |
| Total Return    | 10%               | 9%                  |
| Net Growth      | 4%                | 3%                  |

---

Two unitrusts with the same 6 percent payout, but the net income unitrust has less growth. Too many planned giving officers do not realize this. Only trusts funded with property or that are meant to be invested to produce a small amount of yield for a period of time should be designed as net-income unitrusts.

The higher the required yield, the lower the expected total return. This is the trade-off with net-income unitrusts, and a common result of establishing a unitrust with land or any other nonliquid asset.

## The Makeup Expectation Can Be Costly

With that in mind, let's get back to the $1 million gift of land and the makeup provision. What about spreading out the "owed" money? Because making up the unpaid income within one year is often foolish, one might decide to make up the income over a period of time longer than one year. Over a five-year period, for example, the trust could make up the initial lost income by investing for only one percentage point higher than the stated rate, or 7 percent, but that would also reduce total return. A conservative estimate might show an annual total-return reduction of perhaps three-quarters to one full percentage point, which will have a long-term negative effect on the donor's income.

Exhibit 6.1 shows the effect of investing to recoup income not paid during the first year of the gift, before the land is sold and while the trust is illiquid. Line A is initially higher but then it falls below Line B and stays there. Both lines initially show the result of an investment that has no income or capital growth during the first year. Then, one trust (whose income is shown on Line A) earns income of 7 percent for five years, the amount of time required to make up the initial income that is lost. Line A, the initially higher line, then is invested to earn 6 percent income. During that five-year period when the income is 7 percent, however, the total return is only 8 percent, with only one percent of net growth. This ultimately reduces the amount of income—remember, income from a unitrust is a function of its value—so that the income paid after that five-year period is lower than from the other trust (whose income is shown on Line B). Line B is the line where the income is never made up. In this case, not making up the income is better for the donor. It is also better for the charity. Many planned giving professionals are not aware of this long-term result. Because this is a matter that comes up after the gift is made—usually well after—the planned giving director never deals with the consequences of the decision—a decision that is the result of improper expectations that were established when the gift was made.

Exhibit 6.2 is a two-page printout of the income cash flow and asset growth of the gift with the previous assumptions.

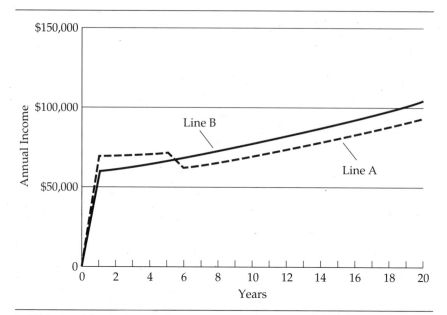

Exhibit 6.1  Nominal Annual Income Payments

Line A shows the effect of using the makeup provision and Line B shows the effect of not making up the deficit. After the first year, when the unitrust has money, the initial annual income from Line A is $70,000 and the total income is projected to be $1.53 million. Although the initial annual income from Line B is $60,000, the total income is projected to be over $1.6 million.

This illustration was prepared using the planned giving software ParaGon™, developed by Blackbaud, Inc.

Both the charity and the donor in this situation end up with more money if the deficit is not made up. Although this is not always true, making up the deficit often will have a negative impact on the donor and the charity; therefore, the planned giving officer should prepare a proposal that compares the two alternatives and takes into account realistic investment expectations.

## Selling the Asset for Less than the Appraised Value

The short-term investment expectation on a trust asset that must be sold to produce income is only part of the problem with net-income unitrusts that are expected to make up their unpaid income. What happens when the trust sells the land for less than the appraised value? This happens frequently. Assume the land, in this case appraised for $1,000,000, sells for only $800,000 after one year, the second year of the trust. The real

# CHARITABLE REMAINDER UNITRUST ANALYZER
Nominal Asset and Income Growth Analysis
Page 1

**GIFT INFORMATION:**

| | |
|---|---|
| Fair Market Value of Gift | $1,000,000 |
| Payment Frequency | Quarterly |
| Full Months until First Payment | 3 |
| Number of Years Analysis Runs | 21 Years |
| Federal Interest Rate Used | 8.4% |

## ASSUMPTIONS FOR THE 6% TRUST THAT DOES NOT MAKE UP THE DEFICIT:

| | |
|---|---|
| Deduction | 417,650 |
| Capital Growth for First Year | 0.0% |
| Yield for First Year | 0.0% |
| Capital Growth for Next 20 Years | 3.0% |
| Yield for Next 20 Years | 6.0% |

## ASSUMPTIONS FOR THE 6% TRUST THAT DOES MAKE UP THE DEFICIT:

| | |
|---|---|
| Deduction | 417,650 |
| Capital Growth for First Year | 0.0% |
| Yield for First Year | 0.0% |
| Capital Growth for Next 5 Years | 1.0% |
| Yield for Next 5 Years | 7.0% |
| Capital Growth for Next 15 Years | 3.0% |
| Yield for Next 15 Years | 6.0% |

### Yearly Growth of Principal and Income

| End of Year | Without Makeup | | With Makeup | |
|---|---|---|---|---|
| | Principal | Income | Principal | Income |
| 1 | 1,000,000 | 0 | 1,000,000 | 0 |
| 2 | 1,030,000 | 60,000 | 1,010,000 | 70,000 |
| 3 | 1,060,900 | 61,800 | 1,020,100 | 70,700 |
| 4 | 1,092,727 | 63,654 | 1,030,301 | 71,407 |
| 5 | 1,125,508 | 65,563 | 1,040,604 | 72,121 |
| 6 | 1,159,274 | 67,530 | 1,051,010 | 72,842 |
| 7 | 1,194,052 | 69,556 | 1,082,540 | 63,060 |
| 8 | 1,229,873 | 71,643 | 1,115,016 | 64,952 |
| 9 | 1,266,770 | 73,792 | 1,148,467 | 66,900 |
| 10 | 1,304,773 | 76,006 | 1,182,921 | 68,908 |
| 11 | 1,343,916 | 78,286 | 1,218,408 | 70,975 |
| 12 | 1,384,233 | 80,634 | 1,254,960 | 73,104 |
| 13 | 1,425,760 | 83,054 | 1,292,609 | 75,297 |

*(continued)*

| | Without Makeup | | With Makeup | |
| --- | --- | --- | --- | --- |
| End of Year | Principal | Income | Principal | Income |
| 14 | 1,468,533 | 85,545 | 1,331,388 | 77,556 |
| 15 | 1,512,589 | 88,112 | 1,371,329 | 79,883 |
| 16 | 1,557,967 | 90,755 | 1,412,469 | 82,279 |
| 17 | 1,604,706 | 93,478 | 1,454,843 | 84,748 |
| 18 | 1,652,847 | 96,282 | 1,498,489 | 87,290 |
| 19 | 1,702,433 | 99,170 | 1,543,443 | 89,909 |
| 20 | 1,753,500 | 102,145 | 1,589,746 | 92,606 |
| 21 | 1,806,111 | 105,210 | 1,637,439 | 95,384 |
| **Totals:** | **1,806,111** | **1,612,222** | **1,637,439** | **1,529,929** |

**Exhibit 6.2**   Income Cash Flow and Asset Growth: Make-Up Provision, Gift of Land

A comparison of the projected cash flow and asset growth of two net-income unitrusts, each funded with land that is sold one year after the gift is made, with stated payouts of 6%, one making up the deficit and the other not making up the deficit.

This illustration was prepared using the planned giving software ParaGon™, developed by Blackbaud, Inc.

estate agent the charity has hired to sell the property has tried for a long time to sell the land, and now has a valid buyer, but the offer is $200,000 less than what everyone had hoped. Add to that $50,000 of commissions and fees and the net trust assets add up to only $750,000. The picture looks gloomier still because now the donor, who has been told to expect a makeup of lost income, will most certainly not see it.

If the donor, who has established a 6 percent net-income unitrust, had been told the income would be made up after one year, the $750,000 would have to be invested for an income return—this is not even total return—of 16 percent. (This is calculated by taking 6 percent of the $1,000,000 appraised value, or $60,000. Because the land is not sold until the second year, from the donor's perspective a full year of income is owed. To make up the deficit *and* pay the second year's income of $60,000, the trust would have to pay out $120,000. An annual investment rate of 16% is required for $750,000 to generate $120,000—and that is just the income.) Even if the hope is to make up the income over six years, the income portion of the total return would have to be over 9 percent. (This is the result of dividing the owed first year's income of $60,000 by 6, the number of years given to make up the income, or $10,000. This is then added to the second year's expected income of $60,000, a total of $70,000. This divided by $750,000 is 9.33 percent.)

Unrealistic at best, this is often the reality after the euphoria of the gift. This puts the makeup issue in an even more dire light. A look at realistic investment projections will show that in most cases, if there is not an unusual income-producing year the income should never be made up. In many cases, it simply *cannot* be made up.

## The Makeup Provision Privilege

As this example demonstrates, thoughtful consideration suggests that the deficit income should normally not be made up when land is donated to a unitrust. Even though the law makes it available, the makeup provision should be considered a privilege, not a right. If the donor, rather than making a gift of land to a unitrust, were to sell the land instead, he would not receive the proceeds until the property is sold. In this non-charitable situation, when a person simply wants to sell land, lost income—or at least lost income that is "owed" the owner of the land—is not an issue during the selling period. A clock does not start to measure lost income while the property remains unsold. The very idea of any income being "lost" on phantom liquidity somehow seems ridiculous. The asset generates income only after it is sold and money is transferred to the trust. Why does transferring the asset to a charitable remainder unitrust create the expectation that income not paid out during that time is due the donor? Contrary to what is discussed at many seminars and implied in much planned giving literature, trustees ought not to think of themselves as obligated to pay money to a donor who would otherwise not receive a benefit during the time it takes to sell a nonliquid asset.

## THE RETIREMENT UNITRUST

The makeup issue is also brought out in retirement unitrusts, where a relatively young donor, say in her fifties, wants to donate money to a unitrust that invests for little or no income until retirement age, at which point the trustee changes investment objectives to produce more income. Unless the donor is the trustee no guarantee can be made, but most charities properly take into account the donor's wishes, and if the charity, acting as trustee, maintains control and determines that any change is not detrimental to the gift, it may informally—not in writing—agree to adjust the investments accordingly. After all, the significant expected growth during the preretirement years will eventually serve the charity all the better. But even then, the donor should not be shown a radical change in investments to make up all that lost income during those years. Even at 65 years old, a donor still has 20 or so years of life expectancy. A change from mostly growth-oriented investments to mostly income-oriented investments during the later years will reduce total growth and generally hurt the donor's income as well as the charity's remainder interest. In this regard the concept is similar to that of the trust funded with land.

Exhibit 6.3 shows the consequences of making up the income in a retirement unitrust, which compares the income expectations resulting from making up and not making up the income of a $1,000,000 trust paying 5 percent to a person who is 54 years old when she makes the gift and who has a life expectancy of 30 years. For the first 10 years the trust is invested for a high amount of growth. The first part of Exhibit 6.3 shows the investment assumptions, and the second shows the expected year-by-year nominal (not inflation-adjusted) cash flow and trust growth.

Exhibits 6.4 and 6.5 vividly compare the incomes of the two options. The first, Exhibit 6.4, shows the nominal (not inflation-adjusted) *annual*

---

### 5% CHARITABLE REMAINDER UNITRUST ANALYZER
#### Nominal Asset and Income Growth Analysis
Page 1

**GIFT INFORMATION:**

| | |
|---|---|
| Fair Market Value of Gift | $1,000,000.00 |
| Payment Frequency | Quarterly |
| Full Months until First Payment | 3 |
| Number of Years Analysis Runs | 30 Years |
| Beneficiary's Age | 54 |
| Federal Interest Rate Used | 8.4% |
| Deduction | $348,460 |

**ASSUMPTIONS FOR THE 5% TRUST WITHOUT MAKEUP:**

| | |
|---|---|
| Capital Growth for First 10 Years | 9.0% |
| Yield for First 10 Years | 1.0% |
| Capital Growth for Next 20 Years | 5.0% |
| Yield for Next 20 Years | 5.0% |

**ASSUMPTIONS FOR THE 5% TRUST WITH MAKEUP:**

| | |
|---|---|
| Capital Growth for First 10 Years | 9.0% |
| Yield for First 10 Years | 1.0% |
| Capital Growth for Next 20 Years | 1.0% |
| Yield for Next 20 Years | 7.0% |

## Yearly Growth of Principal and Income

| End of Year | Without Makeup | | With Makeup | |
|---|---|---|---|---|
| | Principal | Income | Principal | Income |
| 1 | 1,090,000 | 10,000 | 1,090,000 | 10,000 |
| 2 | 1,188,100 | 10,900 | 1,188,100 | 10,900 |
| 3 | 1,295,029 | 11,881 | 1,295,029 | 11,881 |
| 4 | 1,411,581 | 12,950 | 1,411,581 | 12,950 |
| 5 | 1,538,623 | 14,115 | 1,538,623 | 14,115 |
| 6 | 1,677,100 | 15,386 | 1,677,100 | 15,386 |
| 7 | 1,828,039 | 16,771 | 1,828,039 | 16,771 |
| 8 | 1,992,562 | 18,280 | 1,992,562 | 18,280 |
| 9 | 2,171,893 | 19,925 | 2,171,893 | 19,925 |
| 10 | 2,367,363 | 21,718 | 2,367,363 | 21,718 |
| 11 | 2,485,731 | 118,368 | 2,391,037 | 165,715 |
| 12 | 2,610,018 | 124,286 | 2,414,947 | 167,372 |
| 13 | 2,740,519 | 130,500 | 2,439,097 | 169,046 |
| 14 | 2,877,545 | 137,025 | 2,463,488 | 170,736 |
| 15 | 3,021,422 | 143,877 | 2,488,123 | 172,444 |
| 16 | 3,172,493 | 151,071 | 2,513,004 | 174,168 |
| 17 | 3,331,118 | 158,624 | 2,538,134 | 175,910 |
| 18 | 3,497,674 | 166,555 | 2,563,515 | 177,669 |
| 19 | 3,672,558 | 174,883 | 2,589,150 | 179,446 |
| 20 | 3,856,185 | 183,627 | 2,615,042 | 181,240 |
| 21 | 4.048,995 | 192,809 | 2,641,192 | 183,052 |
| 22 | 4,251,445 | 202,449 | 2,667,604 | 184,883 |
| 23 | 4,464,017 | 212,572 | 2,694,280 | 140,615 |
| 24 | 4,687,218 | 223,200 | 2,767,340 | 134,714 |
| 25 | 4,921,579 | 234,360 | 2,848,899 | 138,367 |
| 26 | 5,167,658 | 246,078 | 2,932,735 | 142,444 |
| 27 | 5,426,040 | 258,382 | 3,019,040 | 146,636 |
| 28 | 5,697,342 | 271,302 | 3,107,885 | 150,952 |
| 29 | 5,982,210 | 284,867 | 3,199,345 | 155,394 |
| 30 | 6,281,320 | 299,110 | 3,293,496 | 159,967 |
| **Totals:** | **6,281,320** | **4,065,886** | **3,293,496** | **3,422,707** |

**Exhibit 6.3** Effect of a Makeup Provision: Net Income Retirement Unitrust

A comparison of the projected cash flow and asset growth of two net-income retirement unitrusts with stated payouts of 5%, one making up the deficit and the other not making up the deficit

This illustration was prepared using the planned giving software ParaGon™, developed by Blackbaud, Inc.

income. The second graph, Exhibit 6.5, shows the inflation-adjusted *accumulated* income during a 30-year period. Note that the donor gives up nothing, and even earns more over her 30-year life expectancy, by not making up the income. When this happens—when the donor is expected to receive more actual income over his lifetime with the higher payout than with the lower payout—what is left in the trust is dramatically less with the higher payout. This is intuitive: the higher the payout the less remaining for the charity, but the donor often does not realize the scale of difference.

In this example the donor does earn more income, but that is not always the case. The lower payout could actually return less income to the beneficiary. This is often true when the time the trust is expected to

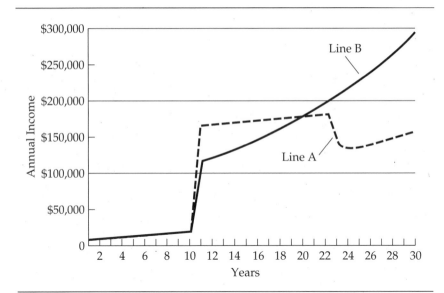

**Exhibit 6.4**    Nominal Annual Income Payments

Line A is initially higher because it shows more immediate makeup of income that was not paid during the first 10 years. That strategy provides less for the donor, however, than the investment strategy shown on Line B. Line A provides an expected annual income of about $160,000 in the final year of the trust, while Line B provides an expected annual income of about $300,000, almost twice as much. The income dip in Line A in the 20th year reflects the completion of makeup payments from prior years.

This illustration was prepared using the planned giving software ParaGon™, developed by Blackbaud, Inc.

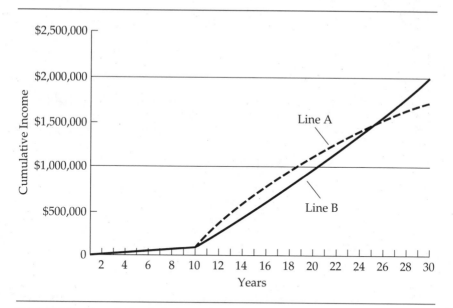

**Exhibit 6.5** Cumulative Inflation-Adjusted Income

Line A shows that the donor initially receives more cumulative income. Line B shows that by the 25th year, the total income is higher without making up the deficit.

This illustration was prepared using the planned giving software ParaGon™, developed by Blackbaud, Inc.

run is short—that is, when the beneficiaries are older or the trust runs for a term of years.

Exhibit 6.6 shows the difference not only in total beneficiary income but in what difference remains for charity at the end of a similar trust that lasts only 22 years. Exhibit 6.6 compares payouts of 5 percent, 6 percent, and 7 percent. The cumulative income is only slightly less, but the charity receives a great deal less.

The difference to charity is so compelling that many donors will readily give up their relatively small income gain for the charity's larger gain. The inflation-adjusted difference to charity in this example is about $377,000, or an increase of about 35 percent, while the inflation-adjusted difference in income to the beneficiary is about $170,000, or a decrease of only 12 percent. Donors who are charitably inclined will be moved, if not always persuaded, by seeing this difference. Many charities consider this the second level of the gift (the first level is to make the gift initially and the second is to agree to the lower payout); it becomes important when the donor sees the difference in what actually goes to charity.

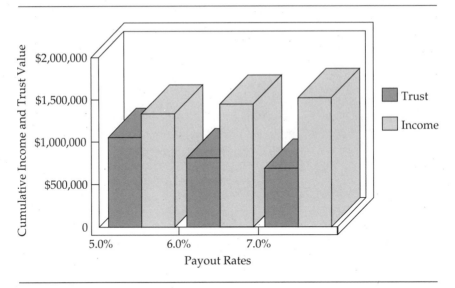

**Exhibit 6.6**   A Comparison of Inflation-Adjusted Cumulative Income and Trust Growth Over a 22-Year Period

The total inflation-adjusted income to the beneficiary is about 12% less with the 5% payout than with the 7% payout, but the charity receives about 35% less.

This illustration was prepared using the planned giving software ParaGon™, developed by Blackbaud, Inc.

## Mortgages Funding a Unitrust

Another problem might occur when a promissory note or a mortgage initially funds a net-income unitrust. This means that not all assets in the trust can be invested in a diversified portfolio. Instead, all or a portion of the value is owed to the trust by a person who has taken a mortgage. In this case the trust acts something like a banker. For example, when land is sold by the trustee, the trust might take on a mortgage instead of an outright payment. The problem arises if the borrower is paying a high rate of interest and, wishing to pay less interest, refinances for a lower amount with a bank and pays off the mortgage or note. If the charitable remainder unitrust has been relying on the high-interest mortgage payments as the source for its beneficiary payouts, a lowering of the payments to the trust or an inability of the trust to equal those payments from interest or dividends in a full investment portfolio will reduce the payments.

For example, if the note was written to pay 9 percent interest to the trust and the borrower, now in a different investment climate, wants to pay it off early, the now-liquid net-income unitrust may not be able to equal the previous income payments to the beneficiary. Planned giving and financial officers need to pay attention to this situation. When interest rates fall, borrowers with high-interest mortgages may want to rewrite their notes to get lower rates. Since charitable trusts don't usually negotiate that way, borrowers may borrow the money elsewhere at a lower rate and then pay off the note. When this happens, if the charity has not warned them, the beneficiaries receive a rude awakening: Their income suddenly and drastically drops.

---

### Example 6.5

Assume that land is sold for $1,000,000 with a 20-year note paying 9% annually in monthly installments. (Normally, the note would not equal the sales price; some actual money would probably be available. But for our example here, we take the note to equal the entire $1,000,000.) Further assume the stated trust payout is 9%. Although this is a high payout under any circumstances, many such trusts have been written that way, and will continue to exist for several more years. The land, in this example, is not sold until the end of the first year, at which time it is sold for its full value. Disregarding sales commissions and other costs, the trust, at the beginning of the second year, has a note valued at $1,000,000 that is being paid with 9% annual interest.

---

The note in Example 6.5, based on amortization tables, pays $107,967 per year, $17,967 more than the stated 9 percent, or $90,000. During the first year, when it is illiquid, the trust incurs a deficit of $90,000 because the value of the trust is $1,000,000 and the stated payout on the net-income unitrust is 9 percent. In this case, when the land is sold at the end of one year, the trust has an excess available during the second year. A deficit of $90,000 would be reduced by at least the $17,967 excess from the 9 percent note, plus any income provided from the other investments (this example does not take into account the monthly payments that are invested when they are received). Even though the trust calls for a 9 percent payout, or $90,000, the donor receives a total income of $107,967 in the second year (the $90,000 that should be paid that year, plus the excess of $17,967 available from extra income) because of the deficit accumulated during the first year, when the trust was illiquid. At this steady state the donor receives nothing in the first year and then is on a schedule to receive over $100,000 per year. This would go on, assuming the values all stay the same, for about five years, until the first-year deficit of $90,000 is made up ($90,000 divided by the almost $18,000 carries the annual excess for almost exactly five years), at which time the donor would receive $90,000 per year. The excess income would be reinvested.

But the borrowers may have other plans. If interest rates fall, they might want to bail out of the deal. Let's say that this happens after three years, and the borrowers pay what they owe. The balance of the loan, based on amortization tables, would be approximately $977,000 (note how much interest and how little of the principal are paid in the first years of a mortgage, one of the consequences of borrowing money). Disregard the actual value of the trust at this point (it would probably be higher than $1 million) and assume the other $23,000 is invested for growth and is earning 3 percent income. Now, all of a sudden, the trust has $977,000 that, at best, can be invested for 6 percent or 7 percent income. Even if the other $23,000 is invested to earn the same income, the total income available to the donor is, at the most, $70,000—7 percent of $1,000,000—and that is a generous expectation. This results in an income drop of over $20,000 from the stated payout rate in the trust, and about $30,000 less than what the donor had been receiving. The borrowers' decision to do this can be abrupt.

It can get worse. The donor who made the gift when he was 60 years old is now 64 years old. (One year passed before the land was sold, and for another three years he received income from the note held by the trust.) If he and his spouse are income beneficiaries, the trust's life expectancy is about 30 years. Where will most planned giving officers be in 30 years? Probably not at the charities where they now work. Deciding today to capture as much income as possible, as suggested above with the 9 percent trust payout, will have a disastrous effect on the total growth of the trust. Over a 30-year period, income against inflation will quickly drop, to say nothing of the remainder value, the value going to charity. It is in fact in the donor's best interests to invest for less income and more growth. This means, however, that by prudently investing the assets the income would drop not to $70,000 but closer to $40,000 or $50,000—a drop of almost 50 percent or so from the $100,000-plus income the donor had been receiving—and was led to expect—when the note was active.

Lower initial income projected to grow over time is less important for older donors. People in their eighties and nineties need income now without planning too far into the future. The need for income restricts the trust's growth, but because the trust's life expectancy is shorter, the asset's value will not drop much against inflation. This should be acceptable to the charity.

The point here has little to do with the specific numbers, but much to do with the ongoing financial oversight necessary to maintain the trust. A similar ongoing stewardship is necessary to keep the beneficiaries satisfied. Managing charitable trusts is not an easy job and the trustee must constantly monitor investment performance and measure it against both donor expectations and the guidelines of prudent management. This is normally done by examining broad market indicators, such as the Dow Jones Industrial Average and the Standard and Poor's 500 Index, as well as inflation, measured by the Consumer Price Index. If the trust is not growing satisfactorily, given payout requirements and investment objectives, the strategy should be changed. Analyzing a trust's progress is not easy, however. Although the *oversight* of planned giving programs is most clearly a task that charities who act as trustees cannot eschew, few charities embrace the chore of making investment decisions themselves. That is the work of professional charitable trust asset managers.

## POOLED INCOME FUNDS

Pooled income funds can suffer a similar fate: Too high a yield may provide a lower-than-expected lifetime income for many donors, especially if they are younger than 75 or 80. Most funds have one of three broad investment objectives: high income, high growth, or a balance of growth and income. Although no strict definition of "balanced" exists, the idea in a balanced fund is to generate both healthy income and growth. This means that the donor is given two expectations: a good income *and* a growing income. The growth part of the balanced portfolio will cause the corpus, and therefore the income, to grow. A balanced portfolio, by the way, might have 40 percent bonds and 60 percent stocks. It also could have the opposite, 60 percent bonds and 40 percent stocks. It could have anything in between, too. No rules—just broad guidelines— determine the actual investment strategy when objectives defined by the words "balanced" or "income" or "growth" are sought. Most charities with just one fund opt for the balanced approach because the combination of growth and income serves the most people; that is, because it tilts toward neither extreme of high income (with little or no growth) nor high growth (with little income), it most adequately serves the widest variety of ages.

The problem arises when the balanced fund is not very balanced. If a 65-year-old donor gave $25,000 to a balanced fund, she might be told to expect an income of about 6 percent or 7 percent. One part of the expectation may be (and usually is) that the fund will initially generate an income of approximately $1,500; the other is that the income will grow by about 3 percent each year. Later, however, the economic climate might change so that income is harder to produce: Actual investment yields may fall, and, with the same mix of stocks and bonds, the income might be only 4 percent. What to do? As with many questions in planned giving, it depends. Some charities choose to adjust the portfolio by purchasing more bonds to produce more income. That's fine for people whose life expectancies are short, but people who will live longer than, say, 10 years will see their income erode against inflation. Further, when yields rise, the prices of those bonds will fall, making the value of the pooled income fund fall. The long-term effect will be a fund with a lower value, which will create a lower income. Almost never—except with short life expectancies—is it prudent to invest too much in fixed-income instruments. As we have seen, high income is generated at the expense of total growth, which in turn lowers future income.

Many charities in this situation stay the course, accepting the lower current yields with an eye on total growth so that future income can be as high as possible. This is a difficult decision, one of prudent investment philosophy as well as determining how to deal with donors who are unhappy with their falling incomes. The variable here, of course, is the age of the average donor in the pool. The older the donors the more likely the prudent move is to switch investments for higher income. With younger donors, the prudent decision is to stay the course throughout the low-interest rate period and accept lower current income with the expectation of a growing income over the years. Younger, in this case, means those under approximately 80 years old. This, too—like the definition of "balanced"—is merely a guideline. For an older person, the inflationary effects on a flat income will not be too detrimental to her purchasing power. (This means that the ever-typical 65-year-old person who dominates life-income examples in brochure prose is young.) This is the problem with having only one pooled income fund, a one-size-fits-all approach. If it is feasible, charities with donors of various ages should consider establishing more than one pooled income fund. Older donors, in their late seventies and older, should be in an income-oriented fund; those in their mid-sixties to late seventies should be in a balanced fund, one in which income and asset value are projected to grow modestly; and younger donors, those in their mid-sixties and younger, should be in a growth fund, one in which the investments produce more growth than the other two. Further, charities should revisit the investment objectives as the donor pool grows older. Ideally, the pooled income fund should tweak its investment objective to become more income-oriented and less growth-oriented as the donors in the fund grow older.

Pooled income funds are popular planned gift vehicles. Most donors who have made a gift to a pooled income fund are still young by most measures. Many years will pass before they die. Their income may not be as important to them as their commitment to charity (although the opposite is true many times), but planned giving officers must know the long-term as well as immediate differences among the three general categories of investment objectives for pooled income funds, and how those differences will affect income beneficiaries. An incorrect decision to place a person in a high-income fund when the gift is made or to buoy income with too many bonds can have disastrous consequences as time passes. Donors, growing older and in need of an income able to fight inflation, might instead see their inflation-adjusted income dropping without any power to change the trend.

## FIXED-INCOME GIFTS

Gift annuities and charitable remainder annuity trusts provide fewer problems for donors than unitrusts or pooled income funds because the income from these two gifts is fixed. For the most part, the negative results of any financial mismanagement of the gift assets will be borne by the charity, not the donor. The assets of an annuity trust need to be exhausted before income stops, and the income provided to the donor of a gift annuity is backed by the charity's assets; the investments of the original gift asset cannot be looked upon as the source of the annuitant's income. As incredible as it sounds, however, annuity trusts have dried up. The problem then affects not only the charitable organization, but also the donor and donor relations. Donors who are told that their gifts were so poorly mismanaged that the assets are all gone—and as a result, so is their income—are usually not happy. Further gifts, from them or the people they talk with, are not likely.

But the most common problem with annuity trusts and gift annuities is not that the income will someday stop. Most trusts are managed well enough to maintain the annuity trust income, and as yet almost no charities have ever stopped paying their gift annuitants because they have run out of money. Instead, the problem with both types of fixed-income gifts is their exposure to inflation. A dollar today is not worth a dollar tomorrow. At an annual inflation rate of 10 percent, a dollar today is worth only 90 cents ($1 minus 10 cents) next year. The following year it is worth only 81 cents (90 cents minus 10 percent, or nine cents). And so on. Inflation is not 10 percent every year but it has been some years. Even if inflation is 5 percent, the average for the last 60 years, in 15 years that dollar will provide a person with less than half her purchasing power.

Too many young people establish gift annuities. Young is anybody under eighty. Again, that is a broad guide, but in economic terms planned giving officers should think of a person as old only when the purchasing power of her income, because of the limited number of years available to spend the income, will not be significantly eroded by inflation. A 65-year-old donor actuarially has 20 years to live, enough time for inflation to significantly erode purchasing power. Even the relatively high payouts from gift annuities are fixed and thus lose their value against inflation. Unless the donor is prepared to see her income erode, she should instead consider the variable income of a pooled income fund or a charitable remainder unitrust. Although the possibility exists that the income will fluctuate from year to year, over time, depending on the unitrust or pooled income fund payout, experience shows that the income from prudently invested portfolios with at least some equities will rise to hedge against if not fully compensate for inflation. Charities need to educate their donors about the effects inflation will have on income.

Some donors who establish gift annuities are motivated by higher rates than those available from commercial investment sources. For the donor who wants to help charity this is natural and part of the planning process. But a gift annuity is for life. A gift annuity is also *not* an investment. It is a payment in exchange for a sum of money donated to a charity. The reason gift annuity payments look so attractive against investment options (other than commercial annuities, which are also not, strictly speaking, investments) is that investments are not intended to exhaust principal; instead investments preserve principal, using a principal amount to generate an income. Charities cannot limit their gift annuity payments from the gifted asset but, mathematically, gift annuities are designed to invade principal. Generally, gift annuities will provide a higher income than an investment. This is why measuring gift annuity payments against investment returns is an invalid comparison. Neither donors nor planned giving officers should be swayed by such fool's logic.

Compare instead the income from the gift annuity and the income from a commercial annuity. Although gift annuities generally provide a higher payout rate than investments, they pay less than what an insurance company pays for the same annuitant. Although the insurance company and the gift annuity both factor in an exhaustion of principal as part of determining the payout, the insurance company does *not* factor in a gift portion. Thus, the lower payment with a gift annuity. On average, the payout rates recommended by the American Council on Gift Annuities are designed to provide the charity with about half the nominal value of the original gift.

Those who talk to donors regularly will sometimes argue that psychological reasons dictate the decision for a fixed or a fluctuating income. A donor, usually a widow who has not participated in the family's investment decisions, might be more comfortable with the security of a fixed income. Even someone in her fifties or sixties might want to make a charitable gift and accept the same dollar level of income from an asset for the remainder of her long life. This argument may be persuasive, but it should not be made in a vacuum. If the planned giving director fails to discuss the impact of inflation on a fixed income, despite psychological considerations, the donor truly does lose. The absence of that point from a discussion of a life-income gift is imprudent.

## BENEFITS FROM A GIFT ANNUITY OVER AN ANNUITY TRUST

If it comes down to the gift annuity or the annuity trust, aside from the size of the gift (because of trust management and administration fees, annuity trusts usually need to be larger than gift annuities), the gift annuity probably is better for many donors because it has the potential for tax-free income, as well as income taxed at capital gains rates. This is true no matter how the gift annuity assets are invested, or even *if* they are invested. The four-tier rule (discussed in Chapter 7) does not apply to the gift annuity. The presumption in a gift annuity is that part of the principal—the amount given to charity—is returned as a portion of the donor's income; therefore the income may be partly tax free. If the gifted asset is appreciated, part of the donor's income will be taxed at capital gains rates, which many times (depending on the donor's tax bracket and the law at the time) is taxed more favorably than ordinary income. How the income from a gift annuity will be taxed is known on the day the gift is made. On the other hand, unless the annuity trust is invested to create tax-free income (which requires a gift of cash or tax-exempt securities) or aggressively enough to create mostly capital gain income (which is usually an imprudent strategy), most or all of the income will be taxed at ordinary rates. Rarely will the donor receive fully tax-free income for life from a charitable annuity remainder trust.

## Total Return Concept for Gift Annuity Investments

The treasurer at Metropolitan Hospital (in Chapter 4) should not have had a problem with the payout rate of Phyllis Emerson's gift. Even though he could not (or thought he could not) invest to receive actual income equaling 6.5 percent, he should have looked at the gift transaction from the perspective of total return. A balanced investment with a total return of 10 percent would yield approximately 5 percent of income and 5 percent of capital appreciation. (This is a broad expectation; the investment might provide between 3 percent and 6 percent of yield, and the capital appreciation would be approximately the difference between the yield and 10 percent.) The remaining amount of 1.5 percent—6.5 percent of needed payout minus 5.0 percent of actual income in the first year—could be made from selling appreciated assets each year. In this way, the investment, if the hospital viewed Mrs. Emerson's gift as something to invest (and most charities do), would increase in value each year. It would increase faster and faster, too.

In that situation the gift was $100,000. Assume the hospital invests to receive a total return of 10 percent. The payout is $6,500. In the following year, the amount grows to $110,000 and the hospital has, after the $6,500 payment, $103,500. During the second year, the value grows to $113,850 ($103,500 increased by 10 percent), but still has to pay only $6,500. The payment is no longer 6.5 percent of the asset's value. Against $103,500, $6,500 equals just a little less than 6.3 percent. This continues until the donor dies. From the charity's perspective, the longer the donor lives, the more the charity will receive. And the dollar amount continues to grow, faster than it would with a fixed percentage. At the end of 20 years, for example, with an original amount of $100,000, a 10 percent total return each year, and a $6,500 annual payment (which is not the same as an annual payment of 6.5 percent), the asset value will grow to approximately $300,500. The payment of $6,500 represents just slightly more than 2 percent of that value. The treasurer ought to be jumping for joy at such a prospect. Indeed, it is the donor, not the charity, who needs to be wary of such an arrangement. If the hospital's cost of operations rises 5 percent on average each year, the present value—the purchasing power—of the $300,500 is about $113,250. This is more than the original gift. The gift's value will grow as long as the initial payout rate is less than the total return. This should not be lost on treasurers or planned giving officers. If the payout rate is above the total return, the opposite happens; the asset value drops, and, in the opposite manner from an increasing asset value, it drops faster and faster as time passes. That is why, except for very elderly donors, the payout rate should be less than the total return expected. Exhibit 6.7 shows the growth of an asset valued at $100,000, a total return of 10 percent, and a payout of $6,500.

Exhibit 6.8 shows a decrease in a gift annuity asset. The gift is $100,000, the payout is 11 percent, and the total return is 8 percent.

Unfortunately, not enough treasurers view gift annuities from the perspective of total return. Too many try to purchase a bond whose income is equal to the gift annuity payment and whose maturity approximates the annuitant's life expectancy. There is no need to do this. The result is a needless decrease in the asset's inflation-adjusted value. Total return is not merely a function of the income from a bond the charity can buy; it

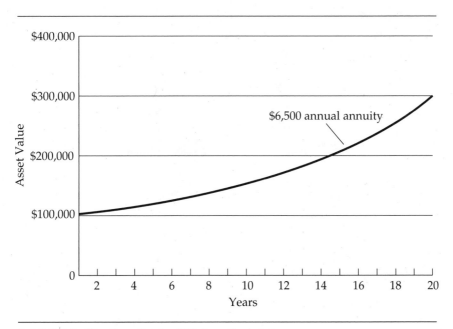

**Exhibit 6.7**    The Growth of a Gift Annuity Asset

A gift annuity asset grows when the initial payout is less than the annual total return. At the end of 20 years, with $6,500 paid annually against a total return of 10 percent, the asset's value grows from $100,000 to slightly more than $300,000.

This illustration was prepared using the planned giving software ParaGon™, developed by Blackbaud, Inc.

should be more than that. Instead, gift annuities should be invested with an eye on total return. The goal should be as much return as possible with as much balance as possible: a broad mix of stocks and bonds, with some high-growth and high-risk investments, some no-growth and certain-income investments, with a smattering of some in between. Even though capital gains can be used to make the annuity payment, the higher the income requirement, the more income the investments need to generate. The job of determining exactly who should make that judgment should be left to a professional investment advisor familiar with the goals of the annuity investments.

These issues should be included in a discussion between Donald Butler, the planned giving director at Metropolitan Hospital, and his treasurer. From the meeting should emerge a valid gift annuity payout policy to assure both the planned giving officer and the finance officer that the program helps the hospital and should grow. The last thing a

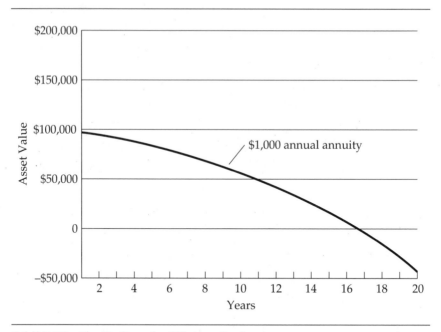

**Exhibit 6.8**  The Decline of a Gift Annuity Asset

A gift annuity asset decreases when the initial payment is more than the annual total return. At the end of 20 years, with $11,000 paid annually against a total return of 8 percent, the asset's value falls from $100,000 to *below* zero.

This illustration was prepared using the planned giving software ParaGon™, developed by Blackbaud, Inc.

planned giving person needs is to be met with self-righteousness from the treasurer when the planned giving officer does his job—acquiring planned gifts. The last thing a treasurer needs, however, is a planned giving department acquiring gifts that have little or no value.

## TRUST ADMINISTRATION

Trust administration, as distinguished from trust management, presents other potential problems. *Managing* trusts commonly involves the investment decisions that affect the growth of the assets inside the trust, as well as the income amounts paid to the beneficiaries. *Administration* is commonly thought to be the reconciliation of management results and income status in the form of reports to the trustee, the donor, and the tax collecting agencies, such as the IRS and any state, county, and local tax authorities. Charities who serve as trustee may or may not perform management and administration functions. Larger organizations have tended to do the work of one or both functions internally, although that is changing. The vast majority of charities, however, hire one or two outside firms, such as a money manager or a bank, to manage and administer their accounts. Within that circle, most charities hire one firm to do both. Many times the charity acts as the trustee, although others, such as the donor, can also be the trustee. Donors who do not receive checks on time or in their proper amounts can become disappointed. Also, trusts as well as donors need to file the proper tax forms.

One of the hidden corners of planned giving is the "four-tier" rule (reviewed in Chapter 7), which affects almost every charitable remainder trust beneficiary's tax reporting. Planned giving officers work at their own peril if they do not understand this rule because donors need to know the tax status of their trust income. One of the trust administrator's jobs is to determine the type of income the trust beneficiary receives each year. This depends on how the investments perform. If enough dividends and interest are produced to cover the amount paid to the beneficiary, all the income is fully taxable as ordinary income, and only the first tier of income is presumed to be paid. To the extent that capital appreciation is used to make the required payout, capital gain income must be reported. This is the second tier. The third tier is tax-free income. The fourth is return of principal, which also generates tax-free income.

- Tier one: ordinary income
- Tier two: long-term capital gains income
- Tier three: tax-free income
- Tier four: return of principal

Because of the four-tier rule the charity needs to know the cost basis of an asset used to fund a charitable remainder trust. Donors should know this, too, even though the appreciated portion is no longer a preference item in the donor's Alternative Minimum Tax calculation. The amount of appreciation is needed to determine when, if ever, any tax-free income can be paid to the beneficiary. It is not necessarily true—indeed it is rarely true—that gift assets invested in tax-exempt securities will produce tax-free income for the beneficiary. This is because if the asset donated was appreciated, and most assets used to establish planned gifts are, that appreciation creates capital gain income well before any tax-free income is allowed. Example 6.6 explains what happens.

---

### Example 6.6

If the donor's cost basis is $100,000 and the value of the gift is $1,000,000, the donor will not realize any tax-free income unless the trust immediately invests in tax-free bonds *and,* excluding gain realized *after* the gift is made, until $900,000 of gain has been reported in the donor's income. For example, if the payment to the donor is $50,000 per year—and the assets are invested in tax-exempt securities for all of that time—18 years would pass before any tax-free income is paid.

---

Only when all the appreciation *since the donor's date of acquisition* has been exhausted will the trust be able to pay tax-free income. This is usually never—or at least a very long time. When a donor expects tax-free income from his trust, not only must the investments be tax-free, but the gifted assets cannot have any appreciation in them either. In almost no circumstances should a donor of appreciated assets be allowed to expect tax-free income from a charitable remainder trust.

The only instance where creating tax-free income might prove helpful is when the donor is so elderly that the flat dollar amount generated by a tax-free bond does not have time to significantly erode against inflation and when the asset is not expected to increase in value. Even then, however, the donor must donate either cash or nonappreciated property to the trust to receive tax-free income. By concentrating on tax advantages, planned giving officers can create too much expectation for tax-free income. Contrary to what many have said, investments earning all or mostly tax-free income are not a good idea for the vast majority of donors.

The administrator of the trust, either the charity or a firm hired by the trustee, needs to keep accurate, thorough records of all gift investment transactions. Correct information must be provided to the income beneficiaries so they will be able to properly prepare their income tax forms. Knowing the donor's cost basis is important when preparing the tax form because the four-tier rule does not allow tax-free income to be paid if ordinary or capital gain income should be paid first. Although a donor may not be able to determine the asset's cost basis easily—and when multiple assets whose dividends have been reinvested have been donated, the process can get complicated—it is important and worth the effort to calculate it. It is the donor's responsibility, and the donor's accountant, stockbroker, or whoever handles the donor's investments should be able to calculate the asset's cost basis. It is *not* the charity's responsibility. If the donor cannot or will not calculate the cost basis, the IRS will assume that it is zero, that the entire gift is fully appreciated. The charity or outside administrator may try to help the donor determine the cost basis, but the IRS talks with the donor, not the charity, in an audit of the gift. The reason the cost basis is important is to determine the amount of income that might be characterized as capital gain, which is taxed, as opposed to return of principal, which is not taxed. This information is also important when one trust administrator assumes responsibility from another administrator. When a charity decides to hire or change a firm, all records on cost basis and gain must be transferred.

Some people feel this is an unimportant point because most trust assets will be invested to earn all or mostly ordinary income. To the degree that capital gain income is provided, it is either short-term capital gain, which is taxed at the ordinary income rate, or long-term capital gain from the inception of the gift. The argument is that rarely, if ever, would the administrator dig so deeply into the trust's investment history, to the point where ordinary income was insufficient and all the capital gain had been exhausted, to create tax-free income from the donor's cost basis, the asset's original principal. While this is often true, for the sake of accuracy—and because one can never know how investments will fare—the donor should provide the charity with the gift asset's cost basis.

## Payments from Life-Income Gifts

Checks should arrive on time and in their proper amounts. A donor should not have to call the charity to ask if the trust administrator has placed a decimal point incorrectly. The initial amount paid out by remainder trusts, pooled income funds, and most gift annuities is pro-rated. This means that a donor who puts $1 million of liquid assets in a 6 percent unitrust on December 15 and whose first annual payment is on January 1 will not receive $60,000. Nor will it be $15,000, as might be expected, if the payment schedule is quarterly. Instead, because the amount is measured against the time that has actually passed between gift date and payment date, the payment will be just under $2,500. (Fifteen days elapse between December 15, the date of the gift, and December 31, the date of the first payment. Fifteen divided by 365 days equals about 4.1 percent; 4.1 percent of 60,000 equals $2,466.) Planned giving officers need to explain this to donors.

But what about incorrect amounts? Bless the donors who don't examine their statements. A fair number simply get their checks and cash them without evaluating whether the amounts are correct. A charity, even when it has hired an outside firm and does not actually write the checks, is often the target of a donor's anger when the check is incorrect. A donor called one charity after three years (and six checks) to ask why his income seemed low for his $100,000 unitrust gift, which, with a stated trust payout of 6 percent annually, certainly should have paid $6,000 the first year, and close to that (because the trust's value did not change by much during such a short time) during the second and third years. The trust specified quarterly payments. The dates of payment were spelled out as well. The trust was not ambiguous about the terms of payment. The donor's records showed that he was paid about half what he was due, and he was calling to find out why.

Incredibly, someone from the firm that was managing and administering the trust said that all the money had been put into bonds and that because they paid income on a semiannual basis the donor was paid that frequently and in the amount the bonds provided. This was *not*, however, a net-income unitrust. That the bonds paid less than the payout and in a different schedule from that provided for in the trust agreement is irrelevant. The dividend schedule of invested assets does not affect the timing of the donor's income. The donor, perhaps like so many others, was completely understanding as the charity switched administration and investment firms. The new firm was obligated to figure out what should have been paid and then paid it, and it reinvested the assets to include a growth component. From that day on, the donor has carefully examined each check before depositing it.

## Trust Reporting

Not only paying income beneficiaries but reporting the proper amount to the tax authorities is important. Another hard lesson to be learned from one charity's experience: Once, a trustee reported on IRS Form 5227—the form used to record all trust investment and payout activity—that the donor received almost twice as much income as he had reported earlier on his Form 1040. This created cause for an audit, an audit the donor did not want, not because the trust income was truly underreported (although it was), but because he had other activity he did not want the IRS to know about. The donor, quite predictably, was upset with the charity, and no further gifts were forthcoming. With no apologies for a donor's other activities, a charity needs to take great care with its reporting function to the donor and to the IRS.

The investment information must be transferred from the asset management company to the administrator. Although this is accomplished most easily when the two functions are performed by the same organization, many charities split the functions between two entities. Also, some charities perform one function in-house and hire an outside firm for the other function. These decisions are complex and require a great deal of analysis and thought. Oversight is the proper function of the trustees, and too many trustees, many of whom are charities, do not do a good job of ensuring that their trusts are being administered correctly.

## Trust Language

Trusts are not always written correctly. This may come as a surprise, but the silliest as well as the most obscure problems can arise as a result of an incorrectly written trust. Two examples will illustrate what can happen. The first: a trust that called for a flat dollar unitrust amount to be paid each year. An oxymoron. The second: several annuity trusts claim to allow for additional contributions. Not allowed under IRC Regulation 664-2(b). But there it is. The responsibility of correctly drafting a trust belongs to the attorney who writes it, presumably the donor's attorney.

Trust administrators and charities who act as trustees need to review trusts carefully. It is easier to address any special concerns correctly before the assets are transferred than after the gift is made. Nonetheless, dealing with the problem of an incorrectly drafted trust falls upon the shoulders of the trustee, sometimes well after the gift is made. Typically, the firm administering the trust discovers the error or errors and needs to reconcile the problem before a proper tax return can be filed. And what about the tax returns filed before the error was discovered and corrected? That tends to be one of the several gray areas in the world of planned giving. Usually, the problem is consigned to history to be forgotten by everyone, and one might hope, ignored or left undiscovered by the IRS.

Clearly, this is the stuff of nightmares for charities already reluctant to enter the world of planned giving. If ever there was a commitment into an unknown and mysterious future, it is that forced by the establishment of a life-income gift. No wonder some trustees at charitable organizations don't want the responsibility. Look at the most successful programs, however, and you will see tangible results and a commitment to address these issues, perhaps because they are seen more as what needs to be done to establish future sources of income and less as headaches. The best way to address this complex area is for a charity, or whoever the trustee is, to ascertain the competency of the charitable trust's administrator. Although many charities can do this well internally, most cannot.

## STEWARDSHIP

But the real problems and headaches for those organizations not inclined to responsibly monitor their charitable trusts lie not in the mechanics of gift administration and management, but in staying in touch with donors. This nontechnical, seemingly nonthreatening, inexpensive process of stewardship is, strangely, where many charities fail. How many donors make their largest gift ever, and then simply fade away because the charity doesn't stay in touch? No one knows for sure, but be certain that the number is too high. Again, because we live in a world of immediate gratification, too many of us tend to think only of the next quarter or the next year, and not years and even decades hence. When a planned giving officer does not know if she will be at a charity for very long, what incentive is there to steward gifts that have already been made? When success is measured by gifts brought in, who has time to spend on those whose dollars already have been counted? Stewardship is often the runt of the development agenda, and only time will tell how serious the problem is.

Successful charities don't make this mistake. They have a long history of cultivation as well as stewardship. One executive director once said that he did not like the term *stewardship* because it borrowed too irreverently from its biblical meaning. His charity, not surprisingly, does not thank its donors very well or very often. In fact, that same person said that donors tire of hearing "thank you." After a while, he said, it sounds insincere. Certainly many major donors do not want to be thanked too often, but perhaps an annual letter would not appear too expensive or insincere to someone who has parted with many thousands of dollars. Again not surprisingly, that charity has no million-dollar donors. Yet the charity down the street, the one that does take the time to sincerely thank its donors in a variety of ways, seems able to attract larger donors, many of whom have given before. Somehow they like the feeling of family. They seem to like to be thanked as well.

We often hear of how long a gift decision gestates. One year. Two years. Five years, or more. But how often do we think about how long a life-income gift affects the  To concentrate on how to acquire planned gifts is proper, but to neglect what happens after is dangerous. Donor relations will suffer and financial consequences—to the donor and to the charity—can be substantial. Although charities spend a lot of time marketing their planned giving programs, the modern planned giving professional must also be proficient in how gifts are managed and administered, know how original decisions—especially the payout rate—affect gifts, understand the makeup provision in unitrusts, and understand how stocks and bonds work. This is in addition to simply staying in touch with donors who have made a major commitment to an organization. In return for a gift that lasts a lifetime, we should honor—with technical intelligence and human compassion—the person who, by donating significant assets, honors our missions.

# CHAPTER SEVEN

# So You Think the CMFR Is a Bit Technical?

*Confusion now hath made his masterpiece.*

**Shakespeare**

As in other professions, planned giving is rich with its own terminology. Much of it is confusing, even to those who solicit planned gifts. Because most donors have not been educated in the school of planned giving, the goal of a planned giving officer should always be to clarify and simplify what can appear to donors daunting and complex ideas and terminology. How many computer manuals do more to confuse people than to shed light? Think how confused a potential donor becomes when she is inundated with technical information about her planned gift inquiry. If we could only know how many people discontinue their charitable pursuits after they have received correspondence warning them that the "annuity trust" about which they inquired must pass the "5 percent probability test." Few of them, perhaps none, were aware that they had inquired about any such trust, and because they were hoping for an income of more than 5 percent, which certainly appears to be contrary to some law or another, why not just forget the whole thing altogether? When we communicate to other people the ideas underlying planned giving, we must strive to be clear and understandable. We are, after all, trying to convince someone to make a gift.

Although this is a book about the art of planned giving, that does not mean the competent planned giving professional need not know or understand many technical—legal, financial, and mathematical—planned giving concepts. The successful person in this profession needs to balance two broad objectives: the ability to understand the way people think (what this book is about) and an abundance of technical matters (what several other books are about).

But what of the more confusing concepts, those with which even planned giving professionals have difficulty? Certain concepts are difficult to grasp, yet need to be understood if the job is to be done properly. Although the following ten terms can seem confusing, planned giving professionals need to thoroughly understand them. The terms are disparate but loosely related. The first three relate to the donor's tax benefits. The following three relate to income, how it is taxed and how it grows. The final four are concepts associated with estate planning. Although they do not nearly exhaust the list (a list that would never be complete), these topics do tend to arise frequently.

- Charitable Midterm Federal Rate
- The bargain sale
- The five percent probability test
- The four-tier system
- Total return
- Future and present value
- Insurable interest
- Transferring assets
- The Generation Skipping Transfer Tax
- Paying gift and estate taxes

## CHARITABLE MIDTERM FEDERAL RATE

First, the name. The name of this rate is not yet universally agreed upon. Although many people call it the Charitable Midterm Federal Rate (CMFR), others call it the "discount rate" or the "interest rate." Charitable Midterm Federal Rate makes sense because it is the *rate* used to determine the value of a *charitable* gift. It is derived from a *midterm* interest rate determined by the *federal* government, specifically the Treasury Department. The CMFR is one of the factors in the IRS's remainder value calculation of a deferred gift. Before May 1989, the planned giving practitioner did not need to worry about this rate because it rarely changed. Prior to May 1989, it last changed in December 1983 from 6 percent to 10 percent. Now, it changes monthly.

But what is the CMFR? What does it do and why is it important? Generally, it has the *effect* of showing the growth in a charitable trust or gift annuity each year. The CMFR is a mathematical expression the IRS uses to predict the effective growth of the gift assets the charitable organization is managing; it is a way of saying that the charity is not slipping them under a mattress. But what kind of growth? Any forecast requires using assumptions. Financial planners and insurance agents use economic forecasting all the time. So does the government. When the Democrats say the budget will be balanced because of a new tax and the Republicans disagree, they will present their differences couched in different growth assumptions. It takes only the flick of a computer button to make a projected loss a projected profit or vice versa. The same is true with the CMFR. It is a growth predictor. The higher it is, the higher the IRS-calculated remainder value is, and the higher (within income limits) the donor's tax deduction.

Warning: The CMFR is not an accurate predictor of a trust's value. It cannot be. One 70-year-old donor makes a gift of $100,000 to an annuity trust paying $5,000 each year. A 9.6 percent CMFR creates an IRS-calculated remainder value of $66,052. A year later, when the CMFR falls to 6.4 percent, another donor whose circumstances are identical receives a deduction of only $59,020. The decrease is $7,000, more than 10 percent of the higher CMFR trust's remainder value. (This disparity is real; the rate in January 1994 was 6.4 percent, and in January 1995, a year later, it was 9.6 percent.) If each donor lives his life expectancy of approximately 16 years, for the 15 years their lifetimes will overlap (one is a year younger than the other) both trusts will presumably be subject to the same investment climate. This means that the trust values, except for that first year's return, will probably be about equal when their assets are transferred to charity. Yet one donor receives a remarkably higher deduction. This does not mean, however, that the exercise is not useful; we must have some established method to measure a future value. It does mean that we must live with that established method and that it is more of a guide than a precise measurement. For planned giving officers, the CMFR is a necessary but artificial assumption; it cannot predict the future.

When deferred gifts were defined by Congress in 1969, the assumed rate of growth—what we now call the CMFR—was 3.5 percent. In 1972 it rose to 6 percent. In 1983, the rate jumped to 10 percent because that more accurately reflected actual investment rates. When this happened, IRS-calculated remainder values—the inflation-adjusted amount deemed to be left in the trust at the end of a person's life expectancy—rose. By 1989, the economic picture had changed, and 10 percent was no longer realistic. Congress wanted to devise a way to better and more contemporaneously reflect economic conditions, so they introduced the variable rate. Panic hit the charitable world. The applicable federal rate used to compute the CMFR itself was not new, but few people knew it existed, and most of them did not understand how it worked. Changing this assumption each month meant that more people would have to be aware of it.

Most people in planned giving use a computer to calculate deductions for their donors, and software companies send the CMFR to their subscribers each month. The number from which the rate is derived can be found in the *Wall Street Journal* (see Exhibit 7.1). Sometime during the

# FEDERAL INTEREST RATES

The following tables, provided by the Internal Revenue Service, show the applicable federal interest rates, the adjusted applicable federal ranges, the adjusted federal long-term rate and the federal long-term tax exempt rate for August 1995.

Revenue ruling 95–51, setting forth this information, will be published in Internal Revenue Bulletin 1995 – 32 dated August 7, 1995.

### APPLICABLE FEDERAL INTEREST RATES

|  | Annual | Semi Annual | Quarter | Month |
|---|---|---|---|---|
| **Short-Term** | | | | |
| AFR | 5.73% | 5.65% | 5.61% | 5.58% |
| 110% of AFR | 6.32 | 6.22 | 6.17 | 6.14 |
| 120% of AFR | 6.89 | 6.78 | 6.72 | 6.69 |
| **Mid-Term** | | | | |
| AFR | 6.04% | 5.95% | 5.91% | 5.88% |
| 110% of AFR | 6.66 | 6.55 | 6.50 | 6.46 |
| 120% of AFR | 7.27 | 7.14 | 7.08 | 7.04 |
| 150% of AFR | 9.13 | 8.93 | 8.83 | 8.77 |
| 175% of AFR | 10.68 | 10.41 | 10.28 | 10.19 |
| **Long-Term** | | | | |
| AFR | 6.56% | 6.46% | 6.41% | 6.37% |
| 110% of AFR | 7.24 | 7.11 | 7.05 | 7.01 |
| 120% of AFR | 7.90 | 7.75 | 7.68 | 7.63 |

### ADJUSTED APPLICABLE FEDERAL INTEREST RATES

|  | Annual | Semi Annual | Quarter | Month |
|---|---|---|---|---|
| **Short-Term** | | | | |
| AFR | 3.87% | 3.83% | 3.81% | 3.80% |
| **Mid-Term** | | | | |
| AFR | 4.63% | 4.58% | 4.55% | 4.54% |
| **Long-Term** | | | | |
| AFR | 5.67% | 5.59% | 5.55% | 5.53% |

ADJUSTED LONG TERM RATE 5.67
LONG-TERM TAX-EXEMPT RATE 5.88

**Exhibit 7.1**   Federal Interest Rate Table

The Federal Interest Rate table from which the CMFR is computed monthly. This table can be found in the *Wall Street Journal* around the 20th of each month. The August CMFR is calculated by reference to 120% of the annual AFR, which in this case is 7.27. That number rounded to the nearest two-tenths of one percent—7.2—equals the CMFR.

Reprinted by permission of the *Wall Street Journal*. © 1995 Dow Jones & Company, Inc. All rights reserved worldwide.

third or fourth week of each month, the *Journal* publishes the "Federal Interest Rates" as an index item on the top of the first page in section C, where stock and bond prices are quoted. Three rate categories—short-term, midterm, and long-term—are found in the boxed chart entitled "Federal Interest Rates," and several rates are found within each of these three categories. Planned gifts are affected by the line that reads "120% of AFR" and the corresponding column that reads "Annual." (AFR stands for *applicable federal rate*, a term used in tax law to impute interest on no-interest or low-interest loans.) The latter number is a two-decimal number that the planned giving computer companies (and others who calculate remainder values) round to the nearest even two-tenths of one percent. If the actual number is 8.05, then the Charitable Midterm Federal Rate is 8.0 because .05 is closer to .0 than it is to .2. When the rate is exactly between the two round numbers, the CMFR is rounded up, not down. This means that 8.50 would become 8.6, and not 8.4. This is done each month.

The Federal Interest Rate Table provides the information necessary to calculate the CMFR for the following month, in this case August 1995. Note that the information is contained in Revenue Ruling 95-51 (the fifty-first revenue ruling in 1995). Simple enough. But that's not all. The donor has the option of using the rate for the month when the gift is made or the rate for either of the two previous months (this is explained in Section 7520(a)(2) of the Internal Revenue Code). If the donor does not use the rate for the month during which the gift is made she must inform the IRS in a written statement accompanying her tax return that she is using the rate of one of the two prior months. In general, if the rate is higher in either of those months, the donor will receive a more favorable tax deduction. Remember, the higher the rate, which, broadly stated, is an assumed growth or investment rate for life-income gifts, the higher the IRS-calculated remainder value, the inflation-adjusted value of what will be someday transferred to charity.

Three situations might influence the donor to choose the *lowest* available CMFR. First, charitable gift annuities provide a trade-off: The higher CMFR provides a higher IRS-calculated remainder value, but a lower portion of tax-free income for the annuitant. Second, for gifts of a residence where the donor continues to live, the higher the CMFR the *lower* the remainder value. Third, a donor who establishes a charitable lead trust usually wants the lowest CMFR because the remainder interest—the value being left to noncharitable heirs, usually children or grand-children—of a non-grantor lead trust is subject to gift tax. In a grantor lead trust, the donor will also usually want to use the lowest CMFR because the income value—the amount on which the donor receives an income tax deduction—is higher.

## THE BARGAIN SALE

A bargain sale takes place when a donor sells an asset to charity for less than its value. The difference between the selling price and the value is a gift. The charity is receiving a bargain, as well as a gift, on the sale. If a donor owns property worth $100,000 and sells it to a charity for $40,000, the charity gets an asset worth much more than what it is paying, and the donor receives a deduction for the $60,000 difference. Simple enough, and would that we could stop here.

Unfortunately, we cannot. The next level of complexity is addressed when an appreciated asset is used in a bargain sale. The donor needs to know not only her deduction, the difference between the value of the property and the price, but the amount of capital gains tax she owes on the sale. The donor is responsible for a capital gains tax based on the appreciation represented in the sale portion of the property. This, too, is not very difficult to understand because the concept is one of proportion. If the $100,000 asset has a cost basis of $25,000, it has an appreciation of $75,000. That means 75 percent of the asset is appreciated, and the donor needs to pay a capital gains tax on 75 percent of the amount she receives. She receives, in this case, $40,000 from the charity on the sale. Seventy-five percent of $40,000 is $30,000. Thus, she will receive a deduction for $60,000, but must pay a capital gains tax on $30,000. The charity does not pay a capital gains tax on property it receives, and neither does the donor. Assuming she is in the 36 percent federal income tax bracket (despite the examples shown in most brochures, not everybody is in the highest bracket), the deduction is worth $21,600 ($60,000 × .36). The donor saves $21,600 in income taxes, yet she must pay a capital gains tax of $8,400 ($30,000 × .28).

Sometimes the donor is interested in making a bargain sale gift of stock in an amount that will exactly offset the capital gains tax that needs to be paid with the income tax that is saved. The following formula shows how to calculate a bargain sale gift if the donor wants to balance the amount saved in taxes with the amount paid in capital gains taxes:

$$N = ADE/(BC+DE)$$

where: $A$ = Total number of shares

$B$ = Fair market value per share

$C$ = Donor's income tax bracket

$D$ = The capital gain per share

$E$ = Donor's capital gains tax bracket

$N$ = Number of shares donated

By inference, $A-N$ equals the number of shares sold.

Example 7.1 uses the formula to show how many shares of stock can be sold and how many given to charity so that the tax paid is exactly offset by the taxes saved by the charitable deduction.

---

### Example 7.1

Assume the donor has 500 $(A)$ shares of stock worth $45 $(B)$ per share, and that the per-share gain is $30 $(D)$. The donor's income tax bracket is 41% $(C)$ and his capital gains tax bracket is 28% $(E)$:

$$N = ADE/(BC+DE)$$
$$N = 500 \times \$30 \times .28 \, / \, (\$45 \times .41) + (\$30 \times .28)$$
$$N = \$4,200 \, / \, \$18.45 + \$8.40$$
$$N = \$,4,200 \, / \, \$26.85$$
$$N = 156.42 \text{ shares}$$

This means that, of the 500 shares of stock the donor is using for this transaction, 157 shares should be donated and 343 should be sold. One hundred fifty-seven shares worth $45 equals a deduction of $7,065. In the 41% tax bracket, this equals taxes saved of $2,897. The 343 shares to be sold with a gain of $30 per share will produce a total gain of $10,290. At a 28% capital gains tax bracket, this results in a capital gains tax of $2,881. The difference between $2,897 and $2,881 can be accounted for by rounding up to the nearest whole share to be given away.

---

As is intuitive, the higher her tax bracket, the more the donor can give away without incurring a net tax. The amount of the gain is also important. The higher the gain, the less she can give away to achieve equality between what she saves and what she pays.

Selling an asset to charity for less than its value, however, is *not* always a gift. A donor who intends to make a bargain sale gift to a charity should contemporaneously put her intentions in writing, stating the fair market value of the asset, the amount she will receive from the charity, and the contribution amount. The document should clearly state her intention to make a charitable gift. A person cannot sell property for $100,000 that she thinks is worth $100,000, and then, upon discovering that the property was actually worth $200,000, claim a deduction for the difference of $100,000. In this situation, the person never had any intention of making a gift and, solely in pursuit of a tax deduction, cannot retroactively make that decision.

A bargain sale also takes place when a gift of mortgaged property is given to charity. If property that is worth $100,000 and has a $40,000 mortgage is given, the donor receives a deduction for only $60,000; the mortgage amount, the $40,000, is considered to be the sales price in a bargain sale to charity. This is true even if the donor accepts responsibility for paying the mortgage. Further, the capital gain attributable to the mortgage is taxed to the donor.

These are the simplest examples. Many other and more complex situations are dealt with under the bargain sale rules, especially as they relate to mortgaged property. Although an attorney well-versed in the rules relating to such gifts is essential to the gift planning process, most planned giving professionals, primarily because of the IRS's resistance to fully clarify its position, wisely tend to avoid mortgaged property, especially when it is to be used to fund a charitable remainder trust.

## THE 5 PERCENT PROBABILITY TEST

For a donor to be permitted to deduct the IRS-calculated remainder value of a charitable remainder annuity trust, there must be at least a 5 percent chance that the trust will not deplete its assets before it terminates. Determining the likelihood of such an event is a calculation called the *5 percent probability test.* In the Internal Revenue Code, 5 percent measures the probability of anything being so small as to be remote; anything with less than a 5 percent chance of happening is quite small. There are times, however, when a remainder value calculation for an annuity trust provides an otherwise deductible value, but, paradoxically, the data are such that the 5 percent probability test is not passed. For example, a $100,000 annuity trust for a 70-year-old donor who receives a payout of 11 percent paid quarterly at the end of the quarter with a CMFR of 9.4 percent will fail the test even though the trust generates a remainder value of $24,493 (see Exhibit 7.2). Setting aside the issue of such a high payout rate, the donor receives *no* income tax deduction even though the remainder value is almost $24,500. As shown in Exhibit 7.2, to pass the 5 percent probability test and thereby provide a deductible remainder value, the annuity trust must not pay more than 9.967 percent.

A formula separate from the one to determine the charitable remainder annuity trust's IRS-calculated remainder value is used to determine whether the 5 percent probability test has been passed. The major planned giving software programs automatically include the calculation when the remainder value is calculated. The amount in Exhibit 7.2 that shows the payout required to pass the 5 percent probability test is calculated

The remainder value and maximum payout to pass the 5% probability test for a trust paying an $11,000 (11% of the trust's initial value) annual income, paid at the end of each quarter, to a 70-year old donor making a gift of $100,000 to a charitable remainder annuity trust. Neither remainder value is deductible because an 11% payout fails the test.

| CMFR | REMAINDER VALUE | MAXIMUM PAYOUT PERMITTED TO PASS 5% TEST |
| --- | --- | --- |
| 6.0 | $ 4,725 | 7.300% |
| 9.4 | $24,493 | 9.967% |

**Exhibit 7.2**   Comparison of Charitable Mid-Term Federal Rate

All else being equal, two different CMFRs of 6.0 and 9.4 show different payout amounts required to pass the 5% probability test. A 6.0 CMFR allows for only a 7.3% payout to pass the test; a 9.4 CMFR allows a payout of over 9.9% to pass the test.

This illustration was prepared using the planned giving software ParaGon™, developed by Blackbaud, Inc.

using software; it is the result of calculating backwards, testing different payout rates with the 5 percent probability test formula.

The 5 percent probability test is a controversial provision, at least in theory, because only the charitable remainder annuity trust is subject to it. Although the IRS has explained this extra requirement in Revenue Ruling 77-374, the portions of the Internal Revenue Code and Treasury regulation sections dealing with income, gift, and estate tax deductions for charitable remainder annuity trusts do not mention a 5 percent test. The charitable remainder unitrust does not have this requirement, probably because a unitrust theoretically cannot reach zero; its income is a percentage of the trust's assets, and the less the trust is valued, the less the income will be.

The 5 percent test is affected by three factors: (1) the CMFR, (2) the trust's payout and frequency, and (3) the age of the income beneficiary.

The higher the CMFR, the lower the payout, and the older the income beneficiary, the more likely the trust will pass the 5 percent test. Conversely, the lower the CMFR, the higher the payout, and the younger the beneficiary, the more likely the trust will fail the 5 percent test. A change in the CMFR can have dramatic results. In Exhibit 7.2 one CMFR is 9.4 percent. A CMFR of 6 percent creates a much lower remainder value of $4,725, and does not pass the 5 percent probability test.

The payout required to pass the test is a much lower 7.3 percent (as opposed to a payout of up to slightly more than 9.9 percent) when the CMFR is 6.0 percent. At least theoretically, a payout of less than the

CMFR will *never* fail the 5 percent test because the payout is less than the presumed rate of growth of the trust (which is what the CMFR is essentially measuring); if the trust is reduced by less than it is growing, it will experience a net positive growth. In a minor way this is adjusted because of the payout interval and whether the payout comes at the beginning of that interval or at the end. If the payout in Exhibit 7.2 were 6 percent and the donor 70 years old, the trust would pass with a remainder value of almost $59,000.

Finally, the older a person is, the more likely the annuity trust will pass the 5 percent probability test. This is because the donor has fewer years of life expectancy. If the donor were 90 years old and the payout 11 percent, the trust would also pass with a remainder value of over $64,000.

## THE FOUR-TIER SYSTEM

The four-tier system relates to how an income beneficiary is taxed on income from a charitable trust. Although it is invoked frequently as a guide to the levels of income taxation, it is widely misunderstood. It is defined in Section 1.664-1(d) of the Internal Revenue Code under "Treatment of annual distributions to recipients—(1) Character of distributions." The regulation says that "ordinary income" is the first tier, "capital gain" is the second tier, "other income" is the third tier, and "corpus" or return of principal is the fourth tier. Capital gain is divided into short-term and long-term gain, and of the two, short-term gain, because it creates fully taxable income, is distributed before long-term gain. "Other income" is tax-free income, such as from tax-exempt bonds. This means that ordinary income, to the degree any is generated from the trust's investments, is paid out first; capital gain income, again to the degree that there is any *and* that all the ordinary income has been paid out, is next; and tax-free income is the last level to be distributed (tax-free encompasses both the third and fourth levels—income from tax-free investments and from principal is untaxed). When you look at it, this makes sense: Within reason, the trust beneficiary is going to be taxed as much as possible.

Because calculating the amount to be paid from each income tier is complicated, only professional trust administrators file charitable trust tax returns, specifically IRS Form 5227, the Split-Interest Trust Information Return. This form is divided into seven parts: (1) the amount and (2) type of income paid out from the trust, (3) an income accumulation schedule listing how much has been distributed during the year, (4) a balance sheet asking for a listing of the assets in the trust, (5) basic information about the unitrust or the annuity trust, (6) any transactions during the year, and (7) information about lead trusts and pooled income funds (Form 5227 may be the only place where those two gifts are linked).

What happens when an asset is donated to establish a charitable remainder trust and the donor must be taxed on that income? Too many planned giving directors and advisors have provided their donors and clients with the wrong information. The question of how the trust income will be taxed usually comes up in the context of a gift of highly appreciated property. Planned giving brochures advertising that gifts with large amounts of appreciation are good because the donors benefit from the tax-free reinvestment do not detail how the income will be taxed, and many people are told that they not only avoid a capital gains tax when the asset is sold but that they will also receive tax-free income when the new asset is a tax-free bond. This is not true.

Two points in the history of the gift asset are important: when the asset was acquired by the donor and the date the asset was given to the charitable trust. The clock for the four-tier system begins when the donor acquired the asset, usually many years before the gift is made, not when the asset is transferred to the charitable trust. Even though the charitable trust is tax exempt, the trust administrator tracks all gains, even those prior to the date of the gift. This means that a $100,000 gift with a cost basis of $10,000 has a gain of $90,000 before *and* after the gift is made. This further means that although the trust can reinvest without incurring a capital gains tax, the income from the trust will, if it is necessary, reflect that gain. This important point is often lost on those who think that an appreciated asset can be contributed to a charitable trust and then immediately provide tax-free income if it is invested in tax-exempt bonds. In fact, a reinvested trust would pay out capital gain income for a fairly long time. For example, a $100,000 annuity trust that pays $5,000 each year and immediately invests in tax-free bonds will generate capital gain—*not* tax-free—income for 18 years. Then, if the asset is still invested in tax-free funds, the trust will provide tax-free income to the beneficiary. Why 18 years? Because the $90,000 gain is exhausted at the rate of $5,000 per year, and at that rate the trust will take 18 years before the capital gain income is distributed. This is what the four-tier rule means when it says that capital gain income will be paid out before tax-free or other income is paid out.

This example also reveals the importance of acquiring the correct cost basis of the donated asset. Even though many times the donor does not readily know the cost basis, it is an important piece of information for planned giving officers to obtain. The IRS contends that an unknown cost basis is the equivalent of no cost basis. Thus, in the context of the four-tier rule, the income beneficiary may pay more in taxes than necessary. In the example above, if the cost basis were $90,000 instead of $10,000, the income would be characterized as capital gain for only two years instead of 18, with tax-free income beginning in the third year.

The practical importance of the four-tier rule to charitable trust income beneficiaries is clear. For two broad reasons, however, the planned giving officer should lead donors to expect fully taxable income while in the discussion stages of making a gift. First, since ordinary income is taxed at the highest rate, any change will be to the income beneficiary's benefit.

The second reason, more complicated and difficult to explain to the donor, relates to prudent investing. Very few donors should enter into a gift agreement with the expectation that the trust will make solely tax-free investments. While not law in and of itself, the "Second Restatement of the Prudent Investor Rule" is a useful guide for the courts; it strongly suggests that a nondiversified portfolio is imprudent. Therefore, without even taking into consideration the four-tier rule, planned giving officers should not frequently talk about tax-free income from a charitable trust.

A unitrust investing solely in bonds will not appreciate very much, if at all, during its term. Neither the income nor the principal will grow, and both will lose value against inflation. Depending on the life of the income beneficiary, this could be devastating. It simply is not prudent to invest in one class of assets. Even though many people think that bonds are safe because they will not lose principal value, they are not so safe when that principal value or the resulting fixed income is exposed to inflation.

Annuity trusts generally should not be invested in tax-free vehicles, because even though the income to the donor is fixed and potentially tax-free, the asset in the trust loses value to inflation. This is not a fair burden for the charity to bear; even though a donor (unless she serves as the trustee) is unable legally to control the trust's investments, charities are usually willing to honor her wishes. Despite that willingness, however, the charity should do everything possible to analyze the results of a tax-free investment portfolio. Even the prudent investor guidelines, however, do not ensure against uncertainty. It may not be so easy to find appropriate tax-free vehicles, especially when the annuity trust payout calls for more income than a bond might produce. Further, chasing a high payout may require the purchase of bonds of dubious quality, which puts the trust at risk of losing the income on the investment and, potentially, the principal. Also, bonds that are callable could be called at any time, exposing the trust manager to the awful decision of quickly buying more bonds or investing for a better total return. The four-tier system should not be an invitation to invest solely in search of tax-free income.

## TOTAL RETURN

Total return is an investment term that means the growth on an investment, including capital appreciation, dividends, and interest. Usually, total return is referenced on an annual basis, although sometimes it refers to growth over a period of many years. Total return is used to estimate how an asset will grow to a point in the future. A stock listed on the New York Stock Exchange will show the price of the stock that day, as well as its dividend. If the stock was worth $10 last year and is today, a year later, worth $11, the appreciation equals 10 percent ($1 divided by $10). If, however, the stock also declared a 20-cent dividend during the year, that dividend is worth 2 percent of the $10 stock value. Thus, the total return—the sum of the appreciation and the dividend—is equal to $1.20, or 12 percent. Many stocks never experience an annual total return of 12 percent, although some do.

Although total return is important in several planned giving as well as many other financial calculations, this concept is particularly important in estimating the growth of net-income unitrusts. A net-income unitrust pays only the income; the trustee cannot use capital appreciation or principal to make the stated payout on the trust (some net-income unitrusts are written to define realized capital gain as income, however). As long as the actual annual income is less than the stated payout rate, the payout to the income beneficiary is less than the stated payout rate (and the capital gain is added to the trust's principal each year).

A donor who compares a 5 percent income with a 7 percent income may think he benefits with the higher annual amount, but this is not always true. Actually, and paradoxically, it is rarely true for two reasons. First, a look at a straight unitrust. If total return can be estimated to be 10 percent for both situations—the 5 percent and 7 percent incomes—the 5 percent income is accompanied by a capital appreciation of 5 percent and the 7 percent income has a capital appreciation of 3 percent. Both have a total return of 10 percent, but the net growth is different. This means that the 5 percent income is growing faster than the 7 percent income, as shown in Exhibit 7.3. After 18 years, the lower percentage payout actually pays a higher income as measured by the total annual dollars paid out. Because many donors live longer than 18 years after establishing a unitrust or pooled income fund, the lower payout usually will eventually provide a higher annual income.

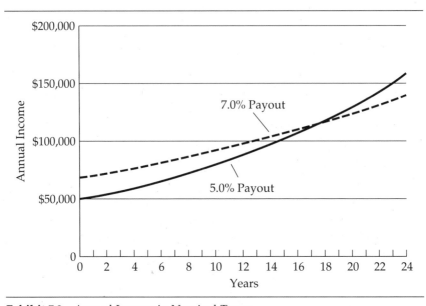

**Exhibit 7.3**   Annual Income in Nominal Terms

This illustration was prepared using the Donor Model software developed by Kaspick & Company.

Second, a look at a net-income unitrust. In investment circles the following maxim is generally accepted: *The more income required from an investment portfolio, the less the total return.* That is, if the trustee must maximize current income (as happens many times with a net-income unitrust), the total return is lower than if the investment objective looked at income—or yield—as a secondary consideration. Many times, different income expectations result in different total return expectations. In Exhibit 7.4, the total return is not 10 percent for both trusts. Instead, total return for the investment requiring a 5 percent yield is higher than the total return for the investment generating a 7 percent yield. In general, although this fluctuates in different economic climates, the total return would be about one to two percentage points less for the investment generating the higher yield. Thus the 5 percent income trust might have a total return of 10 percent, and the 7 percent income trust might have a total return of only 9 percent, or even 8.5 percent. This results in an even more pronounced difference, as Exhibit 7.4 shows, with the lower percentage payout paying a higher income after only 11 years.

When immediate yield is the primary objective, total return is reduced and long-term income suffers dramatically. Thus, total return is

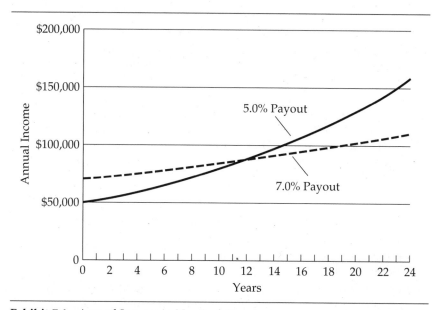

**Exhibit 7.4**   Annual Income in Nominal Terms

This illustration was prepared using the Donor Model software developed by Kaspick & Company.

important when looking at an investment, but its distinct applications are also important when looking at potential growth of various types of planned gifts. This concept applies to unitrusts—both straight and net-income—and pooled income funds, the two life-income gift vehicles whose incomes fluctuate based on the growth of the investment. Donors need to be aware of how their income expectations affect the total growth over the lifetime of a trust and its annual total return. Planned giving officers need to understand these concepts and then be able to clearly communicate them, preferably using easy-to-understand graphs.

## FUTURE AND PRESENT VALUE

The concept of future value is intuitive. Ten dollars today is different from—which is to say, less than—$10 next year because of the invest-ment opportunity available with the $10 today. If a person can invest money at 10 percent annually, the value of that $10 will be $11 next year. This is important when trying to determine by how much a charitable trust will grow given a specified number of years and a fixed investment rate. If a trust is worth $1,000,000 today and is expected to last for 10 years, the investment rate must be stipulated or assumed to determine the trust's future value. If that rate is 10 percent—this is many times called a "growth" rate—by the end of the tenth year, the trust will be worth $2,593,742. This is its *future value.*

One way to calculate future value is to multiply the current value (C) by one plus the interest rate (*i*), and do this for the specified number of years. Using a growth rate of, say, 7 percent, multiply $1,000,000 by 1.07 (.07 is 7 percent) 10 times. That is the slow way, however. A better way is to use a formula:

$$\text{Future Value} = C \times (1 + i)^n$$

A number taken to a power is the number of times the original number is multiplied by its growing self. For example, four squared is four to the second power, and equals four times four, or 16. Four cubed is four to the third power, and equals four times four (16), and that times four again, or 64. (Beyond the power of three it gets complicated; a formula and a calculator become quite useful.) In mathematical notation, $(1 + i)^n$ equals the growth of something. Using the above numbers, the results are: $(1 + .10)^{10}$, or 2.593742. This multiplied by $1,000,000 equals $2,593,742.

Future value is only partially useful, however. The other important calculation is determining *present value.* Calculating the present value of an asset makes it comparable in today's terms, regardless of the future value or the elapsed time. Conceptually, it is the opposite of determining future value. Determining the future value of money means taking a known number today and determining its future dollar amount by "growing" it by an inflation or investment rate. Determining present value, on the other hand, means taking an expected future amount and discounting it, using an inflation or investment rate. Ten dollars to be paid one year from today is not worth $10; because of inflation or the lost investment opportunity on the money, it is worth less. If the investment opportunity is 10 percent, that $10 must be reduced by 10 percent for the year. Surprisingly, or at least not intuitively, the present value of $10 to be paid in one year, assuming an investment opportunity rate of 10 percent, is not $9; instead it is $9.09.

$$\text{Present Value} = C \times \frac{1}{(1 + i)^n}$$

where *i* is the investment rate and *n* is the number of years the future value is being discounted. The formula is not as important as the idea, however; we are trying to take a number invested at 10 percent that will in one year grow to $10. It can't be $9 because a 10 percent growth of $9 is only $9.90. To determine the present value of something we need to reduce a known future amount so that we can measure it against an amount in hand today.

All deferred gifts should be considered in present value terms. To know that a charitable remainder trust will grow from $1,000,000 to $3,0000,000 in 25 years, the life expectancy of the beneficiary, is to know something nice but not very relevant. Without calculating the present value of that $3,000,000, the charity has little idea of what it has raised, especially if the trust is going to fund a specific project, such as a professorship at a university. If it costs $1,000,000 to fund a professorship today, we know that it will be more expensive for a donor who wishes to do the same thing in 25 years. How much more expensive is a matter of judgment, but charities can use an annual cost increase (usually higher than the Consumer Price Index) to estimate how much something will cost in the future. The way to most prudently estimate that rise is to look back over a 20- to 30-year period at annual budget or operating cost increases, and then take an annual average. Assuming for our purposes that the cost increase is 5 percent, a professorship that costs $1,000,000 today will cost $3,386,355 in 25 years. The formula is: $1,000,000 \times (1 + .05)^{25}$. This is an example of calculating the future value. This may or may not be accurate because there is no way of knowing for certain how costs will grow in the future, but one rate or another must be used to project the future cost (or value) of something. To further complicate matters, that future cost is in nominal, or noninflation-adjusted, dollars. We can already see that the two future values—$3,000,000 projected in the trust, and $3,386,355 that the professorship is projected to cost—are different; we know the projected trust asset value will not be enough. The future cost of the project will be higher than the future value of the charitable trust because the trust grows more slowly than the organization's inflation rate; the trust grows at an expected annual rate of just under 4.5 percent, and, as just pointed out, the cost of the professorship is expected to grow by 5 percent each year. Thus, even though the trust's growth to $3,000,000 seems like a lot, when the actual cost of the professorship is considered it is not as high as it first appears.

But to know if there is any growth, especially in today's dollars, we need to reduce the future value by inflation or an investment rate. First, we need to calculate the present value, in this case of $3,000,000, the known (or estimated) amount of the trust in 25 years, and $3,386,355, the known (or estimated) value of the professorship in 25 years. If we use an annual rate of 5 percent to reduce that future amount—this is often called a "discount rate" because the future value is being reduced—to reflect inflation or lost investment opportunity, those numbers become soberingly small. To determine what $3,000,000 will purchase in a world where purchasing power is reduced by 5 percent each year, that number must be reduced accordingly. The future value of the trust, $3,000,000, is reduced to a little under $886,000. The formula looks like this: $1/(1.05)^{25}$, or 3.386355 divided by one; the result is .295, or about 29 percent of the value we are discounting. Since the number we are discounting is $3,000,000, we multiply that by 29.5 percent, which equals $885,908.

The future cost of the professorship, $3,386,355, is reduced to $1,000,000. This is intuitive because we grew the number out and then discounted it for the same number of years at the same rate. A $1,000,000 gift to a charitable trust that grows to $3,000,000 to fund a professorship in 25 years will not be enough. In present value terms, it will fall short by about $114,000, $1,000,000 minus $886,000.

That 5 percent is chosen is not the important decision—although the number chosen should be based on a realistic expectation—but rather that the number remain consistent when calculating the present value of different amounts for a valid comparison. That is, if one charitable trust is projected to grow to $1,000,000 in ten years and another is projected to grow to $2,000,000 in 15 years, in calculating the present value of those two trusts, the discount rate should be the same for both. Using the methodology just described and a 7 percent discount rate, for example, the present value for the first trust is $508,350 and the present value for the second trust is about $725,000. Those two numbers are the result of an effort to measure the money as if it were available today. By calculating the estimated cost of the professorship *tomorrow,* and then discounting it by a cost-increase factor, we know whether the charitable remainder trust has enough money *today.* That is the idea behind present value. The present value of any charitable trust—indeed, the present value of the total of any program—should be calculated to provide accurate and meaningful data.

## INSURABLE INTEREST

Insurable interest is a life insurance term, and applies to the relationship between the insured and the beneficiary, the person or entity to receive the proceeds of the death benefit when the insured person dies. Every state has essentially the same law mandating that a beneficiary to a life insurance policy must have an *insurable interest* in the insured person's life. When a man buys life insurance and names his wife as the primary beneficiary and the children as secondary beneficiaries, there is no question of insurable interest. Life insurance companies assume that a wife and children automatically have an interest in the father's life, a preference for seeing the father live over receiving money upon his death. An insurable interest also exists between business partners. If one partner dies, the business could suffer. The other partner or partners have an insurable interest in the business's continued prosperity.

A parent has an insurable interest in a child and siblings may have an insurable interest in each other, although sometimes a life insurance company may ask for an explanation before it issues a policy. For example, if a parent buys a life insurance policy on his children but does not own any insurance on himself, the company may wonder why a person who does not feel his own life is worth insuring would buy insurance for and be the beneficiary of his children's policy. The insurance company fears that the children may be more likely to have an unfortunate accident than is statistically probable. Life insurance companies think about these things.

Under the right circumstances life insurance also can be a good gift to charity. Many charitably minded people who do not otherwise have the means to make large gifts make gifts of life insurance because they are relatively inexpensive and require little out-of-pocket cost to donors. An existing policy that is already in force and has been for many years is the most common gift of life insurance. In this situation, insurable interest is not a problem. The donor assigns the policy to a charity; the charity then owns it and can either cash it in or wait until the donor dies to collect the death proceeds.

Insurable interest is a problem, however, in charitable giving when a donor buys a new life insurance policy for the sole purpose of making it a gift to charity. Three entities are associated with an insurance policy: the owner, the insured, and the beneficiary. Many times the owner is the insured, and the beneficiary is a spouse, a child, or another party with an obvious insurable interest. During the application process—after the buying decision has been made and before the policy has been issued—the insurance company wants to verify that the owner and named beneficiary have a relatively traditional relationship with the insured. In many states, a charity is not considered to have such status, and a problem arises if the donor names the charity as the beneficiary when the application is being completed. In some states charities do have an insurable interest in the donor, but in many others they do not.

Given the relationships generally required by the insurable interest rules (aside from states that specifically grant charities such status), it is hard to see, with few exceptions, how a charity has such an interest.

Those exceptions might be for donors who have made significant pledges and who may die before the pledge has been fully paid. Charities tend not to enjoy going to probate court to claim pledges.

Insurable interest is normally a problem, however, only during the time before the policy is issued. The easiest way for a donor to make a gift of a new policy is to name her estate as the beneficiary when applying for the policy. Then, if the person dies between the date of application and the date the policy is issued, her will should direct the proceeds of the life insurance policy to the charity. If the first premium is paid and the health requirements are met (either by answering medical questions at the time of application or by taking a physical exam), the insurance company will pay the death benefit if, in the course of underwriting the policy, it discovers nothing that would have prevented the policy from being issued. Then, when the policy is issued, the donor can name the charity the owner and beneficiary. This avoids the insurable interest problem for donors who live in states that do not explicitly declare that charities have an insurable interest in their donors.

## TRANSFERRING ASSETS

There are five basic ways to transfer assets: probate, lifetime gifts, lifetime trusts, contracts, and ownership.

### Probate

Of those five, probate is the most recognized by the general public. Only assets transferred by will, however, go through the probate process. In Latin, the word *probate* means "to prove." The executor of a person's estate must prove the validity of the will in court. The will describes how the decedent wants assets to be transferred to others, and the probate process legitimizes that transfer. A charitable bequest is an example of an asset that is subject to probate; it is a provision in a person's will to pass money or other property to one or more charities.

But many people want to plan their estates to avoid probate. The several books that have been written on the benefits of avoiding probate indicate the public's willingness to learn, as well as provide a measure of the desire to save what are considered to be unnecessary expenses at death. Assets that go through the probate process are usually managed by an attorney whose fee may be measured by the size of a person's estate subject to probate. Further, many people feel the legal fee—whether it is based on the size of the estate or a flat fee—reduces what would otherwise go to their loved ones and to charities. Probate assets are also public assets; a will is open to the scrutiny of anyone who wishes to know what assets a person transferred at death. This is how we know what well-known people did with their estate assets. But we do not know how much those individuals transferred by other methods. Wills are sometimes contested, too. The Howard Hughes will was publicly contested by a variety of would-be benefactors; by contrast, most of the John Lennon estate was not public. Undoubtedly, most of Lennon's estate was not transferred by will. Even though we have heard that his wife and child were the main beneficiaries of his estate, because most of his assets were not named in his will, we may never learn the exact size of his estate or to whom and in what amounts his estate was transferred. Why, then, might a person transfer assets in a will? Flexibility and ease are often cited as reasons assets are transferred by will.

## Lifetime Gifts

During life, a person can give money away. Lifetime gifts can be made to anyone at any time, but to avoid a transfer tax (a gift tax because it is made during life, as opposed to an estate tax, levied at death) a donor is currently limited to a gift of $10,000 per year to anyone other than a spouse, to whom a gift may be made without limit. If the donor is married, she can make a gift of up to $20,000 per year to anyone by splitting the gift with her husband. Anything beyond $10,000 (or $20,000) given to a nonspouse is subject to a gift tax. This does not mean, however, that the person will pay a tax. If the amount given to another person is greater than the annual exclusion, the difference is subtracted from the amount a person is able to shelter from federal estate taxes at death. This amount is currently $600,000.

For example, if a mother gives $100,000 to her daughter in one year, $90,000 of that is taxable (remember, the first $10,000 avoids gift tax consideration). The mother will not pay a tax on that $90,000, however, unless she has used up her entire lifetime exclusion amount of $600,000. This gift reduces that amount to $510,000, assuming no other prior taxable gifts (gifts made in the past that are subject to tax but not necessarily taxed). The $600,000 credit can be used up with a series of large lifetime gifts, and many people may not have any of that amount left at death. That is why lifetime giving is a form of estate planning.

## Lifetime Trusts

A third way to transfer assets is by using an irrevocable or revocable trust established during a person's lifetime. This is usually called an *intervivos trust*, "intervivos" meaning "during life." A charitable remainder trust is a good example of using an irrevocable lifetime trust to transfer assets. As with ownership and contracts, a trust established during life takes precedence over a will in directing property to another party.

## Contracts

A fourth way to transfer assets is by contract, such as life insurance. Life insurance is a contract between the insured person and the insurance company to pay a stated amount to a designated beneficiary. A will cannot change this contract unless the beneficiary is dead and the secondary beneficiary is the estate of the deceased insured person. For example, examine what happens if a person names her son as the primary beneficiary and his wife, her daughter-in-law, as the secondary beneficiary of her life insurance policy, and the son divorces his wife. He then dies and before his mother can change the secondary beneficiary *she* dies. The result is most undesirable: Because a contract is in force, her former daughter-in-law receives the life insurance proceeds, even though she is probably the last person the deceased woman would have wanted to help. The insurance proceeds do not pass through probate. Another example of a contract that passes assets at death is an Individual Retirement Account.

## Ownership

The way assets are owned also determines how they are transferred to others. Jointly owned property is common between married couples. At the death of one spouse, jointly owned property passes automatically to the other and it does not go through probate. Although the rules vary from state to state, the following could happen: A mother might promise her daughter that the daughter, as opposed to the woman's second husband, will receive the house at her death, the daughter will not receive it if the house is jointly owned by the mother and her second husband. It does not matter that the will says otherwise. As with the other two nonprobate death-time transfer methods, how an asset is owned takes precedence over what is said in a will.

## Overview

Estate planning is a complex process, and saving taxes is only one consideration. Except for the annual exclusion for gifts up to $10,000 ($20,000 when spouses split their gifts) and the current $600,000 lifetime exclusion, all assets not left to a spouse or charity are subject to tax upon their transfer; and the estate tax on assets left to a spouse is merely delayed, not avoided. The most important matters in estate planning are personal, not technical. The person should ask herself to whom she wants her assets to go, when she wants the beneficiaries to receive the assets, and in what amounts. When those objectives have been decided, an attorney should be able to determine how to best achieve those objectives with care given to drafting legally enforceable documents as well as with a keen eye on saving taxes.

## THE GENERATION SKIPPING TRANSFER TAX

The founders of this country revolted against aristocracy and royalty. They determined, through the Constitution, that the people would never be subject to laws made by others without the consent of the majority. Part of the modern thinking to keep things fair is that passing assets from one generation to the next is a privilege, not a right; wealthy people are not to be able to pass their wealth from one generation to the next and then to the next without a tax on that privilege. The estate tax and the generation skipping transfer tax are taxes on the privilege of transferring assets at death to others, generally from one generation to another.

In the past, many wealthy people, whose children were already provided for, wanted to transfer assets to their grandchildren. But passing the assets through their children would subject those assets to two rounds of taxation, once when they were transferred to the children and then again when those children transferred assets to their children. Why not establish a generation-skipping trust—providing income to the children for their lives and the principal to the grandchildren—and avoid, or skip, the tax on the intervening generation? The math was compelling. Assuming that a person has $100 million and, upon death, wants to transfer it all to his children, he would pay an estate tax of 55 percent (currently); $55 million goes to the government and $45 million goes to the children. Assuming no increase in value, when the children die and pass along the $45 million to their children, the original person's grandchildren receive only 45 percent of that, or $20.2 million, and the government receives an additional $24.8 million. This is a reduction of almost 80 percent. By skipping the middle generation, the amount transferred to the grandchildren would be almost doubled, and the government would receive much less. In practice, this also could work with property. A person who owns land could establish a life-estate—giving the right to live on the property to the child—and then provide for the passing of the asset to the grandchild when the child dies. The asset would be taxed in the estate of the grandparent and in the estate of the grandchild at death, but not in the estate of the parent. This would avoid tax in one generation.

The federal government feels this tax-avoiding transfer of wealth too closely resembles aristocracy, so it now imposes a tax on the privilege of skipping that generation. Thus, we have the Generation Skipping Transfer (GST) tax. Each person receives a $1-million exemption (married couples are able to split their gifts, effectively creating a maximum of $2 million per couple, similar to the outright gift-splitting provision described earlier in this chapter); beyond that, everything transferred to grandchildren (or other "skip" generations) is taxed at the highest estate tax rate, which is currently 55 percent.

The GST tax can be a factor in establishing a charitable remainder trust or a gift annuity where the income beneficiary or annuitant is a grandchild. The GST tax is more frequently a problem, however, with the charitable lead trust, partly because the asset's remainderman is often a grandchild. Charitably inclined people with substantial family wealth are likely to be interested in establishing a charitable lead trust because of the reduced valuation of the asset ultimately transferred to heirs. Because those heirs are often grandchildren, the GST tax is a problem. A high payout from the trust reduces the taxable value, but it also reduces the actual amount transferred to the grandchildren. Donors who establish a charitable lead trust and wish to take advantage of the $1-million exemption ($2 million for married couples) will reduce or exhaust their exclusion for other transfers to their grandchildren. Although the computations to determine the amount subject to GST tax are complex and the legal implications for a donor are certainly the domain of professional legal advisers, planned giving officers need to be aware of how the GST works and its effect on a donor's estate plans.

## PAYING GIFT AND ESTATE TAXES

Even though the tax rates for gifts and estates are the same—they are called the *uniform tables* and the rates are found in Internal Revenue Code Section 2001(c)—most people do not realize that a gift tax can be much smaller than an estate tax. Although this is counterintuitive, it is simply the difference between dividing and multiplying.

A donor was thinking of establishing a charitable lead trust when he was told about a gift tax liability. The lead trust would have been large, just over $25 million, and $5 million of gift taxes would have been due on the $10 million present value of the remainder interest of the lead trust. The donor decided not to make the gift because of the tax. He preferred to have his estate pay the taxes on the transfer of the asset. This was an unfortunate decision for both the charity and the donor.

The person reasoned that the tax would be the same either way, so he decided to wait. But the wait cost him because he did not understand the difference between the mathematics of transfers during life and death. If a person transfers an asset worth $10 million to his child during his life at the 55 percent tax rate, he will pay $5.5 million (55 percent) in taxes. He must part with a total of $15.5 million, the $10 million gift to his child and the $5.5 million tax to the government. Trying to delay this tax, he may decide to wait until death to make the transfer. But the cost of waiting is great. To transfer that $10 million to his child upon his death, he parts with over $22 million. An estate tax of 55 percent on $22 million is slightly over $12 million; when this is subtracted from $22 million, only $10 million remains. In this second situation, his assets are lumped together at death, then an estate tax is imposed on the right to transfer those assets, and finally the asset is transferred. In the first case (the gift tax), an amount to be transferred is determined and then a tax is calculated; in the second case (the estate tax), a tax is levied, and then, what is left is transferred. It is not just a question of how the pie is divided, but how much larger the pie needs to be in the first place.

Another way to tackle this problem is to think of a paycheck. If a person is thinking of taking a new job in an expensive city, he might think of his desired salary in terms of what he can spend. Let's say he wants to take home—as opposed to earn—$100,000. In a 25 percent tax bracket, to calculate the amount required to do that, we need to divide the $100,000 by 75 percent (that is, 1 minus the 25% tax bracket, the tax bracket's reciprocal), which equals $133,333. The amount of $133,333 is bigger than $100,000 by about 33 percent, not 25 percent, although the tax is only 25 percent. This is because we start out with a need to determine a tax before we get to the available money, as we do with the estate tax. We must *divide* the amount by the reciprocal of the tax bracket. On the other hand, if we started out with a known amount and were taxed on that amount, we would *multiply* the amount by the tax and add the two together. Gift taxes are calculated the latter way. Even though the gift and estate tax *rates* are the same, determining a gift tax—by multiplying the asset value by the tax rate—is always less than determining an estate tax—by dividing the asset value by the tax rate.

The gift tax formula to determine the total needed to transfer an amount to another person is:

$$D = A \times (1 + B)$$

The estate tax formula to determine the same amount is:

$$D = A / (1 - B)$$

where: $A$ = Amount transferred to another person
$B$ = The transfer tax rate
$C$ = The amount transferred to the government
$D$ = The total amount needed for the transfer to the government and the other person

To avoid paying more taxes, the person should have made the lead trust gift.

# CHAPTER EIGHT

# Did You Say Something About an Appraisal?

*What is a cynic? A man who knows the price of everything and the value of nothing.*

Oscar Wilde

If you think of an appraisal as a way to determine the worth of something, and if that value is deductible, you can understand the IRS's interest in appraisals. For years, the IRS grappled with the value of objects donated to charity. In 1984, the year before the current appraisal rules went into effect, the IRS's Art Advisory Panel reviewed over 1,400 charitable gifts of art and determined that a little more than 1,000 of them had been overvalued. Of these, the *average* overvaluation of the gifts was 240 percent. For example: If a person donated a painting he valued at $340,000, the panel reduced the value for tax deduction purposes to $100,000. The summary prepared by the IRS did not include information on an additional 70 gifts that required further examination, gifts that in all probability were also overvalued according to the IRS.

## FAIR MARKET VALUE

We start with the most basic fact of all: fair market value. As defined in Federal Treasury Regulation Section 1.170A-1(c)(2), it is "the price at which the property would change hands between a willing buyer and a willing seller, neither being under any compulsion to buy or sell and both having a reasonable knowledge of the relevant facts." When someone sells her house, its value is often determined not by what she thinks it is worth or even by what she paid for it, but by what the market will bear. An asking price of $400,000 is meaningless if the house ultimately sells for $300,000. The value of that house is determined in large part by what someone else thinks it is worth, in this case the combination of a willing seller and a willing buyer.

What if the house has a leaky oil tank under its front yard, and the seller knows this but the buyer does not? This fact, if known by the buyer, who has three young children who love to play in the dirt in the front yard, would change the buyer's view of the home's value. The property may be worth only $100,000 now, or even less, depending on the severity of the problem and the expected amount of money required to clean it up. In this case, the buyer did not have a reasonable knowledge of the relevant facts, so its $300,000 "value" is inaccurate. People need to know what they are getting when they buy something.

Conversely—and more happily for homeowners—a house's value can rise if more than one person wants it. A bidding war may erupt. If the house is placed on the market for $400,000 but has a beautiful view of the ocean, someone may immediately agree to pay the asking price. But if someone else comes along and says that he would gladly pay $500,000, the house then becomes worth that amount. The price at which something sells—when the buyer and the seller know what is happening—is the strongest indicator of its value.

Now consider a situation where a seller *must* sell. The executor of an estate needs cash to pay estate taxes and must sell property to raise the money. The IRS requires that the estate tax bill be paid within nine months of the date of death. If the buyer knew that fact, she might offer less than the amount asked by the executor. In this case, time works against the seller, who is, in effect, forced to sell the property. The seller is under a compulsion to sell, and a lower selling price in this situation does not mean that the "value" is lower.

## The Appraisal Rules

The appraisal rules, which went into effect in 1985, were created to prevent valuation abuses by donors. They are complex. A person who takes a deduction over $500 for a noncash gift of property must complete the front side of IRS Form 8283, which explains what the gift is, its cost basis, its value, and how the value was determined. If the gift is over $5,000, a qualified appraisal (see Exhibit 8.1a) must be conducted, and its results must be reported on the back page of Form 8283, the appraisal summary form, when the donor sends in her tax return. Gifts valued between $500 and $5,000 do not need a qualified appraisal, and the second part of Form 8283 does not need to be completed for those gifts. There are three general exceptions to the $5,000 rule:

---

### A QUALIFIED APPRAISAL:

1. Must be made not earlier than 60 days before the date of gift or later than the day the tax return upon which the tax deduction is first claimed is timely filed (including extensions and amended returns)
2. Is prepared and signed by a qualified appraiser
3. Includes the information required
4. Does not involve a prohibited fee, such as a percentage of the appraised value of the property

### A QUALIFIED APPRAISAL REQUIRES THE FOLLOWING INFORMATION:

1. A detailed description of the property
2. The physical condition of tangible personal property
3. The date of contribution
4. Any deal made between the donor and the charity for selling the property
5. Information on the appraiser
6. The qualifications of the appraiser
7. A statement that the appraisal was prepared for income tax purposes
8. The date of the appraisal
9. The value of the property on the date it was contributed
10. The method used to determine the value
11. The specific basis for valuation

---

**Exhibit 8.1a**   Qualified Appraisal Requirements

*Source*: Section 1.176A-13(c) of the Federal Tax Regulations.

- Gifts of publicly traded stocks that are found readily on the stock exchanges. If the gift is valued at more than $500 the front part of Form 8283 must be completed and submitted to the IRS, but no appraisal is needed because their value is not in question.
- Gifts of privately held stock. No qualified appraisal is needed unless their value is claimed to be in excess of $10,000, presumably because the value of stock not publicly traded is so difficult to determine.
- Gifts of art valued at $20,000 or more. Donors must complete Form 8283 and under current law must provide a *complete copy of the appraisal* and, upon request from the IRS, a color photograph or slide of the artwork.

---

### A QUALIFIED APPRAISER IS SOMEONE WHO:

1. Holds himself or herself out to the public as an appraiser or performs appraisals on a regular basis
2. Is qualified to make appraisals of the type of property being valued
3. Is not a person excluded from the definition of qualified appraisers (see below)
4. Understands that a fraudulent overstatement of value will result in civil penalties

### A QUALIFIED APPRAISER IS NOT:

1. The donor
2. A party to the transaction in which the donor acquired the property, such as a real estate agent
3. The charity
4. Anyone employed by or related to the donor, a party to the transaction, or the charity
5. Anyone who is regularly used by the donor, a party to the transaction, or the charity, or who does not perform a majority of her appraisals for others

---

**Exhibit 8.1b**   Qualified Appraiser Requirements

*Source*: Section 1.170A-13(c) of the Federal Tax Regulations.

Qualified appraisals must conform to stringent guidelines, the most important of which are summarized in Exhibit 8.1a. A donor cannot pass off to the IRS a one-page description of property written by a real estate agent as a qualified appraisal. After Congress calculated how much money was lost each year on overvalued gift estimates, it mandated that the Treasury Department make the appraisal rules comprehensive; although they are at times ambiguous, they are more specific and thorough than the rules prior to 1986.

## THE PROBLEM WITH LAND

Despite the thoroughness of the appraisal rules, problems still persist. Determining the value of something not on the stock market or at the deli is an inexact science. Land is a particularly difficult asset to value. Take the case of a home whose presumed value is one amount and the selling price is another amount. The problem can be illustrated when the ultimate selling price is lower than the appraised price.

Land and homes on Squam Lake in New Hampshire are expensive, especially since *On Golden Pond* was filmed there in the early 1980s. Alan Ennico and his wife Ruth (whose gift was described in Chapters 2 and 4), with all the right charitable motives, decided they wanted to put their summer home in a charitable remainder unitrust so they could make a gift and turn non-income-producing property on which they paid property taxes into a growing income for the rest of their lives. The need for simplicity now forces a more generic, although similar, situation.

On September 1, a qualified appraisal determined the value of the home to be $1,000,000. The cost basis—generally the amount the donor paid for the property plus any improvements—was low because the father of one of the donors had given his son the property in the 1960s. At the time the father purchased the land, a little after World War II ended, it cost about $20,000. Although the land was worth $100,000 when the father gave it to his son in 1962, the son's cost basis was the much lower $20,000 because gifts transferred during life retain the cost basis of the person who gives property to another person. Thus, selling the land and then reinvesting the proceeds would have been expensive for the donor. The capital gains tax would have been about $250,000 (the 28 percent maximum capital gains tax multiplied by the gain of $980,000). This would have left only $750,000 to be invested. A 5 percent income from $750,000 is $37,500. Property given to fund a unitrust can be reinvested without paying a capital gains tax because the trust is tax exempt, so a 5 percent income from the $1,000,000 trust would generate $50,000. The property was donated to a net-income unitrust paying 5% annually on October 1, 30 days after the appraisal was conducted, complying with the rule requiring appraisals to be conducted not more than 60 days before the gift. By making the gift the donors would get the full million dollars to work for them.

At least theoretically. One million dollars is what the appraisal said the property was worth, but the true test comes on the open market. When land prices have fallen, even the charm of Squam Lake does not rub off on everyone. By March of the following year, the only interest was from someone willing to pay $500,000, half the appraised price. The charity, acting as trustee, did not want to sell the property for less than its full value, but the planned giving officer was rightfully concerned about the income that was *not* being paid to the donors. When generating the computer printouts to show the donor couple the increase in income each year, he had not taken into account the possibility that they might receive less than the appraised value.

"I'm calling to let you know about an offer we just received," said the planned giving officer to the donors. "It's $500,000."

An audible gasp on the other end of the line indicated that the donors were not receiving the low offer with grace. "But I thought the appraisal said it was worth a million dollars."

The planned giving officer took this to mean that they did not want to accept the offer. "I don't want to take it either, but I wanted to let you know because you still aren't receiving any income from the gift. We had thought the first payment might be on January 1." After digesting the news, the donors agreed to wait for a better offer.

Summer arrived before another serious offer was made. The real estate agent was excited when she called the planned giving officer to tell him the news that someone had offered $750,000 for the property. After many sobering discussions during the past several months, the planned giving officer was glad to report this to the donors.

"Only $750,000?" they asked. They were again disappointed. This is what is meant by donor relations, the planned giving officer decided.

"After talking with the real estate agent, I would seriously consider the offer."

## Why Consult the Donors?

Before looking at the effects of accepting the offer, another question arises. Why is a planned giving officer who works for a charity that serves as trustee of this gift worried about what the donors think? After all, the donors have no legal right to control the sales price. The charity may sell the property for any amount. Why not sell the property at whatever price the charity can get and simply let the donors know later?

There may be a few good reasons why the donors should be consulted in this situation. First, as the planned giving officer has already thought, this is a case of donor relations. The charity would lose a good deal of credibility if after accepting a qualified appraisal for $1,000,000, they then sold the property quickly for much less than that value. Although the charity might not be taken to court on this matter, the donors could create public relations problems for the charity by speaking ill of the charity's ability to manage the process of accepting charitable remainder trusts. And a court date is not out of the question; dissatisfied, litigiously oriented donors might make a case in court that the charity handled its fiduciary responsibilities poorly by improperly selling property for less than its value.

When the land is sold is less important to the charity than to the donors, who in this case are the income beneficiaries, because no income is paid until the trust has money; remember, the property funds a net-income unitrust. Solely from its financial perspective, the charity does not care how soon the property is sold. In fact, if it is never sold during the donors' lifetimes the charity would not experience any financial problems with the gift; the net-income unitrust pays nothing to the income beneficiaries until the land is sold. The charity, having every motive for receiving the highest value for the gift, despite the income expected by the donors, would love nothing more than to receive the appraised value or even more. The donors are confronted with the risk of waiting, not knowing what will eventually be offered, against the risk of accepting a low price, which generates a lower-than-expected income.

So, donor relations aside, why not wait until the appraised price is offered? The charity has two economic reasons to sell the property. First, the asking price may never be offered. Cash in the trust is much better than a promise, and until the property is sold, the only asset in the trust is hope. Surely the land will sell someday, but no one knows for how much. The inexact science of appraising is made evident no more clearly than in the process of transforming a written evaluation into something more substantial. Second, the sooner the charity sells the asset, the sooner it can invest the money. Although land historically rises in value, most investment-minded people would prefer to have a diversified portfolio, invested broadly to hedge against inflation as well as deflation. A trust whose only asset is land is risky from an investor's perspective.

Of course, the donor relations issue is important, and the charity must measure its long-term objectives against those of the donors. In general they are the same: Both want the highest value for the property. But the donors expect an income, at least someday, and because a planned gift establishes a lifetime partnership, their needs are also important to the charity. After a long discussion with the donors, the planned giving officer accepts the $750,000 offer. On September 1, exactly one year after the appraisal was conducted, the charity, as trustee of the charitable remainder unitrust, willingly sells the property to a willing buyer, both of whom have a reasonable knowledge of the relevant facts and neither of whom is under any compulsion to buy or sell. The buyer wants a nice summer home and the unitrust wants liquidity. There is no oil tank, and the lakeshore property is beautiful. The noisy neighbors (alas) whose existence is known by neither the buyer nor the seller prior to the sale, are not relevant facts.

## The Home's True Value

What is the value of the home? One million dollars or $750,000? It depends. For the donors' deduction purposes, it is $1,000,000. For the real estate agent, for the unitrust, for the rest of the world, and as a general indicator of prices on Squam Lake, the home's value is $750,000. This is where things can get a little awkward. The first part of the $400,000 deduction—the approximate IRS-calculated remainder value for two people in their fifties establishing a 5 percent unitrust with an asset worth $1,000,000—was claimed in the prior year; after all, the gift was made then and the appraisal was qualified. But shouldn't the deduction be modified to reflect the sales price?

No, according to many attorneys who have considered this question. If the appraisal was qualified, then the donors should stick to their guns and maintain that the property was worth $1,000,000 on the date of the gift. The IRS regulations do say "the appraisal fair market value of the property on the date (or expected date) of contribution." The clause "or expected date" is relevant in this situation because the appraisal was conducted within 60 days before the gift was made; at the time of the appraisal the date of gift was unknown. If the qualified appraisal says the property was worth $1,000,000 on September 1 and the gift is made on October 1, that value should apply, even if the sales price a year later is lower than the appraised value. This would be equally true if the sales price were higher than the appraised value. The IRS probably would not accept an amended return claiming a higher deduction because the property sold for more than its appraised value.

## IRS Form 8282

Most likely, the IRS will eventually know the property's sales price. This is because Form 8282, the companion of Form 8283, must be filed when the property is sold. Officially entitled Form 8282, it has become known informally, yet usefully, as the "tattletale" form. Form 8282 must be completed and sent to the IRS (1) when any property is sold or otherwise disposed of within two years of the date of gift; and (2) for gifts for which the second side of Form 8283 (the appraisal summary side) was completed and signed by a representative of the charity. The charity has 125 days from the date of sale or disposition of the asset to file Form 8282. The gift was made on October 1 of one year and the home was sold on September 1 of the following year, an eleven-month span. The IRS can challenge the appraisal, claiming it was too high, but it probably will not do so solely on the basis that the property sold for $750,000; it would have to successfully contest the validity of the appraisal to win its argument that the property was overvalued for tax-avoidance purposes.

## The Donors' Income

The appraised value has other consequences as well. The donors think, at first anyway, that they have made a gift from which they will receive a 5 percent annual income. The planned giving officer has been honest about the possibility of a delay in the income, but he never fully explained how the income might be less than expected. In fact, he told the donors that they would ultimately receive any income lost during the time the property was for sale. He was describing a net-income uni-trust with a makeup provision. This is typically known as a "Type 2" unitrust and sometimes as a *net income with makeup charitable remainder unitrust* (NIMCRUT). The trust will pay out only the income up to the stated percentage; it cannot invade principal. If the actual income is less than the stated percentage in the trust, the donors receive the lesser amount. When this happens, the trust administrator keeps track of that amount, annually and cumulatively. The makeup provision means that if, in any year, the trust income is higher than the stated percentage amount, it may pay more than that percent as long as it does not exceed the trust's total deficit—the amount "owed" to the donors. Unfortunately, although the donors are led to expect to recover what the planned giving officer characterizes to them as lost income, making up income is difficult and exacts a price.

Exhibit 8.2 shows a partially realistic situation. The deficit is not made up, at least not in the first three years. The problem is that the donors' expectations are based on the appraised value. Even though no income was generated in the first year, the trust had a value, $1,000,000. This is the amount on which the deficit during that first year is calculated. By the second year, when the property is sold, the value is reduced to whatever remains in the trust. Also, in the second and third years, the trust earns 5 percent income.

## Selling Costs

In this case, the amount funding the trust is not $750,000 but $700,000. This is because, although the sales price was $750,000 and the buyer parted with that amount, sales commissions and other expenses, including

| Year | Trust Value | Trust Income | Annual Deficit | Cumulative Deficit |
|---|---|---|---|---|
| 1 | $1,000,000 | 0 | $50,000 | $50,000 |
| 2 | $ 700,000 | $35,000 | $ 0 | $50,000 |
| 3 | $ 700,000 | $35,000 | $ 0 | $50,000 |

**Exhibit 8.2** How the Trust Value Affects the Income and the Deficit

A simplified view of how the deficit is created when the net-income unitrust is not immediately liquid.

| Year | Trust Value | Trust Income | Annual Deficit | Cumulative Deficit |
|------|-------------|--------------|----------------|--------------------|
| 1 (partial) | $1,000,000 | 0 | $12,500 | $12,500 |
| 2 (full) | $1,000,000 | $11,550 | $38,450 | $50,950 |
| 3 | $ 700,000 | $35,000 | $ 0 | $50,950 |
| 4 | $ 700,000 | $35,000 | $ 0 | $50,950 |

**Exhibit 8.3**   How the Trust Value Affects the Income and the Deficit

A realistic view of the income and deficit, taking into account two fiscal years of a $1,000,000 value.

closing and transfer costs, are subtracted before the trust is finally funded with assets that can be invested to produce an income. As noted the situation described in Exhibit 8.2 is only partially realistic. More likely, the $1,000,000 value would be shown for the first *two* fiscal years of the trust. The gift was made on October 1, so for the rest of that year the trust was worth $1,000,000. Then, on January 1 of the following year, well before the property is sold, the trust enters its second fiscal year. Even though the trust is liquid with $700,000 on September 1 of that second year, the trust was valued eight months earlier, on January 1 of that year, and was not valued again until the following January 1, the beginning of the trust's third fiscal year. Then, and only then, will the trust's value reflect the liquidity in it. Exhibit 8.3 is more accurate.

The $12,500 deficit in the first year—the partial year—equals one-quarter of $50,000. If the gift had been made on January 1 of the first year, the deficit would have been $50,000, but only three months—one-quarter of the year—remained on the October 1 date of gift. Thus, the trust "owes" the donors only one-quarter of the annual $50,000. The trust income during the second year—the first full year—is the amount paid when the trust is liquid with $700,000 in it. Five percent of that amount is $35,000, but the trust is liquid for only four months of the year, September, October, November, and December. Four months is one-third of the year and one-third of $35,000 is $11,550. But even though the trust is liquid with $700,000 that year and afterwards earns income of 5 percent, the $35,000 number is not the important number. This is because the trust was valued at $1,000,000. Remember, the trust is valued again on the first day of its second year, even though that date in this case is only three months from the date of gift. That $1,000,000 value is valid for that whole second year, and the income deficit is calculated against it. Five percent of $1,000,000 is $50,000, but the trust paid out only $11,550, leaving the second year's deficit at $38,450. The cumulative deficit is $50,950.

In reality the $50,950 will probably never be made up, despite what the planned giving officer told the donors. At least, it *should* never be made up. Refer to Chapter 6 for a thorough discussion on this point.

## PREARRANGED SALES

Of course, no prearranged deal can take place, even if an appraisal seems otherwise qualified. That is, the donor cannot already have found the buyer of the property and arranged a sale before the trust is established. The IRS dimly views such a transaction, taking the position that the gift was not really a gift but an arrangement to avoid a capital gains tax. If the IRS is successful at proving its case, the donor is liable for the capital gains tax that would otherwise have been owed (as well as any interest and penalties). If, for example, a property with an appraised value of $2,000,000 and a cost basis of $100,000 is donated to a unitrust, the donor avoids paying the tax on the capital gain of $1,900,000. At a 28 percent rate, the capital gains tax would be $582,000—a lot of money for the IRS to forgo.

No one knows when the line defining *too close* is crossed, but we do know that a purchase and sale agreement is far too close. In that situation, the donor finds a buyer who agrees to a price and is ready to pay. The IRS considers that a sale and not a gift. But what if a donor knows a person who might buy the property? Is that too close? Deciding that is more difficult but planning remains the underlying consideration; the sale must not be prearranged. This means that it can't be decided in writing *or otherwise* before the unitrust is established. Just because it is not written down does not mean that it is not prearranged.

### The Secret Deal

One can imagine a person talking to a potential buyer of his property. They are alone in the elevator of a public building, engaged in the following conversation:

SELLER: I think I'm about ready to sell the property to you.

BUYER: For how much, did you say?

SELLER: Two million dollars.

BUYER: That's what we discussed.

SELLER: But first, I'm giving it away.

BUYER: What? I thought we had a deal!

SELLER: Relax! We do. I just want to put it into a charitable trust so I don't have to pay a half million dollars in capital gains taxes.

BUYER: Are you sure this is legal?

SELLER: I don't know for certain, but I don't think so. If the IRS knew about this I'd be in big trouble. The way I figure it, though, is that I can earn more income from the trust—once you've bought the property—than I could not using a charity and paying capital gains tax.

BUYER: Well, whatever you say. All I want is the property. I can earn a fortune by building apartments on it. Are you sure I'll be able to get it?

SELLER: Don't worry. I'm acting as co-trustee with the charity, so no sale will take place without my approval. I'll just approve your offer.

BUYER: Do you think I'll have to wait to buy the property?

SELLER: No. That's the beauty of it all. I got the appraisal and it says the property is worth $2,000,000, the amount you came up with in your own assessment. The appraisal's a technical IRS requirement to make the gift legal. But I don't think it's legal to make the deal before the land goes into the trust. That's why you can't say anything about it.

BUYER: Okay. But I'd like to get this going as soon as possible.

SELLER: You're ready to go then?

BUYER: In the bank and ready to go.

SELLER: Great. It's a deal. I'll leave on the third floor and walk down the other two flights of stairs. You go on down to the lobby alone. That way no one will see us together.

The IRS wants to avoid this situation. Your donors do, too. The IRS is adamant about making sure that no sale is disguised as a gift so the donor can illegally avoid paying capital gains taxes.

## THE AUDIT

If the IRS thinks that something is amiss in the gift-making process, it will do whatever it can to determine what happened. One can only imagine the following audit, performed well after the gift was made, where a donor tried to avoid the capital gains tax.

"But I'm telling you there *was* a qualified appraisal!"

John Davidson, who two years ago donated a piece of land to the County Hospital, sat frustrated across the small table situated between him and Norman Rivard, the IRS agent conducting the audit.

"There was, was there? Well, we'll see about that. The first thing that disturbs me, Mr. Davidson, is that you say the hospital paid for the appraisal. You should know that the Federal Government considers that a problem."

"But they said. . . ."

"It doesn't matter what 'they' said, Mr. Davidson," his voice stern and steady. "You—not they—are being audited today. And besides, who paid for the appraisal is the least of my problems with this charitable gift."

"You have other problems?" John knew that the gift, as well as the process of making it, was valid. He bought the land from his father in 1970, two years before his father's death. They had acquired an appraisal then to determine its value so that the ensuing sale did not constitute in any way a gift from father to son. The cost was $47,300 for 137 acres of prime property that would become of great interest to real estate developers. "What are they?"

"It seems you were able to avoid a capital gain and a corresponding tax."

Now John was truly perplexed. He knew—hadn't the planned giving director at the hospital assured him?—that donors avoid a capital gains tax when they make gifts to charity. This land had been put into a trust of some sort. A trust that had paid him income for the last two years, and whose assets would someday go to the hospital. John responded with bravado. "Look, I know about that. I can tell you I avoided that capital gains tax fair and square."

"Then maybe you'd like to explain how the land was sold so soon." Here, the IRS agent deliberately slowed his next nine words. "And for so much after the gift was made."

"What do you mean by that? The sale price was exactly equal to the appraised value."

"Exactly my problem, Mr. Davidson. This one doesn't pass what we affectionately call around here the 'smell' test." John looked puzzled. "Don't know what I mean by that, do you? I mean, Mr. Davidson, that something smells rotten about this.

"Let me put it this way. You made the gift on August 22, 1994 to a charitable remainder unitrust. And on August 30, just eight days later, the trustee, who according to this document is you, conveniently sold the land to the Mountain View Construction Company, Inc. for two million dollars." He said the word "million" as if it had only four letters in it. "Doesn't that smell a little fishy to you, Mr. Davidson?"

"No," was all John could come up with. He didn't like where this was heading, but he was hanging on to his confidence.

"No? Well, it looks like you and these Mountain View people had a little deal cooked up before the gift was made. And then you decided you wanted to make a little gift to a charity you'd given *no* money to before then just to avoid paying a tax of—let's see. . . ." He pushed several numbers into an old but fully functional calculator. "Yes, a capital gains tax of $546,756." A pause as the two men looked across the table at one another. Neither said a word for 15 seconds. "That's, of course, assuming your remainder value deduction is accurate. And that the appraisal is valid. Which, I can almost guarantee you, isn't."

"Now, look, I'm getting just a little tired of your attitude. What makes you think the appràisal isn't valid? I just told you, and I can prove it, that the appraiser did a good job. What's your problem?"

"Perhaps the chief indicator is the fact that these Mountain View boys signed over a check for two million dollars—the appraisal amount to the penny—to the trust a week after the gift." The government agent stared at the private citizen. "I don't believe in coincidences, Mr. Davidson."

"What do you mean?" John's confidence was waning. "I'd like to know just what you're getting at." A frown developed on John's forehead and a trickle of sweat began to form on his left brow. "Look, I'm not trying to do anything wrong here. How could I have known that? I took a legitimate deduction. Honest." The word "honest" was sounding a little hollow at this point.

The IRS agent, who had returned to his review of the papers before him, looked up. He stared at John for almost 30 seconds, each second ticking slower than the last for John, when the representative of the most powerful and autonomous collection agency in the country finally voiced words that would stay etched in John's mind for a long time, words that took away any hope he had of avoiding paying an additional several hundred thousand dollars in taxes. Plus interest and penalties. "Really? Mr. Davidson, you wouldn't believe how many times I hear that. Every day."

Rivard sat upright in his chair, pushed the papers aside and then sat forward with his hands folded in front of him. His attention was fully on John. "Do you want to know something else? It seems your sister, one Joanna Terullo, is a major stockholder in the Mountain View Construction Company." He then added "Inc." for emphasis. "Do you want to know what else I think? I think Mountain View had a few extra dollars in the kitty and needed to avoid both taxes on profits and some taxes on retained earnings. So it would work out for both of you. Nice and tidy. What do you think of that, Mr. Davidson?"

John was too stunned to think at that moment. Otherwise he would have been concerned about how closely connected the appraiser, as an employee of the Mountain View Construction Company, was to the transaction. He knew the rules at first glance would allow a person unconnected with him or the hospital to be a qualified appraiser, but given the plan he and his sister had devised, he knew the IRS would have a field day with that. But none of this concerned John right now because he was trying to figure out how the IRS knew his sister, and not his college roommate, was the real stockholder.

The game was up, and John Everett Davidson knew it. It would only be a matter of cross-checking the corporate returns with each of the employees' returns, and then comparing those with his own 1040. Then the questions would begin on how the transaction was made so soon after the gift. Rivard was right. And how many times had Davidson heard that the IRS didn't know this stuff—the hospital called it planned giving—very well? That it was so complicated that the IRS usually simply accepted the transaction.

Rivard said, "Mr. Davidson, based on what I just calculated, taking into account the 45 percent remainder value of the gift and the gain on the sale, both of which I am going to investigate thoroughly, you are seriously in arrears to the United States Government. Your bill totals $698,000 plus change. And that doesn't include a stiff penalty and a whole lot of interest. I think it also might be a good idea for me to trundle around the Mountain View return, as well. And I think I'll take a look at the trust document, too." At that he smiled ever so slightly. He blinked slowly. He then softly observed, practically whispering, with a measured cadence, "And I'll bet you thought we wouldn't care."

## THE VALUATION PROCESS

The IRS does not attempt to deny legitimate charitable contribution deductions. The reason the valuation rules are today so strict is that prior to 1985 the IRS discovered many valuation abuses. Because valuing noncash gifts other than publicly traded stock is an inexact science, Congress authorized a method to address those abuses. That method has resulted in the appraisal requirements. Although the regulations are at times ambiguous, the method has worked well. Yet, as with almost any other tax-related transaction, imprecision in the valuation process leads to occasional abuse, an abuse the IRS understandably wants to stop or at least reduce.

Dealing with the IRS can be unpleasant. Many people have testified to that, and the ability of its relatively small force to collect taxes partly relies on that reputation. Yet an inquiry by the IRS does not have to turn into a war. Most IRS inquiries are routine or mechanical. The vast majority of appraisals are legitimate, as are the vast majority of charitable deductions. Some appraisals are not accurate, and some of those, unfortunately, are not meant to be. Nothing can absolutely prevent an audit, but knowing the appraisal rules and then following them are the best defenses against the tyranny most people fear when they realize they must deal with the IRS.

# CHAPTER NINE

# Why Can't We Get That Gift?

*We must cultivate our garden.*
**Voltaire**

## THE POPULARITY OF PLANNED GIVING

Everyone in development has instant access to technical, legislative, marketing, and other types of information on planned giving. The topic is constantly in the development news with frequent seminars and several good newsletters devoted exclusively to planned giving. As a result, charities are learning a great deal about planned giving. Not only development officers read the news—so do trustees, executive directors, administrators, and presidents. They receive their own mail on planned giving and many times will ask the development or planned giving director about what plans the charity has to raise money through planned gifts. Because of increasing competition and more scrutiny surrounding the separation of money from donors, planned giving enjoys an elite status in the world of raising money. Unfortunately, some people read information on planned giving, see that the annual fund is not growing as it should, and then think that planned giving is the answer to the charity's financial problems. Who could blame them? With articles featuring the tax and income benefits to the donor, readers cannot be faulted for supposing that the only thing separating the charity from the donor's assets is asking for the planned gift.

## THE RELATIONSHIP BETWEEN CULTIVATION AND FUND-RAISING

Unfortunately, far too many board and staff members spend far too little time understanding their charities' missions and their constituencies.

Not unusual is the exchange at a development committee meeting of the Southern Environmental Agency, where the trustees anxiously discuss the issue of raising more money.

"You know," says one of the several trustees attending the meeting on an upper floor of a Houston skyscraper, "I read in the *Chronicle* today that Rice University received a multi-million-dollar gift last week." He looks around the room, most pointedly at the director of development, so that without saying anything everyone knows he is really asking why this particular charity is unable to do the same thing. "It says the gift was part of a capital campaign."

The room stays uncomfortably silent because, although it would be ridiculous to imagine a gift of that magnitude in this charity's future, the implied question's logic is skewed. Trying to equate one charity's success with another's is difficult because each has its own constituency, history, and mission. Also, some are larger and have better fund-raising efforts. Finally, the director of development responds, "Well, John, we really don't know what led up to that gift, do we?"

"What do you mean?"

"I suppose we could find out, but my guess is that the people at Rice probably have been working on this guy for some time now. I saw the article, too, and it didn't say anything—these articles never do, of course—about the cultivation period, or how many visits it took from how many people, or what other assets the donor had. Or what the donor's motivation was. All it said was that the donor was a graduate of the university, and that much of the gift will be left through bequests. I can tell you that the paper probably used the term 'bequest' loosely."

*I'm not really interested in your excuses, Phil.* The trustee would like to say the words but, as no such words are ever spoken at development committee meetings, he could only think them. Instead, he said, "But can't we develop a plan of action to secure these types of gifts?"

"Actually, yes."

"And?" asked the trustee, annoyed that the development director was not more forthright.

Phil was not more forthright because he knew, despite the already tense feelings in the room, that the trustee would like the conversation even less from this point forward. "We need to cultivate."

"What do you mean by that?"

"We need to educate our people better. We need to create a solid development program in which our supporters will understand our mission and want to give to support it. That costs money. I need to step up our informational mailings and better explain our needs. It requires a great deal of work, too, work I am willing to do, actually work I have been doing already. You know that, but I need yours and everyone else's assistance—all of the trustees, the executive director, and anyone else I can get on board. And, in addition to all the commitment, all of this takes time."

"What kind of time?"

"I don't know."

"You don't know." The statement was said in a way that meant the trustee could not believe he was hearing this. Of course the development director knew; he just wasn't saying so, just trying to cover himself by not being specific. Like all the other development directors before this one. This type of sparring had taken place twice before and after each encounter the trustee talked to the executive director about the development director's future employment at an institution other than the one at which he was currently spending too much time at a desk. This meeting was another example of the problem and the trustee promised himself to follow up this meeting with a call to the executive director.

"That's right. There's so much to do and who knows when we can start seeing results?" The development director did his best—actually he felt he was learning well—to contain his anger at what he considered trustee ignorance. How stupid, he thought, that anyone would compare Rice's fund-raising program to the one here. Just because the trustee was a graduate of Rice did not mean that the program here—the Southern Environmental Agency—could ever equal that of an organization that has raised money for many more years than this one has. But during meetings where such tension hung in the air, he simply endured.

"So, you basically want carte blanche to spend money on a program whose success you are unable to predict? Or even guess at?"

"Put that way, I understand where you're coming from, but that's how fund-raising works. Not in a vacuum, but as part of an entire program to further our mission. And I'm sure this Rice gift, even though the paper didn't get into this part of it, is an example of a long period of institutional commitment to development, to say nothing of how long the university cultivated the donor."

"What about Trudeau? Can't he make a gift like that? I know he's got a huge income. And the assets."

"That's true. You know that we've put together a strategy to approach him, but so far nothing. He won't even see the executive director, let alone me."

This only frustrated the trustee even further. "Well, dammit, we just don't have a lot of time. What can we do?"

Another trustee offered a thought. "Perhaps if you ask Trudeau about making a *planned* gift, that will make a difference. I've just gotten this brochure from my college and it says here that people can make enormous gifts while receiving income on their gift for the rest of their lives.

They get a tax deduction, too. A big one, according to this." The trustee looked around the room to see if anyone agreed that this might be a good strategy.

This was a meeting to assess the development effort at a nationally recognized yet poorly funded charity with an annual budget of $15,000,000 and, for the third year in a row, whose annual fund raised just under $1,000,000. Most of the other income came from dues paid by members. The endowment was small and provided little for annual expenditures.

"That still leaves the question," said the first trustee. "What do we do?"

## PLANNED GIVING IS NOT FOR ALL CHARITIES

They can forget about a planned giving program to start with. Perhaps a reorganization of priorities should be the first order of business. Despite its popularity, a program of planned giving should not be launched with the expectation that it will be a panacea for a charity's financial woes; a planned giving program must fit into an overall development effort. As Phil, the director of development, said, some charities need to grasp the more basic aspects of fund-raising. Organizations with a tiny endowment are not accustomed to asking for endowment gifts; organizations with no annual fund are not accustomed to asking for any amount of money. Thrusting a planned giving effort into the fragile mix would create unrealistic expectations and might do more damage than good. Phil is right about the need to commit resources for the right purposes. He knows that much time will pass, even under the right circumstances, before the charity will ever see a gift in the million-dollar range. Yet he also knows that the charity will *never* see one if the trustees do not support the development effort on its most fundamental levels first.

"There's a lot of work involved, and I've been doing my best at trying to identify prospects for large gifts. And we've got a few possibilities."

"Like who?"

"Well, as you say, Jay Trudeau is still a good bet. And then we've got about another ten who look pretty—"

"How good a bet?"

"I'm sorry?"

"How good a bet is Trudeau?"

"Well, according to our research, and I must admit that we haven't done as much as we'd like, he's a big supporter to his college, Carleton College in Minnesota, and if we can get him as interested in us as he is in them, he may be able to help with a deep seven-figure gift."

"But what do you *know* about him?"

"Not much actually. His company's closely held so there are no public documents certifying the value of his holdings. But articles in the *New York Times* and the *Wall Street Journal* have estimated that the company is worth at least 60 million dollars."

The trustee winced and held his look on Phil. "Why can't we tap into money like that? God knows, we need it more than a well-endowed, rich university does." He thought about what he said for a moment. Then he asked, "Okay, so what do we do?"

Phil did not answer right away. He thought about the question, one that he asked himself many times. "I don't know."

"But I thought we were paying your salary to know things like this."

"I wish I had a magic answer, something that could open the door. As I mentioned, the executive director has tried to make an appointment with him several times, but he just won't agree to meet him. He's always busy, according to his secretary." Then Phil stopped to think about saying what he had already concluded. He knew it would not rest well with anyone in the room, especially with this trustee. "Actually, I've given this a great deal of thought and I have a suggestion."

"Well, what's that?" Another trustee asked the question.

"I know this contradicts what I just said, but we're needlessly limiting ourselves to one person, a person who has done nothing so far. I think we ought to forget him."

Although no one else had been talking, a hush fell over the already quiet room. Bodies, when they are not tense, seem to have a quality of quiet sound, if not noise; the sounds of breathing and of legs being crossed are noticeable; even eyes seem to emit some sound with their alertness. But now the room became noticeably more still, almost deathlike.

"I'm sorry, but what did you say?" The talkative trustee rallied with the question in a slow monotone.

## CULTIVATION

"I know this may sound ridiculous, but I think we ought to forget about Trudeau." The development director raised his hand slightly and then rushed along to not allow interruptions. "I mean, we have other people, maybe not as well-heeled as Trudeau, but capable people nonetheless, and I think we ought to concentrate on some of them instead. At least the ones who seem to have taken more of an interest in us."

Another trustee, quiet so far, raised his head to ask, "What do you mean? A moment ago you said he was a good bet."

"Look, as much as we think Trudeau can help us, he's been pretty clear that at least for now, he doesn't want to. He's shown an interest from time to time, coming to a few dinners and making a few small gifts. But he knows why we're calling him, and he's resisting. We're never going to force him to give away any of his money. I think we ought to shift our attention to those who are more likely to help." He looked around the table to see how his comments were received. Then he added, "I don't mean we should take him off our list or anything, just broaden our search." He paused again and said something else. "Okay, I misspoke. He's still a good bet, but not for now. I just can't read him; although I'm optimistic that something will come someday, I want to expand our horizons." Finally, after talking too much because the silence made him uncomfortable, he was finished, determined to resist the discomfort.

The original trustee: "You know, of course, that we don't have much time. We're already in the red this year, and we haven't had a good year in the last five. That's why we hired you, to get us out of this mess."

## EARNING THE RIGHT TO ASK

By now, Phil was beginning to think it might be best to offer his resignation, but then he thought, _why?_ No one else is going to do a better job, and he had the best strategy, or at least he thought he did. "Well, yes, you did. But I must respectfully submit that the problem was pretty big when I got here—"

"Almost a whole year ago, I might add."

"A year ago we didn't even have a list of prospects, let alone major prospects. We also had done nothing in the way of community relations. I don't mean to sound defensive, but a lot of things have to happen before we can ask for the big gift." He paused to look around the room at the seven trustees, some of whom came a great distance to attend, and then said quietly, "We need to earn the _right_ to ask."

"Now what does that mean?"

"All I mean to say is that we have done so little in public relations that I don't feel comfortable asking for large amounts of money yet. I mean, we have yet to come through with what I think is a plausible mission statement, and our literature has been so obscure that I don't think we have done what we need to do before we can ask for the big gifts."

"But we're a national organization, and we've been around for over a hundred years. How long do we have to wait?"

"It's not the amount of time that's important, but how we've used it so far. Believe me, right now we're doing everything we can to make up for lost time, but it's going to take a while before we can ask for major gifts. And, while I'm on it, I think it's very risky for us to hope that one or two or even these ten individuals—who in the best of circumstances might make a gift—can bail us out of our financial difficulty."

The mood was somber and not even the querulous trustee was able to think of a response to what had just been said. Phil continued, "As I said, we ought to continue doing what we're doing now; that is, mailing to our constituency on a regular basis, not just fund-raising material but also clear and compelling information about all the good work we're doing. We also clearly need to identify more potential supporters, and I'm looking into direct mail programs that might be right for us. That'll cost money but the statistics show that over the long haul it's worth it."

"But we don't have a lot of extra money to spend on an activity that's not going to produce results," said another of the seven, quiet until now. "I've been listening very carefully to everything you've said, and I can see what you're saying, but where are we going to get the money to continue if we can't raise it now?"

"I think the annual drive is holding its own, actually, and I don't think that we'll go down the tubes with this if we're careful. All I'm saying is that we just can't expect large donations from people, largely because we have not put ourselves into a position to ask. Not yet anyway. Look, the endowment is about 10 million dollars. That's a lot, but not for us, so we're not getting enough income from that, really. And the consultant we hired reported last month that we were not ready for a capital campaign because we don't have enough support yet."

The understanding trustee spoke. "I don't know about the rest of you, but I think Phil has done a pretty good job so far, and what he says makes a lot of sense. We're practically starting from scratch. Remember, before Phil, we had a lot of people who stayed just a few months and it wasn't all their fault. We had a few doozies, but I suspect that we, the trustees, weren't providing the right direction for the public relations and development effort. I'd like to see us act with a little patience here, and not panic or overreact." The trustee thought about what he said and continued. "We've been spending a little of the endowment principal for the last few years, and I think we can continue to do that for another year or two, if we need to. I hate doing that, but I think it's our only option. We've cut back on staff enough—probably too much—and I don't see how we can save any more money on operations." As he said this, he also knew that this organization, in existence to do good work now for more than 100 years, could actually go out of business if things didn't improve. Despite many successes, the organization was in trouble because of years of neglect in the development department.

Phil responded. "I think you're right. This organization has a lot going for it, and we need to keep our course. That means, at least to me, and I suspect to all of you too, that we build the foundation and grow from there. As I say, we've been doing a lot of things and more people know about us today than they did even a year ago. Pretty soon, we'll be able to ask for some large gifts. And others will be putting us in their wills, but they have to be convinced that we're going to be around for a while and that our cause is worthwhile. Only then will we be able to earn the right to ask."

## THE CHARITY'S MISSION

This organization has a lot of work to do. Before large gifts come small ones. Before any gifts comes the successful message of the charity's mission. Before the message can be sent, it must be clearly understood and written by the staff and trustees. Against such a stark backdrop, fund-raising is born. But planned giving grows as an extension of an already healthy life. Only when the program is healthy can planned giving become a part of it.

The question might be, What negative impact on the community would result if the charity ceased to exist at noon tomorrow? Trustees who cannot clearly and persuasively defend their charity's existence do not fulfill the purpose of serving as trustees and do not deserve to be the caretakers of the public good. This basic idea is important not only for charities that have never had a successful fund-raising program, but for all the others that must constantly review their missions and their ability to attract funds. What would be produced if the trustees at all of the almost 600,000 charities in the United States sat down to write out an answer to the question posed above? Would more than a small percent be able to satisfactorily defend their missions, their purpose, their value to society? Maybe. Maybe not. But it's a worthwhile exercise and the success of that exercise will speak to the potential success of any effort to persuade others to support the cause with their money.

A good mission statement is clear and concise. It cannot be too long— a page or two at the most—but must accurately tell the story. Does the private school admit everyone? Or only those most academically capable? Does the hospital emphasize research? Does the conservation group allow for any compromise with tree cutters? Why support one organization and not another if their goals are similar? Most mission statements include phrases like "for the betterment of society" or "to educate with the highest principles of character" or something else equally vague. While these thoughts are noble, they are also flabby. A good ninth-grade English teacher would fail the authors of these statements on the grounds that they use big words to say nothing. Precision is everything—in the newspaper articles you read this morning, in the memo you wrote your boss yesterday, in this book—and most mission statements, the most public guide to the charity's conduct, fail the test of precision. And failing the test of precision is a clear indicator of unclear thinking.

Most charities, like most people, want to be everything to everyone. They want not to exclude. But the process of being precise is one of exclusion. The more precise about who you are, the more clear you are about who you are not. If you are short, you are not tall. If you are fat, you are not thin. If you emphasize sports, you usually do not emphasize academics. You may have room for several goals, but each is an entry on a ladder of priorities, and one must come before another. This is difficult, but it is necessary to admit what is true if you are to convey why people should support your charity. Another question to ask might be, If your charity were to do one thing, and one thing only, what would that one thing be? This is not so much an exercise in reduction but clarification. In fact, most charities do only one or two things well. In their daily lives for the most part they do a good job, and their personnel know the charity's strengths as well as its weaknesses. Before it is finally answered, the question might be posed to *all* those who work at the charity.

Concentrating on this seemingly basic issue might appear to be a far cry from planned giving or even fund-raising, but understanding a charity's mission is one of the most fundamental components of earning the right to ask others to support it. The charity whose trustees are meeting in Houston wonder why they cannot get the kind of gift Rice University has just received. It too is old. It too is established. It too does good work. What is the problem?

The problem with this group, as with many others, is that they have not taken the time to define themselves or cultivate their constituency. Despite their public recognition, they have not committed themselves to their worth to society. They sponsor educational forums throughout the United States on ways to preserve the environment, including recycling newspapers and cutting up nonbiodegradable six-pack holders so animals are prevented from strangling themselves. The group also takes special care to educate policymakers in Washington and in each of the state capitals about the effects of too much deforestation. And lately the organization has begun efforts to predict the long-range effects of ozone depletion. One hundred years ago a group of people undertook what they thought was a remarkable mission to help society, and, although the problems and the manifestation of that effort have changed during that time, the caretakers of today must remain true to that mission. The organization's worth to society—the good it does—is self-evident, but the trustees need to clarify their mission to themselves and to their supporters. They must become less flabby about their commitment before they can ask others to support it. They have never done that, although they may be about to begin. Yet the processes of defining a mission and living up to it are just that—processes. They do not happen once. In fact, they happen all the time; more precisely, they are or should be ongoing. The process of cultivation, part of living up to a mission, is more like breathing than eating, a constant backdrop to other activities. True adherence to the mission makes the fund-raising process easier and morally dignified.

So where does planned giving fit in?

## PLANNED GIFTS DO NOT NEED A DEPARTMENT

A planned gift can arrive at any time, so the development director must be able to recognize it. Just because a charity's fund-raising effort is not large or sophisticated or established does not mean it does not have its able supporters. It may have fewer of them but they are out there. In that sense, planned giving, if not a planned giving program, *is* for all charities. Phil needs to know what to do when a prospect tells him that he would love to help but cannot because all of his assets are tied up in highly appreciated securities. Phil needs to know enough to tell the prospect that a gift of some of those securities could be transferred to a trust that will pay more income than the securities currently provide, and without creating a capital gains tax. A small program is no excuse to walk away from that prospect. The Southern Environmental Agency, an environmental organization with a deep history, whose mission is similar to others', needs to help that prospect make the gift. Otherwise, this conservation-minded prospect may seek out another group to receive his gift. Or the person might make the gift but, from a tax perspective, unwisely.

That has happened before. A donor called to say that she was told by her attorney that she needed to make a charitable contribution for deduction purposes, so she was going to sell some stock worth $10,000 with a $1,000 cost basis and then give the proceeds to the Southern Environmental Agency.

Instead of saying thank you, Phil should have known to tell her to make a gift of the stock directly to the charity. He would have been able to secure a gift approximately 34 percent bigger than what the donor actually gave. Instead of receiving $10,000, however, he received a check for $7,480, the result of paying a 28 percent capital gains tax on $9,000. This may not seem like much, but the difference easily and legally could have been sent to the charity. But Phil did not know that. Multiply that amount by several gifts, and Phil's ignorance begins to cost his charity some real money.

He also did not know enough to ask what the donor meant when she said that she was told she "needed" to make a charitable gift. Many financial advisors seem not to realize that the charitable deduction—unlike other deductions, such as the home-mortgage deduction, for example—requires a postdecision parting of assets. Nothing is "saved" by making an outright charitable gift. What is given simply costs the donor less. Although pointing this out potentially could have cost the environmental group a gift, it also could have opened the door to more discussion, and given more assurance to the donor that this group cared about her financial situation and would take responsibility for her money.

But neither of those questions occurred to Phil because he did not know what issues to raise.

Another time, a prospective donor, sincerely interested in preserving the environment, asked how much income he could expect at his age if he established a charitable remainder unitrust. He explained that several years before he had made a gift to his church. He said that the church gift provided him with an income for life and that he would like to make another, this time to the Southern Environmental Agency. After the conversation labored on for 30 minutes, most of it taken up by discussing the most recent press reports on the charity's activities, Phil said he needed to get more information on the unitrust. When Phil followed up his meeting with a phone call, the prospect politely told Phil that he had reconsidered. Such a conversation does not foster trust in potential donors who want to make a gift but who also want to be certain—or as certain as possible—that their money is in good hands. Donors of planned gifts need to know their money is safe. Charities who are not comfortable asking for large amounts of money typically send messages, however subtle, that they might not be the best place to give, that they are unable to assist with the design of the gift, unable to manage the money well, unable to administer the gift, and unable to follow through with the donor after the gift is made. This, despite the good works of a charity.

This charity, like most others, may never raise the amounts of money the large, well-established organizations raise, but that does not mean that it does not have an obligation to itself and to its mission to be alert to planned giving opportunities. But the reason this particular charity has not received the kind of gift Rice University did has less to do with prospects than with attitude and commitment. This organization has hired and fired several development directors, and Phil is about to leave, because the charity's culture of fund-raising lacks long-term goals and strategies. The prospects for a capital campaign, not surprisingly, are not good and the development staff spend more time figuring out how to make the bad news seem better than they do trying to raise money. They feel exhausted, having called and cajoled with little success. Without a large, sincere commitment with its sights on the horizon, in addition to the current year's balance sheet, this charity will fail at most of its fund-raising efforts.

## THE PITFALLS OF COMPLACENCY

What can the charity do now? Although the trustees might realize that the emphasis should be different from what it has been for many decades, it must do something quickly. It is now spending from the endowment, which will eventually run out of funds if that continues. Spending the endowment's principal is akin to scheduling a charity's demise. So what to do?

The only real answer, short of an empty promise, is to prevent this situation from arising in the first place. This means that financially healthy charities who are not raising the money they need or who do not possess the endowment they should have must spend time and money *now* to outline a long-term strategy. The trustees must assess themselves, identify problems, and then take action. Typically this will involve a consultant. Not simply a fund-raising consultant, although such a consultant will be necessary. More important and immediately needed is a new, outside person who can honestly and without preju-dice evaluate the charity's organizational health, including morale and commitment to purpose, as well as the charity's fund-raising potential. The consultant will instruct the trustees how to be better trustees, how to identify the organization's mission, and how then to nurture it. In addition, the consultant's report may recommend the removal of the executive director or the development director. It also may suggest that some trustees should step down. In other words, the charity must be brutally frank in its self-assessment and come to terms with the painful reality of its situation, as well as how to correct it. A disappointing annu-al fund is a symptom. Not enough donors is a symptom. The problem is inadequate cultivation, which is usually the result of an inadequate effort to appreciate why the charity exists; its mission is unclear or unclearly stated. Take note: The pilot does not turn the engines off while the plane is flying merely because it is in the air, and charities should not turn off their cultivation efforts simply because they are not almost bankrupt.

As for this charity in deep trouble? Perhaps Trudeau will make his gift. Perhaps not.

# CHAPTER TEN

# Trustees and Planned Giving

> ... No sense have they of ills to come,
> Nor care beyond today.
>
> **Thomas Gray**

## THE CARETAKERS

Trustees of charitable organizations play a unique role in American society. They are the caretakers of the organizations our government has deemed better than itself at solving so many of our social ills. Without charities, despite the good intentions of governments and individuals, many of those ills would never be addressed. That is why the tax code provides two major incentives for charities defined in Section 170(c) in the Internal Revenue Code: (1) tax-deductible donations and (2) tax-free growth of their investments.

Financial supporters of charities are permitted to deduct their gifts. Deducted donations to charities represent money not collected by the Internal Revenue Service, and it comes from the pockets of all taxpayers. If a charity receives $1 million of contributions from people in the 35 percent tax bracket—and they itemize—the government loses $350,000 per year, the income tax on the donated money. Over 10 years lost tax revenue from these deductions equals $3,500,000. Further, charities' investments grow free of income or capital gains tax. This is a big benefit. Ten million dollars invested at 10 percent for 10 years grows to almost $26 million. That same amount, if taxed at a blended rate (ordinary on the income and capital gains on the sale of appreciated assets) of 35 percent would grow to only $19 million in 10 years. The significant difference of $7 million between the two results represents taxes not paid, and the lost revenue is subsidized by the taxpayers. This, added to the lost taxes attributable to the deductions in this example, means all taxpayers are subsidizing the charity with over $10.5 million over a 10 year period. Multiply this by approximately 600,000 charitable organizations who can collect tax-deductible donations and invest their endowments tax free, and the amount the IRS does not collect becomes noteworthy—some trillions of dollars. Either the government must reduce the budget by that amount or it must find other tax dollars to make up the difference. Either way, the money comes from all our pockets.

The government does not easily give up this money; it is serious about the purpose of charities. When the IRS issues a letter granting a charity the status described in Section 501(c)(3) of the Internal Revenue Code, it issues a lot.

And the charity must respect that. But when we speak of a charity, at least in terms of defining and maintaining its charitable mission, we speak of its trustees. Its trustees are its caretakers. They are responsible for its present *and* its future—for staying true to its mission and societal obligations—and of course, they still must oversee its budget, the salary of its executive director, the building repairs, and many other ordinary matters. Too many trustees do not obligate themselves seriously enough to ensure a charity's future. Instead, they mire themselves in the mundane affairs that demand lots of time and energy. Further, too many trustees see their appointment as a personal benefit, much like seeing their names on the social register. They are chosen, in large part, not because they have a vision or even management skills, but, too often, because they either know someone on the board or because they are wealthy, or both.

## A COMMITMENT TO THE FUTURE

A group of trustees was listening to a consultant, invited by the executive director for the occasion, explain the virtues of a planned giving program when one of them asked if it was true that the money raised from the effort would not be available for many years. When the consultant replied in the affirmative, the trustee said that he felt there was no reason to continue the meeting because his job did not include taking care of the organization's future; his job was to ensure the present. Without that, he said with conviction and sincerity, there would be no future. He told the consultant and what he may have considered the charity's mutinous executive director that the annual fund, a capital campaign for current and outright gifts, and corporate donations provide current resources, instead of vague promises, and that the charity's fund-raising efforts are best spent on these programs. Thank you for your time, and make certain you close the door on your way out. End of discussion.

End of charity, too. Not immediately, but eventually. As contrived and ridiculous as the scene appears, it has happened; many times at many organizations, trustees have abdicated their responsibilities in one way or another. A fundamental part of the job of a trustee for a charitable organization is ensuring its future. The idea behind being a charity, in fact, is to address social issues, the kind that tend to stay with us, the kind that are not resolved within the span of a board meeting or two. Maladies like poverty, hunger, domestic violence, disease, and lack of education, among countless other issues, are not likely simply to be cured and go away. These are the issues that are too large—because of the scope of the politics and the attendant adverse economics—for any other entity, such as government or business, to address. That is why charities in this country exist. That is their only reason for existing. For a trustee, then, to claim no obligation for the future of a charity is an abandonment of responsibility in the baldest terms. Anyone who thinks that his responsibility ends with the approval of the annual budget hasn't the courage or vision to serve as a trustee. He has, therefore, no right to guard a charity's mission.

Yet many do.

## TRUSTEE NEGLECT

The elderly heiress knits during the discussion of the charity's budget. The finance committee chair is explaining how costs, particularly health insurance costs, have risen faster than expected, leaving a large deficit in next year's budget. The discussion centers on whether to continue paying the complete premium for all employees or to have them contribute toward their health insurance premiums.

"The choices are not good," the chair explains, "but the committee recommends that we increase employee participation from nothing per month to $100 per month for staff with families and $50 per month for single employees. This would allow us to reduce our deficit by a significant amount."

"Plus, this would get us into the real world a little more," says a member of the finance committee. "It's almost unheard of to completely subsidize health insurance premiums for employees. No one that I know of, either in the private or charitable sector, does this nowadays. They can't afford to."

"But," says the executive director, a salaried employee herself, "we've had a tradition here of doing this for everyone. This is one way we can compensate for relatively low salaries, as well as stay competitive to attract good people." This is an awkward insertion because no one else around the table is an employee, and no one can refute the idea without worrying about offending her.

"That's true," says another trustee. "I've looked into this matter from a financial perspective, too, and we don't pay well. I'd like to think about other ways to cut the budget."

"But we've looked at all the other ways. We're already cutting as it is," responds the finance chair again. "This is just one of several ways we're hoping to control our expenses."

Meanwhile the elderly heiress is busily knitting, saying nothing and listening to nothing. After an hour-long discussion a vote is called. Now, listening to the question before them, she rouses herself to say that she doesn't think that the employees should have to pay anything for their insurance. She has heard nothing, at least consciously, about the reasons put forth for the motion. Her opinion is based not on what has been said but on what she *feels* is right. She commands authority because she is the largest contributor to the organization. She has been on the board for years, although her effectiveness long ago waned. She does little more than attend meetings and make life miserable for the development staff, who try to raise a great deal of each year's operating budget from her.

Her late entry in the debate exasperates the chair of the finance committee and the others who have carefully considered the matter, especially because enough of the others decided against the measure. The charity will continue to pay 100 percent of the health insurance premiums for all employees. The problem is not so much that the wrong decision was made—its merits can be debated—but that the duties of a trustee extend beyond mere attendance at meetings.

Everyone who has attended a board meeting, either as a trustee or as a contributing staff member, knows the feeling. Sometimes a trustee simply shows up, explaining most often how busy he is at work or, seemingly as often, how much he enjoyed his most recent vacation, without having prepared for the board meeting. When the meeting actually starts, the change in the person's attention is obvious as he looks at the materials before him for the first time, thinking to himself, and trying to convey to others, that he is serious about the mission before him. Would it be so impossible for trustees to prepare themselves for the meeting? When will trustees realize that the job means more than merely showing up?

Perhaps even worse than having uninformed trustees make vital decisions is that most questions are not debated in consideration of their effect on the charity's mission. Instead of asking if the charity can afford a project, trustees should ask themselves whether a project fits into the charity's mission and then, if so, determine how to pay for it. The budget is important, but the driving force behind decisions needs to be long-term mission, with less emphasis on short-term financial considerations.

## MONEY TALKS

If someone walks into almost any development director's office with a check for $100,000, that person will certainly get immediate attention, and perhaps interrupt an otherwise important meeting.

"Mr. Smith." The development director's secretary interrupts a meeting between the development director and the president of the organization. "I have a Mr. Jones in the office who says he needs to see you."

"Without an appointment?"

"That's right."

"Well, tell him I'm in a meeting and schedule him some time later in the week."

"I will, but he asked me to give this to you." She then hands an envelope to her superior. He opens it to find a letter stating that he would like to make a large donation to the charity, in the vicinity of $100,000, and asking if it would be possible to see the development director.

"Excuse me." The important meeting with the president has become less important and the development director returns immediately to his office. This would not have happened for a $10 check. One hundred thousand dollars is a lot of money. A lot of people would change their schedules to accommodate such a donor.

What goes on in people's minds when someone with means enters a room? For those with less, the monied person seems somehow more able. Not in any particular way, perhaps, but the person has an aura of ability, of intelligence. It is as if the fact of having money equates with being able to solve problems or do things better—simply to be a better person. This is in contrast to much of what we learn about poverty, about how contented are those who understand the shortcomings of mere objects. How those who are smart, really smart, tend to help others and therefore do not earn as much as they could. This, coupled with what we hear about how wealth, especially unearned wealth, produces lazy, uncaring people, should make monks of all of us.

But all this flies away when a person with money actually shows up. Except for the formulaic, false contempt some show when confronted with a wealthy person, most of us tend to mentally pause in awe for a moment when someone of means walks in the door. This does not mean he is more capable, but we think he is. After all, if this person made, or simply possesses, all that money, he must be able. He must be smart. He must be better. How smart are the wealthy? Some are smarter than others, and most certainly the possession of money is not the key. A true examination of how most of us react when talking with a person of wealth—and why—would require a book-length study on its own; it is sufficient here to say simply that development professionals, and those who practice planned giving in particular, see many people of wealth. Many planned giving professionals, although too few, have seen enough wealthy people to understand their humanity.

As a result of the charity's need for gifts, trustees are often thought of first as donors and second as keepers of the mission. The mistaken belief that a person of material means is also committed to and skilled at overseeing a charity and is a person of social conscience is the primary reason why so many charities attract so many ineffective trustees. Is it any wonder that trustees chosen in this manner would find difficulty in taking care of the future? Or establishing and maintaining a planned giving program, the very embodiment of planning for the future?

## A TRUSTEE'S JOB DESCRIPTION

Not all trustees are bad, of course. The vast majority are not. That is obvious and should be unnecessary to point out. But something not so obvious and quite necessary to point out, partly because in the polite tones of the charitable world these things are never discussed openly, is that too many trustees do a bad job. They're not bad people but they're bad trustees. They do not appreciate their roles and they are often unable to perform well the technical functions of overseeing a charitable business, let alone manage a thoughtful vision of the charity's future. There are few outlets for formal training on how to be a trustee. Because trustees at charities are volunteers, serving as a trustee is not a career path.

Yet it is as important to the charity as any career path that does pay an income. A conscientious executive would never hire an employee on the basis of social stature. Instead, she would examine the applicant's abilities as they relate to the job that needs to be done. A person being considered for a sales position, for example, would need to demonstrate that she can sell. This would be done by showing her past sales record and, during the interview, describing how she will be successful at selling. In addition, the person would need to show an ability to understand the product being sold. A person selling pianos should know something about music. A manager should know something about people and the way they react to motivation. To get the job, a trustee should know something about the product she sells—the mission of the charity. For how can a planned giving program be seriously supported by someone who does not understand the mission?

Instead, the scant advice that does exist on the topic generally suggests a *potential trustee* take a good, hard look at *the charity* to be certain that it is worthy of the potential trustee's efforts. If this is not backwards, it is at the least only half the story. A person needs to be assured that she will be serving a mission she fully supports at a charity that is solvent, and at the same time any charity should—although it too rarely does—take a good, hard look at the potential trustee to be certain that she is worthy of the charity's mission.

What kind of process takes place when a charity chooses a trustee? Many start their searches with their donors, though the righteous may deny this. At colleges and universities, alumni are prime candidates. Neither wealth nor graduate standing, however, is a promising measure of a person's abilities to actually perform the role of trustee. Given the current trustee-selection standards at some organizations, an honestly written job description for a trustee would be too embarrassing to contemplate:

Wanted: trustee of growing and prestigious charity. Job is to effectively oversee charitable activities. Candidate must have given lots of money to charity to qualify. Access to others with money is important. Other qualifications, such as the ability to understand budgets and charitable purpose, although desirable, are not as important.

The problem is obvious. Perhaps a good start would be to think about the role of a trustee as if it were a real job, a job that paid money, a job that has—which it in fact does have—deadlines and measures of accountability, as well as the need for a vision.

The job description might be more useful, however, if it were written to reflect what a trustee *should* bring to the organization:

Wanted: a person who cares about our charity's mission enough to prepare for and attend all meetings, participate in the serious dialogue related to our work, serve on one or two committees, consider the kind of organization we appear to be to the public, and thoughtfully deliberate our continuing role in society during the next five, 10, and 25 years. Ability to donate money—as well as time and effort—is important.

Money, of course, is not unimportant. Every charity needs to look to its leadership for donations. In fact, all trustees should be donors to the annual fund and—as we shall see—to the planned giving program. But the role of trustee means so much more.

## Technical Expertise

The advertisement might ask for people with vision, but trustees also need expertise. Even though charities receive special tax status, they are subject to the same challenges that businesses are. Charities must, for example, balance their budgets, maintain their buildings, prioritize their obligations, and plan strategically. This is in addition to creating policies specific to the organization, which then are implemented by the staff. The board, consisting of those most responsible for the success and oversight of the charity, needs to have expertise in various areas. A person overseeing the endowment should be knowledgeable in investments, a person scrutinizing the budget should know the difference between operating and capital costs, and, although most charities hire outside legal expertise, one or more attorneys should be available to approve contracts for the charity.

Trustees also need management skills. Because many of them chair or serve on committees that meet with staff, trustees must understand and employ good management techniques. A trustee cannot, for example, act as a staff person's direct superior. While staff many times work with trustees, most trustee directives are sent through the executive director of the charity. Further, good management means the ability and stamina to make tough decisions. When things are not going well they usually need to be changed, and trustees must make appropriate decisions, even if they are difficult or unpopular. Trustees at an all-women's college may, for example, vote to admit men, despite opposition from the student body and alumnae. If they have conducted extensive research, including demographics, trends in education, and costs, and then reexamined the purpose of the college, trustees must have the strength to address those unhappy constituencies, satisfied that they have made the right decision.

Running a charity is difficult, and able people are needed to run it, exercising their oversight with technical expertise. The group cannot be ignorant of its responsibilities. This means that charities must examine their needs and fill vacancies with talent.

## A Commitment of Time

In addition to looking for trustees who understand the charity's mission, charities also should be aware of another issue: time. Most good trustees serve on more than one board concurrently. And despite what almost everybody thinks about that, it is not a good thing. It is, in fact, unfortunate. Good people are hard to find and one way many charities determine the potential of prospective trustees—in addition to their wealth—is to look at their commitments to other boards. But is that not one of the *worst* ways to search for trustees? If we go on the premise that a person will need to spend time, energy, and thoughtful effort on a board assignment, does it not make sense to ask the trustee to fully dedicate herself to the charity? Perhaps this is the most difficult limitation to accept. Yet how many colleges does a person attend at once? How many jobs do good professionals hold at once? How many marriages at once? These may seem strange comparisons at first, but think about the importance of a trustee's role; serving as a trustee is in effect an additional job in its own right. It then becomes foolish to think that anyone, no matter how dedicated, experienced, or talented, can do justice to more than one charitable board at a time.

But that is what we have. And it is almost a matter of pride, a sort of social resume builder, to advertise how many boards a person serves on. "We are pleased," goes the public statement to the charity's constituency, "to announce that the full board endorsed the nominating committee's recommendation to select Mary Smith as a new trustee. Ms. Smith was graduated from St. Mark's School in Dallas and Stanford University and is president and chief executive officer of Fine Tuning, the CPA firm for musicians she founded in her home city, Kansas City. She also currently serves as a trustee at the Kansas City Animal Shelter, as the treasurer of the board at the Centerville Aquarium, and as the president of the board at the Program for International Student Studies. We are very pleased to have the experience and the abilities Ms. Smith has to offer."

Well, the charity should be pleased it can fool a few people, perhaps many, but Ms. Smith will probably not be a very good trustee. She is too busy. This is her fourth board assignment. That work, in addition to her regular job as a business owner, is too much. What can a person stretched too thin contribute? In contrast to the public perception that board service is some sort of reward for being rich or socially connected, true board service is true work, although far too few trustees—and charities—see their role this way.

What does it take to do the job properly? Take the development chair as an example. She will be responsible for the charity's fund-raising, including planned giving, which means she must work closely with the charity's development director, as well as with the treasurer or business director. A good trustee will not try to do the job of a staff member, but she will provide proper oversight. This means that she will receive monthly fund-raising statements and should review them to see that the charity is meeting its goals. Also, a good development director will want to be in contact with the trustee to review any major decisions that might need to be made in the absence of a committee or full board meeting. This does not mean that the trustee will want to consult on the opening paragraph of every letter sent to supporters and prospects, but it would mean serious discussions of the general direction of the charity's fundraising efforts. Similarly, the finance chair, while he will not review the brand of peanut butter used in the hospital cafeteria or second-guess the stock selections of the investment manager, will be involved in regular meetings with the asset manager and the treasurer to ensure that the broad investment guidelines are maintained. This type of trustee oversight, while not interfering with the staff's activities, does take time.

Although they should, most charities with planned giving programs do not have a planned giving committee. The function of overseeing the planned giving program is subsumed by the overall development committee's efforts. The chair of the development committee needs to know the annual fund numbers, sometimes even takes part in the annual phonathon, and might go on visits for major or planned gifts. To do this, she must become knowledgeable in planned giving, a time-consuming endeavor. How could a person with such responsibilities dedicate herself in that or a similar capacity to more than one charity?

This may sound limiting to both the charity and the board member. A typical term of a trustee is three, four, or five years. Most charities allow for two successive terms (some have rules and follow them, so that people do not serve forever). Thus, a trustee typically serves between six and ten years at one charity. An average of eight years means that one person, if he serves one charity at a time, can be a trustee for four or five charities during his lifetime. But how many strands of altruism does each of us have? How can we honestly give ourselves to more charities? The sheer work involved should be limiting enough, but when you consider how much heart and soul any one person can give to charitable causes, four or five charities are plenty. To claim otherwise is to claim folly, especially when the state of trusteeship at many charities is already poor. Although it is counterintuitive, board members, unless they are retired, should not, because they cannot effectively, serve on more than one board at a time.

## A Commitment of Finances

Trustee dedication means more than giving time. It also means giving money. The planned giving officer who solicits gifts from board members knows the problem—or at least the symptoms—all too well. If getting 100 percent board participation in the annual fund is difficult, getting full participation in planned giving is almost impossible. This is unfortunate, but to understand why we must return to the role a trustee plays. She serves to further the mission of the charity. What better way to display that commitment than by making a planned gift? In a perfect world all trustees should require themselves to make a planned gift, either outright or deferred. Why? Because it is a measure of commitment.

The question of whether a trustee should make a planned gift may seem to contradict what we have recently been learning, a sort of modern theory of trusteeship that says the measure of effective trustees is not their level of giving, but their level of service. Okay. Merit can be found in that thinking; modern boards need activists and specialists to get the job done properly. Further, some trustees cannot make a large planned gift; they are not wealthy enough.

But who cannot make at least a small provision in her will for a charity whose future is in no small part entrusted to her efforts? While recognizing that many trustees are properly recruited for their abilities and vision—and not for their potential as donors—charities must be realistic: For an appeal to the general constituency to be credible, those at the top must provide their support. If the charity asks others, those whose lives are not burdened by overseeing the well-being of the charity, to make a planned gift, how can trustees be excused? The issue is one of commitment. This goes to the heart of what it means to the organization for one group of people to serve as its caretakers. A babysitter will take the time to feed the children and get them to bed, but only a parent's heart will worry about sleepless nights. A trustee must be more of a parent than a babysitter.

## A Business Outlook

If getting the budget in order is a trying task for charities, imagine the difficulty many boards have starting and maintaining a planned giving program. A business outlook requires trustees to carefully examine the charity's mission in the context of funds available to accomplish that mission. An equally important task for trustees—and this is not mere wordplay—is to examine the available funds in the context of the mission. Although the bills need to be paid, the charitable mission needs to drive or at least influence most major decisions. Far too many trustees think that the end of the next quarter is a proper interval to accomplish big projects and that "long range" means 18 months. Because many trustees are businesspeople, they expect results immediately. Charities do need to be run more like businesses. This is accomplished when trustees bring a business outlook to the boardroom. Not purchasing a computer, for example, because it is expensive, even though the charity's mission is better served with automation, might not be good practice. This is where a unique delicacy emerges. Too many trustees leave their business minds back at the office.

## THE DISTANT FUTURE

Planned giving defies business logic, at least in some ways. Although more charities should be run more like businesses, planned giving is one important activity where charities and businesses appear to diverge. Getting a planned giving program started takes time, and most trustees know that. Any new endeavor does. But the fruits of a planned gift do not ripen for many years, sometimes not before 20, 30, 40 years or more have passed. The deferred part of a deferred gift is the part that goes to charity. So not only does the charity have to wait for the first level of results—donors' commitments to planned gifts—but it then must wait, literally, a lifetime before seeing financial returns.

Keep in mind that the trustees serving at the time a planned gift is established normally will not see anything from the effort; they will be gone from the charity. Time is a key consideration. In business, research and development are undertaken in anticipation of long-range results, but some form of intermediate progress is expected during the lifetimes of those doing the planning. To plan for a future beyond the current board or the staff's tenure requires a different mindset, akin to planning for a child's college education. Fortunately, the recipient of the planning, the child, serves as a constant reminder of the obligation. Planned giving requires that people remind themselves that activities today will produce future results for people now unknown to anyone at the charity, at a time when no current employee or trustee will be associated with the charity.

The further reality is that many trustees will be dead by the time planned gifts established today are available to the charity. Take a moment to think not of what you will be doing five years from now, but of what your life will be like 30 years from now. Will you be employed? Will you be in a retirement home? If so, are you planning now to pay for that? Will your children be able to care for you? Will you, according to the actuarial tables, be dead? If you will be dead, what will your children's lives be like? And their children's? Will the planet be large enough to house and feed your children and their children? Perhaps you have not thought of these things. Perhaps next week's tee time or dinner party is a more pressing concern. That we do not fret over the distant future is not bad; in fact, it is human that we think of those things most immediate to us. But to understand the need for planned giving, we need to think of the distant future. We need the foresight of the college founder, of the authors of the constitution, of the pioneers who founded our hospitals, and of many others whose ideas and actions affect our lives today. Yet we have difficulty planting the seed, owning a vision.

## A FINANCIAL LIFELINE TO THE FUTURE

Another problem must be taken into account. Despite many words to the contrary, the charity's trustees may not be ready to begin a planned giving program. Certainly a charity whose trustees are unwilling to see far into the future is almost defined as a charity unready to begin a planned giving program, but a charity may not have the prospects or the clarity of mission to ask for a planned gift. For a charity to ask a donor to make a commitment affecting her financial and estate plans, the purpose of the gift—how the charity will use the money when the income beneficiary dies—should be clearly defined. (Exceptions abound, of course, where the donor makes the gift primarily to save taxes and earn more money. This matter is addressed in Chapter 14, which deals with ethics.)

The big question here is one of commitment. Commitment requires patience and intelligent conviction. A trustee who sits on the board solely because of his record of making current gifts may not understand or appreciate why a planned giving program is important, and a trustee who questions the need for planned giving is not yet ready to support a program that asks people for gifts that will not materialize for more than a decade or two. This attitude might be acceptable for organizations that do not care if they will exist in another generation, but for those who do, trustees need to know about planned giving. They must generally know how the gifts work, what the advantages are to the donor, and their appeal. They must also understand that a good program does not blossom overnight, and that the difference between the planting and harvest seasons is longer than a few months or a few years. This is easy and obvious to assert, but far too many trustees have no idea how planned giving might fit into the overall development picture.

A trustee who says she needs to pay more attention to paying the light bill and next year's salaries and therefore is not interested in planned giving is much like a parent who says that because the baby needs new shoes right now money cannot be put aside for college. If it is not important to put aside money for college, might it be because there will be no college in the baby's future? The parallel here is that the charity will not need the future income produced from planned gifts because either it will then have plenty of money from other sources or it will no longer exist. How many trustees would be comfortable discussing or relying on either prediction?

Looking into the future is an uncomfortable pastime. No one really knows what will happen, yet every day we make decisions based on what we think the future holds. We buy the car or the house or the new suit because we feel good about our financial futures. Or we do not buy because we are worried about our financial futures. By making these decisions we are not predicting the future but we are reflecting our sense of it. Almost everyone thinks he will have a future, however, and all but the most naive plan for it. Planned giving requires the same of trustees. They must plan for the future to seriously consider planned giving.

It is not fair, although it should be, to compare planning for the baby's college and general future with looking at the future of a charity. It is not fair because the baby is precious and unique to the parent; the charity tends to be neither to most trustees. It *should* be a fair comparison, however, because a trustee's commitment should be more than fleeting. Any planned giving professional who has asked her board members for a planned gift knows all too well that the commitment of many trustees is not deep enough to lead them to make a major gift. So it may help to examine a trustee's commitment to the *charity* before wondering why her commitment to a planned giving program might be less than complete. Trustees are right to explore what it will take to run a planned giving program properly, but when their decision is not to accept planned gifts at a healthy organization, the concern has evolved into an unhealthy paranoia that prevents a charity from forming an important financial lifeline to the future.

## ARE TRUSTEES AFRAID OF PLANNED GIVING?

Worrying about the payroll is easier and more defined than maintaining a long-range vision, so it is no wonder that planned giving is a difficult concept for trustees. That is no excuse, however, to delay. Taking responsibility for planned gift assets is problematic for some boards, and understandably so. Life-income gifts are active for a long time before they are realized as money for the charity, and board members are rightly worried that the money must be properly managed. But the need for caution does not equate to abandoning the idea, any more than the danger of being hit by a car does not prevent people from crossing the street.

Trustees have often been heard to make the excuse that if they were to attempt a planned giving program, they would be taking on too much.

This position is usually the result of ignorance. Gift annuities serve as a good example. Many will argue that the charity cannot accept gift annuities because the charity, with all its assets, is liable into the distant future for payments to the annuitant. (Strangely, the future *is* a consideration sometimes.) This, they will say, jeopardizes the charity's financial strength. Some assert that this position shows how fiscally responsible they are. Although the assets of the charity do guarantee the annuity payments, only the most poorly run charities need to worry about not having enough resources to make the annuity payments. By law, gift assets cannot be obligated to back the annuity payments, but most charities set aside gift assets, individually or collectively, to make the payments.

Because the donor is making a gift, the payout from a gift annuity is usually quite modest relative to what a person would otherwise receive from a commercial insurance company for the same amount of money. For example, a donor who contributes $10,000 might receive an annuity of $800 (or 8 percent) from a charity or $1,200 (12 percent) from an insurance company. Looked at another way, the insurance company might require only $6,000 to provide an annual payment of $800 each year. The $4,000 difference is, from a simplistic but useful perspective, a gift to charity. A gift annuity can also be thought of as a bond the charity issues, only without taking on the obligation of paying back the principal. How many trustees have rejected a gift annuity program but enthusiastically supported the idea of raising money by issuing bonds? Yet the financial differences are in favor of the annuity. The trustee who sees a gift annuity as a potential liability is probably reciting something heard at a seminar and not thoroughly examining how the gift annuity actually works. To date, less than a handful of charities in the 150-year history of issuing gift annuities have been unable to fulfill their payment obligations. It is a good excuse, though, for the uncommitted.

## MEASURING PLANNED GIVING

Yes, planned giving can be measured. Charities need to look at planned giving in a quantitative as well as a qualitative way. Cultivating donors and attracting gifts will always be essential to success, but equally vital are the numbers. The more serious, established planned giving programs measure their success in several ways. First, they look at their expectancy file. This consists of the number of commitments they know of and the amounts they represent, to measure how much money is due them and, approximately, when. Second, they look at the payout rates and the ages of the income beneficiaries to calculate how much each gift will grow or decline by the time the charity receives the gift asset.

Sophisticated charities will further examine the present value—the value adjusted downward to take inflation into account—to see in today's dollars what the planned giving program is worth.

For example, a 65-year-old is the beneficiary of a normal (not a net-income) unitrust worth $1 million and paying a 6 percent income. If the trust has a total annual return of 10 percent, the trust grows by 4 percent each year (the 10 percent total return minus the 6 percent payout). If the donor has a life expectancy of 20 years, the trust will equal a little under $2.2 million. This is valuable knowledge. Charities need to be careful not to budget that money because any one donor's life expectancy may not conform to the actuarial tables, but with enough donors the law of large numbers starts to take effect, and on average a charity will have an idea of how much will be made available and when.

But another calculation must be made to know the present value of that trust. If the charity's annual operating budget increase equals 5 percent, the $2.2 million must be reduced by 5 percent each year for 20 years, the expected life of the trust. This calculation shows that the charity has only about $825,000 in inflation-adjusted value. This is equal to 82.5 percent of the original gift (or the gift's value on the day the calculation was made). This percentage—82.5 percent, in this case—is an important way to measure the value of a planned gift. If the present value is calculated for all deferred gifts, trustees will know a great deal about the program. At the least, this process financially quantifies the charity's lifeline to the future.

A planned giving director's effectiveness can be better measured on the projected inflation-adjusted value than on the total amount brought in. In fact, the values of two $1-million unitrusts established by two people the same age are not the same if one trust pays 5 percent and the other 8 percent. Adapting the calculation in the above example, the 8 percent payout provides a projected inflation-adjusted value of $560,000. The efficiency of that gift is only 56 percent instead of 82.5 percent. The difference is almost $265,000 in *today's* dollar values. Trustees not aware of this are not fully aware of the potential of planned giving or the way planned gifts can help their charity in the future.

## TRUSTEE OVERSIGHT OF PLANNED GIFTS

Once charitable trusts are established, they need to be managed. If the charity is the trustee, the board must oversee the investments and the administration of the gifts. Gift annuity and pooled income fund assets are almost always the responsibility of the charity. Trustees will meet at least quarterly, and many times monthly, to discuss how the endowment is managed. This is not true with planned gift assets. Endowment assets are more exciting to trustees than planned giving assets, primarily because planned gift assets are smaller than endowment assets. Much smaller. Almost all charities manage more endowment than planned giving assets, and because endowments are not divided into small trusts with varying payout requirements they are less confusing. As a result, planned giving assets generally do not receive much attention. The planned giving director often must fight to get the topic on the agenda of a board meeting. A discussion on planned giving is usually scheduled toward the end of the meeting, with a high probability of time running out before the topic actually gets discussed. Then, when it does, the discussion will likely center on how much has been raised recently and the amount of planned gifts currently being managed. Sometimes the question of how the assets are managed arises, but a cursory confirmation that a stock–bond mix is similar to that of the endowment is usually satisfactory to trustees. That life-income and lead trust gifts have varying payout requirements and investment objectives usually is not considered. Trustees satisfy themselves that all is well and then move on to more interesting topics.

One of the more interesting topics is the stock market. Although many trustees and portfolio managers will disagree, nothing can be more useless than discussing how the stock market will perform. Finance and investment experts cannot agree on what the markets will do, so what difference can it make that a manager thinks the markets will move up or move down? It is only a guessing game at best. As useless is the practice of predicting the success of a particular stock or even a category of a particular stock or bond, such as small company stocks, large company stocks, or international stocks. No one—that is to say *no one* on the entire planet—knows how anything on Wall Street will perform.

Of far more value is the practice of analyzing trends in particular market segments with an eye on investing for the long-term. Short-term investments are generally not good for any charity, and any charity looking to make quick gains will almost certainly be disappointed. Stocks most likely to rise quickly are also those most likely to fall quickly; their volatility makes a heavily proportioned investment in them a bad idea, at least if the idea is to make money and sell quickly. Yet such is the fodder of many talks within investment committees.

Because planned gifts are so diverse, however, trustees are negligent if they assume the same investment goals for all their planned gifts. Also, to the degree that trustees do pay attention to planned gift asset management, many times they lump together endowment and planned giving assets, despite the varying income, and therefore investment, objectives of the different trusts. Because payout rates and ages are different, each trust's objectives are, or should be, singular; the endowment does not have the same general goals. At least one study has shown that many boards are delinquent on the matter of planned gift management oversight. Properly managing planned gift assets may be less exciting and more difficult than managing endowment assets, but that is no excuse. The gift incomes of many donors are dependent on how planned gift assets are managed. If a donor loses income against inflation—that is, if the income's purchasing power decreases over time—a donor may want to know why. To be told that the trust invested in bonds just to be safe—as many donors would be told because that is exactly what happens many times—is small and incomplete solace. A charity that acts as a trustee needs to invest planned giving assets prudently, which today means, according to the "Third Restatement of the Prudent Investor Rule," that a portfolio invested wholly in bonds is generally a bad idea, at least for people who are expected to live for more than a few years. Protection of income and assets must take into account inflation. That, in turn, means a trustee generally should diversify assets. Even—perhaps especially, given their various payout requirements—planned giving assets.

## LEADERSHIP

The state of board leadership—at least on the question of planned giving, and most probably on many other questions—at many charities today might not be terrible, but it could be vastly improved. Charities must do more to scrutinize those whom they ask to serve as their leaders. To go short on that question is to go short on the reason the charity exists in the first place. What constitutes leadership is a question worthy of many studies and the answers are hardly scientific or mechanical. A good definition usually includes the ability to motivate and provide a vision.

A potential trustee must ask herself if the charity's mission is worthy and then decide if she can enhance its mission through her efforts and skills. The charity must be sure that its trustees are dedicated. Merely attending meetings, while mandatory, is not enough of a measure of commitment, although getting to even that point would represent a great step forward for many trustees. Both charity and potential trustee need to better understand the kind of work involved. No one is doing or receiving any favors when the job description is too brief or does not accurately convey the true commitment needed. Everyone loses then.

So it all comes back to the mission. The banker who doodles during the government relations report and the heiress who knits during the finance report and the attorney who is preoccupied with his wealthy client's estate plan during the nominating committee's report are not doing their jobs. Yet most charities survive, and even thrive at times, despite their trustees. The ideal trustee understands that involvement should be at the level where policy is determined, budgets established, and priorities, especially long-range concerns, listed. The ideal trustee has a vision and is dedicated to securing that vision. The ideal trustee is difficult to find, and when she turns up every charity wants her to serve on its board. Make no mistake: modern-era trustees need to be as financially supportive as their predecessors, but today they need to be more involved in more decisions than most people are willing to commit themselves to be. Although recognizing the importance of planned giving is just one manifestation of commitment, one element of securing a charitable organization's future, it is an important and often overlooked element. For charities to thrive, the state of trusteeship must change.

# CHAPTER ELEVEN

# Is Planned Giving a Capital Concept?

*There are three kinds of lies: lies, damned lies and statistics.*

**Mark Twain**

## IS THE BILLION-DOLLAR CAPITAL CAMPAIGN IN EVERYONE'S FUTURE?

The headline read boldly: "Capital Campaigns: Bigger, Broader, Bolder." Reporters for the *Chronicle of Philanthropy* had compiled information on the state of capital campaigns and found them to be growing larger and larger. Harvard had just announced a two-billion-dollar campaign.

Think of that. Two billion dollars. With a spending rate of 5 percent, which may or may not allow for some growth against inflation, the annual interest alone from two billion dollars equals 100 million dollars. At first. Then, assuming the investment has an annual total growth—capital growth and dividends—of 10 percent, the *increase* in income during the second year will be five million dollars. Just the increase. The standard for the truly affluent has been said to be not merely an ability to live off the interest their investments generate, but to live off the interest of their interest. The five million dollars is the interest of interest, and of course, with capital growth it continues to increase each year. Putting this into some perspective, a health care agency might have a total annual budget of about five million dollars; a local Red Cross chapter might have a budget of one million dollars; the local shelter about $100,000.

One hundred million dollars. Many charities would do anything for that kind of money. Even for merely the interest on the interest, for the scraps, the leftovers. Some charities do. They lie.

The capital campaign has become a forum for dishonesty. Although capital campaigns are getting bigger, one is compelled to wonder if this is primarily because they are raising more money or raising more expectations or raising their level of creativity. Ask any two charities to account honestly for what they have raised and you likely will find two processes for adding up the gifts, probably neither one fitting snugly into anything a professional—say a banker—might otherwise consider normal. Ask ten charities and you will be likely to get ten different answers. Ask 100 and you may get close to 100. So how are we to measure success? How are we to know if one charity raised more than another? How are we to know if a charity has been honest in its counting methods?

Early major gifts are the nucleus of any capital campaign. Normally, between one-quarter and one-half of the goal is raised before the campaign becomes public. This is to motivate the modest donor to support an already winning cause. All the major donors—except for the surprise uncovered during the course of battle—are visited and their commitments are secured before most of the community even knows a campaign is being contemplated, much less launched. This is the first phase of dishonesty.

Imagine the San Antonio Spurs playing a basketball game against the Indiana Pacers without notifying the public, the press, or even the National Basketball Association and the Spurs somehow convincing the Pacers that the game is not, at least initially, for real. Then, in the final minutes, when the game is already decided, the Spurs declare that they are indeed playing a real game, an important game, and they clear the bench so that the second- and third-string players are able to participate by throwing in a few baskets. Victory is declared when the clock stops, but victory was guaranteed well before the game ended. Capital campaigns are conducted in similar fashion, with planning sessions held and the first gifts obtained before the clock begins to tick. Of course, capital campaigns are not actual contests with an opponent, but they do in fact take on the feel of a contest, and time can be an opponent. But the strongest opponent is prestige, the image of the charity after either a success or a defeat.

Capital campaign goals have increased substantially during the years. The pressure to conduct increasingly larger campaigns and to outperform similar charities is intense. Even if a campaign is successful, the effort might still be considered a failure if the amount raised is too modest and too easily achieved.

Onward and upward. The first one-million-dollar campaign. The first 100-million-dollar campaign. The first one-billion-dollar campaign. What of ten billion? After all, adding zeros is easy. The momentum takes on a life of its own, uncontrolled by reason or even need (although the need is far greater than either the public or the charity usually realizes). Unable to accept failure, nonprofit managers have to discover new ways to raise money.

Deferred gifts.

## DEFERRED GIFTS: AN EASY SOLUTION
## FOR AGGRESSIVE CAPITAL CAMPAIGNS

The setting was quite peaceful, much like the calm before the storm: Although the polished mahogany table in the conference room was littered with reports, the three men and three women who sat around it were discussing what they all hoped would change the charity's financial status. A capital campaign feasibility study had been commissioned by the charity's trustees, who desired to raise $200 million over the next five years. Four of the individuals at the table were trustees; the other two represented the consulting firm that had just completed the study and were now reporting the results. The results were good but not good enough; the constituency, the consulting team predicted, would be able to raise only between $100 million and $125 million.

"Lucky we haven't told anybody about this yet," said the chair of the development committee. "I was so sure we would have no trouble raising that kind of money. I knew it was ambitious, but we haven't had a capital campaign for over 15 years, and then it was for only $25 million." What to do? Include deferred commitments, of course. That way, people don't have to really give up anything now by making a gift and the charity can report the results as if it actually raised more money than it did. No longer do charities simply ask for real money. They now confuse real money with future money. Like the lucky heiress who knows she has been named as a beneficiary in her grandmother's will, charities tend to spend or at least count money that is not yet theirs to spend.

"And what, young lady, can you provide as collateral for this loan?" asks the stern banker.

"Well," she answers coyly, "my grandmother has left me $100,000 in her will."

"Oh? I'm so sorry to hear of your grandmother's death. I've known her for some years now, and I'm surprised I haven't heard of this until now. When did she pass away?"

"Oh, she's not dead. Yet. But I know the money is coming, so won't you please give me the loan?"

At least the irresponsible young woman knows she needs to buy her happiness with real money and has gone to the bank to get it. But she learns that there is a significant distance—sometimes a *very* long road—between a dollar and a promise. Unfortunately, many charities behave as if they do not know this.

Capital campaigns are wonderful and useful activities to raise money for a needed cause. In 1903, when the main school building at Dartmouth College burned to the ground, alumni and other supporters rallied and raised enough money within one year to build a new structure. The president of the college is known to have implored potential supporters: "This is not an appeal, this is a summons!" The scene has been repeated many times at many charitable organizations around the country for similarly worthwhile, even heartrending causes. The capital campaign involves the community in as direct a way as possible to raise the maximum number of dollars for one or several specific purposes. For most charities, however, supporters cannot be summoned, only asked.

Asking is difficult enough. There is no good time to raise money: The economy could always be better; prospective donors are never quite as wealthy as they might want to be; the charity always needs to cultivate more people for a longer time than the campaign schedule will allow. Thus, great is the urgency to raise more money and count it more favorably than it should be or in a way that the auditors might approve of. Sometime after the first capital campaign and before today, someone decided that planned gifts—read *deferred* gifts—should be counted as part of the total toward the campaign goal. This, despite a need for immediate dollars to fund current obligations.

## CURRENT GIFTS ARE NECESSARY

Capital campaigns are developed around a need and a projected ability to raise the money. A typical campaign might include three general components: (1) money for a new wing or building; this is the actual capital portion, the money used to fund projects requiring bricks and mortar, (2) endowment gift to provide annual income for certain programs, and (3) the annual fund for each of the years during the capital campaign.

Assume the need totals $10 million. Further assume that the building (including money to be placed in the endowment as restricted money, the income from which will pay for the building's annual maintenance, and a fund to pay for future maintenance) costs $4 million; that the general endowment needs an additional $5 million, the income from which will be used for increased operating expenses; and that the annual fund total is $1 million. Assume further, although this is almost never the case, that the campaign counsel and the trustees agree that the money can be raised from its known constituency. All of the $10 million is needed immediately, during the course of the campaign, which typically runs from three to five years. The contractor building the structure needs to be paid, the charity needs the endowment's income, and the annual funds needs to be spent. In other words, the charity needs real money within a short, ascertainable period of time.

A normal person might think that gifts toward the goal would have to be in the form of some asset that the charity can spend or liquidate, but that restrictive idea died a while ago, probably when investors began building portfolios with junk bonds and when life insurance agents started selling insurance as an investment with an annual projected return of 12 percent. Common sense loses its appeal in the world of shiny veneers.

Common sense sometimes has tough competition.

For capital campaign purposes, the deferred gift has acquired a new status—partly because of its appeal, partly because raising money is getting difficult, partly because bigger is better and mostly because economics has a logic all its own. Instead of raising money that can be put to use immediately, we now raise promises of future money and sometimes funny money (bequests and other revocable gifts, for example), neither of which, for purposes of the campaign, is real. The vast majority of campaign pledges are honored; a promise of future money is a deferred gift. This allows planners to reach the capital campaign goal with less difficulty. That the goal was set in the first instance because of an immediate need for dollars becomes lost in the shadows created by the bright lights of enthusiasm and optimism.

## Improper Crediting

The reporter for the *Chronicle of Philanthropy* called the consultant to say, "I understand you're taking the conservative view."

"How do you mean that?"

"I mean that many other consultants as well as development directors disagree with you on the matter of crediting planned gifts in a capital campaign. Why don't you think these gifts should be credited? Isn't that a bit conservative? I'm a bit surprised to hear that from a planned giving consultant."

"If you think that adding two and two and arriving at four is conservative, I suppose you have a point. But you must understand that no matter how much we want to celebrate planned gifts—and I'll be the first to give you an idea of how we should celebrate getting planned gifts—we still are left with a basic truth: We need the money in the bank now to spend it now."

Yet the questions linger: "But what do you say about the need for larger campaigns?"

"The *need?* We *need* food and shelter; everything else is a luxury. Some say a need is a luxury enjoyed twice. Going one better than the charity down the street is a matter of pride, a destructive instinct, and can hardly be called a need. If, however, you mean a large goal that, when accomplished, will help the charity truly attend to its mission better, I'm all for that."

"What about donors who want to participate in the campaign but couldn't without using a planned gift?"

"The automobile costs $25,000. If you have only $1,000 you can't buy the car. You can buy a bike, but not a car."

"What about donor relations?"

"What about them? Are we to dissolve all standards to make everyone happy? And what about the donor who does make a substantial outright gift? I think I might question just how good those relations really are if my current gift and someone else's future gift were thought to be the same. The fact is, if my outright gift is the same amount as someone else's deferred gift, I'm giving more than the other guy."

Conservative? Extremism is no vice in the pursuit of honesty. Extremism in the context of honesty is merely accuracy.

## DEFERRED GIFTS AS A WELCOME COMPONENT OF CAPITAL CAMPAIGNS

Deferred gifts, nevertheless, should have their place. They should be celebrated as part of a capital campaign, as they should be celebrated during noncampaign periods. (With all the hoopla surrounding capital campaigns, we tend to forget that gifts made at other times, deferred or outright, deserve credit and acclaim.) This should be done by *adding* to the capital campaign total an amount designated for deferred gifts. Call it the expectancy portion of the campaign, an amount that donors and others know will not be used to satisfy immediate capital needs but is important because the charity needs to establish a lifeline to its future with acknowledged sources; they are established today but will not begin to create income for a long time.

Planned giving, like dessert, should be employed only as an addition. It can never replace the need for an annual giving program or currently needed capital gifts. Nor can the process of cultivation, a requisite for securing any large gift, current or deferred, be hastened beyond the limits of the relationship between prospect and charity. The answer to the question of how to integrate deferred gifts in a capital campaign is, therefore, simple: Do not confuse the two types of gifts, and celebrate both.

## Crediting Deferred Gifts

But what of counting the deferred portion of the campaign? How does a deferred gift actually get credited? CASE, the Council for the Advancement and Support of Education, in a 1994 study on this topic recommends that gifts be counted in capital campaigns in either their current value and their inflation-adjusted value as determined by the IRS formulas. That is, a $100,000 unitrust should be counted as both $100,000 and, say, $40,000, or whatever the remainder value is for the donor as calculated using the IRS formula and tables. Clearly, the gift cannot be double-counted, and the method must be clear. Another recommendation is to separate the two categories of gifts, outright and deferred. This way, goes the logic, the public will know what has actually been established.

That's a step. Separating deferred gifts from current gifts is mandatory. They are two fundamentally different things. A $100,000 deferred gift pays for nothing while an outright $100,000 gift pays for things that add up to $100,000. Why it took so long for the charitable world to recognize and admit this obvious fact is bewildering.

## PRESENT VALUE IS NOT IMMEDIATE VALUE

But if we accept that deferred gifts should not be counted as real money in capital campaign efforts, why count them at the present value? Why not instead count them at their full face value? While this idea is not popular among the many fund-raisers who still think the two categories of gifts should be mixed together with vague lines of separation, those people who are most realistic when formulating crediting policies want to be as accurate as possible. As much as anything else, they feel that the IRS calculation of the remainder value suffices. The calculation even takes into account the life expectancy and the payout rate, so that two people with different ages and different payouts from their gifts will be accurately measured against each other. Why not, then, simply take that value and credit it toward the campaign?

Because that is no more accurate than counting the full value—it is still not immediately available. Why not, for that matter, count nothing? Zero. That is, in fact, the amount that will be available for use in the capital campaign.

The problem is illustrated when the money raised during a capital campaign is scheduled to be used to increase faculty salaries at a college. An endowment campaign of $50 million is to be used to raise the salaries of 250 faculty members who are each paid $50,000 per year. If the money is raised, and the trustees limit annual spending from the endowment to

5 percent of its value, the school should have $2.5 million to spend on salary increases. Divided by 250 people, that works out to be $10,000 per person. The month after the campaign concludes, each faculty member might be led to believe he should receive a $10,000 annual increase. Although the example is simplistic (the spending rule is usually an average over three years; all money raised is not invested at the same time; part of the money could justifiably be spent on noncash benefits, such as health insurance or the retirement program; and the campaign consultants must be paid), the point is self-evident: The money must be in hand to increase faculty pay. If half of the $50 million goal was the result of deferred gifts, they would receive only a $5,000 raise.

Fortunately (or unfortunately, depending on your perspective), campaign goals are not so neat, and navigating the distance from raising a dollar to the way it is supposed to be spent is a complicated business. Let's face it. Nothing is accurate when it comes to counting deferred gifts. The big question is, How comfortable are we with our inaccuracy? How comfortable are we when, after the big celebration of success, we then have to explain to the faculty why the money just isn't there? Tough question.

## COUNT DEFERRED GIFTS IN FULL

But planned giving is full of tough questions. And just because the questions are tough does not mean that we have to be devious in adding up the campaign totals. The solution needs to fit the problem or the goal will never be realized. The problem is how, taking into consideration that deferred gifts should be counted somehow, to include them in a campaign. This is a topic of some interest to many people. A 1989 survey of over 50 of the nation's most prestigious and influential charities showed that almost no one counts deferred gifts in the same way.

That's why the argument to count deferred gifts separately at their full value—and counting them at zero value for the part of the campaign that needs to raise real money—is appealing. The method has the benefit of counting properly as well as celebrating heretofore-thought-to-be-conflicting goals. Those controlling the campaign need to explain the difference clearly, but that can be done with enough communication and education, the price for including both types of gifts in a campaign. In that sense, including even the present value of the gift is too generous. The $100,000 unitrust with a $40,000 remainder means nothing toward the capital campaign. The charity not only does not have the full $100,000, it does not have the $40,000 either. In fact, it doesn't have a dime. For purposes of the campaign, the reason the campaign was undertaken, nothing has happened. The faculty, if not the campaign administrators, will appreciate that fact soon enough. Therefore, count the real money toward the real campaign totals and count the full amount of deferred gifts in the deferred portion of the campaign totals. The two totals can add up to a big total, but everyone should know the difference.

## Treating Different Deferred Gifts Differently

Important questions remain. Should a $100,000 unitrust which pays 5 percent to a 75-year-old person be measured in the same way as a 7 percent unitrust for a 70 year old? Does the fact that a net income unitrust can be invested with a higher total return make a difference in crediting a gift? What about life insurance? Should a newly purchased policy be counted the same as a paid-up policy? Should either be counted at face value? And what if a trust's trustee is someone other than the charity, thus making it impossible for the charity to change fund managers if the investment performance is not good? What if a charity is not an irrevocable remainderman? How should lead trusts, the income from which immediately comes to charity, be counted in a campaign? And what of the bequest? The idea is to uniformly count planned gifts, not only during a campaign, but any time. Each year, because established planned gifts represent a growing portion of fund-raising totals, planned gifts need to be reported in a manner that allows anyone who understands the rules to measure who raised what. Understanding the rules is hard, however, when there aren't any. It's easy to claim victory when anything goes, and especially easy when there is no opponent.

## DEFERRED GIFTS: REVOCABLE VS. IRREVOCABLE

The results of a 1989 research project conducted for the National Committee on Planned Giving indicate what might be the beginnings of an answer to each of these questions. The first step is to decide which gifts are revocable and which are irrevocable. Some deferred gifts are irrevocable, known and guaranteed to be available to the charity at some point in the future, even though we don't know when or how much. If a charity is the trustee of a gift and irrevocable remainderman, the gift is irrevocable. A bequest, however, is not irrevocable. It can be revoked by the donor at any time. Even though the vast majority of bequests are not revoked, donors can change their minds. To be accurately recorded each gift must be designated revocable or irrevocable when made to the charity and recognized accordingly. Exhibit 11.1 shows how this might be done, both for a capital campaign and for general use.

| GIFT TYPE | IRREVOCABLE | REVOCABLE |
|---|---|---|
| Bequests | $        0 | $1,000,000 |
| Unitrusts | $1,000,000 | $2,000,000 |
| Annuity Trusts | $2,000,000 | $        0 |
| Pooled Income Fund | $  500,000 | $        0 |
| Gift Annuities | $  500,000 | $        0 |
| Life Insurance | $  100,000 | $5,000,000 |
| Total: | $4,100,000 | $8,000,000 |

**Exhibit 11.1**  An Accounting of Irrevocable and Revocable Deferred Gifts

Some charities would declare that they raised over $12 million, the matter of determining what is irrevocable and what is not being lost in the quest to add up the dollars. And keep in mind that not one of the deferred dollars—revocable or irrevocable—can be legitimately counted as part of *current* money raised in a capital campaign. Not one gift, unless from a person who sets up a gift during the campaign and then dies before it ends—and who wants to count on that?—will be received in cash. Yet the more cunning would declare that in a $100 million campaign, a campaign whose goal includes only current gifts, just over 12 percent had been raised.

The unitrusts, annuity trusts, pooled income fund, and gift annuities in Exhibit 11.1 are irrevocable because the charity knows it will receive the assets someday. Because no trust is involved, the gift annuity assets are already the property of the charity. (Gift annuities are not deferred gifts, but many charities properly treat them as if they were.) The irrevocable life insurance gifts are either paid up policies or old enough so that the donor is relieved of paying the premiums directly; the cash value and dividends can pay the premiums internally. Even though no one knows their value, there is no doubt that the irrevocable gifts ultimately will benefit that particular charity.

The reason some gifts are revocable is that there is some doubt that they will ultimately benefit that particular charity. The $2 million of unitrusts are in the revocable column because the trust document allows the donor to switch charities at any point during her lifetime. A bequest is also revocable because a person who changes her mind about a bequest intention may direct the money to another charity or to a noncharitable purpose. The unitrust assets must ultimately go to a charity, but they are similarly revocable because that particular charity might not ever receive the gift. Maintaining the distinction is important because deferred gifts are, or should be, kept distinct from other assets. And among deferred gifts, all of which occupy a secondary status to current assets, revocable gifts ought to occupy a third tier of assets and should be tracked separately.

Some life insurance gifts are irrevocable and many others are revocable. The $5 million in the revocable column represents the face amount of policies newly purchased during the campaign. The $100,000 gift is the face amount of a paid up policy. The face amount is the initial death benefit, essentially the amount the charity will receive if the policy is in force when the donor dies.

## THE PROBLEM WITH CREDITING
## THE PRESENT VALUE

What about crediting the same unitrust amount for a single 70 year old as for a couple in their sixties? This is a thorny question because the charity will have to wait longer for the younger couple to die than it will for the other person. Similarly, two unitrust gifts made by two people the same age but with different payouts will probably provide different amounts to the charity, even if the two trusts end at the same time. This is why the present value concept is so agreeable. The process of calculating the remainder value provides an evenness to the process, taking into account the payout and the expected term of the trust.

Why not include the IRS-calculated remainder value—and not the full current value—as the amount in the deferred portion of the campaign totals? This would allow for the real differences in the way various trusts are set up, yet still honestly reflect a separate total. The answer to this difficult question depends on what the charity wants to report. It is almost an irrelevant question, however, because the final value will not (or at least should not) be included in the part of the capital campaign totals that reflect immediately spendable money. The appeal of using the full value is that it fully celebrates the acquisition of a deferred gift. Its drawback is that the charity will receive less than that when the gift is realized and, even further finely tuning the distinction, different ages and different payouts will provide different remainders.

But the remainder, the present value, is a guess at best. Contrasting that unknown with the dishonesty of using the full market value at the time of the gift is the real issue. That is why CASE has left the decision in the hands of the charity.

Taking this a step further, the charity's financial books ideally should record deferred gifts as an item *not* included in the endowment. If the endowment is $200 million and the charity has $50 million of deferred commitments, as measured by their current value, it should not say its endowment is $250 million. For one thing, the spending rule—the trustee-mandated guide many nonprofits use to determine the amount of annual spending each year from its endowment—needs to be calculated on the $200 million and not $250 million (and then only if the $200 million is liquid). If the charity's trustees dictate that 5 percent of the endowment's market value be spent annually, and if the endowment number used were the higher number, $250 million, the charity would actually be spending 6.25 percent of the real assets available and thereby violate its mandate. The other reason that the endowment should not include deferred gifts is that it artificially inflates the endowment's value.

## EXPECTANCY GIFTS ACQUIRED IN ONE YEAR

Whether in a capital campaign or not, a nonprofit needs to keep accurate records of its planned giving activity each year. This is not always easy, but Exhibit 11.2 shows a sample summary of acquired planned gifts in an expectancy file.

Each charity needs to establish its own guidelines for defining revocable gifts. For example, a unitrust that names the charity as the remainderman and of which the charity is trustee should be irrevocable, but a unitrust that allows the donor to choose any charity or remove the charity from the trust should be revocable. The trust itself is not revocable from the IRS's perspective—the IRS does not care which charity receives the remainder as long as it all goes to one or more charities—but for the charity's records the trust may or may not come to the charity. Also, if the charity is not the trustee, the gift might be considered irrevocable because the charity would have no control over the financial management of the trust. This point is more important when calculating the projected trust value, both nominally and inflation-adjusted, than it is on an annual basis, but it is an important distinction nonetheless. All pooled income fund gifts, gift annuities, and retained life-estate gifts should automatically be considered irrevocable.

Life insurance presents a real problem. Clearly, a newly established policy is revocable, even though the charity is the owner, because the donor might not continue to pay the premiums. With most life insurance gifts, the donor pays the premiums, either directly to the charity or to the life insurance company; this practice makes it difficult for the charity to be certain that the policy will remain in force. In that sense the gift is revocable. On the other hand, a paid-up policy is irrevocable because, with all the premiums paid, the insurance company must pay the death benefit when the insured donor dies.

SUMMARY OF OBTAINED EXPECTANCIES
THIS FISCAL YEAR

| GIFT | NUMBER | AMOUNT | % |
|------|--------|--------|---|
| **IRREVOCABLE:** | | | |
| Pooled Income Fund | 6 | $ 49,512 | 8.8 |
| Unitrusts | 2 | $270,507 | 48.0 |
| Annuity Trusts | 0 | $ 0 | 0 |
| Immediate Gift Annuities | 3 | $ 34,154 | 6.1 |
| Deferred Gift Annuities | 0 | $ 0 | 0 |
| Life Estates | 0 | $ 0 | 0 |
| Life Insurance | 4 | $209,467 | 37.1 |
| Other | 0 | $ 0 | 0 |
| **TOTAL IRREVOCABLE EXPECTANCIES** | **15** | **$563,640** | **100** |
| **REVOCABLE:** | | | |
| Bequests | 6 | $ 0 | 0 |
| Unitrusts | 0 | $ 0 | 0 |
| Annuity Trusts | 0 | $ 0 | 0 |
| Life Insurance | 4 | $400,000 | 100 |
| Revocable Trusts | 0 | $ 0 | 0 |
| Other | 0 | $ 0 | 0 |
| **TOTAL REVOCABLE EXPECTANCIES** | **10** | **$400,000** | **100** |
| **TOTAL EXPECTANCIES** | **25** | **$963,640** | |

**Exhibit 11.2**   Summary of Deferred Gifts Obtained in a One-Year Period

The paid-up policy needs to be distinguished, however, from a policy whose premiums are being offset by the policy's cash value and dividends; these policies are technically not paid up, even though most people commonly refer to them as if they were. The premium is still being paid in this case, but the payment is generated by the policy itself—it is not paid by the owner. That the owner may discontinue paying the premiums gives the impression that the policy is paid up, but the distinction is important to an insurance company. The charity needs to decide whether a policy whose premiums are offset—when the insurance company predicts no additional payments will be needed from the owner—is revocable based on the charity's confidence that the insurance company's projections are accurate and that no additional premiums will be required from the charity (or donor). Not many people realize, and few life insurance agents make this clear, that if the insurance company miscalculates the policy's growth and dividend projections, additional premiums will be needed to keep the policy in force.

Exhibit 11.2 records only the deferred gifts *acquired* during the year. Other information, such as that shown in Exhibit 11.3, should be used to show the gifts *realized* during the year; these amounts include what has been transformed from either a revocable or an irrevocable commitment into cash. Generally, these are the donors who have died. As the note to Exhibit 11.3 indicates, the cumulative amounts that are realized during the year differ from what the charity has on its records because many people do not inform the charity of their intentions. Despite the charity's efforts to identify people who have included it in their estate plans, this happens frequently.

The logical next step is to combine all deferred activity, recording all deferred gifts that have been established. Exhibit 11.4 is an example of how that information might be presented. These amounts show the total for all active expectancies, those whose donors or income beneficiaries are still alive. The total amount of irrevocable deferred gifts is almost $3

| | SUMMARY OF REALIZED GIFTS THIS FISCAL YEAR | | |
|---|---|---|---|
| **GIFT** | **NUMBER** | **AMOUNT** | **%** |
| Bequests | 5 | $1,755,000 | 65.7 |
| Pooled Income Fund | 12 | $ 120,000 | 4.5 |
| Unitrusts | 2 | $ 250,000 | 9.4 |
| Annuity Trusts | 0 | $ 0 | 0 |
| Gift Annuities | 15 | $ 150,000 | 5.6 |
| Retained Life Estates | 1 | $ 300,000 | 11.2 |
| Life Insurance | 3 | $ 85,000 | 3.2 |
| Revocable Trusts | 0 | $ 0 | 0 |
| Other | 1 | $ 10,000 | 0.4 |
| **TOTAL REALIZED EXPECTANCIES** | **39** | **$2,670,000** | **100** |

**Exhibit 11.3**  Summary of Realized Deferred Gifts in One Year

The numbers and amounts in this report may exceed those found cumulatively in the subcategory reports because some realized deferred gifts, particularly bequests, might not be known to the charity prior to the gift's realization.

**SUMMARY OF ALL ACTIVE EXPECTANCIES**
**FOR ALL YEARS**

DEFERRED OBTAINED

| TYPE | NUMBER | AMOUNT | % |
|---|---|---|---|
| IRREVOCABLE: | | | |
| Pooled Income Fund gifts | 13 | $ 135,012 | 4.5 |
| Unitrusts | 7 | $ 700,000 | 23.6 |
| Annuity Trusts | 2 | $ 300,000 | 10.1 |
| Gift Annuities | 16 | $ 280,000 | 9.4 |
| Retained Life Estates | 1 | $ 250,000 | 8.4 |
| Life Insurance | 10 | $1,302,700 | 44.0 |
| Other | 0 | $ 0 | 0 |
| **TOTAL IRREVOCABLE** | **49** | **$2,967,712** | **100** |
| REVOCABLE: | | | |
| Bequests | 57 | $ 500,000 | (17) |
| Unitrusts | 0 | $ 0 | |
| Annuity Trusts | 0 | $ 0 | |
| Life Insurance | 21 | $1,200,000 | |
| Revocable Trusts | 0 | $ 0 | |
| Other | 0 | $ 0 | |
| **TOTAL REVOCABLE** | **78** | **$1,700,000** | |
| **TOTAL EXPECTANCIES** | **127** | **$4,667,712** | |

**Exhibit 11.4**   Summary of All Active Expectancies

The amount shown for life insurance is the cumulative death benefit, not the cash value.

Amounts for bequests are not included unless the donor has notified the charity of the dollar amount. The number in parentheses following the bequest amount indicates the number of bequests with known dollar amounts.

million. The total amount of revocable deferred gifts is $1.7 million. The grand total is almost $4.7 million. The information in this report should include updated market values for all gifts so the trustees know the current value of all deferred gifts.

Finally, because deferred gifts are a portion of the overall fund-raising picture, their value should be shown with that of outright gifts. Exhibit 11.5 shows a summary of all gifts, deferred and current, divided into the type of gift, the number of each type, the amount of all gifts

## SUMMARY OF ALL GIFTS:
## OUTRIGHT, EXPECTANCIES OBTAINED AND EXPECTANCIES
## REALIZED THIS FISCAL YEAR

**DEFERRED OBTAINED:**

| TYPE | NUMBER | AMOUNT | % |
|---|---|---|---|
| 1. All Irrevocable Expectancies | 15 (60.0%) | $ 563,640 | 58.5 |
| 2. All Revocable Expectancies | 10 (40.0%) | $ 400,000 | 41.5 |
| **TOTAL EXPECTANCIES** | **25** | **$ 963,640** | **100.00** |

\* \* \* \* \* \* \* \* \* \* \* \* \* \* \* \* \* \* \* \* \* \* \* \* \* \* \* \* \* \* \* \*

**REALIZED GIFTS:**

| TYPE | NUMBER | AMOUNT | % |
|---|---|---|---|
| 1. Realized Expectancies | 39 | $ 2,670,000 | 18.2 |
| 2. Outright Capital Gifts | 17 | $ 7,300,000 | 49.6 |
| 3. Annual Gifts | 6,899 | $ 3,000,000 | 20.4 |
| 4. Gifts in Kind | 2 | $ 100,000 | 0.7 |
| 5. Foundation Gifts | 6 | $ 135,000 | 0.9 |
| 6. Corporate Gifts | 127 | $ 1,500,000 | 10.2 |
| **TOTAL REALIZED GIFTS** | **7,090** | **$14,705,000** | **100.0** |
| **TOTAL REALIZED GIFTS AND IRREVOCABLE EXPECTANCIES** | **7,105** | **$15,268,640** | |
| **TOTAL GIFTS** | **7,115** | **$15,668,640** | |

**Exhibit 11.5**  Summary of All Gifts Obtained and Realized in One Year

within each type, and the percent of the total program each type of gift represents. The Deferred Obtained category has two parts, irrevocable and revocable, and the realized gifts are divided into the different types of current gifts, including realized deferred gifts. This one-page report shows the value of the entire fund-raising giving program.

The purpose of these exhibits and any other financial reports should be accuracy and clarity. Unfortunately, too many charities are neither accurate nor clear when counting up their numbers. The pressure to build larger and larger capital campaigns and noncampaign annual summaries is growing. Charities need to honestly examine how they report their successes, keeping their own goals—and not those of others who would push campaign expectations beyond the charity's capacity to raise money or its capacity for honesty—in primary perspective.

# CHAPTER TWELVE

# The Planned Giving Consultant

*A consultant borrows your watch to tell you what time it is.*

**Anonymous**

The planned giving consulting business thrives. Look through the membership directories of the local planned giving councils, and you will see that the names of consultants pepper the lists. Some of them have retired, some have established a side business alongside a full-time planned giving job, and some work full-time as consultants. All help those charities that either cannot afford full-time planned giving staff or that wish to evaluate their programs from an outside perspective. The consultant is generally hired to determine and then communicate the state of planned giving affairs. Consultants often also play key roles in determining the success of a planned giving program.

## WHY HIRE A CONSULTANT?

What does a charity hire when it hires a consultant? The answer is a matter of some speculation, partly because the levels of talent, experience, and commitment among consultants vary. It is easy to see why charities find themselves in the dilemma of needing a consultant and at the same time unable to assure themselves that they will hire the right person or firm for their needs.

But what are their needs? What do charities want from a consultant? Surprisingly, the most common answer, especially among charities looking at planned giving for the first time, will be that they don't know. Not specifically. They may know that they want to get into planned giving or conduct a checkup on their current program, but beyond that most development officers are unsure. Imagine a development committee that wants the charity to become more active in the solicitation of planned gifts. Some have heard of planned giving through other charities they are connected with, and they see a need for this charity to begin a program. The reasons why a charity would hire a planned giving consultant vary, and the consultant's involvement ranges from hands-on help with staff and donors to an occasional office visit when staff can brainstorm changes in concepts and approaches to their program.

## To Help Start and Maintain a New Program

A charity that wants to begin a planned giving program normally does not have the in-house staff to evaluate its chances for success effectively. Generally, only an outside person, a consultant schooled in beginning and maintaining a planned giving program, has the ability and experience to do the job. A charity new to planned giving will have many questions: Is the constituency able to support a program? What types of planned giving vehicles should be offered? How will the technical and legal work get done? How extensive should the effort be? Should the charity hire additional staff? Each of these questions raises other questions: If the charity decides to offer a pooled income fund, for example, how should it be marketed? And should the charity adopt the sample language issued by the IRS or, because of anticipated exceptions, should it write its own trust language? A consultant can help answer these questions.

As part of the evaluation, a consultant will help identify planned giving prospects. This is not an easy task. Many development professionals think that planned giving is so elite that only those who have given the most are prospects. While many planned giving donors are those who have given much during their lives, many others are also prospects. They may include those who have given modestly but regularly to the annual fund. Those who give regularly have shown a long-term dedication to the charity and are likely candidates for a planned gift. Why the modest annual fund donors? Because the annual fund may not be the right vehicle to express their commitment. Planned giving donors tend to want to make a difference; the annual fund is money spent immediately each year, and a planned gift is usually earmarked for the endowment, the income from which will be used to pay for an ongoing project of the donor's choosing. Many planned giving prospects are at least sixty years old, own low-cost-basis, highly appreciated property, such as stock, want to receive a higher income from their investments than they have been getting, and have demonstrated interest in the charity over a number of years. A good consultant will review donor lists for the type of information that often identifies a prospect.

Further, a consultant can evaluate the potential success of a program and suggest ways to implement it. Most charities new to planned giving—let's be honest here—have no idea what they want or what they need. Planned giving has become such a popular topic that almost every charity wants to begin a program, or at least investigate how planned giving can be evaluated. Enter the consultant. A good consultant will evaluate the potential for success and then honestly report the results to the trustees and development staff. Many times that report, because of an uncertain commitment on the part of potential donors, will include a recommendation *not* to place many resources in planned giving. When a report does recommend going forward for a charity new to planned giving, a good consultant will specify how, realistically evaluating the probability of obtaining new planned gifts.

## To Evaluate an Existing Program

The need for a consultant at a small- or medium-sized charity without planned giving expertise on staff is relatively obvious, but large, well-established organizations also need consultants from time to time and the hiring process is even more tricky for them. Why does a program whose staff has the expertise, whose staff attends conferences and seminars throughout the year, whose staff meets regularly to discuss the issues of the day, need a consultant? Maybe it doesn't. But maybe it should.

Jack Nicklaus needed someone to help him tune up his golf game, even in his prime, and Larry Bird needed a basketball coach to keep his game at a high level. These facts are taken as self-evident—highly skilled professionals need an outside observer to evaluate their performances objectively. The outside observer may be less skilled than the star player at the actual playing, but he is more skilled at *evaluating* than the players are. The same is true with almost everything else, including planned giving programs. Despite a charity's success, from time to time a good consultant is needed to observe, evaluate, and correct weaknesses. Many charities that have good planned giving programs routinely hire a consultant to observe the progress of the program and to make recommendations about its direction.

## WHO HIRES THE CONSULTANT?

The decision to hire a consultant is generally made by a group of people, usually consisting of the trustees on the development committee, the development director, and the executive director. A planned giving committee or director is not usually involved because small charities or charities new to planned giving will not normally have either the trustee committee or the staff position, planned giving being a subset of the larger development program. This decision, as with other major hiring decisions, is normally made by a trustee committee.

"We need to get into the business of planned giving," asserts one trustee during a board meeting. "I'm getting a lot of literature from other charities and all they talk about is planned gifts, the tax deductions, and the increased income. Why can't we get into that kind of fund-raising?"

Preoccupied with this year's auction and annual fund, the executive director and the development director do not have answers. The charity was, however, partially successful at raising major gifts during a recent capital campaign.

The trustee continues. "I think we should hire a person to come in and tell us how we can get going with a planned giving program."

"How much will that cost?" wonders the executive director.

"I don't know. But why don't we allocate some money now for that purpose and start the process as soon as possible? I'd like to see what our potential is. After that capital campaign, I think we're in a pretty good position to evaluate our chances of success. I don't want us to lag behind other charities, and planned giving seems to be the way of the future."

"And what will we try to accomplish with a consultant?" The executive director has difficulty understanding the assignment.

"I'm thinking primarily how we can identify prospects and then get the expertise to go out to talk with them. The capital campaign identified several people who wanted to help us but couldn't because, they said, they did not have the income or assets. In fact, our consultants told us that a planned gift would probably be the only way many of our prospects might be able to make a substantial gift."

"Yet we didn't have the expertise or confidence to go out and ask these people to help by making a planned gift," said the director of development, to everyone but particularly to the executive director.

"Which is where the consultant comes in," responded the trustee. "I think."

So the staff have a directive to hire a planned giving consultant. Despite the desire to hire someone with consulting and planned giving expertise, the first difficult question—and perhaps the most important—is whom to hire. Consultants take no courses and receive no degrees in consulting. Where does the staff go and how should the consultant be chosen?

## WHO ARE CONSULTANTS?

A number of consultants are retired or former planned giving directors, many at well-known organizations, who have found a niche in helping smaller charities acquire needed knowledge. These people tend to know what happens in a planned giving office from their experience. Others, often younger, consult as their primary profession and have spent little or no time working in a development office. Some have legal backgrounds and others know finance well. Most possess a combination of technical skills and life experiences in the field. Further, many function in different capacities. Some are available one or two days each month, the most common arrangement. Others work for one client one or two days per week. Some follow the capital campaign consultant model, spending many weeks at a time on site conceptualizing as well as implementing the program's direction. Many technically know enough to appear to be qualified as consultants, but consulting is more than knowing information; it is a process, one that requires the important ability to assess situations and offer realistic solutions. More than planned giving officers themselves, consultants must be able to work effectively with others.

Many of these people make themselves known to the planned giving world through mailings or advertisements. Others sponsor planned giving seminars and speak at conferences to display their expertise. Conference speaking usually does not earn the consultant money, but she will receive instead a good deal of credibility by being a part of the sponsoring organization's faculty. Conducting a seminar is a way for consultants to educate planned giving officers, as well as to make money while marketing their services.

### The Attorney as Consultant

Jokes aside, attorneys seem to have more credibility than other people, especially when it comes to disseminating legal information. A charity might want to hire an attorney over a nonattorney as a planned giving consultant because the board may feel he is more capable. As the profession of planned giving matures, we see more and more attorneys in the role of planned giving director. Some charities, in fact, require a legal background for their planned giving programs. Is this growing reliance on attorneys as staff or as consultants good?

It depends, of course, on the individual being hired. An attorney unquestionably has had specialized intellectual training that nonattorneys have not had, and thus is likely to possess an ability to interpret the Internal Revenue Code and the Regulations with more ease than someone not so trained. Perhaps the attorney also will be able to deal with a donor's legal advisor better than a nonattorney. A donor's advisor may think the charity has prematurely advised on a matter requiring a legal background if his client—your donor—tells him that you have recommended that he establish a charitable trust. The donor's attorney has been hired most probably to preserve assets, not to give them away. So already the charity and the donor's attorney are working at cross-purposes. If the charity then is unable to convey important technical information, the attorney, already unimpressed with the proposed arrangement, will be likely to extinguish whatever slim chances the gift plan had to begin with.

## CHOOSING A CONSULTANT

The first step in hiring a planned giving consultant is to locate someone who has technical qualifications and who is credible. The National Committee on Planned Giving has a list of consultants, with references, around the United States. All one has to do is call the reference to get going on the search. Depending on the scope and budget of the project, a search can be local, regional, or nationwide. But since planned giving professionals are people who tend to talk regularly with each other despite geographical distance, getting the name of a potential consultant is not difficult. Typically, the process should not be conducted in a vacuum; the chances are high that a development person knows a consultant. The chances that the development person knows another person who knows a consultant are even higher. The problem is not one of getting a name, or even a qualified name (although that too can be a problem), but getting the right name. And that *is* difficult.

### Chemistry

The problem is partly one of chemistry. A consultant—a business owner in many respects—by nature has a significant ego, and not all egos work well together. Because very little in developing a planned giving program, especially in soliciting a gift, follows clear-cut, standardized procedures, the charity is forced to rely on the consultant's *subjective* thoughts as to what will work best. This problem is not unique to planned giving consulting. How any professional—attorney, accountant, doctor, or anyone else—works with clients is partly a matter of chemistry, and the more personal the contact the more important the chemistry. On that level, planned giving consultants need to have excellent chemistry with a lot of people: the development staff, particularly the director of planned giving, the head of the charity, the trustees and, many times, the donors.

So whom to choose? There are no easy answers. A consultant admired by some people is likely to be disliked or at least unappreciated by others.

"I did not like him," might go the conversation between two attendees at a planned giving conference.

"Why not? I thought he was great. Our donors loved him."

"Really? Well, we hired him to do a seminar for some of our top prospects and they all thought he was pompous and arrogant."

"How so?"

"He wouldn't answer their questions directly, for starters. Then one guy, an attorney, asked a question and the consultant almost insulted him by telling him he didn't know what he was talking about, that the question was dumb."

"That's not how he came across with a talk he gave to our group. Admittedly, they were low-key and didn't ask a lot of questions, but everybody liked what he said. He was also pleasant."

"Well, for us he wasn't right."

Different strokes. The process of choosing a planned giving consultant is subjective not only because she will get along well with some people and not so well with others, but because the consultant, being human, will have good and bad days. The same question from a participant at two meetings may be heard differently; the consultant's reaction might be different; the participant's judgment might be different. The process of choosing is necessarily flawed. The planned giving officer must rely on reputation, references, other associations with the consultant, and the consultant's success, or chemistry with others, during the interview.

## Experience

So much for recommending consultants. As noted, what works for one charity might not work for another. This is an inevitable problem given the nature of people. So what characteristics do you start with? Experience is often the most important criterion. Where has the consultant worked and for how long? A person at retirement age who has worked at one organization for many years, an organization that has a solid planned giving program, is perhaps the best type of consultant. As talented and intelligent as many younger people are, long-term experience in a planned giving office is valuable. The consultant knows, first-hand, the value of cultivation and is unlikely to suggest a crowd-pleasing solution, one born of convenience instead of truth, to get the job.

## Realistic Expectations

Two consultants are being considered for a job that demands on-site work two days per month. One trustee asks when the charity will begin to see results. The first candidate explains that it is hard to know, that developing a program takes a long time, that she will need to analyze lists of prospective donors, interview others close to the charity (including current and former trustees), and develop a plan to solicit planned gifts. The trustee is not impressed with the lack of specificity. The other candidate says that results will be forthcoming within six months, that he and the planned giving director have discussed prospects and have already identified—at no cost to the charity—five people who are likely to make planned gifts. The latter response is designed to impress the people who want to see results. No contest—the unspecific consultant who raises more questions than she answers will need to find another client to help. The specific consultant full of promises gets the job.

Of course. Is that not always the result, the easy answer victorious over the thoughtful one? Not always, actually. Charities need to understand how planned giving works, the nature of process. They cannot expect to create a program on demand and realize instant results. Even a charity that has done a good deal of work in cultivating its donors for outright gifts still needs to work hard to implement a planned giving program. From both the technical and human perspectives, putting a program together requires work, dedication and time. People don't make decisions quickly and they will not die quickly. The end-of-quarter mindset brought to the boardroom by some trustees must be thrown out the window when it comes to measuring success by how much money is received from a planned giving program. No consultant can change that, no matter what salesmanship he displays.

Salesmanship is an integral part of planned giving, however. Getting a person to part with her money is difficult. Yet the consultant sells to the charity first and the charity needs to be acutely aware of too much hype, too much glitz, too many promises. He needs to be a salesman but not too much of one, and the charity has the responsibility of knowing the difference. Choosing a consultant is not an easy process. The most important characteristic is honesty. Look for the response that is too quick or sounds too glib. A consultant who promises anything other than a good effort promises too much. A good effort, of course, includes a strict schedule and an adherence to establishing short-term goals, such as a development committee primer on planned giving, or an estate planning presentation to potential donors, or a review of planned giving prospects. But promising anything beyond the knowable and the concrete—promising when a gift will be made, who will make a gift, what size a gift will be or the type of gift that a prospect will make—is irresponsible.

## WHAT CONSULTANTS DO FOR THE CHARITY

### Review the Program's Potential

Consultants are expected to perform many tasks, the most important of which is to design a program, a blueprint of how planned giving donors will be identified and solicited. The least important component of the process—most of the time mistaken to be the most important part—is the technical ability required *after* the gift decision is made. Too many charities make the mistake of asking the consultant if he can draft, or has access to, charitable trust documents. Of if she can calculate the exact remainder value of a potential gift. To wonder how a gift can be structured is misguided at such a nascent point in a planned giving program. The donor must be inspired to make a planned gift based on the works, the mission, of the charity. Telling prospects of the works of Congress and the IRS can come later. Yet the technical issues associated with planned giving are seen by many as the most daunting, and many development people and trustees focus on that aspect of the process instead of the important parts—developing a long-lasting program with the right fundamentals.

This is the first sign of trouble: The consultant who says that she can provide IRS rulings, remainder values, cash flow analyses, and other technical information misses the point when she fails to tell the charity that donors are primarily inspired by its good works. Who cares whether the consultant can calculate a remainder value? Who cares even what the remainder value is on a theoretical gift? Besides, anyone with a planned giving software program can calculate almost anything. A good consultant will engage herself in a discussion about the charity's mission and how it has cultivated its donors over the years.

The credentials for consulting are not established, and anyone can establish herself as a consultant. The larger organization will not have the same needs, either in technical expertise or in time, as the smaller one will. The consultant in the former situation needs to evaluate the program on a broad scale, asking questions such as "Is the program all it can be with the kind of constituency it has?" Or "Has the charity overlooked too many out-of-the-ordinary types of planned gifts?" This could mean an examination of the number of lead trusts, bargain sales, gifts of closely held stock to a unitrust, limited family partnerships, or asset replacement plans.

The consultant might also ask if the solicitation process is properly including a conveyance of the charity's mission. In addition, the consultant might evaluate the history of the program to note trends in giving patterns and the types of gifts that are received. For example, are gift annuities being offered to people who are too young? It is possible that when the program began several years earlier, the emphasis was on getting gifts at almost any cost. Today that same effort needs to be examined in light of the actual amount of remainder value the gifts have. Are payouts too high? Is it possible to notch up the effort to be more disciplined in offering the right gifts for people in the right circumstances for the gift? Can trust payouts be lowered, on average? Should the pooled income fund, started 10 years ago with people in their mid-sixties, change its investment goals to reflect a higher income and less growth for people now approaching their late seventies? Are there people in the donor base who are likely planned giving prospects? Have minimum gift policies been well thought out? These are questions of maturity, not the type of questions asked when a program is starting out. While the idea behind using a consultant for a small charity is to begin a program, the idea behind using a consultant for a good program is to make it better.

## Conduct Seminars

Consultants also conduct planned giving seminars for donors. The difficulty in getting the right person for that job is twofold: finding someone who knows the subject *and* who can convey the information in an understandable fashion. Neither is an easy problem to solve, and surprisingly few experts on planned giving are good at both. Assuming that you know something yourself about planned giving, stand up in front of a mirror—right now—and explain what a charitable remainder unitrust is. Do this within five minutes. (A tight time constraint is necessary because a typical presentation lasts no longer than two or three hours and usually includes a description of gift vehicles and the assets that might fund them, as well as an overview of the income, gift, and estate tax system.) In addition, when a presentation is successful the audience will have many questions. The presentation must be inspirational as well. In addition to education, the main idea behind the presentation is to inspire the audience, which is full of planned giving prospects.

After you have finished describing the unitrust to yourself, will you be comfortable answering a question about using real estate to fund it? Or a question on the tax effects of a nonspouse additional income beneficiary? To say that the unitrust has a minimum payout of 5 percent and the income fluctuates each year depending on the asset's value is not nearly enough. A good consultant will be able to do this well and with a respect for the audience that will convey an interest in their situations. Only someone knowledgeable in the technicalities of planned giving and skilled in educating will be capable of competently presenting this information.

## Draft a Brochure

Almost every beginning planned giving program claims authenticity when it has developed a brochure. Usually the consultant has a hand in the brochure's development. Until something can be left on the donor's bookshelf or coffee table, it seems that the program has no validity. That such a brochure or pamphlet should be produced is not at issue. What the pamphlet should contain is. Some of the nicest, slickest, and most complete planned giving brochures, the kind with all the math, along with pictures and prose, are the product of a great deal of work and a lot of expense. The consultant has labored with the staff to get just the right tone and colors, and the piece is perfect.

It also might be useless. The charity cannot know this, however, at least before the fact. The charity has entrusted itself to the consultant who has advised that such a brochure is necessary. How can the charity, which knows nothing about planned giving, know otherwise? The staff take it on faith that the consultant knows what to do. Which is the way it may have to be, but to develop a brochure without a program or prospects is foolish.

But something must be prepared to send to or leave with prospects. Something must be written to allow the prospect to read about the program in the absence of the charitable representative. A brochure does serve this purpose, but the brochure should make sense in the context of the effort. A four-color tome of 20 pages for a program that has yet to establish its pooled income fund, or register to solicit gift annuities, or receive its first remainder trust gift has a false ring to it, sort of like a facade embarrassingly masking a shallowness. The purpose of a brochure, no matter how established the program, is to inspire; it is rarely to educate. The brochure should inspire its readers to ask for more information, even to request a call or a visit from the planned giving officer. To that end, the brochure should be simple, well-written, and accurate. It should not overstate the case for planned giving. It should be gift-specific; that is, it should not detail all the ways to give. Although many brochures have shown all the ways to give, donors should not be confused with too many ideas at once. The brochure serves the specific purpose of inspiring a donor to make a call or write a letter, and should not bore or attempt to educate him. A good consultant will know the difference and will play a key role in the development of a brochure.

## WHAT CONSULTANTS CANNOT DO

### Provide Legal Advice

A planned giving officer must remember that an attorney-consultant usually cannot provide legal advice to the donor or prospect. Certainly a nonattorney can never provide legal advice, but even attorneys at times cannot provide legal advice. Although this is a hot topic at planned giving conferences and much has been written about this, the issue comes down to one of specificity. Is the consultant telling the donor something so specific that the donor can rely on it if it is challenged in a court of law? In almost all cases, the answer is no. Those in the planned giving world need to be aware of the difference between a general statement that applies to a number of people regardless of their particular circumstances, and a specific statement to an individual advising particular actions. To tell a person that the law allows for each individual to give away $10,000 each year to as many people as she would like without incurring a potential gift tax is one thing, but to tell a person that she can now write a check for $10,000 to her son without incurring a gift tax liability is problematic because the donor may have *already* given away $10,000 to her son this year. The planned giving consultant may not know that, but the donor's attorney might.

Ours is a litigious world. What exactly is legal advice and why do so many planned giving officers—attorneys and nonattorneys—want to avoid dispensing it? Is the consultant providing legal advice if she tells the donor that a unitrust pays a minimum of 5 percent of the asset value each year? Probably not, because this is an established fact that can be found in many places, including the Internal Revenue Code. What about telling a prospect that he will avoid paying a capital gains tax when the trust sells a highly appreciated asset because the trust is tax-exempt? Again probably not. This is true and can be proven by reference to public documents—the IRS Code and Regulations. The ability to read and understand those documents is not necessarily a product of legal training. A legal background is essential in the interpretation of much of what is contained in the Code and Regulations, as well as in many other documents. But it is one thing to a donor that a unitrust has certain characteristics, and another when we say that the unitrust will specifically be the best, or even a useful, instrument for that donor. Not every statement relating to legal matters is a legal opinion. Is telling a person to stop at a red light providing a legal opinion? Even though it would be illegal to run the light, telling the driver to stop would hardly add up to practicing law without a license.

So it is with planned giving. Most of what is disseminated is supported by text in the Internal Revenue Code and nonattorneys would be unable to say anything if telling donors the rules of planned gifts could be construed as providing legal advice. But if telling a donor of the minimum payout in a unitrust or of the saved capital gains taxes is not providing legal advice, what is? The words "This plan is best for you" might be. So would the lack of a qualifier in the above examples, especially the one on saving capital gains taxes. What if the donor has identified a buyer for the highly appreciated land and is talking to the planned giving director because he knows about the capital gains tax benefit? Even though the capital gains tax benefit is generally available to donors, if this donor has found a buyer and a purchase and sales agreement has been signed, the benefit of avoiding a capital gains tax does not apply. Making a deal before making the gift disqualifies the capital gains tax benefit. It is, on the other hand, difficult to think of a needed qualifier for the 5 percent minimum payout on the unitrust.

The consultant with legal training in this situation has no more authority than the nonattorney because the consultant is paid by the charity and not the donor. Despite all the talk of how much planned giving officers help their donors, a charity does not provide legal advice, even if the advice is provided by an attorney. Even if it is free to the donor. Whatever is conveyed cannot be construed as legal advice. Even if the advice were legal in nature and the donor could rely on it, the consultant would create an issue of conflict of interest. For whom does the consultant work? This is most easily established by examining who pays his fee. If it is not the donor, the consultant does not represent the donor, no matter what. The donor needs his own counsel, counsel that he—not the charity—pays. That a consultant is an attorney does not change this fact.

So when it comes to hiring a consultant, if she has a legal background, hire her on the basis of a broad range of talents—including the ability to get along with people—and experience, and view the legal experience as an extra benefit. Do not hire her solely because she is an attorney, and with the expectation that legal advice will now be provided to the donors.

## Do the Planned Giving Director's Job

A consultant should not attempt to do the job of the planned giving director. While he can review donor lists and make recommendations about the type of person who might be a planned giving prospect, he cannot actually compile the list. Nor can he make telephone calls to prospects on behalf of the charity. Only a person from the charity—a member of the professional development staff, a trustee, or other volunteer committee member—should contact potential donors. Further, regardless of who makes the contact, it should be coordinated with the development office. Clearly, this is not the job of a consultant.

## THE CHARITY'S ROLE IN A CONSULTING RELATIONSHIP

### Provide Adequate Resources

The consultant must be provided with enough time and money to make recommendations and ensure that they will be carried out. The consultant must spend time with the planned giving officer and others who are part of making strategic policy decisions; they must be available to assist the consultant in evaluating various aspects of the planned giving program. Adequate time also means a commitment on the part of trustees and staff to work in the consultant's absence. For example, if the consultant asks that a list of prospects be created, the planned giving director must accomplish this task by the time the next meeting takes place. The planned giving director is not serving her cause by not doing the job. The consultant cannot continue and the work will not get done. If she says that she had to work on the annual fund or the auction instead, she is really saying that the planned giving task that was assigned by the consultant, and to which they both agreed, was not important enough. And if it's not important enough, then a consultant should not have been hired to begin with. Even though this sounds obvious, surprisingly many charities find themselves in this predicament.

The other resource is money. Adequate financial resources must be available to carry out decisions made—there must be enough money for printing a brochure or traveling to visit a prospect. Enough money also means a budget for the consultant's fees. If a year-long contract has been approved, all of the consultant's fees should be budgeted; the charity should not fire the consultant should resources—including her salary—disappear.

These matters must be considered before the consultant is hired to work for the charity. A meaningful consulting relationship is designed before the relationship begins. This means that the charity must be as specific as it can be about its needs. It must ask how the consultant works, what activity is provided within the fee structure and what is additional. How expenses are limited should be discussed. To the degree possible, the charity should outline its goals for the relationship, and then ask the consultant to be specific about how she would accomplish those goals.

For her part, the consultant needs to use her experience and add to the charity's list anything she thinks has been missed. For example, the charity might not think of sponsoring a planned giving seminar for its donors and so she might suggest it. The consultant needs to ask as many questions as possible so the charity has a good idea of what to expect in the relationship and how much it will cost.

As mentioned earlier, consultants and charities need to be honest with each other from the very first moment, including during the interviewing process. Expectations are set at the beginning. If charities too need to be honest and commit whatever resources are needed to get the job done, it is the job of the consultant to define the job. That is one important aspect of a consultant's job. Then, once expectations have been set, they must be met—by both parties to the agreement. Allocating the proper resources to meet expectations must be part of the deal.

## Follow the Consultant's Advice

The planned giving consultant is trying to earn a living, just as the planned giving director is. The consultant wants to make money helping other charities acquire planned gifts. Beyond that, he wants to work with those who will listen to him, at organizations where he will make a difference. The worst thing for a consultant is to be hired and then for the development staff to ignore his advice. If the advice is good, follow it; if it is not, fire the consultant. But do not hire a consultant and then ignore his advice. This is a waste of money and is frustrating to everyone involved.

To be told that a prospect needs to be saved for a solicitation of an outright gift, especially if the person has expressed a desire to make a planned gift or cannot make a current significant gift, may be frustrating to a consultant. To be told that the charity really does not want to apply to the state's insurance department to establish a gift annuity program may also be frustrating to a consultant; one of the most popular gifts for small donors is the gift annuity. Also, a consultant will become justifiably frustrated if his recommendations on crediting gifts, especially during a capital campaign, are ignored. Not all consultants agree on these matters among themselves, but if the charity disagrees with its consultant to the point where progress is lost and communications become slow and anguished, it is better for the relationship to be severed. In fact, a good consultant will take the initiative on this matter by describing his position on this eventuality before he is hired.

## THE TERMS OF THE CONSULTING AGREEMENT

"Consultants cost too much money," the head of a charity might say. "How can they justify such outrageous fees?"

Most consulting arrangements are the result of an agreement, signed by a representative of the charity and the consultant. Often, a consultant is chosen after she responds to a Request for Proposal. Despite that, however, the topic of how much a charity pays for expert advice is for the most part unexamined. The consultant usually defines her fee as a daily rate and the charity accepts it, perhaps modifying the amount by an established number of days per month or quarter the person works. But the rate is usually set and it usually seems high. Why it is high is almost never discussed. Typically, a consultant will charge one amount if she is to be on site just once to make a presentation to the board or to donors, or if she is to evaluate a program that takes one, two, perhaps three days. She will then charge a lower daily or hourly amount if the relationship is to be ongoing. But even that lower amount is a lot of money. If a consultant is paid $2,000 per day and works two days per month, she will be paid $48,000 for the year by that one charity. Not all consultants charge in that range, of course, but many do; some charge less and several charge more. As with any business decision the question is not only what a service or product costs, but what is being purchased, the benefits of the product or service. The reason $2,000 a day is expensive is that the number is compared with the salaries of the employees at the charity.

"This consultant is getting $2,000 per day?" the trustee asks incredulously. "Why, that means she's earning over $600,000 per year, and that's outrageous!" The trustee, of course, merely multiplies the daily rate by 300 days, taking into account, in his mind, a sufficient reduction for weekends and holidays. But let us look at the numbers a bit more closely.

The typical consultant does not work 300 days per year, or at least not 300 billable days per year. Weekends and holidays actually reduce working days to about 260 days. Even then, however, with five clients who require two days per month, and an additional 10 board or donor presentations each year, the number of days equals 130. This, at $2,000 per day, is $260,000. But that's not all. No consultant has ever simply worked for the days billed. As with most good attorneys, the line consultants draw between actual work and billed work gets fuzzy and the consultant usually loses. That's just the way it is with consulting and working outside of the supervision of an office.

From the $260,000 the consultant subtracts overhead and social security taxes. Overhead can be quite a lot. If she has even a small office, rent could be about $1,500 per month, and a secretary might cost $20,000. That's $38,000 right there. Of course, the secretary's social security taxes need to be paid, adding $4,000. Health insurance for the two of them might add another $20,000 of costs associated with salary—$10,000 for each person's insurance. That's $34,000 for the secretary. Rent, the secretary's salary, and health insurance add up to $62,000. Add in heat, light, the costs of phones, a fax machine, mailings, office furnishings, and travel not paid for by a charity—such as the first visit to a potential client—and the overhead typically approximates one-half of the total revenues. In this case that could mean about $130,000. This leaves about $130,000 for the consultant, a little over 7 percent of which goes for her half of the social security tax bill. This leaves $121,000, before federal and state income taxes. This may still seem high, but not astronomically.

Now compare that with a person who makes $65,000 as a planned giving director. The charity pays his salary as well as its half of social security and office expenses. Assuming that the overhead costs are about the same—$130,000 with the social security taxes figured in—that brings the total to about $195,000. But many charities provide their employees with retirement plans, partially paid for by the charity. This can average about 5 percent (many times it is higher), so that would add another $3,250. And what about travel time to see donors? The charity's planned giving person also does not work 300 days per year, or even 250. He solicits gifts much less of that time, following through on prospects and attending educational conferences with the rest. In the end the two expense numbers are remarkably close. The idea is not to get them close, though. No one has ever said it's cheaper to use a consultant than to hire a good planned giving director or an assistant, but the cost question is now more in focus.

Further, the consultant has one problem the planned giving director does not have: the element of risk. Risk in our economic society has always been rewarded because of its downside. If the consultant does not have five clients, but three, she loses a great deal of money without lowering her overhead. Certainly after enough time earning less money, overhead would need to be adjusted downward, but the risk is ever-present in a consultant's life. The planned giving director has no such element of risk. He, of course, needs to do a good job, but the job is there if he does well. This is not the case with consulting.

This does not mean that the consultant's fees should not be negotiated or even discussed. A consultant needs to be specific about what he will deliver—not in terms of the gifts raised but of activities accomplished and time spent—as well as what the charity will do. The consultant, for example, will not see donors or take time on the computer to design a tracking system for planned giving prospects. The agreement might specify, however, that within three months she will provide a detailed evaluation of the planned giving program, and how to proceed. This will require visits with several people on the charity's staff and some board members, and the people should be named and the length of each visit specified in advance. Although it is not necessary to determine beforehand where and when all the meetings will be, the agreement should specify that actual expenses incurred will be reimbursed to the consultant, and outline the procedure for claiming them. During the latter phases of the relationship, the agreement needs to spell out how many seminars the consultant will conduct, and, for charities with geographically diverse prospects, where the seminars will be held. The agreement should require the consultant to write up all activity and visits so the charity will have a record. The agreement might also address the question of confidentiality; some donors might tell a consultant things they would not tell the charity, and the consultant should be clear that, if that happened, she would honor the donor's confidence. Within reason, the more specific a consulting contract can be, the better.

Specificity means that instead of saying that the consultant will work two days per month for the next 12 months for a daily fee, the agreement needs to outline how those days will be spent, with specific goals (the number of meetings and activities) attached. This also does not mean the agreement needs to be so detailed as to make flexibility impossible. Flexibility in a consulting relationship is necessary.

Consultants abound and always will. Charities will always need the eyes of another, preferably those of an experienced, mature person who is able to listen, diagnose, and prescribe, as well as to work successfully with trustees, staff, and sometimes donors. This is a rare individual and the charity searching for a consultant needs to thoroughly evaluate each candidate's abilities and willingness to work on its behalf.

# CHAPTER THIRTEEN

# How is Planned Giving Learned?

*Education: the inculcation of the incomprehensible into the indifferent by the incompetent.*

**John Maynard Keynes**

For most people the technical aspects of planned giving are difficult to grasp. To learn planned giving is to learn a great deal about the law, the IRS Code and Regulations, finance, and human relations. Like any major in college, planned giving is full of technical information, generalities, and exceptions. Knowing the topic fully is knowing a lot. Planned giving provides a way for people with charitable intent to make a gift they might not otherwise be able to make. Altruism, therefore, is not the only ingredient of a gift. Although saving taxes is not the equivalent of beating the IRS, most donors are at least intrigued by the possibility of giving more to charity at the expense of the government. Uncle Sam may look stern while he points and says "I Want You!" but we all can say back "You Can't Have Me!" At least not all of me.

The business of giving has also become the business of planning, and an improperly planned gift can be unnecessarily expensive for both the donor and the charity. Planned giving officers need to be aware of protecting the charity's interests by not, for example, agreeing to too high a payout from a life-income gift. Conversely, the donor needs to be satisfied that her gift not only benefits the charity but also herself. How to do these things must be learned in an academic setting. Thus, in addition to the real classroom of planned giving—the donor's office or living room—practitioners learn the art and science of planned giving in a more structured environment—the seminar or conference room.

Seminars and conferences are not the only venue for disseminating information. Many groups have local councils that sponsor regular meetings where planned giving is discussed, many times with a knowledgeable speaker. These sessions are useful and generally allow for questions from the audience, but, because they land in the middle of busy schedules, they do not lend themselves to thoughtful discussions.

## SEMINARS

The careful observer will note that courses on planned giving have not yet found their place among the subjects taught at most colleges and universities. Although the faintest of efforts at the university level, as well as efforts to require certification, threaten the status quo, the lack of formally approved training curricula has meant that most practitioners have learned planned giving through one of the many seminars sponsored by private consulting firms or individuals. In addition, trade associations, such as the Council for the Advancement and Support of Education (CASE), the National Society of Fund Raising Executives (NSFRE), the Association for Healthcare Philanthropy (AHP), and others also offer training in small- and large-group conference settings. The most notable of these has become the intense annual conference of the National Committee on Planned Giving (NCPG).

These splendid gatherings usually last three days, and include, despite the variety of sponsors, an almost uniform array of topics. Broadly, these include the structure of our tax system and the three types of federal taxes, the variety of vehicles and methods to give, estate planning, marketing a planned giving program, donor psychology and—especially to be found in programs sponsored by a consultant or consulting firm—how best to employ the services of a consultant. In addition, sometimes because of budget limitations, people learn planned giving at small one-day or half-day seminars sponsored by consultants and local fund-raising organizations. Most of these are worthy expenditures of time because even though the abilities of the various faculty frequently are uneven, the mere gathering of like-minded individuals eager to learn usually produces energy as well as thoughts. Beyond what is learned directly from the presentation, the apparently idle chatter among colleagues many times spawns valuable ideas.

## "BUT WHERE DO YOU FIND THE DONORS?"

One of these meetings, a half-day presentation on planned giving, once highlighted an interesting dialogue between the speaker and a hapless attendee. The speaker, the planned giving director of a prestigious charity—we'll call him Peter—was speaking to a group about what he does to fill the hours of his day. Peter was knowledgeable and the audience was entranced with the way he spoke of the benefits associated with life-income gifts.

". . . and when this donor sauntered into my office the other day and asked about how he could best give away his $100,000, I told him about both the unitrust and the gift annuity. He was quite old, in his early 80s, and he wanted to make a gift, yet he also wanted to retain a sizable income for himself and his wife. I told him that to begin with, by making a planned gift he and his wife would live at least an extra ten years beyond their normal life expectancy." Great laughter. This old line is always good for a laugh for all the obvious reasons, but also may be true. Although not yet shown statistically, many planned giving professionals believe that donors tend to live longer because they often take better care of themselves and have a healthy outlook on life.

"Then I told him that the gift annuity would provide a larger income at first, some of it would be tax exempt, and the tax deduction would also be larger. Then I told him how the unitrust was more flexible, and that. . . ." And on he went, mesmerizing the audience with the magic of life-income gifts, not an unusual flow, especially at large meetings.

Speakers at these gatherings, highly credentialed, usually from a recognizable organization and occasionally good at public speaking, share their secrets to success. By the end of these sessions, those in attendance are nearly jumping out of their seats to call their offices to see if a particular potential donor might soon be available for an interview. Many flock forward to the speaker after he has finished to ask specific questions. Some measure the success of the presentation by the line of those waiting to ask questions of the speaker. Always the air is filled with excitement and a sense of accomplishment.

At this particular meeting Peter was doing a bang-up job, getting everyone delirious and expanding the general level of thinking about planned giving on several tiers. When he asked for questions, most people longed to know how the deduction was calculated (Why is it that most of the time, all else being equal, the unitrust doesn't provide as high a deduction as the gift annuity?), or what type of asset the donor used to fund the gift (Why is land such a touchy issue?), or what the cost basis was (Might there be a problem completing IRS Form 8283 if the donor does not know the cost basis?).

But one person in attendance at Peter's session, who seemed to take a long time deciding to ask his question, tentatively raised his hand and began his inquiry. "This is all very exciting and you're doing a great job." Polite seminar participants *always* preface a question to a speaker by telling him that the presentation is excellent and that they have learned more in the last thirty minutes than in all the years they have endured in this rewarding business. "But my question is much more basic than all the others I've heard. I'm almost afraid to ask because you might find it stupid."

The speaker responds elegantly and respectfully. He is also controlled and practiced at responding courteously to his subjects. At this point, any hint of a smile disappears and the look turns pensive. "No, no. Please. No question is too stupid or dumb. Just those that aren't asked." A pause and then an expectant smile. This comment sometimes brings on a few giggles, but today the audience anticipates a question that will ring relevant for everyone. No laughter this time, so the presenter encourages the questioner. "Please, continue, and ask your question."

"Well. . . ." The questioner takes a moment to gather himself for what he feels must be basic. "I was just wondering how it is that the donor comes to just drop by your office." He would have been too embarrassed to ask how it is that an 80-year-old could walk—much less saunter—into anybody's office.

Silence. The speaker contemplates the impact of the question, trying to comprehend its meaning. After a few seconds, the embarrassed questioner rephrases it. "What I mean, Peter, is how do you get people to the point where they're asking *you* how to best give away $100,000?" And with real confidence now, "That is, I haven't had many of those come into my office."

Great and spontaneous laughter. Such a silly concern. The laughter, however, is a product of the questioner's lack of guile and a nervousness among the many others in the room, a nervousness born of the knowledge that they too never have donors stroll in unexpectedly to give away their money. Now everyone in the audience, as well as Peter, understands what the questioner meant. "Very good question, uh. . . ." Lecturers say that about every question, especially the ones they think are not, and then try to address the questioner by name.

"John Allison. From the Michigan North Shore Chapter of the Small Charity."

"Oh, yes." Pause. "John." Pause again. "As I said, a very good question and one that I'm sure everyone else here has." That's the truth. However, the purpose of the presentation was to provide an overview of life-income gifts, and although Peter had prepared well with handouts and vignettes about his own daily routine, he was not prepared for the frankness or the simplicity of John's question.

"Well, John. We're fortunate to have a program at Rock of Charities where my primary job is to *respond* to those who inquire about planned gifts. Most of my workday is spent reviewing lists of those who have in some way or another inquired about helping us. I then call the people to set up an appointment. Occasionally people call me or come to my office to discuss their gift planning with me, like the man I was just telling you about. I can tell you that it's not every day this kind of thing happens, but since we began the program it happens every so often." Peter stops here for a moment to determine if he has said the right thing. After all, that's the way it is where he works. "Does that answer your question, John?"

John, more grateful to be now finished with his embarrassment than to have his question answered—for, in fact, it was not—quickly replies, "Yes, thank you," and then sits down. But John is still as bewildered as ever.

The problem here is that Peter's planned giving program really began many decades ago. John's program has not yet been started. He still worries routinely about other development activities. He worries about the $10,000 grant he applied for last spring; he worries about the board of trustees who may or may not approve the purchase of a computer program to help him organize his database efficiently; he worries about the annual appeal that went out one month ago, the one with a $75,000 goal that will be characterized as a disaster if it comes up $5,000 short; he worries about raising enough money to keep his job. He does *not* worry about how to advise a donor who wants to give him $100,000 in exchange for an income for the rest of his life. He finds the idea intriguing, but he has no time to worry about so irrelevant a problem.

Yet he wants to begin a planned giving program. That is why he has attended today's session. He has read articles in the *Chronicle of Philanthropy* and other periodicals. He also has read a book on planned giving. He senses that planned giving might be a way to get his charity out of the daily routine plaguing him since he arrived three years ago, and he wants to know more about what has been described to him (incorrectly) as a panacea. Any program able to produce donors willing to plunk down six-figure gifts is not all bad. John is a smart man and looks for ways to improve himself and his charity. He is not afraid to expose himself to new ideas, nor is he hesitant to apply them. But he has yet to attend a seminar or a conference that shares the secret of producing donors. For John, the gap between mastering the technical aspects and actually beginning a program is never bridged at these gatherings.

## THE SHORT SEMINAR

Although the small, relatively inexpensive half-day or full-day presentation is useful to exchange ideas, meet new colleagues, and take a day away from the office, it does not meaningfully teach. It is said that a seminar is useful if only one worthwhile idea emerges that can be employed back at the office. True enough, but learning planned giving requires more than taking notes for one hour or one morning or one day or even three days. Despite the rush of adrenaline seminars produce, planned giving is no more learned by attending a half-day seminar than flying is learned by sitting in the cockpit of an airplane parked on the ground.

Further, and in defense of Peter, the successful planned giving program takes a great deal of time to mature to the point where people sometimes walk in off the street and ask how to give away their money. Think about that and you will realize that Peter had no answer. None could be forthcoming—at least none that could be employed immediately by John or anyone else upon his return to the office the next day. Asking that question is a little like a student asking how a professor has learned what she knows and what could be done to acquire the same knowledge today. The real work of developing such a successful planned giving program was begun well before Peter's time at his charity and now the position of planned giving director is, legitimately, partly one of designing gifts for inquiring donors. Another part (at least for most people), a more time-consuming and important part, is finding donors. To adequately answer John's question would require more than a planned giving seminar; it would require training in communicating a convincing mission statement to planned giving prospects, educating trustees, and developing a comprehensive marketing and cultivation plan.

And time. In addition to lecturing on these topics, which would take at least several weeks, Peter would have to point out that such development (yes, development means much more than fund-raising) often takes several years, sometimes several decades. Peter is the beneficiary of that work and, quite frankly, John is not. Although a half-day or one-day seminar can address some of the more technical matters of planned giving, it cannot address John's question acceptably. Those who send their development people to such gatherings to learn all there is to know about planned giving will be disappointed and, worse, place an unreasonable burden on their charges.

For what then, if not for comprehensive learning, are one-day seminars useful? Although a thorough review of all aspects of planned giving is impossible, much can be accomplished in one day. One-day seminars need to be humble about what they say they provide, but a review of the techniques and assets used to make gifts, as well as tips on marketing and donor relations, can be quite readily accomplished.

Inspiration, too. Much as an effective planned giving brochure does not teach prospective donors the technical merits of the various planned gifts, the short seminar does not effectively deal with the problem of cultivation or allow for in-depth discussions of the various solicitation techniques. It does, however, perform the important job of whetting the attendees' appetites. Ideally, they will leave the half-day seminar having learned the basics of one or two concrete particulars, and with a desire to learn much more about those topics by reading reference materials and newsletters. To say nothing of the newly found inspiration and confidence to call upon prospects.

The short seminar also has the advantage of time and cost. It allows an otherwise busy development professional to schedule time for compact learning, an important commodity for those who have other obligations. As well, the cost of a one-day seminar is less than for a longer one, important to budget-conscious small offices.

## THE MULTIDAY SEMINAR

The more conventional three-day seminar is more useful and more expensive. In three days a group of 20 to 30 people has time to study more topics more thoroughly, and to benefit from discussing the material with peers during breaks, meals, and evening activities. Many of these seminars also employ role-playing. Under simulated conditions, participants practice planned giving as solicitors and prospects. Although the exercise invariably produces the jitters, as well as many laughs, the process is educational because the attendant nervousness simulates the feeling of a real visit.

But the marketing efforts for these seminars are often misleading. Brochures for multiday planned giving seminars promise a lot. For example, some promise knowledge gained in intricate areas of the tax code, the most useful technical information about planned giving. "How Income Tax Deductions Can Save Your Donors Money" is a good one; it appeals to many people. Or "All You Ever Need to Know About Planned Giving." *All you ever need to know* has a sure-fire ring to it; you can't go wrong. Too frequently, however, seminar teachers choose the explosive slogan whose ability to draw a crowd outweighs its verity. Regardless of how long three days may seem, it is still too short a time for much to be absorbed or retained.

Yet many brochures do accurately indicate a seminar's contents. The prose is much less bold, but it is more honest. Such phrases as "The seminar is interactive" and "This will be a challenging experience" truly do describe the scene at some seminars. Also, specific topics that will be addressed are often described in the seminar's marketing brochure to make the participant feel that she will learn about that topic: "Dealing with real estate in a net-income unitrust," and "The difficulties of gift substantiation" are low-key but specific topics that, depending on the presenter—and the other participants—probably will be covered well. At least the prose is not hype.

Let's take a look at a typical gathering.

## EAVESDROPPING AT THE THREE-DAY SEMINAR

The group began to gather at the hotel conference room in Seattle around 8:45 in the morning. The brochure said that coffee and Danish would be served at that hour and that the seminar would begin at 9:00 sharp. The first arrivals did not know each other, so they busied themselves by carefully pouring their coffee or tea and then inspecting the Danish. They scrutinized the seminar room. It had a large U-shaped table that allowed each of the many participants elbow room and permitted the instructor to walk close to everyone. Most instructors—the good ones—will walk right up, almost to people's faces, and talk so that everyone pays attention. Eagerly and anxiously, after the room had been minutely inspected and there was no avoiding each other, they informally introduced themselves.

"Hi, I'm Bud Schultz from Texas. The Lone Star Hospital in Dallas." The accent is Southern and friendly.

"Hello. Diane Myers, from the Devon School in New Hampshire."

"Have you been in the business long?" the Texan asked.

"Actually, I'm only in my second month as Director of Planned Giving. I was a financial planner before then for many years." She stopped to sip nervously at her coffee and to take a bite of Danish. She wondered if he really cared what she'd been doing with her life. "And you?" she asked as earnestly as possible. And so it went for 15 minutes as people strolled in from all types of charities and all parts of the country. People from places like Harvard, the University of Southern California, the Children's Hospital in Los Angeles, the Sierra Club, the ACLU in New York, and 12 other charities.

By the appointed hour, the instructors—there were two at this seminar—appeared and called the group together. Despite the participants' initial nervousness, the world of fund-raising, and in particular planned giving, attracts outgoing, intelligent people who usually have little difficulty meeting others. The members of the group quickly began to know each other. In a few minutes most found that they had something in common: another fund-raising conference, a mutual professional colleague, or a summer residence on the same lake. They might even have shared potential donors.

On the table in front of each person was a large notebook, its more than 300 pages filled with information about taxes, gifts, and marketing.

Toward the end were articles taken from magazines and newspapers, mostly trade publications, addressing various aspects of planned giving. At first glance, the information was daunting. Many pages were filled with calculations that make little sense, and made the attendees feel somewhat like geometry students glancing through a calculus textbook for the first time. "Unitrust" appeared at the top of one page, followed by "Bargain Sale" several pages later. Perhaps, some might think, planned giving is too difficult to master. The new vocabulary alone is complex, and it is warning enough for some. The annual fund, from whose ranks at least one participant at this seminar has risen, provides refuge from all this technical and legal complexity.

Still more daunting was the quiz the instructors handed out. And on the first day! Questions were difficult: "What is the American Council on Gift Annuities?" Must be a congressional creation. "A Pooled Income Fund has a maximum payout of 9 percent—true or false?" Oh, true. Why not? I think I heard the business manager talking about one of those the other day. "Name three major features distinguishing an Annuity Trust from a Unitrust." Three? What about one? What about a hint as to what these words mean? "The appraisal rules require IRS Form 8283 to be completed for which—gifts of over $500 or over $5,000?" Appraisal rules? Again, true or false: "The gift tax rate is equal to the estate tax rate." The questions indicate what is to come for three days. More coffee.

To some newcomers to planned giving, it appeared that the seminar leaders must have been on a sadistic binge when they created these questions. Then this—and after the others, it must be true: "Because this information is so complex and technical, only large, well-established organizations should have planned giving programs—true or false." Amen. Some around the table believed that they might better enjoy organizing the phonathon.

"You should first know that planned giving is not as difficult as it seems." The words were the first, after introductions, from Elliot, one of the two instructors. "You can learn planned giving, and you will—at least the most important fundamentals—during these next three days. But this means that our time will be spent with complex ideas and some of you will get tired. Don't worry, though; this is natural. We'll try to make it as enjoyable as possible, but hard enough so that when you leave here on Thursday you can go back to start—or improve—your program, no matter how little time you actually have to devote to planned giving." Each individual in that classroom had a unique background and different reasons for entering the profession of planned giving. The two instructors, because planned giving is not yet a credentialed field (not even for them), had to at once address a variety of skill levels and attitudes. For fewer than three complete days, this classroom would be an intellectual as well as cultural melting pot. Theirs was a difficult job.

## PROFESSIONAL EXPERIENCE AND TRAINING

### A Profile of One Seminar Participant

Take, for example, one person's situation. Diane Myers came to this seminar because the director of development at her place of employment, the Devon School, a private secondary school in New Hampshire, had told her the best way to learn planned giving, at least to get a handle on it, was to attend a seminar. The brochure describing this one had crossed her desk two months ago. "Make Planned Giving Easy," it said on the cover, and on the inside, "Talking to Your Donor With No More Double-Talk." The brochure went on to maintain that those who attended would learn all about taxes, the many ways of giving, how to "help your donor," and how to "increase your institution's endowment." What could be better? Not much, she decided, and because she had been hired as the new planned giving director, she had better quickly learn something about this field.

Not that she came to her new job completely unprepared. She was, in fact, a certified financial planner, and before she raised two children she had made a handsome living planning other people's finances. Her studies included estate and tax planning blended with a good deal of psychology. As a practitioner, she felt that she understood the nuances of financial planning, helping people like herself prepare for an unpredictable future. What did they say in one of her first courses on life insurance? Out of 100 people, by the time they reached sixty-five, 95 were either dead or dead broke. Few people actually plan correctly, she learned, and she wanted to help people realize that although the future is tomorrow plans must be made today.

The job in planned giving seemed so right when she read the ad in the *Chronicle of Philanthropy:*

#### Director of Planned Giving

The Devon School seeks a highly qualified, experienced professional as Director of Planned Giving. We are seeking someone with 3–5 years of experience in the field of financial, estate or charitable planning, and a bachelor's degree. A law background or the Certified Financial Planner designation will be a plus.

The Devon School is one of the oldest private secondary schools in the United States, located in Bragdon's Crossing, NH. The select-

ed candidate will be a self-starter and will regularly and enthusiastically look forward to a great deal of travel and meeting new
people.

The position is available July 1. Excellent benefits. Salary com-
mensurate with experience.

Another ad looking for God. One might wonder how many institutions seek employees who are less than "highly qualified." She felt
good, however, about taking on a new job. After 15 years, she felt a
need to again orient herself to her own goals, to begin anew the process
of becoming a person whose priorities were not always dictated by her
children. Unburdened of being a single mother to children who needed her around the clock, Diana Myers boldly sent Devon her resume.
Didn't they now call it a *vitae* or something Latin? Wasn't a French word
good enough any more? So much had changed since she last worked for
someone other than her two children.

Sent boldly but hardly with confidence. Oh, sure, they say they want
someone with a background in finance or fund-raising, but they're probably looking for a man. The little she had learned about charitable planning—there was only one chapter and no test on this subject in her CFP
studies—told her that most people who make bequests were old men,
usually in their late seventies. Wouldn't Devon want another old man,
or at least *a* man, to go talk to these rich old men who were planning
their deaths and what would happen afterward? And did she really
want a job talking to people about what would happen with their
money after they died? One of the least appealing aspects of being a
financial planner was talking about the need for life insurance; the subject of death always had to come up. And wasn't she glad when she quit
her practice to take care of her children, at least in part because she
knew, or thought she knew, that she would no longer have to talk to
other people about dying?

Although she felt she was capable of doing the job on a technical
level, it had been several years since she practiced her trade. But the
concepts behind financial and estate planning generally had not
changed, and she knew that the techniques used in planned giving,
while an elite slice of estate planning, could not be all that difficult to
master. She wondered, however, if she could become a part of the
atmosphere at Devon. She was not, after all, a graduate of the prestigious independent secondary school. She had attended a public high
school. Could she be accepted as a fund-raiser among the alumni as well
as the others in the development office? Technically capable, she was
still emotionally uncertain. And Diane Myers's story was just one of 20.

## Diverse Backgrounds

From where did the other 19 come? Some came from another department in the organization's development office. Many times a person will move from annual giving to planned giving; the corporate giving office and, at colleges and universities, the office of alumni relations also often provide new planned giving officers. Others came from other professions. More and more attorneys are entering planned giving, many times, they say, because they did not enjoy the rigors or politics of a law office, and find refuge and sanity as well as intellectual stimulation in the planned giving office. Some, like Diane Myers, also come with financial backgrounds, including investment management and insurance. They find that they can apply their mathematical and financial knowledge in a practical way to real people doing good things for good organizations.

Many planned giving officers are former teachers. One of the best backgrounds is teaching. Planned giving officers teach every moment they are with a prospect. The ability to communicate is paramount. Knowing the facts is important, but not knowing how to convey concepts can be lethal in the profession of planned giving, where each donor is different, with different intellects and attitudes, linked only by a love of the charity. Of course, it does not matter what a person's background is if he cannot or does not learn taxes and the gift vehicles, such is the importance of the technical aspects of planned giving. But a desire to learn and to be with people, as well as a sense of mission—much like what is demanded of donors—are also key ingredients of a good planned giving professional.

## TECHNICAL ISSUES ADDRESSED AT SEMINARS

The first day of the seminar was, by any measure, difficult for a newcomer to planned giving. The group learned the various types of gifts—such as remainder trusts, pooled income funds, and gift annuities—and the various ways those gifts can be funded. Then the instructors moved directly into taxes—income, gift, and estate taxes—the difference between ordinary income and capital gains income, and the level of tax on each. To learn the most from this experience, several people asked questions as new topics were introduced, challenging the seminar leaders.

"Wasn't the capital gains tax rate a lot less than the rate for regular income?"

"Yes, a long time ago," Ann, the other instructor, responded, "but now the two rates are almost the same."

"Almost?"

Then, the Alternative Minimum Tax (AMT). "In 1969, the same tax bill that produced unitrusts and annuity trusts produced this—a tax for the rich who otherwise would not pay much tax."

"Why is there a situation where the rich don't pay a tax?"

"Some rich people are able to make investments that exclude income from being reported on the regular tax form."

"Like what?"

"Well, like accelerated depreciation of real property placed in service before 1987, for one thing. And investments in pollution control facilities placed in service after 1986. Things like that."

Things like that. "What are those?"

"Well, a lot of these things—we call them adjustments and preference items—are the domain of qualified CPAs and other financial advisors. Don't worry about the particulars."

"So what does all this have to do with charitable giving?"

"Actually, nothing," Ann answers. "But for six years, the appreciated portion of a noncash gift was a preference item when calculating the AMT. You wouldn't believe the problems that caused."

"What do you mean?"

"For a while, between 1987, when that provision of the expansive Tax Act of 1986 went into effect, and 1993, many charities could substantiate the reduction or complete loss of charitable gifts of property, gifts many planned giving officers were certain would have been made had those would-be gifts not been subject to the AMT calculation."

"So, what you're saying is that this AMT is no longer a problem for people who make property gifts to charity?"

"That's right."

"So why are we talking about this?"

Ann thought for a moment before answering. "Because it reminds us all how fickle Congress can be when it comes to charitable giving. It was ludicrous—and that's being polite—to think that the 'wealthy' were unfairly avoiding their share of taxation by being charitable. After all, when a person gives an asset to charity, the asset is gone, forever. Further, the charity has full use of that asset. Combine that with the 30-percent-of-adjusted-gross-income limitation and you have no economic incentive to give away money. None. Yet some people in Congress believed—and many still do believe—that the wealthy are getting something for nothing. The charitable deduction is a fragile privilege, and we have to constantly fight to make sure Congress protects charities, which, after all, protect society. That's why the deduction is allowed in the first place, to encourage people to support the public good in their own private way."

Lunch time. Some participants actually understood what had taken place up to that point, while others were completely confused. Diane understood a little because she was able to call upon her tax planning background. But even she had never really dealt with many of these issues. Few of her clients ever had to pay an AMT, the charitable deduction notwithstanding. Back in her day, the only AMT preference item she knew about was the amount by which capital gain income was reduced, the 60 percent of that income excluded from tax on the regular tax form 1040. Now that's not even a problem, she supposes from the tenor of the class so far.

And then there's Bud, whose hospital hired him because he was such a great volunteer. He knew nothing about financial planning. He just liked to talk to people about the hospital that saved his wife's life five years ago. The hospital's development director thought that Bud was out of his league, and if Bud weren't the type to take advantage of learning new things his boss would think the tuition money would have been better spent on a golf membership for him. Not because Bud is dumb, but because he had no idea that this was what he signed up for when he took the planned giving job. Some discover at a seminar like this that they are in the wrong profession, but many more are like Bud. They do not have a technical background but are adept enough to learn what is necessary. They shine, however, as Bud soon learned about himself, when they sit with prospects who want to make a planned gift as much for the personal relationship that develops with the planned giving officer as for the charitable cause they wish to help.

## MARKETING THE CHARITY'S MISSION

In the afternoon, to lighten things up a bit, the instructors put technical issues aside and took up the matter of marketing planned gifts. Questions relating to advertising a planned giving program were raised. The group learned that marketing planned gifts is very much the process of marketing the organizational mission—if prospects do not buy into the cause, they will not make planned gifts.

One participant observed, "You say marketing and you talk of the mission. Everybody else talks about selling the tax benefits."

"Well, that's what planned giving might seem to be," responded Elliot, one of the two seminar leaders. "Partly because so much emphasis—and we do that a lot, even here—is placed on the technical aspects of getting the gift. But I feel—and I think Ann, my teaching colleague here, feels the same way—that the mission of the charity is what really motivates the donor. After all, every charity with a 501(c)(3) status has the same ability to offer tax benefits."

When five o'clock came everyone, including the instructors, was exhausted. Diane and the others felt that they had learned so much in one day that not only could they learn no more, they were suspicious of what they had already learned. What more could be accomplished in two more days?

## REDUCING THE COST OF A PLANNED GIFT

Homework, for one thing. The instructors had the participants take back to their rooms one sheet of paper with a calculation showing the tax benefits of making a planned gift. Ultimately, the idea was to show the true cost of the gift. The assignment took into account the donor's charitable income tax deduction for making the gift and the capital gains taxes saved by using an appreciated asset to create an income. This was compared to selling it, paying the capital gains tax, and then reinvesting the net proceeds.

The homework assignment looked short enough but not very simple:

### Homework Assignment

Sixty-two-year-old John Smith has $100,000 of appreciated securities whose cost basis is $20,000. They pay an annual dividend of 3%. He wishes to establish a Charitable Remainder Unitrust. Assume the remainder value is $45,000 and that he is in the 30% tax bracket. Calculate the following:

1. Taxes saved because of the deduction
2. Capital gains taxes saved
3. Total taxes saved
4. Net cost of the gift

Diane dutifully spent time that night working on the homework and came prepared the next day to explain how the donor saves money by giving it away. First thing, the instructors went right to the assignment.

### Income Taxes Saved Because of the Deduction

Ann began, "All right. Question number one. How much does the donor save in income taxes from the charitable deduction?"

"$13,500," said someone from California.

"That's right. How did you calculate that?"

"By multiplying the 30 percent tax bracket by the $45,000 remainder value."

"Good. And remember, donors subject to any state or local taxes, those who are able to deduct charitable gifts, will get an even higher tax benefit. Keep in mind, though, the 30 percent limit is against adjusted gross income (AGI), which means that if the donor's AGI is less than $150,000—which is what $45,000 is 30 percent of—the donor will have to carry forward some of that deduction. In this case, the donor needs an AGI of $150,000 or more to deduct the entire amount in one year, and can have as little as $25,000 to deduct the whole amount over six years, assuming no complications, such as another charitable gift." Ann then explained, "Thirty percent of $25,000 is $7,500, the deductible amount each year; that multiplied by six—the year of the gift plus the five years available to carry forward the unused portion of the deduction—equals $45,000."

Ann continued. "By the way, the 30 percent AGI limitation is not the same as the 30 percent tax bracket we're using here for our example. Don't get those two confused—the 30 percent tax bracket plus the 30 percent limitation a person can deduct from his adjusted gross income. That the two numbers are the same in this example is merely a coincidence."

Ann paused to see how many people understood the concept. As a way of finding out, she asked if anyone could calculate the AGI required to deduct a $100,000 gift in one year. The response confirmed her suspicion that this was not an easy concept for beginners.

After no one spoke for a while, one person raised his hand and said, "$300,000?"

"That's not bad because you seem to have the general idea. But let's get the math right. Thirty percent of something is not the same as a third. In this case, the answer is $333,333. Thirty percent of that equals $100,000. It's easy to do it the other way—knowing the AGI is $100,000, for example, and figuring out the deduction limitation—but, because sometimes donors want to calculate how much they can give based on their income limitations, it is useful to also know how to go the other way on this question."

## Capital Gains Taxes Saved

Elliot, the other instructor, prepared to pick up the discussion here and looked around to see most people taking notes. Satisfied, he continued. "Next. Number two. How much in capital gains taxes is he saving?"

No one spoke or showed a hand immediately. "Come on." The leader encouraged the students not to be afraid to make a mistake. "I really don't care if you're right, but I do want to know what you're thinking. How do you determine the capital gains the donor is not paying by making the gift?"

Diane spoke up. "I don't know, but I'd say $80,000, the amount of the appreciation."

"Okay," Elliot responded slowly, trying to decide how to let her know kindly that she was not correct. "Let's take a look at this one. It's a little difficult." He then went to the board at the front of the room and calculated some numbers. Despite desires to the contrary, math is an important part of understanding planned giving. "Diane is right in thinking that the appreciation is $80,000," John explained, "because the asset is worth $100,000 and the cost basis is $20,000. The $80,000 difference is the capital gains. But the *tax* on that if the donor sold the asset would be only 28 percent of that, or $22,400. He then wrote:

$$\$80,000 \times .28 = \$22,400$$

"Simple enough," he said when he looked back at the class. "Remember, the maximum capital gains tax rate—at least as of today—is 28 percent." Any questions? There were none, and someone from an Illinois hospital knew right away that the answer to the third question was the sum of both taxes saved—$35,900.

## Net Cost of the Gift

But a debate grew out of the fourth question, the net cost of the gift.

"I think that's simple—you just add the taxes saved from the deduction to the capital gains taxes saved and you get the total—the answer to the third question—and subtract that from the $100,000," a man from a United Way agency opined. "That would be, let's see . . . $64,100."

"But what if the donor was not going to sell the asset?" someone else wondered aloud.

"What?"

"Do you 'save' the capital gains taxes if you weren't going to pay them anyway? It seems to me that you don't save something if you don't spend something you wouldn't spend anyway."

Ann broke in on this after several others offered opinions that showed that the debate could go on longer with no resolution. "This is the kind of thing that gets us into trouble. Everyone here is right, of course, depending on his or her perspective. I caution you, however, not to use the capital gains tax savings as a benefit of making the gift until you know that the donor is thinking of otherwise selling the asset and then reinvesting it. If he isn't, look at it more conservatively. She then handed out two computer-generated sheets showing how the donor's savings looked (Exhibits 13.1 and 13.2). After the class took a few moments to study the sheets, Ann reviewed their contents. "The

IRS-calculated remainder value, the deductible amount, is actually just over $45,000, and we can see the benefits of the gift in each assumption, an increased yield of over 92 percent when compared with not making a gift, and an increased yield of almost 50 percent when the gift is compared with selling and then reinvesting the asset. Either way, since the stock was generating only 3 percent of annual income for the donor, the numbers look good.

"Interestingly, though—and you can see this at the bottom of the second page (Exhibit 13.2)—while the tax savings may be more when the donor avoids the capital gains tax, the immediate increased yield will be less. The donor almost doubles his income when he compares it with his current stock dividend. But we are increasing it by only a little less than 50 percent when we assume he sells the stock, pays the capital gains tax, and then reinvests into something comparable to what the unitrust will invest in. The reinvestment amount will also grow each year, just like we would expect the unitrust to grow."

The tax points were made and slowly the class began to grasp their application in the world of planned giving.

## OTHER TOPICS IN THE LONG SEMINAR

The remainder of the second day and the entire next day were spent with a more rigorous examination of each of the trust vehicles and other gifts, as well as their applications, estate planning and marketing. The instructors even had time to organize a mock interview between a planned giving officer and a prospective donor. Although this went well—lots of good questions and embarrassing silences as the participants were unprepared to answer them—Diane felt that it did not truly duplicate the real world of the interview. So much had to be confined to a few minutes, so much information that would have been gathered from previous interviews and some from potential future interviews that included the donor's advisors. Yet it was plain that the interviewing process was not easy, that people would ask the strangest questions, and that the group, because they had not yet mastered the information, was not yet ready to respond to some of the problems the mock prospective donors brought out. "What about my kids?" was a favorite. Or "Does the pooled income fund guarantee a minimum income?" Or "My broker told me all about those unit trusts, and I'm not interested." Unitrusts and unit trusts are often incorrectly interchanged.

By the end of the three days, Diane felt overwhelmed, but as a former financial planner she understood the concepts well enough. Her problem was the question of why people make gifts. These three days

## CHARITABLE REMAINDER UNITRUST
### Comparison Report—Gift vs. No Gift

**Donor's Name: John Smith**

### GIFT INFORMATION:

| | |
|---|---|
| Value of Gift | $100,000 |
| Type of Gift Asset | Appreciated Securities |
| Cost Basis | $20,000 |
| Fixed Unitrust Percentage | 5% |
| Payment Frequency | Quarterly |
| Full Months until First Payment | 3 |
| Length of Trust | Lifetime of Beneficiary |
| Beneficiary's Age | 62 |
| Federal Interest Rate Used | 9.6% |
| Charitable Deduction | $45,144 |

### GIFT COMPARISON:

The following information is useful if the donor wishes to examine the potential initial income difference between making a gift to a charitable remainder unitrust and keeping the asset:

| | GIFT | NO GIFT |
|---|---|---|
| 1. Value of Gift | $100,000 | $100,000 |
| 2. Charitable Deduction | $45,144 | 0 |
| 3. Value of Deduction (30%) | $13,543 | 0 |
| 4. Donor's Investment (Line 1 – Line 3) | $86,457 | $100,000 |
| 5. Income (%) | 5.0000% | 3.0000% |
| 6. Income ($) | $5,000 | $3,000 |
| 7. Effective Yield (Line 6/Line 4) | 5.7832% | 3.0000% |
| 8. Increased Yield with Gift | 92.7733% | |

No planned gift should be made in the absence of a charitable intent or solely on the basis of financial expectations.

Note: This illustration is for educational purposes only and is merely intended to provide information based on certain assumptions. The donor or others should not interpret this information as legal, tax, or financial advice. Therefore, before entering into a planned or deferred giving arrangement with any charitable organization, the donor should seek competent and relevant professional legal and tax opinion.

---

**Exhibit 13.1**   Report Comparing the Initial Income With and Without a Gift

This illustration was prepared using the planned giving software ParaGon™, developed by Blackbaud, Inc.

# CHARITABLE REMAINDER UNITRUST
## Comparison Report—Gift vs. Sell and Reinvest

**Donor's Name: John Smith**

## GIFT INFORMATION:

| | |
|---|---|
| Value of Gift | $100,000 |
| Type of Gift Asset | Appreciated Securities |
| Cost Basis | $20,000 |
| Fixed Unitrust Percentage | 5% |
| Payment Frequency | Quarterly |
| Full Months until First Payment | 3 |
| Length of Trust | Lifetime of Beneficiary |
| Beneficiary's Age | 62 |
| Federal Interest Rate Used | 9.6% |
| Charitable Deduction | $45,144 |

## GIFT COMPARISON:

The following information is useful if the donor wishes to examine the potential initial income difference between making a gift to a charitable remainder unitrust and selling the asset and reinvesting the income:

| | GIFT | SELL AND REINVEST |
|---|---|---|
| 1. Value of Gift | $100,000 | $100,000 |
| 2. Charitable Deduction | $45,144 | 0 |
| 3. Value of Deduction (30%) | $13,543 | 0 |
| 4. Donor's Investment | $86,457 | $100,000 |
| 5. Capital Gain | $80,000 | $80,000 |
| 6. Capital Gains Tax Paid (28%) | 0 | $22,400 |
| 7. Investment Amount (Line 1 – Line 6) | $100,000 | $77,600 |
| 8. Reinvested Income (%) | 5.0000% | 5.0000% |
| 9. Reinvested Income ($) | $5,000 | $3,880 |
| 10. Effective Yield (Line 9/Line 4) | 5.7832% | 3.8800% |
| 11. Increased Yield with Gift | 49.0515% | |

No planned gift should be made in the absence of a charitable intent or solely on the basis of financial expectations.

Note: This illustration is for educational purposes only and is merely intended to provide information based on certain assumptions. The donor or others should not interpret this information as legal, tax, or financial advice. Therefore, before entering into a planned or deferred giving arrangement with any charitable organization, the donor should seek competent and relevant professional legal and tax opinion.

**Exhibit 13.2** Report Comparing a Gift with Selling and Reinvesting the Asset

This illustration was prepared using the planned giving software ParaGon™, developed by Blackbaud, Inc.

had shown her all the tax and income benefits of making a gift, but the root question—why?—still had not been addressed.

Making it more awkward was the presence of one particular development director, Scott Walker, who did not yet have his certified financial planning degree (although he announced that he was almost there), and kept insisting that the financial benefits many times clearly outweigh the charitable reasons for making a planned gift and that it really is a waste of time to approach people for whom making a gift is *not* financially beneficial.

## BUT WHY DOES A DONOR GIVE?

During the last part of the third afternoon, the instructors raised the question of employing the tax and financial information the students had learned in the context of using these benefits as motives for making a gift. Scott said he felt that this business was really great because people now didn't need a charitable motive to give away their money since they could do so well financially investing it with charity. This comment prompted other comments, and soon a debate grew.

The group was almost boisterous when Elliot took the position—perhaps to fuel just such a debate—that, indeed, given the tax and income advantages of making a gift, the charitable impulse was really only an unnecessary appendix to the gift planning process.

"Are there any questions?" Silence.

"Diane?" The question caught her by surprise.

"I'm sorry?"

"I just noticed what I took to be a look of confusion in your eyes, Diane, and I wanted to be certain you took in the material we just covered."

She remembered only that Elliot, an attorney, had been talking about the charitable impulse and how many people nowadays don't care about charity. This led her, she supposed, to wonder why she came into this business. "Well, I guess I don't have any questions right now."

"That's interesting." His eyes did not leave hers. Why wouldn't he simply ask somebody else?

"Why is that so interesting? I think you are quite clear on all your points and I believe I understand them all. So far."

"Well, I think it's interesting because I just made what I think is a controversial statement and none of you has taken issue with me." He removed his eyes from Diane and began to look around the room at the other 19 people who represented 12 other charities from around the United States.

"Please remember one thing. We have learned much these past three days. Technical topics like the federal gift tax, income tax deductions, remainder values, the Charitable Midterm Federal Rate, remainder trusts, lead trusts, and more. And we've also talked about marketing, donor solicitations, and issues you all need to address back in your own offices about how to implement a planned giving program.

"But remember that the world of charitable solicitations is one of people talking to people, of helping a person donate to support a cause. That's why all these fancy technical gizmos exist.

"A few moments ago I told you that many people make gifts because they want to make money. Further, taking up the position that your colleague Scott Walker has proposed, I said that the charitable impulse is essentially dead, that people are now making gifts regardless of which charity benefits, or even *whether* a charity benefits." Elliot paused to look around the room again. The time allotted for the seminar was used up. In a few moments people would need to leave for the airport. Darn! Why does this topic always have to come last, when there's no more time?

Mr. Scott Walker, the assistant director of Special Gift Planning at the Society for Wayward Children in Pittsburgh, confidently attended this seminar as an experienced planned giving officer. Not yet the director in his office, he had three years behind him in development, one year at a hospital, and two years employed at two colleges. He also spent three months at an ARC—Association for Retarded Citizens—in York, Pennsylvania. Scott had participated enthusiastically during the three-day seminar, with opinions and answers on almost all the topics covered. This topic was no exception.

"I know exactly what you're getting at. You've been saying all along that donors receive benefits from planned gifts that they don't get from other ways of making gifts. So now there are some people who are taking advantage of these benefits and making gifts without really being charitable. Right?"

Elliot hesitated, and then said, "Okay."

"Well, it comes as no surprise that these people see what's in the IRS Code and say, 'What's in it for me?' I think it's perfectly logical that we've come to this point. And I see nothing wrong with taking the breaks we deserve. I mean, so what if the person's not so charitable? If charity gets something and the donor does too, the only guy with a problem is the government. And that's the whole idea, isn't it?"

"But then you run the risk of the IRS taking all these benefits away," offered the person from the Sierra Club. "We can't really go out and sell these things as if they were tax shelters, can we?"

"And why not?" Mr. Walker would not let go. "Most financial planners I know are saying exactly that, especially after the 1986 Tax Act when so many other tax shelters got the boot. The charitable deduction is the only one left."

"Other?" someone else asked. "Is that what the charitable deduction is? A tax shelter?"

Then, several of the participants began talking at once, wanting to argue with what seemed an unseemly position, but not knowing how. "It just doesn't seem right to me," said one.

And another, "What happens if all the financial promises fall short, and the donor gets mad because he thought he made an investment? What then?"

The discussion had become the liveliest of any during the entire three days. But the grandfather clock in the corner of the seminar room chimed three times. "I'm sorry, but I must be getting along," said someone. "Traffic on Friday afternoons is horrible, and I have a four o'clock flight back to Dallas. I hope you won't think I'm rude to leave now, but your brochure said that the seminar would be over by 2:30." A few others in the room reluctantly mumbled their agreement that they too must leave to catch planes or beat traffic.

"I know, I know," said Elliot, with a raised voice, holding his hands up to signal that he still wanted their attention. "I'm sorry that we have overrun our time. This happens more frequently than I would like, but it seems we always get into discussions at the end of these seminars that just get everyone going at the last minute. I'd like to continue our thinking on this subject, though, and I want you all to stay in touch. You know how to reach either Ann or me if you have any questions about anything we covered this week, and I will be especially interested in hearing about your five calls to planned gift prospects next week." Most of the attendees were finished packing up their materials and were on their way out the door.

"And, oh yes," Ann said quickly. "Please be sure to fill out and return the evaluation survey. These seminars are as good as they are because of people who have attended before you, and they will be improved for others because of your comments." She paused to be certain everyone heard her, and then ended the seminar. "Thank you all for coming and good luck when you get back to the office." Exhilaration. A success. Good memories. And a lot on taxes.

## SEMINARS AND TECHNICAL INFORMATION

If anything—and the better seminars will be at least honest about this—the world of planned giving is difficult. It is not as "Easy as 1–2–3," and these people did not learn "All There Is to Know—And More!" Instead, perhaps mainly because the questions they pondered did not have easy or quick answers, they learned that although seminars like this can expose them to many of the topics that comprise planned giving, they can obtain specialized knowledge only after a great deal of hard work. Those for whom this was the first planned giving seminar will not yet feel very comfortable talking with a donor.

Imagine having recently learned about unitrusts, not yet an expert, and then sitting with a donor *and* the donor's advisor. "And you say that my client won't pay tax on his trust income if, once his highly appreciated gift asset is sold, the trust then invests in tax-exempt investments? What about the four-tier rule?" Although the attorney jokes sometimes fly rapidly in the confines of the lecture hall, it is best that not even the most expert of planned giving professionals make the mistake of offering an incorrect recommendation. Advisors can get pretty nasty. They and their clients know when someone doesn't know what he is talking about. A discussion about a charitable gift cannot be constantly interrupted with reference to notes or promises to get back to the person. No matter what any brochure says, no seminar can convey what only experience can—the comfort level to understand and respond to what a donor might ask. And even then, experience may not be enough. Specific legal matters require a qualified attorney.

The admissions offices at the better colleges and universities do not mislead their applicants. They say that the work will be difficult and the entrance requirements demanding. Perhaps someday, when those who teach planned giving—primarily the consultants whose advertisements are the most strident—are as concerned about teaching as they are about the income such seminars generate, marketing materials for planned giving seminars will be equally honest. Even the associations who support the various sectors of the nonprofit community—those whose motives to teach are apparently less financial than educational—however, need to be more sensitive than they currently are to what a participant will actually learn at one of their sessions. Learning planned giving is not quick and it is not easy.

Diane, for example, gloomily likened planned giving to selling insurance because each is a process of planning for death. Although it is true that the money from most planned gifts becomes available to the charity upon the donor's death and life insurance becomes available at the insured's death, the true professionals realize and communicate that the purpose of their activities is to benefit those whose lives and missions continue, that the planning helps others. That is what planned giving does for a charity. Because most planned gift assets eventually are placed into a charity's endowment, they allow a person's efforts during life to benefit others forever.

Like the high school and college classroom, the seminar chamber is the incubator of the learning seed, where the foundation of what is yet to be built is formed. In education, there is no other way. Although the examples used in seminars are almost always simplistic and therefore unrealistic, they still serve the vital function of defining the terms within which and the process by which planned gifts are made. One does not condemn the first-grade teacher for avoiding sex education. Things can get complicated in later life, and, although what one learns at age six has little to do with decisions made by an adolescent, much of the decision-making ability brought to the complex question was learned when the world was simpler. Such is the function of planned learning and the planned giving seminar.

Back to the office, then. One thing always mentioned and sometimes discussed at most planned giving educational forums is what to do back at the office. Mentioned and discussed perhaps, but most often ineffectively. There are no rules, no standards even, for the daily planned giving activity at different charities. These participants' lives are no different. As excited as they are in the immediate aftermath of the seminar, they each have a different job to do when they get back to their offices. The culture at one organization will be different from that of others, even among similar charities. The tools of this trade, although technically complex, are simple enough for most serious-minded professionals to understand, but their use as a part of identifying donors, making appointments, seeing people, and marketing the effort—the real work of planned giving—is hardly uniform. Hence John Allison's dilemma at the Michigan North Shore Chapter of the Small Charity, from where he looks for guidance to start a planned giving program. No course of instruction will produce donors at his door. In his case, learning the technical aspects of planned giving, while intellectually challenging, does not directly further his job to identify people in alignment with his charity's mission. The Michigan North Shore Chapter of the Small Charity is no Rock of Charities.

Yet, if together for only a short time, these convened people discovered a unity. The need for discovering common ground and establishing camaraderie, as much as for exploring new ideas, keeps the professional associations going. Especially at small charities, planned giving offers little in the way of a collegial family except through these outlets. Not many CEOs or directors or presidents are likely to engage willingly in the planned giving officer's quest for answers to dilemmas that only solitary work can normally resolve. That and an association from time to time with others who at least know the questions, if not always the answers.

No laboratory can predict the outcome of activity carried out in a noncontrolled environment. Even the best role-playing with the most sincere players inside the confines of an educational laboratory cannot hope to simulate the conditions that confront planned giving officers as they trudge into the homes and offices of those who may or may not make a gift to charity. By inviting themselves onto the agendas of others, those who solicit major gifts enter the lives of others; their hopes and dreams, their happiness and sadness, and sometimes their misery. Conferences and seminars provide only the briefest examination of the tools of the trade. Like that of almost any automobile, this profession's user's manual is difficult to read and quite inadequate for most confrontations. Yet the tools of taxes, gift structures, and marketing strategies are at least a solid foundation upon which the genuine efforts of persuasion can be built.

# CHAPTER FOURTEEN

# Did Someone Mention Ethics?

*A bad moral state, once formed, is not easily amended.*
**Aristotle**

## THE MODEL STANDARDS OF PRACTICE FOR THE CHARITABLE GIFT PLANNER

On May 7, 1991, the National Committee on Planned Giving and the American Council on Gift Annuities (then the Committee on Gift Annuities) adopted the *Model Standards of Practice for the Charitable Gift Planner,* consisting of ten guiding principles.

### Preamble

The purpose of this statement is to encourage responsible charitable gift planning by urging the adoption of the following Standards of Practice by all who work in the charitable gift planning process, including charitable institutions and their gift planning officers, independent fund-raising consultants, attorneys, accountants, financial planners and life insurance agents, collectively referred to hereafter as "Gift Planners."

This statement recognizes that the solicitation, planning and administration of a charitable gift is a complex process involving philanthropic, personal, financial, and tax considerations, and as such often involves professionals from various disciplines whose goals should include working together to structure a gift that achieves a fair and proper balance between the interests of the donor and the purposes of the charitable institution.

Ethics is a strange thing. Getting everybody to agree on what the word means is difficult, and perhaps impossible. No one seems to be able to agree on its application either. The *American Heritage Dictionary* says the following of ethics: "The study of the general nature of morals and of the specific moral choices to be made by the individual and his relationship to others." That particular definition of ethics also refers to a "moral philosophy." Also, the definition continues, ethics are "the rules or standards governing the conduct of the members of a profession." And then, "The moral quality of a course of action."

These are impressive words—"morals" and "standards" and "conduct"—but what do they mean? It is one thing to send a message through oratory, but quite another to send a message through action. We often speak of doing the right thing, but who does *not* want to do the right thing? Yet clearly not everyone—at least in everyone else's opinion—*does* the right thing. Perhaps everyone does not agree on what the right thing is. This is a tough, age-old issue. Our most concrete examples of what is wrong—murder, for example—are based on generally accepted principles. Some have been around longer than others and are the product of ancient philosophy. Today, we accept without question that murder is wrong. It is so wrong, in fact, that it is against the law and punishable in the most severe way. When behavior becomes so accepted, a law is passed; to behave otherwise is to break the law. Logically, then, ethical behavior, while perhaps generally accepted, is not *so* generally accepted as to have become the law. If it did, the question would be whether it is legal, as opposed to ethical.

This is why ethics, by its definition, is not a study of absolutes or a process that results in a right or wrong answer. Even the seemingly concrete example of murder has its gray area. What about murdering a person whom you know is going to murder you? Or murder a loved one? What about during war? Although these situations have their precedents for explanation, they do raise questions that the basic inquiry of the morality of murder does not address. And if something so absolute as murder has its gray area, almost everything else must, too. Ethical behavior does not have the weight of law, and generally it does not have the financial suasion of business decisions. Ethical behavior stands in a place by itself. This is why ethical guidelines are controversial.

## WHY CHARITIES RECEIVE PREFERENTIAL TREATMENT

When it comes to right and wrong in planned giving, the questions might seem banal were they not related to how our society is structured and how it views itself.

Philanthropy—our charitable sector—is considered the third leg of our society. Government and private business are the other two. Charities fit into neither of those categories, yet must satisfy one and act like the other to succeed. By being given the status of a charity—as defined in Section 501(c)(3) in the Internal Revenue Code—an organization fills a role that neither government nor business does well. In a large but true sense charities do for the common good what nothing else does. The list of American charities includes organizations dedicated to every imaginable cause. Education and religion are among the most recognized charitable efforts in the country, but the list also includes groups dedicated to end diseases, some familiar and many unfamiliar; institutions to care for the sick and the needy; and research centers, whose goal is to disseminate information on countless subjects. You would see those parts of society that government cannot address and business will not. That is why the government provides beneficial tax treatment, allowing donors to make tax-deductible contributions and charities to invest without taxation on their income or gain.

As a result of this special status, charities are more responsible to society as a whole than many people think. To put the tax benefits first—as far too many fund-raisers do—as a reason to help a charity, is to get it backwards. First, charities exist to help society. Second, government recognizes their value to society by providing tax incentives to keep them in business. Congress did not invent the charitable deduction and then go looking for charities to do their good work. This issue, as it is understood or misunderstood, is at the heart of most ethical issues in the world of planned giving.

## PERSPECTIVE

When a person reads the law, how can it be that one person interprets the words one way and another person sees something different? In the controversial case of the "Accelerated Charitable Remainder Trust," several people made a gift to a charitable remainder unitrust and then, through a quirk in the IRS Code, received tax-free income, as opposed to capital gains income. The quirk is the issue; some do not think the way the words are written is a quirk. Intelligent people read the same words differently. It could almost be a cultural difference. The attorney for a donor sometimes sees the world differently from the way a charity or the IRS sees it.

The meeting at the restaurant in Santa Fe brought together a donor, his legal advisor, and a representative of the charity, who was not an attorney but who knew the fundamentals of charitable giving. The donor's attorney wanted her client to make a gift of appreciated securities to a charitable remainder annuity trust.

"At your age, Sol, this is the only way to go." Sol was 89. "A charitable remainder annuity trust provides you with a guaranteed income for the rest of your life." The advisor then looked at the planned giving director to see if this information was correct. "Isn't that right, Jon?"

Jon, whose mouth was full at the moment because he wanted to keep himself busy to ease the anxiety of not knowing what the attorney would say, was happy that the advice was to make a gift. Jon simply bobbed his head up and down at this most inopportune moment to be brought into the discussion. That's right, he thought. Sol would receive a fixed, guaranteed income for the rest of his life. This would make it a little better from a safety standpoint for the donor, although Jon had been used to talking about unitrusts, whose income would fluctuate but potentially could rise.

"Guaranteed?" Sol asked.

"Absolutely." The attorney glanced alternately between her two luncheon companions. "The income is guaranteed by the assets of the synagogue." This time the attorney did not feel the need, apparently, to look over to Jon, whose mouth was now quite empty and who was prepared to respond. This was unfortunate, because, in fact, this time the attorney got it wrong. Jon knew that this information was incorrect, that the attorney was thinking instead of a charitable gift annuity, not a charitable remainder annuity trust (the latter's income is guaranteed only by the assets in the trust). Jon made a quick decision not to interrupt, thinking that the distinction was so minor that it did not merit an explanation. The 89-year-old man might not make the gift, Jon thought, if he became suddenly burdened with this new and contradictory—and probably irrelevant—knowledge, forcing him to think about the difference between two gifts that, from his point of view, would create the same deduction and similar income benefits.

The attorney pointed out that because the donor's capital gains tax on selling his assets would be so high the annuity trust would be best, especially since Sol's income would be increased from 2 percent of the asset's value to almost 10 percent.

What would you do in this situation? Jon is probably right to think that making the distinction at this point would confuse the donor and slow the process down. But the fact is that the attorney got it wrong and if, for some reason, the trust ever becomes too small, the income will stop. And it would stop without the charity backing the assets. Jon is in a dilemma.

The answer to that question, while interesting and debatable, is not the centerpiece of a discussion on ethics. Instead, the example is shown to point out that often advisors approach the question of making a gift from a very different perspective from that of the charity. The attorney was looking at the gift from the perspective of a hugely increased income for her client. In her zeal for that, and in not knowing very much about planned giving, the attorney got an important fact wrong. But, because of the attorney's zeal, Jon made a decision not to interrupt. Those in the charitable world owe it to themselves to understand the perspectives of others. Planned giving, because of its unique blend of personal and philanthropic considerations, lends itself to questions of ethics in philanthropy as no other aspect of fund-raising does. When attending a meeting or a conference, when discussing all the technical matters that affect the profession of planned giving, during the informal times for talk and visit, planned giving practitioners many times will debate what amounts to the ethics of different situations.

## THE AFTER-DINNER CONVERSATION

The time before and after the formal sessions of conferences and seminars is remarkably productive. Imagine that the scheduled dinner on the second evening of a three-day national planned giving conference is over, and a group of five people from the same dinner table decides to meet afterward to continue discussing some of the more interesting points that were raised during the meal and in various organized presentations during the previous days. This group had no intention of talking for long, but such is the chemistry of winding down at the end of the day when like-minded people with similar but distinctive experiences convene. Despite their efforts, they almost never avoid discussing business. The difference between a time like this and the time during the seminar is that feelings are looser and people are more likely to be honest and forthright, as well as more talkative.

The imagined discussion that fills the rest of this chapter addresses each of the *Model Standards of Practice for the Charitable Gift Planner.* They are given in an order intended to replicate the flow of what could easily be a typical conversation:

- *Gary* is the planned giving director at a large university whose planned giving program establishes approximately $7 million each year in life-income gifts.

- *Louise,* an attorney, is the development director at a hospital that raises about $1 million annually in planned gifts. Because the hospital does not have a director of planned giving, Louise serves in that role as well as oversees all other development activities at the hospital.

- *Cliff* is a practicing attorney and many of his clients make planned gifts. Although he is not employed by a charity, he is a member of his local planned giving council.

- *Sharon* sells life insurance and also does not represent a charity. She has involved herself in planned giving by establishing programs at charities to accept gifts of life insurance and by promoting the concept of asset replacement.

- *Derek* was hired three months ago as the planned giving director, a newly formed position, of a small United Way agency. The agency has never had a planned giving program, although it has received several bequests recently. A former teacher, he is new to the profession of planned giving.

## FULL DISCLOSURE, COMPENSATION, AND THE PUBLIC TRUST

*FULL DISCLOSURE: It is essential to the gift planning process that the role and relationships of all parties involved, including how and by whom each is compensated, be fully disclosed to the donor. A Gift Planner shall not act or purport to act as a representative of any charity without the express knowledge and approval of the charity, and shall not, while employed by the charity, act or purport to act as a representative of the donor, without the express consent of both the charity and the donor.* **(The third Standard of Practice)**

*COMPENSATION: Compensation paid to Gift Planners shall be reasonable and proportionate to the services provided. Payments of finders fees, commissions or other fees by a donee organization to an independent Gift Planner as a condition for the delivery of a gift are never appropriate. Such payments lead to abusive practices and may violate certain state and federal regulations. Likewise, commission-based compensation for Gift Planners who are employed by a charitable institution is never appropriate.* **(The fourth Standard of Practice)**

*PUBLIC TRUST: Gift Planners shall, in all dealings with donors, institutions, and other professionals, act with fairness, honesty, integrity and openness. Except for compensation received for services, the terms of which have been disclosed to the donor, they shall have no vested interest that could result in personal gain.* **(The tenth Standard of Practice)**

## Commissions

"So let's continue on the topic of commissions." Sharon, the life insurance agent, was speaking. "I didn't understand where you were coming from, Gary, when you said you'd never accept a commission for getting a gift."

"That's how this business works, Sharon," said Gary, the university planned giving director. "Nobody gets a commission. We're all paid a salary and accepting a commission would violate an ethical standard."

"But what if you *did* get paid a commission, and you didn't receive a salary? What if everybody who raised money for charity were paid on the basis of what he raised? Wouldn't that be more fair?"

"No. Not at all."

"Why not? What if you're no good?" she said with a smile. "What if you don't raise any money?"

"If I don't do my job, then I don't have a job. It's pretty simple. Commissions don't need to be part of the compensation structure."

"But why not?" insisted Sharon. "I don't want to sound too impolite, but I don't see why commission is such a bad word around this profession. Even lawyers are paid a commission sometimes."

"They are?" asked Derek, the new planned giving director at a United Way agency. "I didn't know that."

"That's not quite right, but I think what she means," suggested Cliff, the attorney, "is that some attorneys in trial cases share in a portion of what they win for the plaintiff. The attorney generally gets about a third of the jury award."

"I guess I knew that," said Derek, "but I somehow don't think of attorneys as commissioned."

"We're not, not really," replied Cliff, "but the legal profession allows it, defends the system quite emphatically, actually. Most attorneys—not trial attorneys, though—bill by the hour. By the way," he continued, "not all lawyers agree on that point, and we have our own ethics committees looking at that question. Congress has looked at it from time to time too, but the American Trial Lawyers Association has always been able to stop any movement to change the rules."

"Okay. So what about commissions in fund-raising? And in planned giving?" asked Sharon. "It seems to me that paying a commission would be the purest form of compensation because you literally get paid based on performance. Why is this profession so dead set against it?"

Gary was silent for a moment. He knew in his heart that paying commissions was wrong, but could not rationally explain why. Sharon argued in favor of commissions so clearly that he paused to consider her logic. It was irrefutable. "I know how I feel," he eventually confessed, "but I can't explain it to you right now."

"Perhaps I can help," offered Louise, the hospital director of development. "I took a course for fund-raisers in planned giving two years ago and I remember a question raised about how the profession of charitable fund-raising is different from anything else."

"And what does that mean?" asked Sharon.

"I'm not sure, but I get the impression that if a person were to receive a commission based on what he raised, it would somehow take away the purity of the charitable process."

"But I just said that commissions would be the purest form of earning money. Now you're saying that it's impure and that there's something pure about fund-raising."

"That's right," said Louise.

"I'm sorry, but that sounds like a bunch of gobbledygook," replied Sharon. The others laughed. "I'm serious," she insisted. "I just defined 'pure' and now you're turning that completely around. How is charitable fund-raising different from any other job?"

At this, Derek fell silent, too. Sharon continued, "I mean, you *work* for a charity. It's your livelihood. You're not a volunteer. Gary, are you a graduate of the university where you work?"

"No."

"Then you're not even an alumnus pretending to give back to your alma mater. Where's the purity? You have a job. You may love your job and you may do it well, but you work there just like anybody else works anywhere else. You just happen to raise money. The more you raise, the better your university is, right?"

"Yes."

"So what's the difference between that and a sales job?"

"I think I can put my finger on it," replied Louise. "This is not an ordinary job. We're doing this to do well for society. When money comes into our charities, it is spent for the betterment of society. I think that's what that portion of the *Model Standards* refers to."

"I still don't get it," said Sharon. "Like I'm not doing anything for society? I pay taxes with the money I earn, just like you. And I do well by doing good, to borrow a phrase I heard at one of today's sessions. When I sell a life insurance policy and a person dies, his widow has money to live on, money she wouldn't have had before I showed up. This keeps her and their children off welfare. It provides food, shelter, and clothing. It also provides a dignity they wouldn't have had otherwise. And I get paid on commissions." Sharon began to sound irritated. "So I ask again, what's unethical about taking a commission for raising money?"

Gary, who had been pondering the matter for some time, again spoke up. "Let me give this another try. First, let me say that I like your questions. I've been in planned giving for over 15 years, and I'm adamantly against paying commissions to anyone in this field. But until this moment no one has ever probed the issue so logically, not with me at any rate. Now, understand this, I'm still against commissions, but you're raising some good points."

Gary stopped for a moment to gather his thoughts. "To you, Sharon, this probably sounds as if the people in fund-raising think they're better than the people in other professions. But that's not what's driving this issue. What's driving the issue is abuse. Abuse and self-interest."

Sharon, as well as the others, looked confused but interested. "Go on," someone encouraged.

"Does anybody remember the news stories in the late eighties about the telemarketing firm that was hired to raise money for a charity but gave the charity only a few cents on every dollar raised?" Cliff was the only person who nodded. "You'll have to take my word for it, then. Paid solicitors were hired to call potential donors and the charity ended up with only about ten cents on every dollar raised."

"Go on," said Sharon. "What's your point?"

"My point is this," said Gary cautiously. "That type of fund-raising deceives people. I had always lumped that with just any commission-based salesperson. Now, I'm not so sure. I also don't think the argument over commissions will be won or lost based on who does more good for society. Perhaps it will never be won or lost," he added absently. Another moment later, he reenergized himself. "You're right, Sharon. You do as much for society as anybody at a charity. You and a lot of other people who earn their livings by making commissions. Around the halls of many charities, there's a strong and unfair bias against those who earn commissions. Many development people don't respect commission-oriented people or products, even though salespeople are the engine that drives the economy."

"Okay, but what's your point?" asked Sharon again, frustrated that he did not answer the question the first time she asked it. "Now you sound like you're almost in favor of commission."

Gary knew he was on thin ice here. He never had to argue this point before; it was always a given among his colleagues at the university and those who worked at other charities. He was confronting the problem head on and in person; his resolve was less in doubt than the logic behind it. "I guess it's not the logic of the argument that makes the point, but the spirit."

"Now you're starting to sound sanctimonious."

Gary sensed that she would not be satisfied. Nor should she be, he thought. "Perhaps. But let me continue. It's not so much that we do good work for our charities and that no one else does good work for their employers, or even that there is no honor in commissions. But we deal more with the public trust."

"What exactly does that mean?" Sharon sounded defensive. This had become a two-way debate between Gary and Sharon, but the others did not seem to mind.

"Our employers, unlike yours, are subject not only to the standards of good business practice, but also to those imposed by Congress on the recipients of tax dollars. People *buy* things from business, but they *donate* to charities. For what it's worth, I see a difference. People give primarily because they want to help a charity and if they see that their money is primarily going to the fund-raiser and not to the charity, they're right to get upset."

Cliff, the practicing attorney, jumped back in the debate. "So you're saying that charities *are* unique."

Gary thought that over for a few moments to determine if that was what he was actually saying. "That's right."

"But," said Sharon, "commissions don't make the problem. The telemarketing example you cited a moment ago certainly wasn't fully the result of a commission-oriented fund-raising effort. Other things must have been wrong with that process."

"They were," said Gary. "Too much overhead and not enough oversight by the charity. But when a person knows that part of his donation—a fixed percent at that—is going to a fund-raiser, not only is the incentive to give reduced but the trust between a charity and its public might be eroded."

Gary decided to provide an example. "Although everyone knows it takes money to run a charity, there's something different when a donor *knows* that a percentage of her gift is going to the person who obtained the gift. The more the donor gives, the more the fund-raiser makes. If I make a big gift, I wouldn't be happy knowing that the person, not the charity, will earn money directly related to the amount I give. If the commission is 10 percent, and that's probably low by most sales standards, and I give $10,000, the charity gets only $9,000 and the fund-raiser gets $1,000. This essentially amounts to paying a transaction fee for the privilege of giving away money. That would be a disincentive to me as a donor." He then added, "This is different from a planned giving officer doing well for his charity and hoping to receive a pay raise for his efforts. The gift and the pay are not so closely aligned."

Gary then continued with his second assertion. "This, in turn, erodes the trust between a donor and a charity. This is a little more esoteric, so please bear with me. Everyone knows that a business is out to make a profit for its shareholders. Although charities don't have shareholders, they do have a public, a public who depends on them to provide a service. Life insurance is a perfect example of how commissions work well; the agent is paid directly based on her ability to sell. The insurance industry has, over the past 100 years or so, determined that paying commissions to people to sell their products is cost-efficient. The buyer of the insurance knows this, however, and understands that paying a commission as part of the annual premium is a cost of doing business. If the people who support the charity or those who depend on its services know that one person is financially benefiting directly from gifts, the purpose of the mission is eroded and the trust with its public is tainted." Gary stopped for a minute to organize his thoughts. "I told you this is esoteric, but I see a direct link between commission-based fund-raising and how the public perceives the charity."

Everyone around the table gave this some thought, including Sharon. Derek was impressed at the argument. Never having even contemplated the issues himself, he was not now going to confess that he had, until this moment, secretly thought that paying a development director directly on the basis of the amount he raised was perfectly acceptable. Until a moment ago he had sided with Sharon's argument. Now he felt differently. Louise, the other silent person at the table, had agreed with Gary all along, but was also unsure of how to defend the position without sounding like she was somehow better than other people in other professions. She liked Gary's reasoning.

But Sharon did not. "It still sounds sanctimonious," she said finally. "I don't know how to respond to your argument except that I still don't see a difference here."

"Then let's agree to disagree. For now, I'm comfortable with that difference, and our profession has gone on record as not accepting commissions."

## Finder's Fees

"I have another question," announced Sharon. "I'm the non-charitable gift planner in this group, so I guess I'm the right person to ask. What do you do when a financial planner sends a donor your way in exchange for a finder's fee?"

"This happened at my hospital about a year ago," said Louise.

"What?" asked Gary, the university planned giving director.

"Someone wanted to talk to me about naming the hospital as a remainderman in his client's charitable remainder unitrust."

"You were interested, of course," said Cliff, the practicing attorney.

"Who wouldn't be? But the conversation really got interesting when the guy said that we'd be named as a 50 percent remainderman for a fee of $52,000."

"What?" Derek almost fell off his chair in surprise. "Fifty-two *thousand* dollars? For half the gift? Was the guy out of his mind?"

"Actually, that's how I reacted," replied Louise, "but after I finished putting my tongue back in my mouth, I was intrigued. So I asked him a little bit about the offer."

"He wasn't offering much," said Gary.

"No, he wasn't. The deal was this. If we paid the money up front, the donor—whose name I never got, by the way ...'"

"I'm not surprised," interrupted Cliff. "Sorry. Go on."

"That's okay. You're hearing this for the first time, so you're going through the same shock I went through," Louise continued. "The person, a financial planner, said that he had a client who wanted to name us as one of two remaindermen in a unitrust. I figured that must mean the guy was trying to extract—'extort' might be a better word—a little over $100,000 in fees from charities. Supposedly, the trust was worth $1 million at the time and he said that it would grow a great deal during the donor's lifetime. I did find out that the donor was 72 years old and the payout was 10 percent."

A silence fell about the table. After almost a full 15 seconds passed, Gary spoke. "This kind of thing really ticks me off. Who are these people? I'm not even concerned that a gift might not come our way if we don't pay for it. The donor in this case is not a donor, not in the real sense of the word. The financial planner—bottom-of-the-barrel kind of guy, in my opinion—probably told his client that he could save a lot of taxes by putting together a charitable remainder trust. He could get an income tax deduction, avoid paying a capital gains tax when the assets are reinvested in the trust, *and* get a higher income than he's been getting all along from his current investments. Great deal, the advisor tells his client. The only problem, he explains, is that a charity has to get involved. 'So what kind of charity are you interested in?' he asks. It doesn't matter to the financial planner. In fact, I'm sure that a lot of these 'clients' don't have a charitable bone in their bodies, which would be okay except that they're establishing charitable trusts."

Gary's anger was building. "I went to a seminar for retired people a few years ago in Sun City, near Phoenix, and the presenter was one of these guys—maybe this guy—and he had the gall to tell his audience that the charitable remainder trust was one of the last great tax loop-holes and that charity was just a necessary evil in the process. He used an example of a 12 percent unitrust—which makes a 10 percent payout look modest—with ridiculous growth assumptions."

"I can't believe this," said Sharon. "We've had a lot of talks and I've read several articles about life insurance in the process of charitable giving, but I've never heard any of this before."

"Perhaps you're not devious enough," said Cliff, the practicing attorney.

Gary continued. "Don't worry. Asset replacement—he called it 'Wealth Replacement'—was part of the deal, too. He didn't miss a trick."

"What's 'asset replacement'?" asked Derek, the new planned giving director at the United Way agency.

Louise answered. "That's when a donor buys an insurance policy to replace the asset going to charity. A lot of times a donor wants the assets to go to his kids, so he doesn't make the gift, which is logical enough, even though he'd like to do something for charity. Purchasing life insurance allows him to name the kids as the beneficiary *and* make the gift." She looked at Sharon and said, "Correct me if I'm wrong. You're the life insurance expert here."

"You're doing just fine, Louise," said Sharon.

"But how does he buy the insurance?" Derek asked.

Louise continued. "He uses the tax dollars saved on the deduction, as well as the increased income from the gift, if there is any, to pay the premiums. Actually, the donor—the person whose life is insured—isn't the owner of the policy. His kids usually are. That's because the donor wants to keep the insurance proceeds out of his estate so they aren't taxed."

Derek seemed satisfied with the answer, although he still looked confused.

Sharon then said, "Louise is right, Derek, but it's pretty complicated. So for now just know that it's a way to satisfy charity and use life insurance to pass assets to the kids." She then returned to Gary's earlier comment. "Gary, you said a moment ago that the financial planner in Sun City didn't miss a trick, and you were talking about asset replacement. What's wrong with asset replacement?" she asked. She did not like the idea of linking something she thought was legitimate with something that wasn't.

"Nothing," replied Gary. "Except that, first, it's not for everyone all the time, as this guy suggested, and, second, this guy made it part of an overall slimy presentation." Sharon, unable to object, stayed silent.

"Anyway," said Louise, returning to the topic of paying a fee for a gift, "I told the advisor that we weren't interested in paying a finder's fee."

Cliff was doing some calculating. "A little over $100,000 is only a little over 10 percent of the $1 million gift. Let me play devil's advocate for a moment." This interested the other four. They liked Cliff, sensing he was different from the kind of attorney ridiculed in a few of the presentations that discussed the difficulties of working with legal advisors who knew little of planned giving. "A moment ago, we were talking of commissions. Ten percent isn't much as things go. Do you put this finder's fee problem in the same category as accepting commissions?"

"This is worse," said Gary.

"Why?"

"Because this is almost thievery. The charity gets nothing."

"So?" Cliff was still playing the devil's advocate, or so Gary, Louise, Sharon, and Derek hoped. "So what if the charity gets nothing? The financial planner's client—I wouldn't call him a donor—isn't doing it for a charitable reason anyway."

"But," said Louise, "he's using a device meant to help charity."

"Again. So what? Sometimes you use a car when a bike would get you there just as easily."

"And no one gets hurt," said Gary.

"Who gets hurt here?"

"Everybody." This time Derek stepped in.

The four others looked at Derek after this uncharacteristically confident outburst. "I mean, this is no good for anybody."

"But who gets hurt?" Cliff repeated his question.

"The government, that's who," replied Derek. "Every time somebody doesn't use the charitable deduction for the right purpose, the taxpayers pay. The deduction comes out of all our pockets."

"There couldn't be much of a deduction, not with a 10 percent payout," said Sharon.

"It's not just the deduction," replied Derek, with more confidence now. "You were talking about a public trust a few minutes ago. Because most people think that charitable giving means giving charitably, paying for a gift violates the public trust. Besides, with a 10 percent payout, that gift won't be worth anywhere near a million dollars. And then, when you take inflation into account, well it's just ridiculous to think anything would be left for the charity."

"Maybe so, but how is preventing all that enforceable?" Cliff seemed to stump everyone with that question. He looked around for a moment before saying, "Actually, I've got my own answer for that question." The others looked with anticipation. "The IRS won't hesitate to attack a program on its principle in addition to its technicalities. If a program doesn't live up to the spirit of the law, and the IRS sees a tax-avoidance scheme going on, it will make it clear that it will try to stop it."

"But this isn't about tax avoidance so much as it is paying a finder's fee. So what do you do with the guy who wants to *sell* you a gift?" asked Derek.

"Gary said earlier that he knew about this, and I did what Gary says he would have done," said Louise. "We refused the gift."

"The finances of it looked pretty good, though." Cliff was speaking again. "A fee of just a little over 10 percent to get the gift. That's $52,000 of a potential $500,000."

"We did that calculation, I'm embarrassed to say. Our finance office actually considered taking the gift on that basis. They even did a present value calculation, using 7 percent a year for 15 years, approximately the donor's life expectancy. We kept the gift value the same, even though the advisor said it would grow a lot. We didn't think it would grow a lot, not with a 10 percent payout. In fact, I thought it would lose money, but we used the original figure just to keep things simple. We took the $500,000 we'd get in 15 years, and reduced that by 7 percent per year. That was about $180,000, as I recall. Financially, it looked like a decent deal. If our assumptions were correct, we'd make about $128,000 on the transaction."

"But you didn't do it," said Gary. "Why not?"

"Because it would've been wrong."

"Back to the old deductive reasoning powers," said Sharon, the life insurance agent. "Can't you ever get something solid on this stuff? Can't anything be wrong because there's a reason, and not just a feeling?"

"That's precisely the issue here," said Gary, the university planned giving director. "This is so hard for you to comprehend because it's hard for all of us to decide what's right and wrong. I know a dozen planned giving people who would have eaten up that gift and paid the fee. As Louise just pointed out, even though the value of the fee, taking inflation into account, was not 10 percent, but actually closer to 30 percent—paying $52,000 to get something worth $180,000—it still could make economic sense."

"If the charity has the money," said Derek.

"Yes, if it has the money. But don't you see, Sharon, this is not all about money."

"It isn't? I thought you were raising money for your charities. Why isn't it all about money?"

Gary thought Sharon had an irritating way of asking the right questions. "Okay. It is about money. But it's about more than that. Why do you think the *Model Standards* forbids paying fees? Why is it that *every* planned giving council in the United States has to abide by those standards to be a member of the National Committee on Planned Giving?"

"I don't know, Gary. You tell me. I'm sure there's a good reason. I just haven't heard it yet."

Louise interjected at this point, sensing that Gary was running out of patience. "Yes, you have, Sharon. You're just not seeing it the same way. Like we agreed before, we're trying to be good. When a person wants to collect a fee from a charity in a transaction involving a person with no charitable intent, we all have problems.

"Sharon, would you agree that charities exist for reasons other than tax benefits provided to those who support them?"

"Of course."

"Then, to me anyway, it stands to reason that a person who supports a charity should do so for reasons beyond the tax benefits. In fact—and this will sound radical to our fee-collecting colleagues out there—people give to charities because they want to help philanthropic causes. The financial advisor who calls a charity to collect a fee in return for the privilege of being named as a remainderman is short-circuiting the system, and the whole idea of philanthropy."

Sharon considered this for several moments before saying, "I do understand that. I don't want you to get the wrong idea. I like charities and planned giving, and I'm not in favor of abuse. But until this moment, I had never heard the argument put forth so well. No offense to you, Gary, but I wasn't seeing the picture I needed to get this right."

"That's okay. You're the first person who ever challenged me like that on this point. I guess I needed to examine it more critically than I had before. I thought it was a self-evident truth."

"It is," said Cliff. "Not everything right has to be logical, at least within our limited reasoning capacities. It does help, however, to walk through it all to see if it makes sense. What Louise just said is what we all need to hear from time to time to maintain faith in our principles. There's nothing wrong with asking the question. Sharon did everyone a favor by being so hard-nosed."

## DONATIVE INTENT

*PRIMACY OF PHILANTHROPIC MOTIVATION: The principal basis for making a charitable gift should be a desire on the part of the donor to support the work of charitable institutions.* **(The first Standard of Practice)**

## Advertising

Louise brought up an issue she had been wondering about for a while. "I have some donors who I know aren't making their planned gifts solely on the basis of donative intent. How do you make this part of the deal? I don't mean the obvious examples we just discussed, where the donor is barely in the picture. I'm talking of those who come to you claiming that they want to make a planned gift."

"Good question. Everybody asks it, but no one seems to have an answer."

"I don't know," said Cliff, the private attorney. "I think most people are clear about that."

"Clear, perhaps, but unable to police it." Gary looked at the others to see if another view might be forthcoming. "Look. I'm the first to say it: Donative intent is important. But how do you make certain what's in the donor's mind? I'm not a mind reader."

"I saw an advertisement in a major newspaper recently that touted the tax benefits of a charitable gift," said Derek.

"What's so remarkable about that?" asked Cliff. "That's done every day."

"I thought it was interesting. The headline said that the charity could manage the money better than the donor could, and that the donor would get a higher income from the asset than she's getting now. It didn't say much about the charity."

"That *is* scary," said Sharon, the life insurance agent. "Even though I sell mutual funds and other investments, I'd never approach a donor that way."

"I saw an ad not too long ago from one of the big investment firms that boasted a high-paying unitrust. It actually admitted that very little would be left for charity but that it was a great deal for the donor and his family."

"That's pretty aggressive marketing, but I give up," said Gary. "This stuff is going on all the time, but what can we do about it?"

Louise, from the hospital, asked, "The ad about promising the higher income. Was it for gift annuities?"

"I think so," Gary replied.

"That's *so* stupid."

"Why?" asked Cliff, who thought he knew what she would say, but wanted to hear it.

"It seems as if everybody in planned giving has lost his marbles. Comparing the return from a gift annuity to one from a stock, bond, or CD is not valid."

"Why not?" asked Sharon, the insurance agent.

Gary thought for a moment and then said to Louise, "Look, you sell annuities, right?"

"Right. Although I wouldn't say we 'sell' them. We 'issue' them to our donors."

"Okay. And Sharon here, who sells life insurance, might understand this better than anyone. What happens when a person signs up for a gift annuity?" Gary looked around but did not want an answer. "A person gives his money away and gets an income, an income that's partly based on a *return of principal.*"

"Go on," said Louise. She did not yet understand Gary's point.

"With a stock or bond or CD, you're investing, not annuitizing. You get your principal back at the end of your investment. With a gift annuity, like a commercial annuity, you don't. That's why gift annuity rates look so attractive. Right, Sharon?"

"Yes," said Sharon. "I've done some work with this in reinsuring a gift annuity. That's when a charity buys an annuity from an insurance company to guarantee the payments. The reason it makes sense, from my perspective at least, to reinsure a gift annuity is that the charity pays less to an insurance company for the same income to a same-aged donor than the amount of the gift. That frees up the difference for the charity. For example, if you pay 9.1 percent to an eighty-one-year-old on a $10,000 gift annuity, you need to guarantee $9,100 per year for the rest of the person's life, about nine years or so. My insurance company doesn't need $10,000 to pay that amount to that person. We would need only about $6,000. Remember, there's no gift element in a commercial annuity. The $4,000 difference is available to the charity. If you looked at the $9,100 as a return on $6,000, the return would be over 15 percent. That's no return, or at least anything an insurance company would count on. Instead, the annuity pays partly principal back to the annuitant.

"I'm not trying to promote reinsuring gift annuities here," said Sharon. "Whether a charity does that is up to them. The point here is that insurance companies, like charities, pay back more than a return. They pay back principal."

"What?" asked Cliff and Derek in unison.

Sharon explained, "Let's say a ninety-year-old person wants to get a gift annuity and you pay about 10 percent right now. That's a good return compared with stocks or bonds. But that's because it's not a return; it's not an investment. With a gift annuity, the money you get each year is based on getting part of the principal back each year. That's why part of the income is tax-free. You don't get your money back as you plan to do with an investment. A more valid comparison would be with a commercial annuity with an insurance company. I guarantee you that because there's no gift, the income would be more from the insurance company than it would be from a gift annuity. That's what I was getting at a minute ago."

"Why is that?" asked Derek, the new planned giving director at the United Way.

"Because of the gift element," answered Gary. "Sharon's right. Charities aren't competing with ordinary, personal investments, but with insurance companies. Actually, we're not competing with the private sector at all."

"So," said Cliff, the attorney in private practice, "when I see the ads for gift annuities in my alumni bulletin, I shouldn't be thinking of them as regular investments?"

"That's right," said Louise. "In fact, the American Council on Gift Annuities doesn't like the words 'investment' and 'return.' They prefer 'payment' because they don't want to imply that they compete with marketplace investments. Gift annuity income is guaranteed. I like to think of it this way: We don't compete with investments, but by using the techniques Congress has given us to encourage giving, we can reduce the cost to the donor of making a gift. The income and tax benefits are factors, but the reason the money is better off at a charity is the good the money ultimately will accomplish there."

"So why the aggressive ads?" asked Derek.

"That's the ethical question," said Gary. "This isn't rocket science. Anybody who writes ads should know better and, assuming they do, they're intentionally fooling people."

"What does this have to do with donative intent?" asked Derek. "I understand the math but don't most people make gifts because they want to help charity?"

"No question," responded Louise. "*Most* people do. But some don't, and ads that highlight returns speak to the lesser angels in us all, to paraphrase Lincoln."

"So?" Derek looked around. He felt he was becoming unpopular but wanted to further his questions. "Don't all charities play up the financial return?"

"What?" asked Gary.

"We tell people why they should make a gift, and we do that by telling them about the income, at least to one degree or another. An old copy of a college alumni magazine had a planned giving ad listing 100 stocks, most of which you'd recognize, all of them on the New York Stock Exchange. It didn't matter much that the stocks were all bunched together in such small type that it was difficult to read them. The headline read: 'If You Own Any of These Stocks We Can Double Your Income.' That's powerful stuff. The college's pooled income fund was paying over 7 percent income then and all the stocks, mostly blue chip companies, were paying low dividends, under 3 percent."

Gary's eyes lit up. "That sounds like a really great idea. What a nice way to get someone's attention."

"Precisely my point," said Derek. "You don't seem to have any trouble with that, but you don't like the ad with high-paying gift annuity rates. Yet in both cases, the charity casts itself as competing against other investments." He looked around the table for a reaction. Everybody was deep in thought about the apparent contradiction.

Cliff responded first. "You're right. It may be that *every* ad for planned giving does that to some degree or another."

"So now we're talking *degree* as opposed to fact," said Derek. "To me, that's a problem. We're quick to condemn what looks bad. But look close enough and you see what we condemn is very much like what we praise."

Louise, the attorney and hospital development director, was next. "I don't know about the rest of you, but I think Derek has a valid point. Just by going out to get a planned gift that pays the donor income for the rest of his life, we're engaged in the practice of convincing someone that his money is better off at our charity than at some financial institution. We can't be hypocrites about that."

"Let's say that Derek is right, and I'm inclined to think he is. Where does that leave us? Should we just ignore the income and tax benefits of making a gift? How do you think we ought to do our marketing?" asked Gary.

Finally. "We're back to the matter of donative intent, aren't we?" said Sharon, the life insurance agent. "It seems to me that all your ads should emphasize your charity's mission and then, almost as an afterthought, the income or tax benefits."

"You're right, of course," said Gary, "but that's a tall order. In this world of competition among charities and appealing to donors' self-interest, policing ourselves is going to be very difficult."

Cliff answered, "Yes it will be. But the more you police yourselves, the less likely Congress or the state attorney general's office will feel the need to do it for you. I recommend that we stay tuned to this matter over the next several years. It's a tough one; the Supreme Court said once that donative intent is not a legal requirement to make a deductible gift. That's smart because who can tell? You've just said that the line is blurry. But because the philanthropic sector is so important and special, we owe it to ourselves to constantly search out what is right and good, in addition to what is legal. Even if it's legal today, if it's not good and right, it won't be legal for long."

## The Accelerated Charitable Remainder Trust

Derek then thought of one of Louise's earlier comments about what the IRS will do when it sees a tax-avoidance scheme. "What more were you going to say about tax avoidance and the IRS?"

Cliff broke in. "The Accelerated CRT became a problem when some creative planners took advantage of the ability to not make a unitrust payment until the beginning of the first quarter of the following year. It involved a standard unitrust—the kind that does not pay a net income—where the donor put highly appreciated property in a unitrust on January 1, and the annual payment was due on December 31 of that same year. The example the IRS used was for $1 million and the whole thing was appreciated, 100 percent."

"I'm told this happens frequently," said Louise.

"This happens frequently?" asked Cliff.

"Many times a payment is made at the beginning of the first quarter of the following year. This was discussed yesterday in the technical part of a seminar on trust administration. What's the issue with that?" asked Louise.

"The problem is that the donor characterized his income for the first year as return of principal, as opposed to capital gain income. The payout was 80 percent, by the way."

"By the way?" asked Derek incredulously. "That's ridiculously high."

"The term of the trust was two years."

"This is getting really weird," Sharon, the life insurance agent, added.

"It is, but that's not the weird part," said Cliff. "Despite its popular moniker, the IRS's problem is with neither the high payout nor the short term of the trust. In fact, it is not accelerated at all. That is, if you take the word accelerated to mean that the scheduled endpoint has been moved closer. This trust was always intended to be only two years."

"And the IRS has no problem with that?" asked Sharon.

"No," said Gary. "The deduction formula takes those facts into account."

"That's right," said Cliff. "The problem has nothing to do with that, but everything to do with the plan to give the donor tax-free income instead of capital gain income, which he would—and should—receive under the four-tier rule."

"The what?" asked Sharon.

"That's what makes the accelerated CRT problem a problem," explained Gary. "The donor said that he received the first year's income as return of principal. Therefore, he argued that the income should not be taxed. Assuming no income was generated by the asset during the first year, the first payment should be capital gain and not tax-free income. The four-tier rule is spelled out in the Internal Revenue Code."

"That's right," said Cliff. "The income was tax free, or so the donor thought. Think of that. He gets a check for 80 percent of the gift's value, which is $800,000. All tax free."

"$800,000 that should be capital gain income," said Gary.

"Which," added Sharon, "would be, at the 28 percent tax bracket, about $220,000 in taxes. But what would the charity get?"

"About 7 percent was the IRS-calculated remainder value on the trust, as I recall," Cliff added. "I did the IRS calculation on my computer. The deductible number was about $72,000, using a Charitable Midterm Federal rate of 9.4 percent. But that was only the calculation. If there's no growth in the asset, after taking out 80 percent after the first year, there's $200,000 left. Then, another 80 percent payout, or $160,000, will leave only $40,000 for the charity. Of course, the asset should grow a little." Then he thought about it. "But it couldn't. Not with an 80 percent payout. The charity's really going to get only $40,000, or 4 percent of the beginning amount."

"Actually, it could. A little." Gary was speaking. "The payout isn't until the end of the year, and the charity has $200,000 at the beginning of the second year, and it would grow. Say it grows by 10 percent. That means it's worth $220,000 by the end of the second year. Eighty percent of that is $176,000, which leaves $44,000 for charity."

"Let's not get mired in the details," said Louise. "No matter how you cut it, charity's not getting much. But the donor didn't care, did he?"

"No," Cliff replied. "Again, it was a case of using a charitable instrument to further a private cause. In this case, to avoid taxes."

"That's what I was getting at earlier," said Gary. "This business of avoiding taxes as a sole reason for making a charitable remainder trust makes me really uncomfortable."

## COMMUNICATION BETWEEN ADVISORS AND CHARITIES

### Consulting Advisors

*CONSULTATION WITH INDEPENDENT ADVISORS: A Gift Planner acting on behalf of a charity shall in all cases strongly encourage the donor to discuss the proposed gift with competent independent legal and tax advisors of the donor's choice.* **(The sixth Standard of Practice)**

"Cliff, you mentioned earlier that a donor should see his advisor before making a decision."

"That's right, Louise."

"Then how should we deal with the situation where the advisor works against our interests, not for them?"

"I think I know where you're heading, but why don't you explain what you mean."

"I don't know about the rest of you, although I can't imagine that you haven't run into this same situation, but sometimes I've gotten the distinct impression that when I send a donor off to see her attorney, the attorney squashes the deal. I'm not saying the attorney is doing anything wrong, but I can't help feeling that the attorney doesn't know much about planned giving and may be afraid of it. For whatever reasons, the gift doesn't get made. When I call the donor to follow up, I'm told that her attorney said that the gift was not in her best interests."

"You're being kind," said Gary. "I run into that all the time. The whole thing is despicable. It's as though there's some sort of conspiracy. 'You want to make a planned gift? A what? Oh, that's ridiculous. Did some dimwit from a charity put that malarkey in your head? Don't you know you're giving up the asset forever? Forget that. It just doesn't fit into your plans.' That's what I think goes on sometimes."

Derek, the new planned giving officer at the United Way, agreed. "They just don't understand planned giving and they don't want to lose their fees when the estate gets settled."

"Now that's harsh," replied Cliff, the attorney. "I know what you're getting at, and there are lots of attorneys who don't understand planned giving, or charity for that matter, but I'd like to think that most of us are not merely looking at what size estate we're probating to figure our fee."

"Then what *is* going on with attorneys?" asked Louise, who started this discussion.

"The problem is one of perspective. Attorneys are hired by clients to protect assets while planned giving people, people in all sorts of charitable development actually, are hired to take those assets away. There's not much mystery in that."

"It does create conflict, doesn't it?" asked Derek.

"Sometimes. But attorneys don't see themselves as against charities. The problem—and on this point I can speak from experience—is that attorneys aren't always sure that the person—your donor and my client—has thought the whole thing through. The attorney will ask a few questions to get a feel for the person's desires."

"Such as?" Derek persisted.

"Gary just gave one. Are you aware that this asset is no longer available to you? Forget the income for a moment but think of not having access to the principal. Such questions many times indicate that the person hasn't thought of the consequences. In that context, I'd turn the question back to the planned giving people and ask whether *you're* doing a competent job of reviewing with the donor all the consequences of making a gift."

"I'd like to get to that in a moment," said Gary. "But first I want to look at the times when the gift is good and the attorney is not helpful. We all can continue to increase our knowledge of the tax consequences and other effects of making a gift, but certainly you'll agree that there are times when an attorney does no one any good by stopping a gift plan."

"Sure, I'll agree to that. And more. The state of legal advice in the realm of charitable estate planning is inadequate. For some reason many attorneys not only give legal advice, they also think they should tell their clients what they should do." The others looked confused. "If a person says that he wants to help a charity in his estate plans, it's not my role to say otherwise. My role at that point becomes facilitating the process. That's something you need me and my brethren for. But whether that person should have a charitable intent to begin with is not my call.

"Same for other plans. If a husband says he wants everything to go to his wife at his death, I won't argue with him, but I'll show him the best way to do that. Most people think that they should leave everything outright to their spouses, and they would write their wills to say that. I tell them, those with large estates anyway, that they can save a lot of taxes by setting up a trust to protect assets from taxes. No real difference to the spouse, but a huge amount more goes to the children. See the difference? I'm not telling them what their values or goals should be, but I do tell them how to best accomplish their objectives given the legal picture in estate planning."

"I like that," said Louise. "But how can we work with attorneys so that the donor doesn't change his mind?" The others agreed, wanting to know the same thing.

"You may not like this, but this is how I see it," responded Cliff. "Provide as much information as possible—without practicing law yourself—so that your prospect goes to his attorney with as much knowledge and comfort as possible about the gift plan. A good attorney won't want to sway your prospect into not making the gift if he really wants to do it."

"So you're not saying. . . ."

"No. I'm not saying that you should tell your prospect *not* to see an attorney. We may be bad," Cliff said with a smile, "but we're not so bad that you should steer people away from legal advice. Or that you can do the entire job yourselves. Let me be clear about this. You need to show your prospect why the plan is good for him, and you need to do that after having been convinced that he's really interested in your cause. Once that's done, the person knows he wants to make a gift and, because of your help, knows basically how to do it. By the time I see him, I know what he wants to do and I make sure, knowing the rest of his estate plans, that it fits into his overall picture. Believe me, I want to see the gift happen as much as anybody. I just want to prevent anything foolish from taking place."

"I understand that," said Gary, "but I still sense an antagonism among attorneys toward planned gifts. I can't tell you the number of times I've lost a donor to an attorney who didn't know what she was talking about."

"Are you sure you lost a donor?" asked Cliff.

"What do you mean?"

"Are you certain that the person was a donor, a person who wanted to make a gift?"

"Okay. Maybe not everyone was completely certain he should make a gift, and the attorney or the accountant showed him the consequences. But others, I'm sure, did want to make a gift. Those are the ones I'm talking about."

"Yes, and that's where we agree. Too many attorneys think their job description includes thinking for their clients. But your prospect still needs to be comfortable with the gift idea so that when the attorney challenges the concept, he'll be able to say that he's certain he wants to make the gift."

"But why do attorneys take such a different view?" asked Derek.

"I don't think it's all that different, actually. To be brutally frank—I'm not paid to give my clients' money away. They hire me to *preserve* their assets, not to give them away."

"What do you mean by that?" Sharon joined the conversation.

"You hire an attorney to protect your personal interests. Charity is not a personal interest, not in the same way as protecting assets for loved ones is. You have an automatic conflict, unless the client is specific and, in my view, strong, about his wish to help charity."

"But what about the tax benefits?" asked Derek.

"What about them?"

"Don't you tell your clients that they can save taxes by making a gift?"

"No, I don't." Derek looked surprised at this admission, so Cliff explained. "Keep in mind that I write a lot of charitable gift agreements and bequest provisions. So before you think of me as the bad guy, understand that I want to help your cause. But, you also need to know that I'm not going to say something stupid to my clients, such as save taxes by giving money away to charity.

"Quite simply, a person doesn't benefit himself financially by giving away money. No gift, planned or otherwise, can do that. Not when compared with keeping the asset. A million dollars taxed at 50 percent will give the kids $500,000 at their parent's death. Sure, giving the asset to charity will save taxes, but the kids get nothing. See? If the guy wants to help his kids, giving it to charity is not in his best interests."

Gary rejoined the discussion. "So your advice is to be sure our donors really want to make the gift before we send them to their attorneys, *and* to be sure we send them to their attorneys."

"Exactly," replied Cliff.

"That makes sense," said Louise. "I've always thought attorneys, and other advisors, were the bad guys, the ones who stood in the way of a gift. Now I see the other perspective, one I should've seen because I'm an attorney myself. This approach makes my job a little harder because I've got to do more work with the prospect, but I hope it'll be worth it."

"Your job is even harder than that," said Cliff. "Not every attorney knows much about planned giving and not all of them care to find out what the client, your donor, really wants."

## Consulting Charities

*CONSULTATION WITH CHARITIES: Although Gift Planners frequently and properly counsel donors concerning specific charitable gifts without the prior knowledge or approval of the donee organization, the Gift Planner, in order to insure that the gift will accomplish the donor's objectives, should encourage the donor, early in the gift planning process, to discuss the proposed gift with the charity to whom the gift is to be made. In cases where the donor desires anonymity, the Gift Planner shall endeavor on behalf of the undisclosed donor, to obtain the charity's input in the gift planning process.* **(The seventh Standard of Practice)**

"Speaking of the advisor's role in all this, Cliff, do you make sure that the charities for which your clients make gifts are notified?" Gary wondered aloud.

"Yes." The answer was short and undeliberative, as if Cliff knew the question was coming. After realizing that a single-word answer would not suffice, he continued. "I always tell my clients to inform the charity of their intentions. Not to do so would, I believe, inhibit the point of the gift."

"What do you mean?" asked Derek.

"If a person wants to set up a remainder trust, for example, I tell him that the remainderman should be informed. Usually the donor wants to have control over the gift, particularly the investments and administration. But if I write up a trust document for a gift that a financial planner has arranged, I always advise the donor to tell the charity."

"That should be obvious," said Louise.

"But it's not, not to everybody. More than once I've actually not written a trust agreement when I suspected that the donor and the financial advisor wanted to keep the charity out of the loop. One, I remember, was for a unitrust paying 14 percent. And that was for the life of two people in their fifties. They wanted the remainder to go to a United Way agency in our state, Derek, but didn't want them to know. Looking back, they might as well have been kept in the dark because there isn't going to be anything left of the gift. The financial planner simply didn't know what she was doing, putting together a gift like that."

"That's the point of all this." Gary, silent for a few minutes, had been thinking about Cliff's comments. "The charity can usually tell the donor if the gift is good. That's in addition to telling the donor how the money will be used and, of course, thanking him or her. But my biggest fear is that a financial planner, attorney, or accountant puts together a gift that doesn't make sense and that the donor wouldn't want to do if he knew the truth."

"Like what?" asked Sharon.

"Like the possibility that nothing will be left for charity. Most people don't know much about planned giving, and when their advisors tell them about it, they look at it more as a tax shelter than anything else, with maybe a little help to charity. I hear too many people say that this is a win–win situation, a phrase that makes me angry because a properly constructed gift—with a good payout, the right ages, the right assets, and the right intention—does benefit charity. But nobody ever *makes* money with a planned gift."

"I think we've touched a button here," observed Derek. "What do you mean that nobody ever makes money?" He was reminded of Cliff's earlier comments. "I thought that with all the tax and income benefits, a donor could actually be better off by making the gift than by not making it."

"But the donor doesn't have access to the asset any longer," Louise added.

"That's true, but there's more," said Gary. "I did a comparison once, taking everything into account—how the asset would grow in the gift and outside the gift, the taxes paid on the income, the estate tax comparison, and what would end up with the kids, and I decided—although I know other people could come to a different conclusion—that the donor is not really any better off making the gift. I saw that the IRS would be better off, at least on the stream of income, with the gift than without it. These gifts usually produce more income than the donor had before and it's usually fully taxable. I know that sounds radical, but that's what I learned." The group took this in with surprise.

"I'd wondered about that," said Derek. "We're always talking about benefits to the donor."

"Yes, but that's in exchange for a gift to charity. There's a trade-off, a trade-off we don't always admit. It's certainly not a win–win situation." Gary said the words with disdain. "But it's more than that. It's the issue of control. If a donor is going to give a major gift to a charity, why shouldn't the charity know? Why should the financial advisor control that situation, often to both the donor's and the charity's detriment?"

"Sometimes," Sharon, the life insurance agent, said, "the donor wants to remain anonymous."

"But then, you—the financial advisor—should tell the donor that you still need to tell the charity, even if he's anonymous, so that the charity knows what's going on." Sharon had not thought about this before, but could see the point.

"That's part of the *Model Standards*," said Louise.

"But I'm a financial planner, not a planned giving officer. Why do I have to abide by those standards? I don't mean to sound as if I'm against them, but where do they get the authority to tell me how to conduct my business?"

"Good question," said Derek. "When I first read them earlier this year, I wondered who'd be affected. I saw that the National Committee on Planned Giving and the American Council on Gift Annuities endorsed them in 1991. But do they have the power to control everyone who writes a planned gift?"

After a pause, Gary said, "No, they don't. And that's the difficulty with them. I like to think of them as a sort of constitution, but they're really less than that. More a list of suggestions than anything else."

"Might be something a professional designation would cover," Cliff said, sensing that it might be controversial. "If you don't follow the rules, and these would be some of the rules, then you're out of the profession."

"That's great for those who are certified, but what about the others, those who talk to people about gifts but aren't connected to planned giving otherwise?" Gary asked.

"That's a problem. But at least the profession would be taking an important stand. Charities would have more leverage to warn their constituencies that if they're approached by a financial planner or other advisor urging them to make a planned gift, they should contact the charity. I admit it won't cure all the problems, but it would be a start in the right direction."

"I like it, but I have to think about it." Given the silence after Cliff's thoughts, Gary seemed to be speaking for the group.

## DISCLOSURE

### Competence

*COMPETENCE AND PROFESSIONALISM: The Gift Planner should strive to achieve and maintain a high degree of competence in his or her chosen area, and shall advise donors only in areas in which he or she is professionally qualified. It is a hallmark of professionalism for Gift Planners that they realize when they have reached the limits of their knowledge and expertise, and as a result, should include other professionals in the process. Such relationships should be characterized by courtesy, tact and mutual respect.* **(The fifth Standard of Practice)**

*FULL COMPLIANCE: A Gift Planner shall fully comply with and shall encourage other parties in the gift planning process to fully comply with both the letter and the spirit of all applicable federal and state laws and regulations.* **(The ninth Standard of Practice)**

Derek picked up the questioning again. "Cliff, you said that we should not practice law. What did you mean by that?"

"You need to have a level of competence in *your* profession, but specific legal advice should be the domain of attorneys."

"That's the rub," said Gary, the university planned giving director. "How much is enough information?"

Louise now: "I know I don't go far enough in many cases and I'll bet a lot of others don't either. For example, how many of us know anything about Medicaid and the costs of living at a retirement home? When assets are given away, as you said earlier, they're absolutely gone, never to be retrieved, no matter what. It doesn't matter how bad things get. The charity can't give the money back. Who knows what will happen? In a way—and I know I'll regret saying this—I don't know how we can morally accept any gift of that nature, seeing that the donors might need it someday. Who knows?"

"No one," said Gary. "But I've been down this road before, and I think that I can justify it by comparing it to an outright gift of the same size. We don't have a problem with a person who gives an outright gift of a million dollars. We don't say, you might need this in your old age."

"No, but maybe we should," said Sharon, the life insurance agent, whose job was to make sure that people had enough money after a loved one dies.

"Actually," said Derek, "I think we do. We do that with planned gifts and, in a way, we do that for outright gifts. How many people want to give away their entire estates, all their holdings? If we knew someone was thinking that, we'd advise against it. Wouldn't we?"

"Most of us would," said Louise. "But that still doesn't make us knowledgeable about their estate and family situation. To do a truly thorough job we need to know more about the prospect's family and finances. A lot more. Our job, I'm coming to realize, isn't simple. That sounds ridiculous, I know, because no one here thinks planned giving is simple. But it's even more complicated, I fear, than we're all currently thinking. The more I heard during today's sessions on techniques and tax matters the more I realized that our job spills into so many other areas. Law, accounting, taxes, finance. Here we are, supposedly basic fund-raisers, and we're doing a lot more than asking for money."

Gary agreed. "Yes. In a real way we're acting as advisors. We have to draw a line short of formally becoming advisors, but we have the obligation to explain all tax and income benefits, as well as consequences. All the implications, both good and bad."

## Full Disclosure

"How many planned giving people do that?" asked Sharon.

"About as many as there are insurance agents who explain the truth about insurance," responded Derek.

"What's that supposed to mean?"

"Simply that insurance agents are no paragons of honesty when it comes to explaining things."

"Like what, for example?" Sharon was feeling defensive.

"Like the offset premiums." And for emphasis, "For example."

"What are you talking about?"

"Do insurance companies advertise that most of their cash value policies need to have their premiums paid outside the policy—by the owner of the policy, that is—for only a certain number of years?"

"Yes." Although the others could not, Sharon could see what was coming.

"Well, well. I have a *written* guarantee from an insurance agent promising that after six years of paying premiums my policy would be flush enough with cash that each year it would get the premium from the cash reserves, and the company would no longer need my payment to keep the policy in force. That was ten years ago. Two years ago I got a notice saying there wasn't enough money in the policy to do what was originally thought possible, and that for a few years I would need to make additional annual premiums."

"Interest rates have gone down dramatically since then," Sharon said.

"That does me a lot of good."

"What did the company say when you said you had a written guarantee?" asked Louise.

"They practically laughed. Of course, the agent who sold the policy no longer works at the insurance company, and I was stuck. The company said that it wouldn't matter, though, because their agents aren't allowed to make those kinds of promises and the company can't be held liable for them. So I'm paying the extra premiums because buying a new policy would be out of the question and letting it lapse is a dumb idea."

Sharon felt embarrassed, but carried on. "You're right. On all counts. I can't tell you how angry I get at some insurance agents. Making promises like that is wrong and the practice infuriates me."

"Well, I don't want to get off the subject," said Gary, "but how does this relate to planned giving?"

"I'm sorry," answered Sharon. "I was just thinking that some planned giving directors are sometimes guilty of not explaining all the implications of a gift."

"Like which ones?" asked Derek.

"There are lots of examples," replied Gary. "We say 'deduction' many times when we mean 'remainder value.' That might not sound like a big deal, but to be honest we should say '*potential* deduction' because the donor doesn't always get to deduct the entire amount."

"I've got another example," said Derek. "How many of us tell the donor she can put our name in as a remainderman *conditionally?*"

"What?" asked Sharon.

"How many trusts are written with the charity as an irrevocable remainderman? Wouldn't we be doing our donors a favor by telling them that they can have the trust drafted in a way that lets them change the charity?"

"I'm uncomfortable with that," said Gary, the university planned giving director.

"Why? If we're trying to do the ethically right thing, why are you uncomfortable with that idea?"

Gary thought this over. He had been held hostage to his heart, as opposed to his mind, twice before during this conversation and wanted to be certain he had a logical answer. "Okay. If we've done the work of identifying a person who wants to help *our* cause and we set up the plan and take charge of managing the trust as trustee, I think we have a right to be the irrevocable remainderman."

"What if," asked Derek, "you explained that and the donor felt otherwise? What if she decided not to make you the irrevocable remainderman?"

"Actually, I have no problem with that." Gary felt confident. "So, I suppose I should go ahead with the explanation—something I know very few people do. Then, if they don't make us the remainderman, fine, I can live with that. But I still think that we're entitled to be the irrevocable remainderman for doing all the work." Gary paused to think some more. "It would be ridiculous for a donor to change his mind after making an outright gift."

"That's because the donor can't change his mind. The asset—and its income—are gone," said Derek.

"Yes, but what if it wasn't? What if a gift is for the endowment and the income is used each year to fund a project at the charity? This happens all the time, but nobody ever says that the donor can have the right to change charities, to have the income go elsewhere." Gary stopped to look around the table, and then said with conviction, "This is one area I'm confident about. I'll concede that we should review the question with the donor, but at the same time I fully expect to have my charity named as the irrevocable remainderman in a charitable trust."

"I'm not as comfortable," confessed Louise. "These are not outright gifts. The donor could change his mind later on and be upset that he can't do anything about it."

"But then we'd have nothing more than a bequest, where the gift is uncertain."

"Bequests have a 90 percent success rate," countered Louise. "I'd be willing to live with that in exchange for the donor's good will."

"Then who'd act as trustee? What about overseeing the management and administration of the trusts?" asked Gary. "We're trustee of many trusts. Some people have set up their own trusts and we're not involved, but for the vast majority we act as trustee and we hire the investment manager. I know that the university wouldn't handle the administration and management without guarantees. Besides, we feel that the trust, and the beneficiary's income in the case of unitrusts, are better when we're trustee than if the donor were left to do it himself."

"That's a good argument," said Derek. "I hadn't thought about this before. I just assumed that we would be the irrevocable remainderman whenever we could, but Gary's giving me a reason why."

Even Louise seemed to agree. "I admit I hadn't thought about the more practical aspects of the problem, but I'm still uncomfortable."

"The question's hardly resolved. I just take the stance that we should tell the donor everything about retaining the right to change the remainderman, and then try to convince him not to retain that right. I can live with that."

## Explaining the Gift's Tax and Income Implications

*EXPLANATION OF TAX IMPLICATIONS: Congress has provided tax incentives for charitable giving, and the emphasis in this statement on philanthropic motivation in no way minimizes the necessity and appropriateness of a full and accurate explanation by the Gift Planner of those incentives and their implications.* **(The second Standard of Practice)**

*EXPLANATION OF THE GIFT: The Gift Planner shall make every effort, insofar as possible, to insure that the donor receives a full and accurate explanation of the proposed charitable gift.* **(The eighth Standard of Practice)**

"What else do we need to tell our donors?" asked Gary. "Do we tell them everything else they need to know before they make the gift? I'm not talking about knowing what their advisors know or even their general estate plans. Are we telling them what they need to know about the gift?"

"For example?" said Derek.

"For example, how many annuity trusts have you established for a donor in his or her 60s?"

"I had a widow in her 60s who established an annuity trust," said Louise, the hospital director of development. "She was quite happy with it, too. Still is."

"Still is," Gary said. "But her fixed income will erode as she ages. The purchasing power of her annuity payments will go down, and I'll bet she doesn't even realize it."

Louise looked at Gary. "I didn't bring up that fact with her at the time. But she said that's what she wanted to do. She was a new widow at the time—her husband had just died of cancer in our hospital—and, appreciating all the care he received, she wanted to do something for us. An annuity trust seemed just the right thing for her."

"Telling her about inflation may not have made a difference," said Gary. "I've seen a lot of situations like that. But that doesn't mean we shouldn't bring inflation to their attention. A person in her 60s has 20 or 30 more years to live, and inflation can do awful things to a fixed income." Gary paused and looked at the others. "I'm not saying we should tell everything, but I'm afraid we don't tell enough about the implications of the gifts we establish."

"What else do you feel you should discuss with the donor?" asked Cliff, the attorney.

"One thing that I've noticed," replied Louise, "is that the income from a unitrust, especially a net-income unitrust, doesn't always go up, the way it does in our income projections. And when it does, it doesn't go up as smoothly as the graphs show."

"I've noticed that, too." Derek joined in here. "I was looking at the income from two unitrusts, each about five years old. The first and second years' income was good, increasing a little each year, but in the third year, the income dropped. It dropped the fourth year and then, last year, it stayed at the same level as the year before. I looked at the correspondence my predecessor had with the donor of one of the trusts prior to the gift, and he sent her a projection that showed an annual income increase of 6 percent. In five years, the income should have increased by a little over 30 percent, yet so far it has risen only about 4 percent."

"Exactly," said Sharon. "This is the problem many life insurance agents have. They think that income always goes up. We definitely have an obligation to tell our donors—your donors and my clients—the truth about income. Over time, markets should rise, but that's not the case for any given year." Sharon then displayed her financial acumen. "In fact, now that you mention it, the more aggressive the portfolio, the more likelihood the trust will vary each year, both up and down. Aggressive stocks are more volatile. How many of us tell *that* to donors?" The four others looked around the table at one another and their conspicuous silence told them that this was not something any of them shared with their donors. "It's important because a person, especially an elderly person, might not be able to withstand a drop in income."

"This isn't in the same league, but what about the deduction limitations?" Derek asked. "I mean, a little while ago Sharon said that we talk about the IRS-calculated remainder value as if it were the deduction, and she said that it isn't sometimes. I thought it was the deduction."

Sharon replied. "I was referring to the 30 percent ceiling of adjusted gross income. If a person's income is low and the remainder value is high, the person might not be able to deduct the whole remainder value."

"Although that's not usually a big problem, it can be an issue and we ought to be more clear about explaining that to prospects," added Gary.

"What I'm hearing," said Cliff, the attorney, "is that there's a lot to tell people and you're struggling with how much. And, I infer, when."

"True enough," Louise responded. "We don't have all the answers, but I'm beginning to realize that we need to tell our donors more. After this conversation, I'm no longer comfortable with what I've been telling them."

"I like what I've heard tonight," said Cliff. "But let me tell you something that should make you feel good." The others looked at him with anticipation. "In 1970, well before I knew anything about remainder trusts, a large university established an annuity trust worth $1,000,000 for a woman who was then 62 years old. The payout was high, 9 percent, but the planned giving director, according to his correspondence with the woman, was certain it wouldn't present a problem. The university, under pressure to agree to a high payout and hoping to increase the trust's value over time, took a very aggressive investment stance. In the first year, the trust went from $1,000,000 to $1,050,000. Taking into account the

$90,000 payment each year, that amounted to almost a 14 percent return. The treasurer was patting himself on the back for his wisdom. He calculated what the trust would be worth at that rate at the end of 25 years, the woman's life expectancy, and was happily looking forward to the results.

"During the next two years, however, the trust nose-dived and lost a full 50 percent of its value. By the end of 1974 it was worth only $510,000."

"That's when the markets took a plunge, '73 and '74," said Sharon. "I wasn't around either, but we discussed that in one of my Certified Financial Planner classes."

"So," Cliff continued, "the university saw a problem. By this time, the $90,000 annual payment represented almost 18 percent of the trust. That meant the trust would have needed to earn 18 percent just to make the payout, let alone realize any growth. That would've been bad enough, but the treasurer decided to bail out of the investments and take a safer route with more bonds in it. This was a bad decision for two reasons. The stock market came back in 1975, but the trust wasn't holding many of the now-recovering stocks, so it lost an opportunity to recover. Second, the investment grew by only 6 percent a year after that, *before* the payment. A little more than six years later, the trust was empty." Cliff looked at the others. "The donor lives, but the trust is dead. And so is her income."

"And so is the purpose to which her gift would've been put," said Gary.

The group looked gloomy, as if a close friend had died. After a long moment, Louise said, "That's the first time I've ever heard about a trust going belly-up. Until now, I thought it was only a theoretical possibility, but you've brought the issue to life."

"I thought this was going to make us feel good," said Derek.

"I know it's not a good story, but from what I gather from tonight's conversation, none of you will have that problem. I attribute a great deal of the problem to the times. This was right after remainder trusts were defined in late 1969 by Congress, and no one had a lot of experience with them or with the payout issue. Certainly not the one you brought up earlier, Gary, about the impact of inflation on a fixed income. Back then, charities were just getting the word out, and I'm sure that any donors who came along were welcomed and accommodated at almost any cost."

Digesting this news, Derek asked, "By the way, Cliff, how do you know this?"

Cliff looked at Derek, then at the others, and then smiled faintly. "The treasurer who is no longer at the university is one of my clients. He told me the story. And he still has difficulty sleeping."

## Professionalism

Cliff wanted to address another issue that had bothered him for the last several minutes. He was thinking of their discussion of how a professional designation might address the question of providing substance for the *Model Standards,* and wanted to explore the matter more fully. "I'm a lawyer, so I don't have to worry about this, but it seems to me that you do. This discussion makes me think of planned giving as a profession that needs to review these questions regularly. Do you think it should have more structure?"

"Are you suggesting that the planned giving profession should have a certification or some professional designation?" asked Derek.

"*That's* an interesting question," Gary responded. "This profession— if we can call it that—has been struggling with that question for some years now."

"And the answer?"

"The answer's unclear. Many people are opposed to the idea because they say it won't prove anything, that a professional designation can't transform a bad gift planner into a good one. They say that so much of our business is people-oriented that the problem is not technical proficiency but human interaction."

"But surely," said Cliff, "you can't mean that a minimum level of technical competence can be *bad* for the profession?"

"No," said Gary, somewhat reflectively. "But a lot of people, many of them among our most senior people, by the way, have opposed the idea of a professional designation. I think it's partly because many of these senior people grew up in a world where planned giving was itself nascent. They took their jobs seriously and did them well, and they see their abilities as the result of hard work, of spending a lot of time with people. Also, I have to admit, these people—you'd know their names— are the types of people we aspire to become. They have a point."

"The argument," said Louise, "as I recall it, went to the heart of whether we're a profession, that the idea of a profession is one of credentials. The definition of a profession, in fact, is that it is an occupation requiring training in a specialized field. Right now, although we have many good seminars and conferences to attend, none of them provides a credential. There are a few places that are starting to grant degrees in planned giving—sort of like the American College that issues the Certified Life Underwriter designation for insurance agents—but a degree from any of these places is not a prerequisite to be a planned giving director."

"That's how it is in life insurance, too," said Sharon. "The CLU designation, which I have, is not required. Someone almost literally can walk in off the street and sell life insurance. Yet that's not entirely true. To sell life insurance, every agent must pass a state exam. So life insurance agents have that hurdle. It's not much of one, but at least it's a minimum requirement. The CLU designation shows that a person is really serious about the profession."

"I think that's the problem in planned giving," said Gary, from the university. "We don't even have that small level of required competence. People *can* walk in off the street to be a planned giving director."

"That's not good," said Cliff, the attorney.

"No, but why does the profession refuse to deal with the subject?" asked Sharon.

Gary answered. "Because the feelings are strong about not restricting what's necessary to learn and what's not. Most of the good people have learned a lot on their own, at seminars and conferences like this one. Many of them read and study on their own. We have newsletters that deal with many of the issues. Also there are classes available now, even courses with degrees. They're new, though, and not yet required by charities. That might change in the future. For a long time I was against the idea of a professional designation, but with the increase in topics, and the number of people who are entering planned giving, to say nothing of potential litigation, I'm starting to feel that we need something."

"Some charities require that the planned giving person be an attorney. Is that right?" asked Cliff.

"Yes," said Louise. "My hospital's one of them."

"Why?"

"I really don't know. I can't represent the donor's legal interests and I don't represent the hospital's. A law degree isn't necessary to my work." She thought about this for a while, and then continued. "Perhaps it's because of a presumption that I can get around the IRS Code and Regulations a little easier than a nonattorney."

"But surely, a planned giving designation would not require a law degree?" Gary was incredulous.

"No," Louise responded, "it probably wouldn't."

Cliff then said, "I asked the question only because the requirement at admittedly only a few charities seems to be a prerequisite of sorts. It seems that there should be some prerequisite for planned giving so that charities—and donors—know what they're getting. As Sharon said, those being approached to buy life insurance take comfort in knowing that the soliciting agent has passed a state examination. Donors have no such assurances. In many ways, because gifts are large and the decision-making process takes into account more complex issues, the stakes are higher. I don't know all the issues, of course, but it makes sense that planned giving should have its own designation."

Derek said, "This isn't an issue that will be resolved tonight, but I think we need to have a professional designation. If we're going to call ourselves a profession—and most of us do—then we ought to think like professionals and start a designation program."

## NO EASY ANSWERS

The early evening had turned to early morning, and everyone was suddenly tired. Because human nature calls for clean endings, these five people wanted to agree on matters that they were slowly coming to realize had no clean endings or solutions.

By definition, ethical issues have no clear resolutions. The points of decision are too blurry and personal, and not fully endorsed by a profession or by society. Thus the study of ethics will be with us forever, and some questions will never be answered definitively. So if no answers are forthcoming, why the effort? Why spend time on matters that are, for the most part, destined to remain unresolved? Because people care. Despite their inability to define and rationally defend many positions, they care about what is right and what is wrong.

Ethics crosses the line from knowing to sensing or feeling. We study that gray area of not knowing when we study ethics. The idea behind an ethics initiative is not so much to answer all the disputes but to make sure all parties to the dispute know what the others' perspectives are. It is a process of educating. Some may feel that the effort has no backbone, that what is right is right, what is wrong is wrong, and that should be the end of it. But if issues were that clear, ethics wouldn't be the question; the law would.

As our five individuals ready themselves for bed and when they wake later in the morning, they will have no new answers to the questions they raised when they were together. But the very fact that they discussed them, that they were open to the ideas of others, that their environment was casual and encouraged thought-provoking consideration, made the issues more real and understandable to them than they had been before.

Here's to many more discussions like that.

# EPILOGUE

# The Sources of Philanthropy

*The devil's had it long enough.*
**Anonymous**

In the movie *The Star Chamber*, a superior court judge about to be honored as the Southern California Legal Association Man of the Year excuses himself a few moments before he is to be introduced and commits suicide in the men's room. He does this because, despite his reputation, he had betrayed the legal principles on which his life was supposed to have been based. The judge was part of a group that in an effort to efficiently serve justice actually violated an important principle of justice. A group of men who thought legal technicalities were the principal reason why otherwise guilty defendants were not convicted took into their own hands the task of judging these legally acquitted individuals. Then, when the defendants were found guilty by the Star Chamber—as they inevitably were—the newly convicted people were sentenced, usually to death. The sentence, too, was carried out privately.

*The Star Chamber* is about hypocrisy. The man who ended his life was overwhelmed by the severity of his wrongdoing, and the hypocrisy of allowing himself to be honored so publicly—the local hospital had named its new wing after him—became too much for him to bear. In the context of his role in the wrongful deaths of many people, as well as by denying a justice system he was thought to serve so ably, the judge arguably did the right thing. Perhaps a story of hypocrisy is an unusual way to conclude a book examining the human dimensions of planned giving and philanthropy. But perhaps not. A real Star Chamber once existed in England. And, accept it or not, hypocrisy exists in philanthropy.

As trustees and staff at charities throughout the United States look back at the histories of the organizations where they serve and work, they emphasize the positive: an educator who moved to the middle of

New Hampshire to teach Native Americans; the religious social worker in New York City who knew that the homeless and hungry would not be served by either government or business and so did it herself; the nurse who saw that the Civil War wounded needed more than the military could provide and provided it; the group who saw both nature and government losing the battle against the businesses who wanted to claim the California forests and joined the fight. Many charities had noble beginnings, and throughout their histories have remained true to their missions. In large part, their nobility is due to efforts to achieve their goals with inadequate income from fees or dues; thus, their reliance on private philanthropy. This is why we see charities in such a special light and why we can easily distinguish their purposes—and problems—from those of business and government.

One of those problems is hypocrisy. Although charities have noble causes they do not always have noble supporters, and the matter of accepting charitable support from those whose experiences and intentions are questionable has always plagued charities. Determining charitable intent is—or should be—of broad concern among all fund-raisers. The *sources* of charity is a matter that transcends the planned giving arena and falls squarely in the lap of philanthropy. Go to the nation's oldest and most highly regarded universities; go to the most well-known art and science museums; go to the hospitals with the most advanced technology. Go to these and many other fine charities and you will be in awe of their work. You will see society's good at its best. You will see in action de Tocqueville's observations regarding the unique charitable impulses in America. Your heart may swell with happiness and pride.

Undoubtedly, if you are associated with such a charity, you are proud to be part of such goodness. Some beginnings were surprisingly modest: John Harvard (who, contrary to the assumptions of many, did *not* found the famous university) was memorialized after leaving his books to the college. And today, many people without large checkbooks, such as former Speaker of the House Tip O'Neill and teacher-astronaut Christa MacAuliff, who was killed when the space shuttle *Challenger* exploded in 1986, are appropriately commemorated at charitable organizations for their service to society. But you are also likely to be told that so-and-so gave millions to fund this project or that building. Buildings and projects require a great deal of money; these days anything less than a million dollars does not buy much when it comes to carving a name in granite. Money plays an enormous role at charities. While the names of those who have done good are often reserved for entitling giving clubs, the names of buildings and important, highly publicized projects are the almost exclusive domain of those who have given, and given big. Although charities tend to be grateful for the gifts they receive, today the matter of money—not just a person's good deeds—is the driving force behind recognition. Well-known benefactors pay dearly to be remembered.

Yet many of the benefactors whose influence on charities is visible today—those who gave the money for buildings and projects—earned their fortunes in ways that might seem contrary to the purposes of the charity. How many Eastern campuses have a building named after a Rockefeller, for example? Several. And one large foundation wears that name as well. It is one of the most revered names in all of philanthropy, and many charities owe a great deal of their ability to do their work to at least one Rockefeller. But where did the money come from? John D. Rockefeller created a monopoly and, according to generally accepted historical accounts, ruthlessly drove others out of business and into poverty while acquiring his millions (although many years passed before critical accounts of the time, such as Ida Tarbell's unromantic exposé of Standard Oil of Ohio, were socially acknowledged). Rockefeller, who established his oil company in 1870, made secret deals with railroads in exchange for a reduction in prices, thus driving competitors out of business. It took an act of Congress and many other laws to stop him.

Howard Zinn, in *A People's History of the United States*, recounts that several of the wealthiest Americans in the late 1800s, many of whom are now enshrined in philanthropy, employed similar business practices. Of J. P. Morgan, Zinn explains how dividends were paid to stockholders of the U.S. Steel Corporation: "By making sure Congress passed tariffs keeping out foreign steel; by closing off competition and maintaining the price at $28 a ton; and by working 200,000 men twelve hours a day for wages that barely kept their families alive." Rockefeller's name is on many campuses across the country. So is Morgan's. So are the names of many others who made their money by conducting themselves in a manner that today would be either illegal or unethical. The seeds of philanthropy, indeed.

But this line of logic might be taken too far. Certainly not all wealthy people, then or now, earned their fortunes illicitly or employed unethical business practices. Further, the unfair critic will take an absolute standard and apply it across the ages: Thomas Jefferson owned slaves and therefore could not have been an enlightened man; Abraham Lincoln suggested sending African Americans to a foreign island so he could not have been a great leader; Richard Nixon left office in disgrace and therefore could not have advanced the cause of international relations with his historic visit to the People's Republic of China. The difficulty with absolutism—without relative perspective—is that it is categorical and does not take the times into account. If everyone were judged on an absolute or present-day standard, no one would pass the test of goodness. The same can be said of John D. Rockefeller and J. P. Morgan.

Yet the story of how generous the robber barons were to our charities, as well as to our entire society, is instructive: More than a handful of the people upon whose largess many fine charities were built did not themselves share, or at least practice, the vision of society's goodness as reflected by those charities. For how can taking away another person's job be reconciled with charitable gifts to help society? And—so that this is clear—many of the more substantial charitable gifts were *not* induced by an income tax deduction. The charitable income tax deduction was not created until 1919, three years after the federal income tax was established in the Thirteenth Amendment. Perhaps some will argue that the deductibility, the tax-savings aspect, of charity today plays a role in gift-making decisions, but the big philanthropic names of the nineteenth and early twentieth centuries had something in mind other than tax savings.

But what, then? Why would people who were in many ways ungenerous be so generous in others? Perhaps for the same reason that many people are generous today—ego. What drives any charitable instinct? Many people say they give because they want to help a mission or because they were touched by a charity's work. This is good, of course, but the act of helping others—except for truly altruistic individuals (and psychologists skeptically argue whether altruism actually exists)—is strongly related to a sense of self in relation to those others. That sense of self has its roots in ego and is played out in the desire to do something good for oneself. So far, neither Congress nor the IRS has been able to attach a monetary value—a *quid pro quo*—to the impulse to help others, even though such help is gratifying to the donor. And, with luck, that will never happen.

Ego is not a bad thing. Without it, an individual is deprived of one of three basic psychological characteristics. Ego is the conscious part of the personality, most immediately controls behavior, and is most in touch with external reality. The superego, another major component of a person's desire to help charity, reflects a person's perceptions of moral standards of the community; it is mainly unconscious although it includes the conscious. The id, the third major division of the psyche, controls a person's demands for immediate gratification. All three in balance contribute to a healthy mind. But somewhere, sometimes, a line is crossed. Some people have an enlarged sense of worth and wish to impose it on society. Perhaps that is what John Rockefeller did. And, of course, Rockefeller, although among the most well-known, is not the only name on such a dubious roster. Many, many other people can be added, with one of the most recent being Michael Milken, the convicted and celebrated junk-bond trader who used inside information illegally to create his vast empire and annual income of more than $100 million—kind of a modern-day robber baron. After learning that he had cancer (and having time to think about it in prison), he established a private charity to research cancer. What is *his* motive? Should society celebrate his efforts, efforts essentially to save himself from the dreaded disease? The answer to such a cynically structured question might be a resounding no. But what if others—many others—are saved by the money Mr. Milken invests in his project? Would that make him a better man? Would his potential personal benefit make him a lesser man? The answer is so subjective that each person who cares to know the situation must answer for herself.

But if we can answer in the positive—that a person who damages society and then helps it does good—what does that say about the state of philanthropy? Does it not debase the very idea of good? For how can good be married with bad and still be good? Because the good influences the bad? Perhaps. But what if the bad influences the good? What if charity is being used, not from a tax perspective—an all-too-obvious motive—but from the perspective of an oversized ego or superego, a much more subtle motive? What if those who have a great deal of money and the same amount of ego want to influence society? Is this bad if the result is good? If so, can the argument be made that the ends justify the means? The answer to this question, which must be asked hypothetically at least once during the campus stay of every college student, has serious consequences. If the answer is no, then no money with a tainted history should ever be accepted, no matter the good it does. If the answer is yes, the very idea of right and wrong is called into question, and situation ethics rules over an absolute standard. The answer is not easy.

But to decide the answer, you must be aware of the question's importance. Trillions of dollars have been donated to charities and many of the biggest benefactors have associated their names with them. But many of those benefactors are not model citizens. With the application of an absolute standard much of that money would not have been around to help educate and feed and otherwise help many millions of people. Besides, who among us—including you, dear reader—can be confident of having lived an exemplary life? That you are not wealthy and prepared to be a major charitable benefactor does not excuse you; a double standard is not permitted. The deal is that the right to throw a stone means you must be prepared to be hit with one. To decide the question, you must decide—using our examples in this case—whether John Rockefeller and Michael Milken were essentially good or bad people. Not whether they were guilty of any wrongdoing—Congress and the courts have already decided that—but whether they were good or bad. This, of course, is an unfair question. But the very unfairness of it, in a way, answers our other question: Should charities judge their donors on the basis of how those donors earned their money?

We say we search for truth when many times we mean that we search for an easy answer. But few matters requiring thought are easy to decide. Few alternatives are fully with or without merit. Whether an income tax should be levied must be decided by weighing both its positive and its negative attributes, the cost of the work to be done versus its value to society. When the Chicago Bulls lose a basketball game to the Phoenix Suns, the score is not 100 to 0. The losing team scores some points. It often scores many points, just not as many as the winning team. The win–loss column is definitive but the state of the opposition is less clear. The opposition almost always has merit, whether in basketball or in other contests.

So it is with groping for an answer to our question of whether charities should judge their donors on the basis of how those donors earned their money. My answer, for what it is worth, is no. Charities would impose upon themselves the impossible and highly subjective task of searching out the source of their donations and passing judgment on their worthiness. Only rarely can a charity know for certain that a specific gift is tainted; charities cannot, and should not, be expected to evaluate everyone's business practices and private lives. A charity cannot be expected to pass judgment on its support or its supporters. When the matter of charitable support arises, John Rockefeller should be considered guilty of nothing.

Yet in a moral society the job of judging needs to be done. The very idea of charity is to help society, and understanding the relationship between the source and the ultimate disposition of money is important. If judging is not the job of the charities, then it must be that of the donors. We must rely on the goodness of donors to honorably assist society in furthering its goals. That is not the way a perfect world might be built, but it is the way ours is structured. Charitable organizations must rely on donors to ensure their success.

The story about the suicidal judge in *The Star Chamber* instructs. What if, with all his doubts and pangs of honesty, he had revived himself and come to the stage to deliver his speech? What would he have said? Would he have told his admirers the truth? Would he have said that during his distinguished career he had broken not only the letter but the spirit of the law to suit his purposes? Such a speech would be worth listening to. Truth in place of hypocrisy would be refreshing, although difficult to hear. For that matter, what would a similarly guilt-ridden donor say, if in appreciation of the vast sums he had given to a charity he was awarded an honorary degree and asked to make a speech before a college's graduating senior class? How might the speech go? Imagine a warm noon in late May, full of the expectations of a few thousand members of the graduating senior class and their parents, as well as the faculty, administration members, and local media.

*I am being wrongly honored today.*

The speaker begins without bestowing the usual appreciation to those who invited him to the ceremony.

*I mean no disrespect to your president, who so gloriously recounted my accomplishments just moments ago. But, although all of what he said is technically accurate, it certainly does not tell the whole story.*

The audience, unaccustomed to this type of introduction, thinks he jokes, the way many accomplished speakers begin their talks. This is, after all, a day of great hope and promise. The speaker will certainly—won't he?—address the anxiety of these naive seniors about to embark on their lives in a world not surrounded by protective faculty and brick buildings. Wrongly honored? Impossible. Let the speaker move on, as he most surely will, to the predictable and comfortable prescriptions for dealing with the future.

*I'm embarrassed to be here today, addressing all of you aspiring graduates of this fine school. I'm embarrassed because my story is, quite frankly, one I'm not proud of. Yet here I am before you as your graduation speaker.*

The audience slowly realizes, with incremental levels of discomfort, that this is no joke. An anxious silence of trepidation, as opposed to the polite quiet of a receptive, passively aware audience, envelops everyone. No one speaks or even whispers to his neighbor, as might be the case during a more conventional talk. Rigid, anxious attention.

*As you all have just been told, I have recently made a large gift to this school, a gift of $30 million. I have made the gift to establish a building and an endowed chair for the study of moral applications of science. After all, isn't that what you are all about here? Isn't that what you learn, especially with nuclear technology mushrooming around the world? Although I did not have the privilege of attending this college, I remember when I was a student and being exposed to some of the best minds in the history of humankind. I remember long discussions on ethics and the nature of leadership, both topics you will address in your careers, whether you are in the halls of corporate America, in the lowest or highest levels of government, or at home with your spouse and children.*

*The idea behind how we behave in relation to others, no matter the circumstances, is complex, and you have only just begun to know of this complexity. Life will teach you the rest. God knows, it's taught me more than I ever imagined. Or, in a way, more than I really wanted.*

*Why am I embarrassed? Why is it difficult for me to stand here before you to accept your gratitude in public? Well, a little history perhaps. As you know from the introduction, I attended college—not here, alas—on a full scholarship. My parents were killed in an automobile accident when I was a child, and I was raised by my grandparents. They did not have a great deal of money, and my father, who was thought to have had a successful business, died with debts that exceeded his assets. I'm told he didn't believe in insurance, so nothing was left for my grandparents to raise me. In fact, back in those days, the creditors required that my grandparents pay off the debts. They were not wealthy, however, and so took several years to work off the debt. To say the least, I had no money to go to college without financial assistance.*

*I was graduated with honors, as you also know from the introduction. My first job was with one of the well-known life insurance companies where I learned about financial planning and investing. By chance I met someone with an investment firm in New York, and then, after a mildly successful start selling life insurance, I began to work as a stockbroker. 'That's where all the money is,' I was told. And it was. In the wonderful satire of my profession,* Bonfire of the Vanities, *a person not unlike myself is the protagonist, in this case a successful bond trader whose wife describes his ability to earn income as much like that of someone serving a piece of cake and taking some of the crumbs for himself. The actual cake is made by someone else and its pieces are purchased by others. But someone has to serve it. The server neither makes it nor consumes it; he's the middleman. But, in the profession of trading stocks and bonds, the middleman makes a lot of money. Those crumbs are a big deal.*

*Those of you who read the newspapers' business pages know that my investment firm, while well known and historically a bedrock for sound investment advice, has gone through some major changes recently. My firm's managing director and other high-ranking officials are now in jail, while several others have retired in disgrace. I and a handful of others stayed above suspicion because, according to the newspaper accounts, we did nothing wrong. In fact, recent* Wall Street Journal *reports have lauded the way I handled myself in the face of adversity and temptation. In a technical sense this is true. But in a real sense, the kind of sense that you are supposed to learn about here, that is not true.*

*I am here to tell you that although I have never broken any laws—laws of any kind, not only those enforced by the Securities and Exchange Commission—I am embarrassed about accepting your praise and admiration.*

*I am not alone. I know people who have invested money with me who have earned that money by illicit means. I not only know it, I can prove it. I am not here to indict anyone but I am here to confess, so please listen carefully. I took their money and in turn I earned more money from it for myself. Of course, not all the money I earned can be traced to illicit means. Most of it can be traced to hard working, honest people. But maybe 10 percent—which is a lot— can be traced to something illegal or unethical.*

*But put this into context. The very building we are all in front of today was financed in the 1930s by one of the most well known oil barons of his time. If we were to peek into the life he led, we might see that what he did to make his money would be, in large part, illegal today. Take, for a start, the way he put his competitors out of business. He hired a person to infiltrate a competitor and learn of marketing plans so that he could beat his opponent to the punch. He also drove the price so low his competitors could not match it, and then they went out of business. This would be illegal today. So what? It was not illegal then. The point here is that this man knew it was wrong. But what's wrong is not always illegal.*

*My crime then? Among several examples I could cite, my crime was knowing about a crime and then profiting from it. The most dramatic example that comes to mind is that I once earned $10 million from a transaction that I then used to purchase stock of a large company, a company I knew would do well. And it has; I have more than quadrupled my investment in the last four years. Not bad. I knew the person whose transaction earned me the money, and I also knew he got his money by selling drugs. He was a friend of mine—I can tell you this today because he was well known in corporate America—and he died three years ago. I did not sell the drugs, but there it was, money freshly laundered through a bank in the Cayman Islands. How did I know? He told me. And you ask, why did I take it, knowing it had been earned illegally? Because $10 million is a lot of money, especially to earn essentially in one day. Philosophically, it would be easy to say I should not have accepted it. Yet three-quarters of it— of its original amount and its earnings—now funds the construction of a new building on this campus and will soon endow a department to study the ethics of science.*

*The SEC saw nothing wrong. I broke no laws. But I am apologizing nonetheless. Perhaps I am responding, finally, to a lifelong problem, a problem that started long ago. Do you have any idea how much tainted money I have used to build my own fortune? Of course you don't. Just after being graduated from college, I went to Morocco and smuggled hashish to the United States in camel saddles. That money financed many activities that led to making more money. Selling life insurance was not necessary—nothing was—but it was my feeble attempt at forgetting a past that could be excused by the excesses or naiveté of youth. But once I started, as with an alcoholic, it was hard not to keep going; when the opportunity presented itself, I began again. Today, because of that start and knowingly investing the tainted money of others, I am a wealthy man.*

*The building for which ground was broken at an elaborate ceremony just weeks ago has been paid for—by the donor's own admission—by money wrong-fully acquired. This is quite a dilemma, isn't it? At least the way I see it. I stand here today, therefore, not as someone who imparts great words of wisdom, words usually, in my experience, not worth much, but instead as someone who asks a tough question: What moral authority do I bring with my gift, a gift which, in this case, will be used to further the study of moral values? I don't know the answer. I leave that to the administration of this fine school, and to you, dear audience, to ponder and then decide.*

*Most certainly, this was not the speech you expected today, but it's the one I've written over and over in my mind for the last several years. I feel better for having given it, even if you don't. Thank you. And good luck in figuring out what to do with your dilemma.*

The audience, stunned, does not applaud. Instead, the people—including the college president who introduced the speaker—stay in their seats for what seems many minutes until the president rises to thank the speaker. The conveyance of gratitude is flat, lifeless, and brief, allowing the audience to leave without having to confront the truth of the talk. Predictably, many complain of the hypocrisy, but some admire the *lack* of hypocrisy. A prize with a price.

What would you do? Not as the donor, but as the charity? The donor who just finished his speech at graduation has come to peace with him-self, or at least has relieved himself of a great burden, but that burden has landed in the lap of others, others who need to address the issue. Should the speaker's money be returned with such an admission of wrongdoing? Perhaps, but perhaps not. After all, a great deed will be done with the money.

Despite the inevitable discomfort, let us ask this question of the sources of philanthropy: Is it ethically permissible for donors to further the social good with gifts that are tainted with behavior or business practices contrary to the social good? Philanthropy as we know it, despite the many stabs at truth and goodness charities make many times every day, every year, may not yet be ready for the answer.

# Index